Praise for Jack Turner's

S P I C E

"*Spice* is an erudite and engaging account of how foodstuffs can change the flow of history."
— *The New York Times Book Review*

"Jack Turner handles his subject with discernment and confidence, his style appropriately brisk and animated. . . . Impressive and reassuring is his combination of sympathetic understanding and tough-minded rationalism. Although he never condescends to the past, neither does he ever blur the line that separates fascinating lore from the objective truths of science." — *Los Angeles Times*

"A nifty grab bag of a book. Entertaining and informative."
— *San Jose Mercury News*

"A hugely enjoyable book, written with erudition, style and wit." — *New Scientist*

"Jack Turner possesses the two ingredients most essential for the great historian — scholarly detachment allied to a passionate obsession with his subject. He also writes uncommonly well. A splendid book." — Philip Ziegler

"Based on research that is broad and deep, Turner succeeds remarkably well in capturing the evanescent attractions of spice." — *The Orlando Sentinel*

"Stimulating. . . . *Spice* is stuffed with memorable details. . . . Turner writes with pace and intelligence."
— *New Statesman*

"*Spice* is deliciously rich in odors, savors, and stories. Jack Turner quickens history with almost bardic magic, pouring his personality into his narrative without sacrifice of scholarship."   —Felipe Fernandez-Armesto

"Turner's banquet . . . is, as he admits, a ramble, but it is a fascinating one—urbane, anecdotal and easily digestible."
                                                    —*The Scotsman*

"Sumptuous. . . . Turner quotes well and widely from literature, and has a flair for anecdote."
                                        —*The Guardian* (London)

"Turner brings serious scholarship to bear on his subject, quoting from all manner of obscure texts in ancient languages. But his gentle, ironic wit makes him a lighthearted companion. . . . The book shimmers with life, with real people springing from every page, some of them millennia old. . . . Turner's enthusiasm carries it all forward with terrific momentum."   —*The Tablet*

"A fascinating and scholarly book that can help you improve both your cooking and your sex life. An excellent piece of work."   —Peter Mayle

JACK TURNER

SPICE

Jack Turner was born in Sydney, Australia, in 1968. He received his B.A. in Classical Studies from Melbourne University and his Ph.D. in International Relations from Oxford, where he was a Rhodes Scholar and MacArthur Foundation Junior Research Fellow. He lives with his wife, Helena, and their son in Geneva. This is his first book.

SPICE

The clove, from bud to flower.
Matthioli, *Commentarii in sex
libros Pedacii Dioscoridis
Anazarbei* (Venice, 1565)

Previous pages: Southeast Asia and its spices. Jan Huygen van Linschoten, *Discours of Voyages in ye East & West Indies,* translated by W. Phillip (London, 1598)

SPICE

THE HISTORY OF A TEMPTATION

JACK TURNER

VINTAGE BOOKS
A DIVISION OF RANDOM HOUSE, INC.
NEW YORK

FIRST VINTAGE BOOKS EDITION, AUGUST 2005

The Library of Congress has cataloged the Knopf edition as follows:
Turner, Jack.
Spice / Jack Turner.—1st ed.
p. cm.
Includes bibliographical references and index.
1. Spices—History. 2. Cookery (Spices)—History. 3. Spice trade—
History. I. Title.
TX406.T87 2004
641.3'383'09—dc22
2003064084

Vintage ISBN: 0-375-70705-0

Author photograph © Helena Fraser
Book design by Peter A. Andersen and Pamela G. Parker

www.vintagebooks.com

Printed in the United States of America
10 9 8 7 6 5 4 3 2 1

TO HELENA

"The true figure of Ginger." John Gerard,
The Herball or General Historie of Plantes
(London, 1636)

CONTENTS

●

III
BODY

IV
SPIRIT

●

THE IDEA OF SPICE

A certain Christopher Columbus, a Genoese, proposed to the
Catholic King and Queen, Ferdinand and Isabella, to discover the
islands which touch the Indies, by sailing from the western
extremity of this country. He asked for ships and whatever was
necessary to navigation, promising not only to propagate the
Christian religion, but also certainly to bring back pearls, spices
and gold beyond anything ever imagined.

—PETER MARTYR, *De Orbe Novo,* 1530

One day at Aldgate Primary School, after the dinosaurs and the pyra-
mids, we did the Age of Discovery. Our teacher produced a large, illustrated map, showing the great arcs traced across the globe by Columbus
and his fellow pioneers, sailing tubby galleons through seas where nar-
whals cavorted, whales spouted, and jowly cherub heads puffed cotton-
wool clouds. Parrots flew overhead while jaunty, armor-clad gents
negotiated on the beaches of the newfound lands, asking the natives if
they would like to convert to Christianity and whether by chance they
had any spice.

Neither request struck us ten-year-olds as terribly reasonable: we
were a pagan, pizza-eating lot. As for the spices, our teacher explained
that medieval Europeans had been afflicted with truly appalling food,
necessitating huge quantities of pepper, ginger, and cinnamon to disguise the tastes of salt and old and rotting meat—which, being
medieval, they then shoveled in. And who were we to disagree? It made
a lot of sense, particularly relative to the generally perplexing matter
of schoolboy history, whether it was frostbitten Norwegians dragging
their sleds to the South Pole, explorers dying of thirst in the quest for

nonexistent seas and rivers, or knights taking the cross to capture the Holy Sepulchre from the Infidel—all, from a schoolboy's perspective, strangely perverse and pointless pursuits. The discoverers were somehow more intelligible, more human: our food at school was lousy, but theirs was so dismal that they sailed right around the world for relief. And to an Australian ten-year-old this was not only plausible but highly relevant: so this was why Australia had been colonized by the English.

There was indeed some truth in my potted ten-year-old perspective, albeit radically streamlined. The first Englishmen in Asia were indeed looking for spices, as were the Iberian discoverers before them (whereas Australia, not having any spice, was left till later). Spice *was* a catalyst of discovery and, by extension—that much-abused phrase of the popular historian—the reshaping of the world. The Asian empires of Portugal, England, and the Netherlands might be said with only a little exaggeration to have sprouted from a quest for cinnamon, cloves, pepper, nutmeg, and mace, and something similar was true of the Americas. It is true that the hunger for spices galvanized an extraordinary, unparalleled outpouring of energies, both at the birth of the modern world and for centuries, even millennia, before. For the sake of spices, fortunes were made and lost, empires built and destroyed, and even a new world discovered. For thousands of years, this was an appetite that spanned the planet and, in doing so, transformed it.

Yet to modern eyes it might seem a mystery that spices should ever have exerted such a powerful attraction, however bad the food: mildly exotic condiments, we might think, but hardly worth the fuss. In an age that pours its commercial energies into such unpoetical ends as arms, oil, ore, tourism, and drugs, that such energies were devoted to the quest for anything quite so quaintly insignificant as spice must strike us as mystifying indeed.

In another sense, however, the attraction of spices is still with us. Let your remote control lead you far and wide enough through the nether regions of American television, and sooner or later, amid the chat shows and the monster truck racing, you will come across a soft-porn channel by the name of Spice. Any possible confusion about its contents—I first took it for a cooking channel—is soon dispelled by ads for a cast of pneumatic-chested sirens, served up and devoured by rippling, oiled hunks. The name was chosen, I suppose, to strike a suggestive note: to hint of exotic, forbidden delights, while at the same time forewarning of strong flavors—sultry scenes in the suburbs and breathless encounters poolside. A little will titillate, too much and your senses are overwhelmed.

Which is probably true enough. But while the Spice channel might suggest something about the creative proclivities of American television, the reader may think it has little to tell us about spice. Yet in fact the erotic associations of the word are part of an old tradition. Spices have always been sexy—and so it would seem they still are, at least in TV land. Spices have an ancient aphrodisiac reputation, of which the word's sexual overtones are but the faint, figurative residue. Besides the Spice channel, these associations have resonated with many others, among them no less of an authority on the topic than Barbara Cartland, the author of more than seven hundred romantic novels and the aphrodisiac cookbook *Food for Love,* the preface to which promises to bring "spice into your life!" Long before the invention of television or the romantic novelist there was the Song of Songs, with its lyrical evocation of the loved one as "an orchard of pomegranates with all choicest fruits, henna with nard, nard and saffron, calamus and cinnamon, with all trees of frankincense, myrrh, and aloes, with all chief spices."* Consciously or otherwise, in linking spices and love Cartland partook of a literary tradition reaching as far back in time as ancient Palestine.

Of course, "spice" suggests much more than veiled erotic allusion. Besides romance, if that is the word, there are the Romantics, for whom spices were inextricably linked with images of a fabulous Orient in all its mystery and splendor. The word comes poetically charged. In *A Midsummer Night's Dream* Titania tells Oberon of her conversation with a changeling's mother in the "spiced Indian air"; in the dour surrounds of a New England farmhouse, Herman Melville imagined the "spiced groves of ceaseless verdure" growing on the enchanted islands of the East. For countless others spices and the spice trade have evoked a host of vague, alluring images: dhows wafting across tropical seas, the shadowy recesses of Eastern bazaars, Arabian caravans snaking across the desert, the sensual aromas of the harem, the perfumed banquets of the Moghul's court. Walt Whitman looked west from California to "flow-

---

*Nard is an aromatic plant of the Himalayas that was widely used in ancient perfumes and unguents. Calamus is an aromatic, semiaquatic perennial herb, widely distributed from the Black Sea to Japan, put to similar purposes. Frankincense and myrrh are powerfully aromatic gum resins native to southern Arabia and the Horn of Africa. Frankincense was primarily used in ancient incense. Myrrh was put to purposes as diverse as incense, seasoning, and embalming.

ery peninsulas and the spice islands" of the East; Marlowe wrote of
"Mine argosie from Alexandria, Loaden with spice and silks, now under
sail . . . smoothly gliding down by Candy shore." In a similar vein Ten-
nyson waxed lyrical of the "boundless east" where "those long swells of
breaker sweep / The nutmeg rocks and isles of clove." Spices and the
trade that brought them have long been one of the stocks-in-trade of
what Edward Said has labeled the orientalist imagination, their reputation for the picturesque, glamour, romance, and swashbuckle enduring
from the tales of Sinbad to several recent (often equally fabulous) non-
fiction potboilers. We can still appreciate the nostalgia of John Masefield's poem "Cargoes," with its

> *Stately Spanish galleon coming from the Isthmus,*
> *Dipping through the Tropics by the palm-green shores,*
> *With a cargo of diamonds,*
> *Emeralds, amethysts,*
> *Topazes, and cinnamon, and gold moidores.*

All of which was a world away from the "Dirty British Coaster" laden
with "Tyne coal" and "cheap tin trays" of Masefield's day.

Or, for that matter, our own day. Much of spices' own cargo is still
with us. The word alone continues to evoke something more than a
mere seasoning, a residual verbal piquancy that is itself the echo of a
past of astonishing richness and consequence. By the time these quintessentially Eastern products reached the West, spices had acquired a
history laden with meaning, in which respect they are comparable to
only a handful of other foods, the weight and richness of their baggage
rivaled only by bread ("Give us this day our daily bread"), salt ("the salt
of the earth"), and wine ("In wine is truth"—but it is also the liquor of
death, life, deceit, excess, the mocker or mirror of man). Yet the symbolism spices have carried is more diverse, more spiked with ambivalence than these parallels would suggest. When spices arrived by ship
or caravan from the East, they brought their own invisible cargo, a
bulging bag of associations, myth, and fantasy, a cargo that to some was
as repulsive as others found it attractive. For thousands of years spices
have carried a whole swathe of potent messages, for which they have
been both loved and loathed.

To explain why this is so, how spices came to acquire this freight, is
the purpose of this book. Contrary to the certainties of my faraway

classroom, this was not an appetite amenable to a simple explanation: there was a good deal more to the attraction of spices than culinary expediency; nor, for that matter, was the food of the Middle Ages quite so bad as moderns have generally been willing to believe. This is a diverse and sprawling history spanning several millennia, beginning with a handful of cloves found in a charred ceramic vessel beneath the Syrian desert, where, in a small town on the banks of the Euphrates River, an individual by the name of Puzurum lost his house to a devastating fire. In cosmic terms, this was a minor event: a new house was built over the ruins of the old, and then another, and many others after that; life went on, and on, and on. In due course a team of archaeologists came to the dusty village that now stands atop the ruins where, from the packed and burned earth that had once been Puzurum's home, they extracted an archive of inscribed clay tablets. By a happy accident (for the archaeologists, if not for Puzurum), the blaze that destroyed the house had fired the friable clay tablets as hard as though they had been baked in a kiln, thereby ensuring their survival over thousands of years. A second fluke was a reference on one of the tablets to a local ruler known from other sources, one King Yadihk-Abu. His name dates the blaze, and the cloves, to within a few years of 1721 B.C.

As startling as the mere fact of the cloves' survival might seem, what makes the find truly astonishing is a botanical oddity. Prior to modern times, the clove grew on five tiny volcanic islands in the far east of what is today the Indonesian archipelago, the largest of which measures barely ten miles across. Because cloves grew nowhere else but on Ternate, Tidore, Moti, Makian, and Bacan, these five islands were the sixteenth-century equivalent of a household name, the Moluccas of mariners' fables and merchants' fantasies, spoils contested by rival empires more than half a world away. Cervantes found in the rivalry between Ternate and Tidore a suitably exotic setting for his novel *The History of Ruis Dias, and Quixaire, Princess of the Moluccas.* Yet as colorful as the Moluccas seemed to a sixteenth-century readership, in Puzurum's day they were surely beyond even the reach of fantasy. For this was an age when Mesopotamian scribes etched their cuneiform narrations of the hero Gilgamesh, when the wild man Humbaba stalked the cedar forests of Lebanon, when genii and lion-men roamed the lands over the horizon. Yet many centuries before compasses, maps, and iron, when the world was an inconceivably more vast and mysterious place than it has since become, cloves came from the smoking, tropical cones of the Moluccas to the parched desert of Syria. How this occurred, who brought them, is anyone's guess.

Since the incineration of Puzurum's cloves there have been many more famous spice seekers sprinkled through history. There are the names we learned at school: Christopher Columbus, Vasco da Gama, and Ferdinand Magellan, gambling with scurvy, shipwreck, distance, and ignorance to find the "places where the spices grow"—with spectacularly mixed results. There were, besides, the colossal, heroic failures: Samuel de Champlain and Henry Hudson hunted in vain for nutmeg in the snowy wastes of Canada; the Pilgrim fathers scoured the cold Plymouth thicket; others froze among the bergs of Novaya Zemlya or left their bones bleaching on some forgotten shore half a world from their objective.

The stories of their spice odysseys have filled plenty of books already. However, the pages that follow do not pursue the twists and turns of the spice routes, nor the (generally sorry) fates of the traders who traveled them. This book is not a history of the spice trade, at least not in a conventional, narrative sense. I have not sought to retrace the winding pathways that brought cloves to Puzurum or nutmeg to the king of Spain, least of all to show how spices "changed the world." (All writers and publishers who embrace this view too avidly would be well advised to read Carlo Cipolla's hilarious, acid parody *Le Poivre, moteur de l'histoire* [Pepper, Motor of History].) In fact, I am less concerned with how spices shaped history, than with how the world has changed around them: why spices were so appealing; how that appeal emerged, evolved, and faded. In focusing on the appetite that the spice trade fed, this is not so much a study of the trade as a look at the reasons why it existed.

These reasons were more diverse than we might at first suppose. Taste was only one of the many attractions of spices; they brought many more exotic flavors to the table than we might imagine. Intertwined in their long culinary history there is another older still, one that until recent times was seldom far from the minds of their consumers. Besides adding flavor to a dry and salty piece of beef or relieving the fishy tedium of Lent, spices were put to such diverse purposes as summoning gods and dispelling demons, driving off illness or warding against pestilence, rekindling waning desire or, in the words of one authority, making a small penis splendid—a claim that would gratify the creative talents behind the Spice channel. They were medicines of unrivaled reputation, metaphors for the faithful, and the seeds of purportedly volcanic erotic enhancement.

But if they were much loved, they were also viewed with mistrust. There was a time not so long ago when the more straitlaced residents of the Maine coast were liable to hear themselves dismissed as "too pious to eat black pepper"—a recollection, perhaps subliminal, of a time when spices had been forbidden foods. More than exceptions to a rule, these dissenters help explain an appetite that was ripe with ambiguity and paradox. For when the critics—and they were many—explained what was so objectionable about spices, they tended to single out the reasons that their admirers found for liking them: the merits of flavor, display, health, and sexual enhancement transmuted into the deadly sins of pride, luxury, gluttony, and lust. These were anything but innocent tastes, and therein lay much of their attraction. It is only by viewing spices in terms of this complex overlap of desires and distaste that the intensity of the appetite can be adequately accounted for—why, in other words, the discoverers we learned about in Aldgate Primary School found themselves on foreign shores demanding cinnamon and pepper with the cannons and galleons of Christendom at their backs.

All authorities are inclined to inflate the importance of their chosen topic, yet it is my hope that this anatomy of an appetite is not mere antiquarianism. As writers as diverse as Jared Diamond and Günter Grass have observed, food has played a huge role (and a curiously neglected one) in shaping the destinies of humanity—a fact that seems unlikely to change in an age of environmental degradation. Within this field spices occupy a special place. Notwithstanding the fact that they are, in nutritional terms, superfluous, the trade that carried them has been of fundamental importance to two of the greatest problems of global history: the origins of contact between Europe and the wider world and the eventual rise to dominance of the former—hence, in a nutshell, the academy's interest. However, in the pages that follow I avoid the larger questions of cause and effect in favor of a more intimate, human focus. This book is written with a sense that history too often comes deodorized, and spices are a case in point. The astonishing, bewitching richness of their past has suffered from being too often corralled into economic or culinary divisions, the essential force of their attraction buried in a materialist morass of economic and political history. Narratives of galleons, pirates, and pioneers are more readable but, ultimately, no more explanatory of why that trade existed.

Insofar as I have a thesis, it is that spices played a more important part in people's lives, and a more conspicuous and varied one, than we might be inclined to assume. As whimsical as the claim may seem, there is a deeper historical point. For in the final analysis the great historical developments associated with supplying Europe with spice sprang from a demand: from the senses, hearts, and breasts of mankind; from the shadowy realms of taste and belief. In people's emotions, feelings, impressions, and attitudes toward spices all the great, spice-inspired events and dramas, all the wars, voyages, heroism, savagery, and futility had their elusive germination. The very existence of the spice trade, Columbus's voyages in search of the phantom spices of the Americas, archaeologists' discovery of four-thousand-year-old cloves in the Syrian desert—these are events that can be endlessly speculated upon by historians and archaeologists with ever greater elaboration and sophistication. Yet it is easy to overlook the question from which the others derive: why the trade existed in the first place. It all sprang from desire.

❍

Very obviously, a subject as ephemeral as this demands flexibility from reader and writer alike. The story of spice consists of a thousand unruly, aromatic skeins of history, and several years spent trying to untangle them has taught me that they refuse to be neatly woven into the straighter, clearer-cut threads that historians conventionally spin across time and space. In lieu of a narrative, I have tried to isolate such traditions as can be drawn out from the huge rattlebag of facts thrown up by such a diffuse topic, to tease out the more important continuities of spices' past and follow them down through time. The result bears a resemblance to polyphony, albeit without the satisfying resolution.

The book begins with a brief discussion of what historians have called the Spice Race, the crowded decades at the end of the fifteenth century and the beginning of the sixteenth, when Europe poured quite extraordinary energies into the search for spice. The following chapters consider the chief hallmarks of the appetite that drove that search, under the headings of cuisine, sex, medicine, magic, and distaste: palate, body, and spirit. An epilogue touches on some of the reasons behind spices' fall from grace, how it was they ceased to be so esteemed, downgraded to the mildly exotic foodstuffs they are today. These are broad horizons, with scant regard for conventional or chronological arrangement, yet I would argue that the merits of the thematic approach outweigh the drawbacks. Medieval and occasionally even modern authorities looked back centuries or even millennia for precedents and justification of their own use of spices; indeed, one of my concerns is to show the extent to which these traditions have survived since remotest antiquity. This is not to suggest that a set of beliefs pertaining to spice survived intact from beginning to end. But I would argue that spices have their traditions, reverberating with echoes and recollections; that the apparently straightforward act of eating them has been more laden with historical baggage than we might at first assume.

There are other advantages in flitting across time and space. If the narrative wanders from one time and place to another, this is exactly what spices themselves have always done, cropping up in defiance of the received wisdom, in places where, by rights, they should never have been. The drawback, of course, is that any one of these themes could warrant several books of its own, and since day two I have felt overwhelmed by the embarrassment of riches. The problem has no easy solution other than a broad brush and a carefree ruthlessness in its use. Where I have resorted to particularly sweeping statements, I have tried to flag some of the complexities and nuances of the academic debate, where there is one, in the sources at the back of the book.

●

It might be helpful at the outset to clarify what exactly I mean by "spice." The list below is far from comprehensive, nor is it intended as a technical guide. There is, in fact, no single, satisfactory definition: ask a chemist, a botanist, a cook, and a historian what a spice is, and you will get very different responses—for that matter, ask different botanists, and you will get different definitions. The history of the word itself, its changes and devaluation, is a theme running through the book.

The *Oxford English Dictionary* is, as ever, a good place to start: "One or other of various strongly flavored or aromatic substances of vegetable origin, obtained from tropical plants, commonly used as condiments or employment for other purposes on account of their fragrance and preservative qualities." Broadly, a spice is not an herb, understood to mean the aromatic, herbaceous, green parts of plants. Herbs are leafy, whereas spices are obtained from other parts of the plant: bark, root, flower bud, gums and resins, seed, fruit, or stigma. Herbs tend to grow in temperate climates, spices in the tropics. Historically, the implication was that a spice was far less readily obtainable than an herb—and far more expensive.

Environment may also account for spices on a more fundamental level. Chemically, the qualities that make a spice a spice are its rare essential oils and oleoresins, highly volatile compounds that impart to the spices their flavor, aroma, and preservative properties. Botanists classify these chemicals as secondary compounds, so called because they are secondary to the plant's metabolism, which is to say that they play no role in photosynthesis or the uptake of nutrients. But secondary does not mean irrelevant. It is generally accepted that their raison d'être is a form of evolutionary response, the plant's means of countering threats from parasites, bacteria, fungi, or pathogens native to the plant's tropical environment. Briefly, the chemistry of spices—what in the final analysis makes a spice a spice—is, in evolutionary terms, what quills are to the porcupine or the shell to the tortoise. In its natural state cinnamon is an elegant form of armor; the seductive aroma of the nutmeg is, to certain insects, a bundle of toxins. The elemental irony of their history is that the attractiveness of spices is (from the plant's perspective) a form of Darwinian backfiring. What makes a spice so appealing to humans is, to other members of the animal kingdom, repulsive.*

Historically, of course, neither chemistry nor the curiosities of natural selection could be known, and there were other qualities that marked out a spice. Before the European discovery of the Americas the rare and fine spices were, practically by definition, Asian. There was no shortage of other, homegrown aromatics native to the Mediterranean basin, among them many spices now widely associated with Eastern cuisine, such as coriander, cumin, and saffron. (In medieval times England was a major producer of saffron—a reminder that traffic along the spice routes went both ways.) Moreover, many substances formerly counted as spices are today classed otherwise. Early in the fourteenth century, the Florentine merchant Francesco Balducci Pegolotti wrote a business guide in which he listed no fewer than 188 spices, among them almonds, oranges, sugar, and camphor. When Lady Capulet calls for spices, Juliet's nurse takes her to mean dates and quinces. Generally,

---

*They can be toxic to humans too if taken in sufficient quantities. Protracted nutmeg abuse, for example, can cause cancer of the liver.

however, spices were alike in being small, long-lasting, of high value, and hard to acquire. Above all, the word conveyed a sense of their uniqueness; there was no substitute. To say a spice was special was tautological; indeed, the words have a common root. And just as a sense of their exceptionalism was embedded in their name, so it was integral to their appeal.

By any measure the most exceptional of the spices, and far and away the most historically significant, is pepper. The spice is the fruit of *Piper nigrum,* a perennial climbing vine native to India's Malabar Coast. Its tendrils bear clusters of peppercorns on dense, slender spikes, turning a yellowish red at maturity, like red currants. On this one plant grow the three true peppers: black, white, and green. Black pepper, the most popular variety, is picked while still unripe, briefly immersed in boiling water, then left to dry in the sun. Within a few days the skin shrivels and blackens, giving the spice its distinctive wrinkly appearance. White pepper is the same fruit left longer on the vine. After harvest the outer husk is softened by soaking, left to dry, and rubbed off in water or by mechanical action. Green or pickled peppercorns are picked while still unripe, as per black pepper, then immediately soaked in brine.

Pepper has several look-alikes, the cause of much confusion, that all belong to different species. Melegueta pepper was widely used in medieval times but is now confined to specialty stores, a fate shared by long pepper. (The latter is doubly confusing for sharing an Indian origin with black pepper, whereas Melegueta pepper is native to Africa.) The attractive pink peppercorns commonly sold in combination with the other peppers are entirely unrelated—the plant, native to South America, is in fact mildly toxic, recommended more by its appearance than its taste.

The clove, on the other hand, is unmistakable. The spice is the dried, unripe flower bud of *Syzygium aromaticum,** an evergreen tree reaching a height of twenty-five to forty feet (eight to twelve meters), thickly clothed with glossy, powerfully aromatic leaves. A walk through the perfumed groves of Zanzibar or the Indonesian islands is an unforgettable experience; in the age of sail, mariners claimed they could smell the islands while still far out to sea. The clove itself grows in clusters colored green through yellow, pink, and finally a deep, russet red. Tim-

*Sometimes also called *Eugenia caryophyllata.*

ing, as with pepper, is everything, since the buds must be harvested before they overripen. For a few busy days of harvest the more nimble members of the community head to the treetops, beating the cloves from the branches with sticks. As the cloves shower down, they are gathered in nets and spread out to dry, hardening and blackening in the tropical sun and taking on the characteristic naillike appearance that gives the spice its name, from the Latin *clavus,* "nail." The association is common to all major languages. The oldest certain reference to the clove dates from the Chinese Han period (206 B.C. to A.D. 220), when the *ting-hiang* or "nail spice" was used to freshen courtiers' breath in meetings with the emperor.

For reasons of both history and geography, the clove is often paired with nutmeg and mace. The latter two are produced by one and the same tree, *Myristica fragrans.* The tree yields a crop of bulbous, yellowy orange fruit like an apricot, harvested with the aid of long poles, with which the fruit is dislodged and caught in a basket. As the fruit dries it splits open, revealing a small, spicy nugget within: a glossy brown nutmeg clasped in a vermilion web of mace. Dried in the sun, the mace peels away from the nutmeg, fading from scarlet to a ruddy brown. Meanwhile, the aromatic inner nutmeg hardens and fades from glossy chocolate to ashen brown, like a hard wooden marble. Legend has it that unscrupulous spice traders of Connecticut conned unwitting customers by whittling counterfeit "nutmegs" from worthless pieces of wood, whence the nickname the "Nutmeg State." A "wooden nutmeg" was a metaphor for the fraudulent or ersatz. Schele de Vere's nineteenth-century *Americanisms* cites the "wooden nutmegs" of the press and Congress who "have to answer for forged telegrams, political tricks, and falsified election returns."

Adulteration, conned customers, and mistaken identities are recurrent themes in the history of spice, bedeviling the historian's sources just as they did, historically, consumers. The problems were particularly acute with cinnamon—a fact, we shall see, with some considerable ramifications and over which scholars continue to wage arcane debates to this day. The tree that bears the spice, *Cinnamomum zeylanicum,* is a small, unassuming evergreen, resembling a bay or laurel, native to the wet zone of Sri Lanka, in the island's west and southwest. The spice is formed from the inner bark, which is stripped from the tree with knives, cut into segments, and left in the sun to dry, curling into delicate, papery quills. Cinnamon's best-known relative is cassia, the bark of *Cinnamomum cassia,* originally a native of China but in historical times widespread throughout Southeast Asia. This and several other members of the family were long considered the poor relations—cassia has a coarser, ruddy bark, with a more pungent aroma. (It is also easier and cheaper to produce; much of the "cinnamon" sold in the modern West is in fact cassia.) It is disconcerting though hardly surprising to find the medieval consumer more attuned to the difference.

For even the most indifferent there can be no mistaking the last major spice, ginger. *Zingiber officinale* has been cultivated for so long that it is no longer found in a wild state. Of all the spices it is by far the least fussy and by far the easiest to transplant. The plant will no longer go to seed of its own accord but must be propagated manually, with root-stalk cuttings. (During long oceanic voyages, Chinese navigators grew the spice in boxes to ward off scurvy.) Provided that the ambient soil and air are sufficiently hot and wet, the slender, reedy stems soon sprout, flowering in dense spikes colored pale green before maturing through purple and yellow. The spice is the root, or tuberous rhizome. But as amenable as it is to transplantation, before the technology of refrigeration, air travel, and greenhouse, no European had eaten fresh ginger, at least not in Europe. The spice arrived after a long journey by ship and caravan, occasionally candied in syrup but more commonly and conveniently in dried form, either powdered or whole, in the distinctive, gnarly lumps still occasionally to be seen in a Chinese grocery.

These, the archetypal, tropical Asian spices, are the main subjects of this book—the dramatis personae. Occasionally the narrative strays beyond, for, as we have seen, "spice" was never a clear-cut category. There were others that rose into and fell from favor. But these were foremost, whether on grounds of cost, origin, reputation, or the sheer longevity and intensity of demand. They were in a class of their own. And while spices are the immediate subject, in a broader sense the book is necessarily about Europe and Asia, the appetites that attracted and the links that bound. For the most part, however, the scene and action of the following chapters are written from a European perspective, partly on account of my own linguistic limitations but also in deference to what might be termed the law of increasing exoticism. A fur coat is standard in Moscow, a luxury in Miami. When the world was an immeasurably larger place, so it was with spices, and particularly these spices. The further they traveled from their origins, the more interesting they became, the greater the passions they aroused, the higher their value, the more outlandish the properties credited to them. What was special in Asia was astonishing in Europe. In the European imagination there never was, and perhaps never again will be, anything quite like them.

I

THE SPICE RACE

THE CLOVE TREE
Cristóbal Acosta, *Tractado de las drogas y medicinas
de las Indias orientales* (Burgos, 1578)

CHAPTER I

●

THE SPICE SEEKERS

When I discovered the Indies, I said that they were the richest
dominion that there is in the world. I was speaking of the gold,
pearls, precious stones, and spices, with the trade and markets
in them, and because everything did not appear immediately, I
was held up to abuse.

——CHRISTOPHER COLUMBUS, letter from the third voyage,
written from Jamaica, July 7, 1503

THE TASTE THAT LAUNCHED
A THOUSAND SHIPS

According to an old Catalan tradition, the news of the New World was
formally announced in the Saló del Tinell, the cavernous, barrel-vaulted
banquet hall in Barcelona's Barri Gòtic, the city's medieval quarter.
And it is largely on tradition we must rely, for aside from a few sparse
details the witnesses to the scene had frustratingly little to say, leaving
the field free for painters, poets, and Hollywood producers to imagine
the moment that marked the watershed, symbolically at least, between
medievalism and modernity. They have tended to portray a setting of
suitable grandeur, with king and queen presiding over an assembly of
everyone who was anyone in the kingdom: counts and dukes weighed
down by jewels, ermines, and velvets; mitered bishops; courtiers stiff in
their robes of state; serried ranks of pages sweating in livery. Ambassadors and dignitaries from foreign powers look on in astonishment and
with mixed emotions—awe, confusion, and envy. Before them stands
Christopher Columbus in triumph, vindicated at last, courier of the

ecosystem's single biggest piece of news since the ending of the Ice Age. The universe has just been reconfigured.

Or so we now know. But the details are largely the work of historical imagination, the perspective one of the advantages of having half a millennium to digest the news. The view from 1493 was less panoramic; indeed, altogether more foggy. It is late April, the exact day unknown. Columbus is indeed back from America, but he is oblivious to the fact. His version of events is that he has just been to the Indies, and though the tale he has to tell might have been lifted straight from a medieval romance, he has the proof to silence any who would doubt him: gold, green and yellow parrots, Indians, and cinnamon.

At least that is what Columbus believed. His gold was indeed gold, if in no great quantity, and his parrots were indeed parrots, albeit not of any Asian variety. Likewise his Indians: the six bewildered individuals who shuffled forward to be inspected by the assembled company were not Indians but Caribs, a race soon to be exterminated by the Spanish colonizers and by the deadlier still germs they carried. The misnomer Columbus conferred has long outlived the misconception.

In the case of the cinnamon Columbus's capricious labeling would not stick for nearly so long. A witness reported that the twigs did indeed look a little like cinnamon but tasted more pungent than pepper and smelled like cloves—or was it ginger? Equally perplexing, and most uncharacteristically for a spice, his sample had gone off during the voyage back—the unhappy consequence, as Columbus explained, of his poor harvesting technique. But in due course time would reveal a simpler solution to the mystery, and one that the skeptics perhaps guessed even then: that his "cinnamon" was in fact nothing any spicier than the bark of an unidentified Caribbean tree. Like the Indies he imagined he had visited, his cinnamon was the fruit of faulty assumptions and an overcharged imagination. For all his pains Columbus had ended up half a planet from the real thing.

In April 1493, his wayward botany amounted to a failure either too bizarre or, for those whose money was at stake, too deflating to contemplate. As every schoolchild knows (or should know), when Columbus bumped into America he was looking not for a new world but for an old one. What exactly he was looking for is clearly delineated in the agreement he concluded with the Spanish monarchs before the voyage, promising the successful discoverer one tenth of all gold, silver, pearls, gems, and spices. His posthumous fame notwithstanding, in this respect Columbus was only a qualified success. For in what in due course turned out to be the new world of the Americas, the conquistadors found none of the spices they sought, although in the temples and citadels of the Aztecs and Incas they stumbled across riches that outglittered even the gilded fantasies they had brought with them from Castile. Ever since, it has been with the glitter of gold and silver, not the aroma of spices, that the conquistadors have been associated. But when Columbus raised anchor, and when he delivered his report in Barcelona, seated in the place of honor alongside the Catholic monarchs, ennobled and enriched for his pains, the perspective was different. The unimagined and unimaginable consequences of his voyage have clouded later views of causes, privileging half of the equation. Columbus sought not only an El Dorado but also, in some respects more beguiling still, El Picante.

Why this was so may be answered with varying degrees of complexity. The simplest answer, but also the shallowest, is that spices were immensely valuable, and they were valuable because they were extremely elusive and difficult to obtain. From their harvest in distant tropical lands, spices arrived in the markets of Venice, Bruges, and London by an obscure tangle of routes winding halfway around the planet, serviced by distant peoples and places that seemed more myth than reality. That this was so was as much a function of the geography as the geopolitics of the day. Where the spices grew—from the jungles and backwaters of Malabar to the volcanic Spice Islands of the Indonesian archipelago—Christians feared to tread. Astride the spice routes lay the great belt of Islam, stretching from Morocco to Indonesia. As spice was a Christian fixation, so it was a Muslim milch cow. At every stage along the long journey from East to West, a different middleman ratcheted up the price, with the result that by the time the spices arrived in Europe their value was astronomical, inflated in some cases to the order of 1,000 percent—sometimes more. With cost came an aura of glamour, danger, distance, and profit. Seen through European eyes, the horizon clouded by ignorance and vivified by imagination, the far-off places where the spices grew were lands where money grew on trees.

Yet if the image was beguiling, the obstacles that stood in the way seemed insuperable—prior, that is, to Columbus. His solution was as elegant as it was radical. It was not inevitable, said Columbus, that Eastern goods should arrive from the East; nor that Westerners should pay such a premium, thereby lining the pockets of the Infidel. The world being round, was it not simple logic that spices might also come around the other way: round the back of the globe, from the west? (Contrary to one hoary myth, hardly any well-informed medieval Europeans were flat-earthers. That the earth was spherical had been accepted by all informed opinion since ancient times.) It followed, then, that all one had to do to reach the Indies and their riches was head west from Spain: the ancients had said so, but thus far no one had put the idea to the test. With a little endeavor spices would be as common as cabbages and herrings. Columbus, in not so many words, proposed to sail west to the East, to Cathay and the Indies of legend; or, in the words of one of his intellectual mentors, the Florentine humanist Paolo dal Pozzo Toscanelli, *"ad loca aromatum,"* to the places where the spices are.

It was an idea of hallucinatory promise—not for the promise of discovery for discovery's sake, nor even because the idea was particularly original, but because of the fiscal rewards. In the event of success Columbus's scheme would deliver his Spanish patrons a limitless source of wealth. For the small outlay required to fit out the expedition—a sum roughly equivalent to the annual income of a middling Castilian nobleman—Columbus proposed to drag the Indies out of the realms of fable and into the mainstream of Spanish trade and conquest. Though the story of his voyage has been endlessly mythologized, buried under a mountain of romantic speculation and scholarly scrutiny, in effect his success depended on convincing a coalition of investors and then the Crown that his relatively inexpensive plan merited the gamble. There were experts who disagreed, but in fifteenth-century Spain no more than in a modern democracy did expert opinion or the weight of evidence always carry the day. With a powerful syndicate and capital on his side, those who labeled him crackbrained no longer mattered. His voyage was possible because he got the backing and the cash, and he got the cash because of the promise of more—vastly more—to come back in return. Today he would be labeled an entrepeneur of a particularly bold and inventive hue.

Hence, very briefly summarized, the scene in the Saló. And if the returning discoverer's choice of exhibits made a good deal more sense then than now, so too, in his defense, did his mistakes. Very few Europeans had been to the real Indies, and fewer still had looked on the spice plants in their natural state. Reports of spices and Indies alike arrived rarely, often heavily fictionalized, a situation that left the fertile medieval imagination free to run riot, and few had imaginations more fertile than did Columbus. A month after first sighting land he had seen enough for his own satisfaction, writing in his log that "without doubt there is in these lands a very great quantity of gold . . . and also there are stones, and there are precious pearls and infinite spicery"— none of which he had thus far laid eyes on. Two days later, as his small flotilla picked its way through the coves and reefs of the Caribbean, he discerned hidden treasures beyond the palms and sandy beaches, convinced that "these islands are those innumerable ones that in the maps of the world are put at the eastern end. And he [Columbus] said that he believed that there were great riches and precious stones and spices in them." The evidence was lacking, but his mind was made up. He had set out to find spices, and find spices he would. Desire was father to discovery.

Yet for all Columbus's confidence there was, undeniably, something odd about his "spices"—not least the fact that they did not taste, smell, or look like the spices he and his patrons knew from their daily table. But Columbus would not be disillusioned. Indeed, on the subject of spice the logs and letters of his voyages read like a study in quixotic delusion. His imagination was more than equal to the challenge of an intruding reality, far outstripping the evidence. Within a week of his arrival in the Caribbean he had the excuse to dispel any doubts: a European, unfamiliar with the plants in their natural habitat, he was bound to make the odd mistake: "But I do not recognize them, and this causes me much sorrow." It was an escape clause that would stay obstinately open for the rest of his life.

So Columbus kept looking, and he kept finding. He was far from alone in his wishful thinking. His men claimed to have found aloes and rhubarb—the latter at the time imported from China and the Himalayas—although, having forgotten their shovels, they were unable to produce a sample. Rumors flitted among the excited explorers; sightings abounded. Someone found some mastic trees.* The boatswain of the *Niña* came forward for the promised reward, notwithstanding the fact that he had unfortunately dropped the sample (a genuine mistake or a cynical manipulation of his commander's optimism?).

---

*Mastic is the resin of *Pistacia lentiscus,* an evergreen shrub native to the eastern Mediterranean, much sought after in medieval times for use in dyes, perfumes, and varnishes and as a flavoring. In medieval times the major producer of mastic was the Greek island of Chios, where Columbus's Genoese countrymen acquired the spice.

Search teams were dispatched, returning with yet more samples and the caveat, by now customary, that spices must be harvested in the appropriate season. Everywhere they were bedeviled—and shielded—by their innocence. On December 6, 1492, lying off Cuba, Columbus wrote of the island's beautiful harbors and groves, "all laden with fruit which the Admiral [Columbus] believed to be spices and nutmegs, but they were not ripe and he did not recognize them."

What Columbus could see for certain, on the other hand, was the potential of great things to come. If the first samples of Indian spices left much to be desired, his evidence and testimony were at least enough to convince the Crown that he was onto something.* Preparations for a second and much larger expedition were immediately put into place, a fleet of at least seventeen ships and several hundred men sailing from Cádiz on September 25, 1493, carrying with them the same freight of unfounded optimism. In the Caribbean forests Diego Álvarez Chanca, the expedition's physician, found evidence of fabulous wealth tantalizingly out of reach: "There are trees which, I think, bear nutmegs, but they were so far without fruit, and I say that I think this because the taste and the smell of the bark is like nutmegs. I saw a root of ginger which an Indian carried hanging around his neck. There are also aloes, although not of the kind which has hitherto been seen in our parts, but there is no doubt that they are of the species of aloes which doctors use." As he shared his commander's illusions, so Álvarez also shared his excuses: "There is also found a kind of cinnamon; it is true that it is not so fine as that which is known at home. We do not know whether by chance this is due to lack of knowledge of the correct time when it should be gathered, or whether by chance the land does not produce better."

However, not all these spice seekers were quite so naive or gullible as their cavalier tree spotting might suggest. In order to assist in the search, each of Columbus's expeditions took along samples of all the major spices to show the Indians, who would then, so it was hoped, direct them to the real thing. Yet such was the strength of the Europeans' conviction that even the real thing failed to clear up their misunderstanding—rather, the reverse was the case. During the first voyage, two crew members were sent on an expedition into the Cuban

---

*Not everyone was convinced. Some present in the Saló felt that the Indians were in fact Moors and that Columbus had sailed somewhere down the coast of Africa.

An early and fanciful depiction of
Columbus's arrival at Hispaniola.
The illustrator mistakenly
depicted the merchants in oriental
headgear, arriving in Mediterranean galleys. From a copy of
Columbus's *Letter* to Ferdinand
and Isabella, printed at Basel,
1493

hinterland with samples of spices, reporting back on November 2, 1493:
"The Spaniards showed them the cinnamon and pepper and other spices
that the Admiral had given them; and the Indians told them by signs
that there was a lot of it near there to the southeast, but that right there
they did not know if there was any." It was the same story everywhere
they went. "The Admiral showed to some of the Indians of that place
cinnamon and pepper . . . and they recognized it . . . and indicated by
signs that near there there was much of it, towards the south-east."

The Spaniards' mistake was, then, of the sort that has always bemused
strangers in a strange land: shortcomings of intelligence; problems of
communication; finding what they wanted to find. The script was
repeated with every new landfall. The Indians, already sufficiently puzzled by the pale, bearded strangers, were accosted with samples of dried
plants they had no way of recognizing. Anxious to get rid of them, or perhaps keen to help but reluctant to admit ignorance of the directions—a
still-flourishing Caribbean tradition—the Indians fobbed the visitors
off with a wave of the hand and a vague report of gold and spices "further
on." The Spaniards, incapable of rejecting their convictions and refus-
ing to believe the awful possibility of their self-deception, willingly

accepted the version of events that suited them best. Exceptions to their expectations were discarded as anomalies, not the smoking gun of falsification. No one could see that the empire had no spice.

Everywhere they went, on this and on subsequent voyages, it was the same story. Yet before long the excuses started to wear a little thin, and in due course Columbus's inability to make good on his promises of gold and spices would contribute to the loss of his credibility. On each of his four voyages to the Caribbean, he was compelled to turn for home with little more than paltry samples of gold and his indifferent "spices," just enough to save him from ridicule, leaving others behind to carry on the search, each time with his excuses at the ready. Ferdinand's patience with his dreamy admiral wore thin, as did the patience of those who served under him. An anonymous memo of 1496 stated what was becoming increasingly clear to all but Columbus: that the island's so-called spices were worthless. One who had his feet more firmly planted on the ground and was perhaps the first to appraise the realities of the situation was a crew member of the second voyage, Michele de Cuneo. Writing from the island of Isabella during the second voyage, on January 20, 1494, he was quick to accommodate himself to a spice-free America. When an expedition was dispatched into the hinterland, returning with two Indians, their failure to find any spices was compensated for by their samples of gold: "All of us made merry, not caring any longer about any sort of spicery but only of this blessed gold." And indeed gold was where the future lay.

Even now, however, and for decades after, the hope of American spices lingered on. As late as 1518, Bartolomé de las Casas was still prepared to believe that New Spain was "very good" for ginger, cloves, and pepper. Remarkably, Hernán Cortés, the conqueror of the Aztecs, was perturbed by America's elusive spices—this in spite of his having delivered a quite colossal fortune into the royal treasury from the conquered empire of Montezuma. In a string of letters to the king he repeatedly promised to find a new route to the Spice Islands and offered a string of shamefaced apologies for his failure to deliver any cloves or nutmeg in the treasure ships now regularly sailing back to Castile. His men, he pleaded, were still looking. In his fifth letter of 1526, like Columbus before him, he asked for a little forbearance. Given time, he promised, "I will undertake to discover a route to the Spice Islands and many others. . . . If this should not prove to be so, Your Majesty may punish me as one who does not tell his king the truth."

Fortunately for Cortés his bluff was not called. He found no spices, but neither was he punished. For several decades more the conquistadors kept looking, yet all, like Columbus, found themselves chasing a will-o'-the-wisp. In the south of the continent, Gonzalo Pizarro set off on a deluded and ultimately fatal quest for cinnamon, plunging from the icy heights of the Peruvian *altiplano* into the Amazonian jungle, half a planet away from the real thing. Others sailed north, searching for nutmeg and a northwest passage deep in the icy wastes of the Canadian backlands. In due course the New World garnered new dreams and new fortunes from gold and silver; after, came sugar, fur, cotton, cod, and slaves. It was not for well over one hundred years after Columbus first looked that the myth of America's spices was finally dispelled.

Yet the search was not quite the failure it seemed at the time. The Central American jungle yielded vanilla, and Jamaica allspice—its hybrid taste and pepperlike appearance the source of much confusion. There were, besides, other vegetal riches ripe for the plucking: tobacco, maize, potatoes, tomatoes, chocolate. Columbus himself brought back pineapple and cassava. Centuries later, Asian spices were eventually introduced to the Americas, with such success that the island of Grenada is now a major producer of nutmeg; the island republic features a nutmeg on its flag. Even Columbus, his delusions and false dawns notwithstanding, himself found one reasonable approximation to a spice. In his log for January 15, 1492, he writes of Hispaniola that "there is also plenty of *aji,* which is their pepper, which is more valuable than [black] pepper, and all the people eat nothing else, it being very wholesome. Fifty caravels might be annually loaded with it [from Hispaniola]." Peter Martyr, the Italian humanist at the Spanish court, noted that five grains of the new plant brought back by Columbus were hotter and more flavorful than twenty grains of Malabar pepper. Columbus himself was taken aback by its heat, reporting to the king and queen (like many an unwary newcomer since) that he found Caribbean food "extremely hot." The natives seemed to put their pepper into everything.

Not even such a dreamer as Columbus could have foreseen the future success of his *aji:* It was, of course, the chili, and it was growing wild all over Spain's new possessions. Within decades the plant had spread so rapidly around the world that Europeans traveling in Asia expressed confusion as to its origin, just as we too might wonder at the possibility of Thai or Indian food without its bite. But in 1493, the future pop-

PIPER INDICVM.

A double misnomer: Columbus's "Indian pepper," in reality the American chili. From Pietro Matthioli, *Commentarii* (Venice, 1565)

ularity of the chili was unknowable and would in any case have come as scant consolation to those who had their hopes or money invested in the chimerical spices of America. Given its ease of harvest and transplantation, the chili was never the major money-spinner that the true Eastern spices had been for thousands of years. In respect of spices, which is to say in respect of one of the primary reasons why it was discovered, the New World was something of a disappointment.

CHRISTIANS AND SPICES

> After the year 1500 there was no pepper to be had at Calicut that was not dyed red with blood.
>
> —VOLTAIRE, *Essai sur l'histoire générale et sur les moeurs et l'ésprit des nations,* 1756

Outside his native Portugal, where past glories live long in the memory, Vasco da Gama has generally been remembered as Columbus's less eminent contemporary. It is a somewhat unfair assessment, for in a number of senses da Gama brought about what Columbus left undone. In sailing to India five years after Columbus sailed to America, da Gama found what Columbus had sought in vain: a new route to an old world. The one might be thought of as the complement to the other, as much in terms of their objectives as the achievements of their missions. Between the two of them, however dimly sensed at the time, they united the continents.

The greatest difficulty of Columbus's voyage was that it was unprecedented. In navigational terms, the outward crossing was uncomplicated. Barely out of sight of Spanish territory in the Canary Islands, his small flotilla picked up the northeasterly trade winds that carried them across the Atlantic in little over a month. In comparison, da Gama's voyage lasted more than two years, covering some 24,000 miles of ocean, a distance four times greater than Columbus had sailed. When Columbus sailed to America, he had to chivvy his men through thirty-three days without sight of land; da Gama's crew endured ninety. Their voyage was, in every sense, an epic — literally so, inasmuch as it provided the inspiration for and subject matter of Portugal's national poem, the magnificent, sprawling *Lusiads* of Luís Vaz de Camões, its 1,102 stanzas an appropriately monumental and meandering tribute.

As tends to be the way with epics, the drama was supplied by a combination of heroism, foolishness, and cruelty. After saying their last prayers in the chapel of the Torre do Bélem, the crew bade farewell to wives and family before setting out on their "doubtful way" (*caminho duvidoso*), directing their three small caravels and one supply vessel down the Tagus on July 8, 1497. Passing the Canaries, they headed south down the African coast, skirting the western bulge of the continent toward the Cape Verde Islands. Next they turned their prows south and west into the open ocean, hoping thereby to avoid the calms of the Gulf of Guinea — so much they already knew from the many earlier Portuguese expeditions that had sought African gold and slaves for decades. Dropping below the equator, they passed from a northern summer into a southern winter whose gales, now deep in the southern latitudes, slung them back east to Africa. Even now they were still far to the north of the Cape of Good Hope, and they had to fight a torturous battle against adverse currents and winds before they could finally round the bottom of the continent. When they finally left the Atlantic for the Indian Ocean, they were already six months from home.

Thus far their course had been scouted by the exploratory voyage of Bartolomeu Dias a decade earlier; now they were entering uncharted waters. With scurvy starting to grip his exhausted crew, da Gama cautiously worked his way north along the continent's east coast, in an atmosphere of steadily mounting tension. Stopping for supplies and intelligence at various ports along the way, the Portuguese met with mixed receptions, ranging from wary cooperation to bewilderment and outright hostility. A lucky break came at the port of Malindi, in present-day Kenya, where they had the immense good fortune to pick up an Arab pilot familiar with the crossing of the Indian Ocean. By now it was April, and the first gatherings of the summer monsoon, blowing wet and blustery out of the southwest, propelled them across the ocean in a mere twenty-three days. On May 17, ten months after leaving Portugal, a lookout smelled vegetation on the sea air. The following day, through steam and sheets of scudding monsoon rain, the mountains of the Indian hinterland at last rose into view. They had reached Malabar, India's Spice Coast.

Thanks to good fortune and the skill of their pilot, they were no more than a day's sailing from Calicut, the principal port of the coast. Though they naturally had little idea of what to expect, the newcomers were not wholly unprepared. With their long experience of voyages down the west coast of Africa, the Portuguese were accustomed to dealing with unfamiliar places and peoples. On this as on earlier voyages, they followed the unsavory but prudent custom of bringing along an individual known as a *degredado,* generally a felon or an outcast such as a converted Jew, whose role it was to be sent ashore to handle the first contacts with strange peoples. In the not unlikely event of a hostile reception, the *degredado* was considered expendable. And so, while the rest of the crew remained safely on board, on May 21 an anonymous criminal from the Algarve was put ashore to take his chances.

A crowd rapidly formed around the exotic, pale-faced stranger. To the bemused Indians little was clear other than that he was not Chinese or Malay, regular visitors in Calicut's cosmopolitan marketplace. The most reasonable assumption was that he came from somewhere in the Islamic world, though he showed no signs of comprehending the few words of Arabic addressed to him. For want of a better option he was escorted to the house of two resident Tunisian merchants, who were, naturally enough, stunned to see a European march through the door.

Fortunately, the Tunisians spoke basic Genoese and Castilian, so some rudimentary communication was possible. A famous dialogue ensued:

> Tunisian: "What the devil brought you here?"
> *Degredado:* "We came in search of Christians and spices."

The answer would not have pleased the Tunisians, but as summaries go this was an admirably succinct account of the expedition's aims.

Spices figured no less prominently in da Gama's motivation than they had in Columbus's voyage five years earlier. The Christians too were more than a matter of lip service; to some extent commercial and religious interests went together. Yet of the two the spices offered richer pickings, and there could be little doubt which mattered more in the minds of the crew and those who came after them. The anonymous narrator who has left the sole surviving account of the voyage goes straight to the heart of the matter:

> In the year 1497, King Manuel, the first of that name in Portugal, sent four ships out, which left on a quest for spices, captained by Vasco da Gama, his brother Paulo da Gama and Nicolau Coelho. We left Restelo on Saturday 8th July 1497, for a voyage which we hope God allows to end in his service. Amen.

Their prayers were not in vain. Whereas Columbus was an entire hemisphere off track, the Portuguese had hit the mother lode.

When da Gama's *degredado* splashed dazedly ashore in May 1498, the Malabar Coast was the epicenter of the global spice trade; to some extent, it still is. Located in the extreme southwest of the subcontinent, Malabar takes its name from the mountains that sailors see long before the shore comes into view, a suitably international hybrid of a Dravidian head (*mala,* "hill") grafted onto an Arabic suffix (*barr,* "continent"), the latter supplied by the Arab traders who dominated the westward trade from ancient times through to the end of the Middle Ages. The mountains are the Western Ghats, whose bluffs and escarpments form the western limit of the Deccan plateau. The coast, a low-lying, fish-shaped band of land squeezed between sea and mountains, was, and is, a center of both spice production and distribution. Calicut was the largest but not the only entrepôt of the coast. A string of lesser ports received fine spices from further east for resale and reshipment west, onward across the Indian Ocean to Arabia and Europe. From the jungles of the Ghats merchants brought ginger, cardamom, and a local variety of cinnamon down from the hills, punting their goods through the rivers and backwaters that maze across the plain to the sea. Above all, they brought pepper.

Pepper was the cornerstone of Malabar's prosperity: what the Persian Gulf today is to oil, Malabar was to pepper, with similarly mixed blessings for the region and its residents. The plant that bears the spice, *Piper nigrum,* is native to the jungles that cloak the lower slopes of the Ghats, a climbing vine that thrives in the dappled light, shade, heat, and wet of the tropical undergrowth. Though it has long since been transplanted around much of the tropical world, connoisseurs of the spice claim that Malabar still produces the finest. Like practically every other aspect of life in Malabar, pepper's cycle of harvest and trade moves to the seasonal rhythms of the monsoon. (The word derives from the Arabic *mawsim,* "season.") In late May or early June, the rains sweep in on a front of gusty southwesterlies from the Arabian Sea: the "burst." Over the next few months, the first blooms appear on the pepper vines as the upper slopes of the Ghats are drenched in a daily, Wagnerian deluge of inky clouds and crashing thunderstorms. By September, the rain falls less heavily, and the clouds and mists boil away up the valleys and gorges. A long, sultry heat descends on the hills. In November, the winds flip 180 degrees, blowing mild and dry out of the northeast as the hot air of the Central Asian summer is sucked southward, down the subcontinent from the Himalayas, across the Indian plain to the ocean. In this hot, dry atmosphere the pepper berries cluster and swell; their pungent, biting flavor ripens and deepens. By December, they are ready for harvest. Walk any distance in rural Malabar before the return of the monsoon, and you are likely to have to make a detour around a patch of peppercorns left out to dry in any space available.

Thanks to the combination of spice and monsoon, when Malabar first emerged into history the coast was already a crossroads frequented by traders and travelers from around the Indian Ocean world. The spices were the end, the monsoon winds the means. There were communities of Chinese and Jews there from the early centuries of the Common Era, the latter constituting one of the oldest Jewish communities outside the Middle East. Long before then there had been visitors from Mesopotamia: pieces of teak—another attraction of the coast— were found by Leonard Wooley at Ur of the Chaldees, dating from

The pepper harvest, depicted as a bucolic event closely
resembling the European grape harvest. The pepper is
shown growing on a tree, not as in reality on a vine.
Ambroise Paré, *Des monstres et prodiges* (Paris, 1585)

around 600 B.C.* By the time of Christ, when da Gama's native Portugal was still a bleak and barren wilderness of Lusitanian tribesmen
peering out on the sailless waters of the Atlantic, Greek mariners were
arriving in Malabar in such numbers that one recherché Sanskrit name
for pepper was *yavanesta,* "the passion of the Greeks." Thanks largely to
its vegetable wealth, Islam was established here from the seventh century onward, Indian Muslims thriving, settling, and converting more
than half a millennium before their Moghul coreligionists stormed
down from Central Asia. Even in da Gama's day there were a handful of
intrepid Italian merchants who had arrived by the long and dangerous

---

*Contacts may well have been still older. Excavations of Mesopotamian cities of the third
millennium B.C. have turned up specimens of the Indian chank, a conch shell found only in the
coastal waters of southern India and Sri Lanka.

overland route from the Levant. When da Gama dropped anchor, Malabar was the most important link in a vast and vastly profitable network and had been so for centuries.

For those who profited thereby, da Gama's arrival represented an almighty spanner in the works; for the Portuguese, a coup de théâtre. Now for the encore. Surviving the voyage out was one thing, but the Portuguese had still to find their way through the perilous shoals of Malabar politics, in which respect they were utterly in the dark. It seems that da Gama had expected to find in India a situation similar to the one the Portuguese knew from their trading voyages to West Africa, where they could barter trinkets of low value for stellar returns, and so he was taken aback to find the rich and sophisticated Indians demanding payment in gold and silver. As with Columbus's experience in the Americas, his misconceptions had tragicomic results. On his march into Calicut to meet its ruler, the zamorin, da Gama was so overwhelmed by this proliferation of peoples and religions, and so confident of finding the eastern Christian lands of Prester John, that he mistook a Hindu image of Devaki nursing Krishna for a more familiar mother-and-son pairing. Though puzzled by the teeth and horns on some of the statues of the "saints," he promptly fell to his knees and thanked the Hindu gods for his safe arrival.

This was, however, an isolated and definitely unwitting display of religious tolerance. Da Gama regarded himself every inch the righteous crusader and was out to garner profits no matter the means; thus Indo-Portuguese relations were practically bound to get off to a rocky start. In his first meeting with the zamorin, da Gama promptly set about aggravating an already fraught situation with a mix of religious bigotry and peevish ignorance. The truculent tone of the new arrival might have been calculated to cause offense. The zamorin was a civilized, sophisticated ruler used to receiving traders from around the Indian Ocean world and one, moreover, most definitely unused to the tepid tribute and paltry gifts—honey, hats, scarlet hoods, and washbasins— offered by the Portuguese. Who were these uncouth newcomers that they should treat him, the Lord of Hills and Waves, like some naked barbarian chieftain?

On all sides there were confusion, misunderstandings, and suspicion. Da Gama was briefly detained ashore, further fueling his already ripe paranoia over the "doglike" behavior (perraria) of the Indians. On board the Portuguese vessels there was a steadily mounting nervousness that the Moors had poisoned the zamorin's mind. Their fears were justified, if self-fulfilling: it was, after all, only rational for the Moors, sensing an opportunity to nip this new threat in the bud, to have encouraged the zamorin to imprison or indeed execute the ungracious newcomer.

The zamorin, however, hedged his bets. He granted da Gama's men freedom to trade, and throughout the months of July and August they carried on a desultory exchange in an atmosphere of mutual recrimination and distrust. After a summer of escalating tension, da Gama sailed for Portugal in bad odor, leaving a mood of foreboding behind. As he raised anchor, he angrily threatened a group of Moorish merchants, warning them that he would soon be back. He had every reason to be as good as his word, for he left with the fruit of the summer's efforts, a respectable cargo of spice.

Unlike Columbus's altogether less convincing souvenirs from the Indies, there was no doubting da Gama's evidence. But spices aside, exactly what else he had found would not be perceived for several years. In his report to the king, da Gama painted a somewhat distorted picture. Even now he was convinced that Hinduism was a heretical form of Christianity. After two months in the country, he seems to have concluded that the unmistakable polytheism of Hinduism was some sort of misconceived Trinity. But what was clear to all was the prospect of great things to come, and King Manuel was not one to shirk such a golden opportunity. The doubters' faction at court and the voices of caution had been routed. The way to India and its riches lay open. Preparations were immediately put in place for a second, larger fleet.

It sailed on March 8, 1500, under the command of Pedro Álvares Cabral, his thirteen ships and more than thousand-strong crew dwarfing da Gama's scouting trip of three years earlier. If da Gama's mandate was reconnaissance, Cabral's was empire building. Once his fleet arrived in India, some of the uncertainties and anxieties of the first voyage crystallized into ruthless, imperial intentions. (En route to India, Cabral discovered Brazil—another unforeseen consequence of the search for the Indies.) Arab and Gujarati traders, Jews and Armenians already established in the trade—all were infidels, ergo enemies. Contrary to a long-cherished notion of liberal and nationalist Indian historians, the Portuguese were not the first to bring violence to the ocean, but they certainly did so with unprecedented expertise. They were, moreover, the first to claim ownership over more than a localized corner of its waters, and to do so in the name of God. When Camões versified his countrymen's feats, he had Jupiter, in a Virgilian touch, dispense imperium to the conquering Portuguese: "From the conquered riches of the Golden Chersonese, to distant China and the farthest islands of the East, the whole expanse of the ocean shall be subject to them." And this, substituting "God" for "Jupiter," was exactly how King Manuel saw matters. On the king's orders, Cabral was to seize control of the spice trade by any means necessary. Portugal's work was God's work.

For a time, it looked as though God was on their side. Da Gama had made the gratifying discovery that Arab traders had no answer to the fearsome naval artillery of the Portuguese. Now it fell to Cabral to flex his muscles. On his arrival in Calicut, he demanded that the zamorin expel all Muslim merchants, which, naturally, the zamorin refused to do. Calicut's prosperity, after all, was built on the twin pillars of free trade and respect for foreign shipping. Relations went from bad to worse. As the zamorin stalled, Cabral seized a large and heavily laden Arab ship preparing to sail for the Red Sea, provoking a riot in which fifty-three Portuguese trapped onshore were killed. In response, Cabral turned his artillery on the city. The savage two-day bombardment forced the zamorin to flee for his life. Having had the temerity to resist the Portuguese *diktat,* Calicut and all within were now fair game. The Portuguese seized or sank all Muslim shipping they could lay their hands on; Muslim merchants were hung from the rigging and burned alive in view of their families ashore.

Calicut's fate was just a taste of things to come. In the years that followed, similar treatment was revisited on the city and other Malabar ports, often provoked by local squabbles but all to the strategic end of establishing a royal monopoly over trade in the Indian Ocean. Henceforth traders of all nations would require a permit to sail waters they had sailed freely for centuries. The goal was nothing less than to make the Indian Ocean a Portuguese lake. All competition would be taxed or blown out of the water.

And so, in their clumsy, bloody way, Portugal's pioneers in the East set about building an Asian empire. It would last, in parts, for nearly five hundred years, the first of all European empires in Asia and the longest lived. Unlike its successors, however, this new empire was not based on the occupation of territory, the filling in of the blank spaces on the map, so much as it was aimed at the acquisition of a network of trading stations and forts. The empire would rapidly diversify, but it is fair to say that spices provided the early impetus. What mattered was

control over the centers of trade, above all the spice trade. In its forma-
tive years Portugal's Estado da India was, as one historian has dubbed
it, the pepper empire.

It was certainly spice that impressed Lisbon and its rivals. Looking
back on the golden epoch of the conquests from an age of imperial
retreat, the Jesuit historian Fernão de Queyroz (1617–1688) claimed
that da Gama's legacy and ownership of the spices in particular could
not fail "to astound the world." Viewed from Europe, it was the Italians
who were most astounded, for it was they who stood to lose the most.
By the time Asian spices arrived in Mediterranean waters, the trade was
effectively monopolized by a handful of big Venetian merchants, for
whom da Gama's démarche opened a terrifying prospect. Incredulity
and caution on the first reception of the news of da Gama's voyage
turned to dismay when news of a second and then a third expedition
came in. In 1501, two Portuguese ships laden with spices arrived in
Flanders and immediately set about undercutting the Italians who had
long dominated the market. Venetian merchants in Alexandria and the
Levantine ports and marketplaces soon found prices soaring, and for a
few years the spice galleys returned empty. La Serenissima trembled.
There was scant consolation in the sneering nickname conferred on Portugal's King Manuel, the upstart "grocer king."

This Manuel knew full well. In letters to various crowned heads of
Europe, penned within days of da Gama's return, King Manuel crowed
his success, styling himself "Lord of Guinea, and of the Conquest, the
Navigation and Commerce of Ethiopia, Arabia, Persia and India,"
boasting of the vast profits that would now flow through his
kingdom—and away from Venice. Among the recipients of these
letters were the Spanish monarchs Ferdinand and Isabella, his parents-
in-law; given the poor returns of their own investments in spices, they
must have found it particularly galling to learn of Manuel's successes
among the glittering riches of the glorious East, at a time when Spain's
explorers were still scraping around a scattering of heathenish
Caribbean islands. This Manuel fully appreciated, and for good measure he had his letters printed into pamphlets for public consumption.
One particularly gloating missive invited the Venetians to come and
buy their spices at Lisbon, and indeed, in the desperate year of 1515,
the Venetians had no alternative.

For a time it looked as though events in far-off Malabar had sparked
a revolution in the old Mediterranean order. During the summer of

da Gama's return, the Florentine Guido di Detti gloated that the Venetians, once deprived of the commerce of the Levant, "will have to go back to fishing." The Venetians feared as much themselves. In July 1501, the Venetian diarist Girolamo Priuli estimated that the Portuguese would make a hundred ducats from every one they invested; and there was no doubt that Hungarians, Flemish, French, Germans, and "those beyond the mountains," formerly wont to come to Venice for spice, would now head for Lisbon. With this gloomy prognosis in mind he predicted that the loss of the spice trade would be as calamitous "as the loss of milk to a new-born babe . . . the worst news the Venetian Republic could ever have had, excepting only the loss of our freedom."

For all those who envied Venice its riches, it was an appealing prospect, but they were to be disappointed. As far as business was concerned, the Venetians were no babes in arms. In the longer run, Portugal's grasp of the spice trade proved more slippery than it had at first appeared. Historians long took Manuel's boasting at face value, taking it for granted that da Gama's voyage had succeeded in neatly redirecting the spice trade from the Indian into the Atlantic Ocean, but this was far from being the case. After a few disrupted decades as the shock of the early Portuguese conquests reverberated back down the spice routes, Alexandria and Venice staged a comeback. In the 1560s, there were so many spices for sale at Alexandria that a Portuguese spy suggested that the Portuguese should abandon the Cape route altogether and ship their spices via the Levant in order to cut costs. So great was the flow of illicit spices through the Portuguese blockade that there was speculation that the Portuguese viceroy was in tacit revolt against the king.

That Portugal failed to monopolize the spice trade is not, in retrospect, so remarkable. Even with their fearsome cannons, the Portuguese effort to lord it over the Indian Ocean, so far from home, was an extraordinary act of hubris. Manuel's vainglorious titles were little more than a fantasy. With their religious bigotry and cavalier attitude to established networks, the Portuguese rapidly accumulated enemies who would in due course cost them dear. Though they were unable to face the Portuguese ships in a shooting match, smaller, swifter Arab vessels enjoyed remarkable success in avoiding the Portuguese blockade and generally raising costs. For the Portuguese Crown every fort, every cannon, and every man under arms represented a loss of profits. Violence was bad for business. Beset by enemies on the outside, the Portuguese empire proved remarkably porous from within. Subject to strict rules, compelled to buy and sell at prices set by the Crown, and facing the likely prospect of an early death from some foul disease, shipwreck, or scurvy, the Portuguese in India, most of whom had gone east to enrich themselves, had few legal means of doing so. Endemic smuggling, corruption, and graft were the inevitable result. There were too many temptations to plunder and little to stop it. The costs of the pepper empire raced ahead of returns. For all the sound and fury (and the poetry), this was a creaking, leaking empire—"There is much here to envy," as one of da Gama's descendants summarized matters.

In May 1498, however, all such future complications were far from the minds of da Gama's crew. There were more pressing matters to attend to. As they walked dumbfounded through the streets of Calicut, ogling the opulent houses of the great merchants, the huge warehouses bursting with spice, the mile-wide palace, and the rich traders passing on their silken palanquins, they naturally thought they had hit the big time. Their first priority was getting rich quick—or simply making it home. Da Gama contrived to make this already daunting task infinitely more difficult by sailing too early, before the monsoon winds had shifted. The crossing to Africa, three weeks' sailing on the outward leg, took three months. Thirty crew members died of scurvy, leaving a mere seven or eight able-bodied mariners on each of the ships. The third caravel was abandoned, "for it was an impossible thing to navigate three ships with as few people as we were." By the time they finally returned to Lisbon, only 55 of the 170 or so who had set forth remained. Da Gama himself survived due to the hardiness of his constitution and, in all likelihood, thanks to the superior quality of the officers' rations. (The nutrients in the wine and spices reserved for officers may have made the difference.) Among the casualties was his brother Paulo, who died in the Azores only a few days' sailing from home.

Even in purely financial terms, the initial results were less spectacular than they had hoped. The two ships that returned to Portugal were compact, designed for discovery, not cargo. As a result, the expedition brought back a substantial but scarcely earth-shattering haul of spices. The survivors brought little more than curios, in some cases paid for, quite literally, by the shirts off their backs. But in the hazy days of da Gama's return, when the king himself hugged this once obscure nobleman and called him his "*Almirante amigo*," any future problems were far from anyone's mind. For if da Gama's experience foreshadowed the extreme hazards of the sea route to the Indies, it also gave a stunning demonstration of its promise. As they offered prayers of thanks in Bélem, where they had knelt two years earlier, all the survivors had reason to hope that the spices they had brought back were harbingers of greater things to come. The financiers rubbed their hands; from Antwerp and Augsburg the great banking houses of Europe looked on remote little Portugal with new interest.

What was clear was that the old order had been rattled, and there was good reason to believe that it would shortly be turned on its head. A decade after da Gama's arrival in India, an itinerant Italian by the name of Lodovico de Varthema (ca. 1465–1517) traveled through the Portuguese Indies and beyond, witnessing the prodigious infancy of Europe's first Asian empire firsthand. He spoke for many in 1506: "As far as I can conjecture by my peregrinations of the world . . . I think that the king of Portugal, if he continues as he has begun, is likely to be the richest king in the world." At the time, it seemed a reasonable surmise. Measured by the spicy mandates of their missions and in the assessment of the day, Columbus looked the failure and da Gama the success.

DEBATE AND STRYFE BETWENE THE SPANYARDES AND PORTUGALES

Behold the numberless islands,
scattered across the seas of the Orient.
Behold Tidore and Ternate,
from whose fiery summit shoot rippling waves of flame.
You will see the trees of the biting clove,
bought with Portuguese blood. . . .

—CAMÕES, *The Lusiads,* 1572

As the competition between Spain and Portugal for the spices of the East escalated into an all-out race, not all the victories went Portugal's way; nor was the competition, though always bitterly contested and often bloody, wholly without agreements and treaties. But like its modern counterpart, the fifteenth-century treaty could have unpredictable effects—on occasion not so much preventing conflict as redirecting or even provoking it. This gloomy fact of international life has its prime late-medieval exemplar in the Treaty of Tordesillas, signed by ambassadors of the two Iberian powers in the Spanish town of the same name on June 7, 1494.

In its planetary terms the Treaty of Tordesillas was perhaps the single most grandiose diplomatic agreement of all time. Following Columbus's return in 1493, the Spanish Crown moved quickly—by the standards of fifteenth-century diplomacy—to clarify the scope of any future voyages: who was entitled to discover what. The issue was referred to the Vatican, the ultimate arbiter of matters earthly and divine, and later the same year Pope Alexander VI duly issued a papal bull on the matter. To Spain he granted sovereignty over all lands west of a line of longitude running 100 leagues (about 320 miles) west of the Cape Verde Islands. Spain thus had title to the lands visited by Columbus, while the Portuguese retained the right to their discoveries along the West African coast.

For Portugal, however, this was not good enough. Sensing some national bias on the part of the Spanish-born pontiff, Portugal's King João II demanded a revision, which was duly achieved after prolonged negotiations in the northwestern Spanish town of Tordesillas. In effect, the pontiff's planetary partition was shunted west. According to the new, revised terms, each Iberian power was assigned a zone on either side of a line of longitude running 370 leagues (about 1,185 miles) to the west of the Cape Verde Islands. To the Portuguese went all lands to the east; to the Spanish, everything to the west. They agreed, in effect, to divide the world between them, as neatly as an orange split in two.

Yet as cut and dried as the arrangement seemed, the treaty muddled as much as it clarified. In its ambiguities and uncertainties it was pregnant with the seeds of future conflict. Critically, and fatally for any treaty, it was impossible to determine with any degree of accuracy when its signatories were in breach of its terms. With the invention of chronometers sufficiently precise to measure longitude still several hundred years in the future, there was no way of accurately measuring the division. The demarcation was for all intents and purposes a legal fiction. Navigators heading west into the Atlantic had to rely on dead reckoning to determine whether they were in the Spanish or the Portuguese zone.

More seriously, the framers of the treaty, like everyone else in 1494, labored under serious delusions concerning the shape of the world they purported to parcel up. In the short term, this worked to Portugal's advantage: ignorance of the shape and extent of the lands visited by Columbus, in particular the great eastward bulge of the South American continent, gifted Lisbon legal title to Brazil. But Brazil was at this stage regarded as little more than a supply stop on the road to India. More pressing was the dispensation on the other side of the planet. The real prize in everyone's mind was control of the fabulous, far eastern Indies. Whom did they really belong to, Spain or Portugal? (The possibility that the Indies might belong to the Indians did not enter into consideration.)

It was here that the unanswered and effectively unanswerable questions of Tordesillas were the stuff of Portuguese nightmares. The world being round, it was self-evident that the line of division ran in a great circle, all the way round the globe. When João succeeded in revising the treaty, in effect he gambled on giving Spain hundreds of leagues of Asian waters in return for more of the Atlantic and the right to Africa. But more in the west meant less in the east. The question was, Where lay the slice? Where was the "antimeridian," and who owned the title to the Spice Islands? Cosmographers could argue the point endlessly, debating the circumference of the earth with arcane and ingenious suppositions, but there was no way of knowing who was right.

With fleets setting off every year and the pace of discoveries accelerating, the issue could not long remain academic. Indeed, as discoveries in the East proceeded apace, the debate became more complex and more fraught with geopolitical implications. After da Gama's first voyage in 1497, successive Portuguese expeditions pressed deeper into the heart of maritime Asia. The first stop was the island of Sri Lanka and its cinnamon. In 1505, the first Portuguese expedition extracted "tribute" of 150 quintals* of cinnamon from the king of Gale—the first of a sorry string of similar, steadily escalating exactions. Six years later, the Portuguese crossed the Bay of Bengal and seized, after a brief and bloody siege, the entrepôt of Malacca. Dominating the strait of the same name between Sumatra and the Malay peninsula, Malacca was the richest port of the East, its prosperity dependent, like Singapore's today, on a position astride a natural bottleneck. Here Gujarati, Arab, Chinese, and Malay ships came to trade for spices and all the exotica of the East.

*A quintal is a commercial hundredweight.

The cinnamon harvest as imagined by someone who had
never seen it. The spice is stripped from the tree trunk
before being loaded onto the camel's back. In reality these
two stages of production took place on different sides of
the Indian Ocean. Paré, *Des monstres et prodiges*

(The name is probably derived from the Arabic *malakat,* "market.")
Malacca was the choke point through which all Eastern spices headed
west. In the judgment of the first Portuguese arrivals, Malacca was the
richest seaport in the world. A few years after its fall, the adventurer
and chronicler Tomé Pires (ca. 1468–ca. 1540) claimed, with the
hyperbole typical of these years, that "whoever is lord of Malacca has his
hand on the throat of Venice."

Even now, however, the real prize lay still further east, somewhere in
what the Malays called "the lands below the winds." From somewhere
in the scattered islands of the archipelago came the most elusive and
costly spices of all: cloves, nutmeg, and mace. In 1511, all that was
known by the Portuguese was that they came from the mysterious
"Spice Islands," at this stage more a vague yet alluring notion than a

place on the map; there were, in fact, no European maps of the Moluc-cas, or none worth navigating by. The obscurity shrouding the islands did not prevent, but rather engendered, speculation. For what limited intelligence they could garner, the Portuguese had to rely on the sec-ond- or thirdhand reports of Arab, Javanese, and Chinese navigators, plus the extremely sparse accounts of one or two European travelers who claimed, with varying degrees of plausibility, to have been there. Most painted a picture of a place straight out of Sinbad's voyages. The cosmography of Kaswini (ca. 1263) located the clove on an island near Borneo, whose residents had "faces like leather shields and hair like tails of pack-horses." They lived deep in the mountains "whence are heard by night the sounds of the drum and tambourine, and disturbing cries, and disagreeable laughter." The eleventh-century traveler and geographer Alberouny of Khiva told tales of a fabulous island of Lanka:

> When ships approach this island, some of the crew row to shore, where they deposit either money or such things as the natives lack, such as salt and waist cloths. On their return the next morn-ing, they find cloves in equal value. Some believed that this barter was carried on with genii; one thing was, however, certain: no one who ventured into the interior of that island ever left it again.

Other Arab accounts of the islands were still vaguer and more vivid, as with Masudi's (890–956) *Meadows of Gold:*

> No kingdom has more natural resources, nor more articles for exportation than this. Among these are camphor, aloes, gillyflow-ers [cloves], sandal-wood, betel-nuts, mace, cardamoms, cubebs and the like. . . . At no great distance is another island from which, constantly, the sound of drums, lutes, fifes and other musi-cal instruments and the noise of dancing and various amusements are heard. Sailors who have passed this place believe that the *Daj-jal* [the "dark messiah" or "Antichrist" of the Muslims] occupies this island.

Embroidered as these fictions were, the sixteenth-century reality lagged not far behind. For the spices they sought grew on only two tiny archipelagoes, each of which is barely larger than a speck on the best modern map. Needless to say, no such maps existed in 1500. To locate them among the sixteen thousand or so islands of the archipelago was to find a needle in a haystack.

The northernmost of those specks is the home of the clove, in what is today the province of Maluku, in the easternmost extremity of Indonesia. Each of the five islands of the North Moluccas is little more than a volcanic cone jutting from the water, fringed by a thin strip of habitable land. From the air, they resemble a row of emerald witches' hats set down on the ocean. Ternate, one of the two principal islands, measures little more than six and a half miles across, tapering at the center to a point more than a mile high. In the phrase of the Elizabethan compiler Samuel Purchas, Ternate's volcano of Gamalama is "angrie with Nature," announcing its regular eruptions by spitting Cyclopean boulders into the atmosphere to an altitude of 10,000 meters, like the uncorking of a colossal champagne bottle. A mile across the water stands Tidore, Ternate's twin and historic rival, like Ternate a near-perfect volcanic cone, barely ten miles long, its altitude a mere nine meters less: 1,721 meters to Ternate's 1,730. From the summit it is possible to see the other three North Moluccan islands, marching off in a line to the south: Moti, Makian, and Bacan beyond. Together they represent a few dozen square miles in millions of miles of islands and ocean. At the start of the sixteenth century and for millennia beforehand, they were the source of each and every clove consumed on Earth.

The nutmeg was equally reclusive. Provided the winds are right, a week's sailing southward from Ternate will bring the well-directed traveler to the tiny archipelago of the Bandas or South Moluccas, nine outcrops of rock and jungle making up a total land area of seventeen square miles (forty-four square kilometers). Here, and here alone, grew the nutmeg tree.

Size and isolation conspired to keep the Moluccas' obscurity inviolate. The first European with a plausible claim of having seen nutmegs in their natural state (though many have doubted his claim) was the early-sixteenth-century Italian traveler Lodovico de Varthema. He found the islands savage and menacing and the people "like beasts . . . so stupid that if they wished to do evil they would not know how to accomplish it." Spices aside, there was practically nothing to eat. He made a similarly disparaging assessment of the northern Moluccas, where the people were "beastly, and more vile and worthless than those of Banda." The Portuguese historian João de Barros (ca. 1496–1570) considered the land "ill-favored and ungracious . . . the air is loaded with vapors . . . the coast unwholesome . . . [the islands] a warren of every evil, and contain nothing good but the clove tree." But regardless of their vapors and "rascal" inhabitants, the Moluccas' cloves, nutmeg, and mace were sufficiently tempting to lure traders around the planet.

Portugal's first expedition in search of the Moluccas left in 1511. In December of the same year, shortly after the fall of Malacca, António de Abreu set off in charge of three small vessels. With the assistance of local guides, the Portuguese found their way to the Bandas, where they filled their hulls to overflowing with nutmeg and mace. With no room remaining for cloves, de Abreu resolved to return to Malacca with two of the expedition's three ships, leaving behind a companion by the name of Francisco Serrão to carry on the search without him.

The northern Moluccas were a more elusive goal for the Portuguese, although in the longer run they would prove a more valuable asset. After various tribulations, including shipwreck in the Banda Sea and getting hopelessly lost among the islands, Serrão eventually made it to Ternate in 1512 on a junk stolen from pirates on whom he turned the tables. Forming an alliance with the sultan of the island, he worked his way into local favor by assisting Ternate in its desultory conflict with neighboring Tidore—a condition as constant as the annual visitation of the monsoon. The original Lord Jim, he married a local woman (who may have been a daughter of Sultan Almanzor of Tidore; if so, an adroit act of marriage diplomacy) and built himself a small fort and trading post—it still stands—from which he sent back a steady stream of cloves to Portugal. He would remain in the Moluccas for the rest of his life.

On the surface, everything was going Lisbon's way. The immediate and troubling question was whether the Portuguese had any legal claim to their conquests. To many experts the possibility of Spanish ownership under the terms of Tordesillas looked like a probability. At the time the earth's circumference was still greatly underestimated, no one having the slightest inkling of the vast breadth of the Pacific. All authorities agreed that the Spice Islands lay only a few days' sailing west of the Mexican coast, a misconception that would not be corrected for several years. According to the document regarded at the time as the single most authoritative description of the world, the *Suma de geografía* of Martín Fernández de Enciso, written in 1519, the eastern meridian as defined at Tordesillas fell at the mouth of the Ganges—which made the Moluccas Spanish.

While the cosmographers speculated, troubling reports and rumors filtered in. The sheer distance the Portuguese had to travel from India east to the Moluccas had come as an unpleasant surprise to de Abreu and Serrão. Given the great distance they had covered, it seemed not at all unlikely that they had passed out of the Portuguese hemisphere and into Spain's. The secrecy with which the Portuguese shrouded their voyages served only to encourage further speculation; one reason why so few contemporary maps survive is that they were treated with the secrecy of classified documents. The Spaniards smelled a rat. To many it looked as if the Portuguese were not conquerors but trespassers.

One of those who shared this suspicion was a Portuguese nobleman from the remote province of Trás-os-Montes, Fernão de Magalhães, or, as he is known in the English-speaking world, Magellan. A veteran of Portugal's early years in the Indies, he had waded ashore at the conquest of Malacca alongside Serrão, whose life he had saved. When his friend sailed east to the Moluccas, Magellan headed west, to India and then back to Portugal. But he never renounced his ambition to revisit the Indies, and the Spice Islands in particular. Over the course of the next few years Magellan and Serrão maintained a regular correspondence via the junks Serrão sent back laden with cloves from Ternate. It was clear from Serrão's letters that the Moluccas lay a good deal further east than the Portuguese authorities would publicly admit. Largely on the basis of his exchange of letters with Serrão, Magellan's suspicion that the Moluccas lay in the Spanish half of the globe grew to conviction.

Conviction soon ripened into action. Magellan wrote to Serrão that he would come and join him soon, "if not by the Portuguese way, then by Castile's"; that is, he would sail west from Europe to the Spice Islands, avoiding the Portuguese zone entirely. The idea seemed eminently feasible. Provided that his assumptions about the circumference of the earth were correct, the voyage would be shorter than the long trip around Africa and across the Indian Ocean. Technically, in strictly navigational terms, there was nothing to stop him; politically, on the other hand, the idea was dynamite.

In its essentials, of course, Magellan's plan was nothing new: the idea of a westward voyage to the Spice Islands was the same as Columbus's scheme a few decades earlier, the main difference being that Magellan was aware of the chief obstacle in his way, in the form of America. Sailing west across the Atlantic, he aimed to drop down south around the bottom of South America or through a southwest passage, then cruise west to the Spice Islands. Only the outlines of what happened next are clear. As with Columbus before him, the first problem was securing the necessary capital. Back in Portugal, all of Magellan's efforts to support his scheme ended in failure. Perhaps feeling personally slighted by the king's refusal to grant him a pension, at some point disenchantment with Portugal and King Manuel set in. He may have been a casualty of court bickering and intrigue—a common fate for returnees from the Indies. Whether or not he divulged the full extent of his suspicions to the king is uncertain but unlikely. If he did, the king would rather not have known: he had no interest in raising any more doubts over his claim to the Spice Islands. Either way, having failed to generate any interest in his plan, Magellan went to Spain in search of richer pickings. Abandoning the land of his birth, he arrived in Seville on October 20, 1517.

Success across the frontier was not long in coming. Freed from the encumbrances of Portuguese court politics, Magellan joined forces with Cristóbal de Haro, the Portuguese agent of the Fuggers, the German banking dynasty that had provided the Portuguese Crown with capital for the early spice fleets. Like Magellan, de Haro had abandoned Portugal in search of a more cooperative royal client, his relationship with Manuel having soured, perhaps as a result of the king's clumsy efforts at price fixing and insistence on a royal monopoly on all trade in spices. Between the two of them, the exiles from Portugal had the capital and the requisite expertise. By 1519, over increasingly shrill protests from the court in Lisbon, they secured the third element necessary for success, in the form of backing of the Spanish Crown.*

Of all the great voyages of the Age of Discovery, Magellan's circumnavigation of the globe has good claim to be the greatest, whether in terms of the privations endured or the sheer audacity of the enterprise. Five black ships sailed from the port of Sanlúcar de Barrameda on September 20, 1519, with a complement of about 270 men. Ambitious as it was in conception, the voyage was hugely complicated by its commander's innocence. There were volumes of speculation, but as yet no one knew where, or for that matter *whether,* the American continent ended; nor, if there was one, where the purported passage was to be found. Magellan may have imagined that the River Plate fit the bill,

---

*There may have been earlier Spanish efforts to sail to the Spice Islands, but they were stymied either by the Spanish Crown's unwillingness to confront Lisbon or perhaps by Portuguese machinations. As early as 1512, the archbishop of Valencia had promoted a plan whereby the Spanish would sail east, contest Malacca, and take possession of the Moluccas.

but sailing upstream they soon found the water turning sweet and their way blocked. Exploring dozens of bays and inlets, each time they were forced to turn back in disappointment. The expedition was wracked by fear, ennui, and fatigue. Tensions between Magellan and his Spanish captains culminated in a mutiny at midnight on Easter Day 1520, suppressed by the execution of one of the mutineers; another was left to the tender mercies of the natives. Only as winter lifted, after yet more fruitless searches up every inlet, did Magellan finally lead the survivors through the maze of sea and islands at the southern tip of the continent, passing through a desolate fire-bearing country—Tierra del Fuego, as he dubbed it—then through 325 miles of icy squalls, mists, and fogs in the strait that now bears his name. This was already an astonishing achievement, but it came at a price. When they entered the Pacific on November 28, 1520, only three of the original five ships remained.

The survivors found the new ocean calm, whence "Pacific." Its tranquillity, however, was deceptive. Like Columbus before him, Magellan had premised his plan on a mistaken assumption of the earth's circumference, but in this case almost catastrophically so. The upshot was that he had no inkling of the vast expanse of ocean still ahead of him. For fourteen weeks the survivors inched north and west, tormented by fickle winds and consumed by doubts, their food and water all but gone, forever imagining that the Moluccas were just over the horizon. (As it was, they were extremely lucky to have taken a course assisted by a westward current—an oceanic conveyor belt. Had they sailed a little further to the north or south, they would almost certainly have perished.) When supplies ran out early in the crossing, the crew was reduced to a diet of ship's biscuits softened in rancid water; when the biscuits were gone, they mixed sawdust with rat droppings and chewed on the leather of the yardarms with teeth that rattled in their blackened, scurvy-ridden gums. When land was finally sighted on March 6, 1521, the crew had been decimated by malnutrition, exhaustion, and despair. They had survived no fewer than ninety-nine days without fresh food or water.

Next came the absurd and ignominious anticlimax. Soon after arriving in the territory of the modern Philippines, Magellan promptly threw away his life in a pointless skirmish with what the chronicler of the expedition calls "an almost naked barbaric nation." It was an utterly pointless death, the result of trying to impress a local chieftain with the power of Christian arms, the more ironic for coming at the end of such a hellish crossing. "Thus did this brave Portuguese, Magellan, satisfy his craving for spices."

Even now, however, the survivors still had much sailing ahead of them. With no clear idea of where they were or where to look, they visited "an infinity of islands, always searching for the Moluccas." Finally Magellan's Malay slave (a relic of his time in the Indies) identified the unmistakable twin cones of Ternate and Tidore rising above the horizon. While the small Portuguese garrison on Ternate looked on in astonishment and dismay, the crew fired their cannons in joy and proceeded to neighboring Tidore, where they bought cloves "like mad." The narrator's relief is palpable: "It is no wonder that we should be so joyful, for we had suffered travail and perils for the space of twenty-five months less two days in the search for Molucca."

After a brief stop for rest and resupply, the shrinking band of survivors made plans for home. At this point Magellan's flagship, the *Trinidad*, sprang a serious leak from its worm-eaten bottom. The crew repaired the hull as best they could and made an unsuccessful attempt to sail back across the Pacific to Mexico, but after a fruitless battle against adverse winds and currents they were compelled to return to the Moluccas, whereupon ship and crew were promptly captured by the Portuguese. Only four crew members would ever see Spain again.

Meanwhile the other surviving vessel, the *Victoria*, headed west.* There were still another nine months of hard sailing before the ship rounded the Cape of Good Hope and turned north, passing along the entire western length of Africa and across the Strait of Gibraltar, to Spain. On September 6, 1522, the *Victoria* limped into its home harbor of Sanlúcar de Barrameda, fourteen days short of three years since leaving. Of the expedition's original complement of more than 270 men, only 18 had survived. A harborside observer commented that the ship was "more full of holes than the best sieve, and these eighteen men more fatigued than the most exhausted horses."

By his premature death, Magellan had forfeited the fortune and glory for which he had abandoned his country; as a Portuguese in service of Spain, he won only the opprobrium of his motherland and the suspicions of his adopted country. (Had he lived to return to Spain, he

---

*The third ship, the *Concepción*, had been abandoned in the Philippines, "because there were too few men."

would, almost certainly, have fallen foul of court intrigue.) The honors went to the survivor who piloted the *Victoria* back into Sanlúcar, a native of Guetaria by the name of Juan Sebastián de Elcano, one of the participants in the mutiny against Magellan at Port Saint Julián. But to the survivor went the spoils. Elcano was rewarded with a coat of arms with the device of a globe set above two cinnamon sticks, twelve cloves, and three nutmegs, flanked by two Malay kings grasping branches of a spice tree blazoned with the caption *"Primus circumdedisti me"*—"You were the first to encompass me."

As the durable Spaniard had outlasted his Portuguese commander, so it seemed on the larger stage of diplomacy. When the *Victoria* limped back into harbor, the tables, it seemed, had been turned. With a claim staked in Tidore, the Spanish Crown now had a physical presence to back up its theoretical claim to sovereignty over the Moluccas. Yet even now there were more twists and turns in store. The border town of Badajoz was the scene of fierce debates between Spanish and Portuguese diplomats, the key issue the still unanswerable question of the Moluccas' exact longitude. (As a matter of fact, the Moluccas were indeed in the Portuguese zone, though that would not be confirmed for many years yet.) The Spanish pointed to their presence on Tidore; the Portuguese called them trespassers; the Spanish flung back the same insult. Talks ground on, one futile deposition succeeding another. In the end, a settlement came not from the diplomats but from the accountants of the royal treasury in Madrid. By the terms of the Treaty of Zaragoza of 1529, the impecunious Spanish monarch, deaf to the pleading of his counselors, traded his claim to the Spice Islands for the sum of 350,000 ducats, so as to pay for the ceremonies attending his forthcoming marriage. The Spanish claim to the Moluccas, purchased with so much ingenuity, sweat, cash, and blood, was thus sold to fund a royal wedding.

It was an ignoble end to the enterprise. Many voices—among them de Haro's—were raised in protest at the king's short-term outlook. With the annual profit from the islands estimated at 40,000 ducats, the settlement represented less than a decade's return. Compounding the investors' disappointment was the fact that so far these profits had failed to materialize. Even the return of the *Victoria* had brought de Haro and the other investors little cheer. Among the quayside celebrations, one of the interested parties prepared a breakdown of the expedition's costs and returns in a document unearthed three hundred years later by the scholar Martín Fernández de Navarrete. Known as the "discharge document," this unadorned summary of inputs and outputs makes for fascinating reading. Though the *Victoria,* at only eighty-five tons, was the second-smallest vessel of the expedition, its leaking hold yielded 381 bags of cloves, the legacy of the frantic buying that followed the crew's arrival at Tidore. The net weight was calculated at 520 quintals, 1 arroba, and 11 pounds: 60,060 pounds, or 27,300 kilograms. There were also samples of other spices: cinnamon, mace, and nutmeg, plus, oddly, one feather (of a bird of paradise?).

In the debit column alongside is a listing of expenses: weapons, victuals, hammers, lanterns, drums *"para diversion,"* pitch and tar, gloves, one piece of Valencian cochineal, twenty pounds of saffron, lead, crystal, mirrors, six metal astrolabes, combs, colored velvets, darts, compasses, various trinkets, and sundry other expenses. Taking into account the loss of four of the five ships, the advances paid to the crews, back pay for the survivors, and pensions and rewards for the pilot, it emerges that once the *Victoria*'s 381 bags of cloves had been brought to market the expedition registered a modest net profit. For the investors it was a disappointment, paltry in comparison with the astronomical returns then being enjoyed by the Portuguese in the East; but it was a profit nonetheless. The conclusion must rate as one of accountancy's more dramatic moments: a small holdful of cloves funded the first circumnavigation of the globe.

THE SCENT OF PARADISE

It is an orchard of delights, With all the sweetness of spices.
—Paradise as described in the *Cursor Mundi,*
a Northumbrian poem written ca. 1325

Columbus, da Gama, and Magellan, the three standard-bearers of the Age of Discovery, were spice seekers before they became Discoverers. Many lesser names followed where they had led. In the wake of their first groping feelers into the unknown, other navigators, traders, pirates, and finally armies of various European powers hunted down the source of the spices and squabbled, bloodily and desperately, over their possession.

After the early successes of the Iberian powers, the spice trade took a Protestant turn. At the close of the sixteenth century, English and Dutch traders made their first appearance in Asian waters, impelled by a desire for spice, as Conrad phrased it, burning in their breasts "like a flame of love." Better organized and more ruthless than any traders yet seen in Atlantic or Asian waters, they fought off the Catholic powers, each other, and all Asian rivals and smugglers for the advantage of bringing spices direct to Amsterdam's Herengracht or London's Pepper Lane.

At the hands of the northern newcomers, Portugal's Estado da India endured a protracted, undignified senescence, though it was barely a century old. Raiders preyed on the corpse and lopped off the choicest pieces. The first Dutch ships called at the North Moluccas in 1599, returning to Amsterdam low in the water from the weight of the cloves they carried: "So long as Holland has been Holland," one crew member claimed, "such richly laden ships have never been seen." The English followed them east in 1601, James Lancaster leading a fleet under the auspices of the newly formed "Company of Merchants of London trading into the East Indies"—better known as the East India Company.* Sailing from the Javanese port of Bantam, an English pinnace reached the Bandas and their nutmeg groves in March 1603. Others followed, setting sail in vessels with such optimistic names as *Clove* or *Peppercorn.* With toeholds on the tiny islands of Ai and Run, James I was, for a time, proud to style himself "King of England, Scotland, Ireland, France, Puloway and Puloroon." For the sake of their nutmeg the latter two tiny islands shade Bermuda as England's first overseas possessions.

Though these early voyages enjoyed mixed results, malaria, scurvy, and inexperience taking a heavy toll, the northern intruders soon struck at the "Portingall" with devastating swiftness. The first assets to go were the remotest, the distant Spice Islands. Here a handful of Portuguese, having long since incurred the loathing of the Muslim population, clung on in a string of moldering forts in a state of permanent siege. Ternate fell in 1605. Shortly after, the Dutch seized the Portuguese fort on Ambon, midway between the North and South Moluccas. Worse was to come, as the conquests of da Gama and his successor

---

*This was, incidentally, the first occasion when the English used lemon juice to ward off scurvy.

Alfonso de Albuquerque (1453–1515) were steadily rolled back. In the disastrous decade of the 1630s, Ceylon and its cinnamon forests fell to combined Ceylonese-Dutch forces—a marriage of convenience the Ceylonese would soon have cause to regret. The Portuguese Jesuit Fernão de Queyroz claimed the Dutch were "so disliked by the Natives, that the very stones will rise against them," but his prediction of independence was some three hundred years premature. Malacca, the bottleneck and entrepôt of the East, surrendered to the Dutch in 1641; the pepper ports of Malabar followed in 1661–1663. Spices were now, in effect, a Protestant concern.

The drama was played out on a global stage. The golden age of discovery was also the golden age of European piracy, when freebooters could plunder their way to royal favor and enrichment. The talismanic figure in this respect was Sir Francis Drake, whose *Golden Hind* was only the second ship to circumnavigate the globe. On the way he called at Ternate in 1579, sailing off with a cargo of cloves and agreement from Sultan Babu to reserve the trade in cloves to the English. For his part, Drake promised to build forts and factories and "to decorate that sea with ships." It was a bargain that would never be entirely fulfilled, yet his treaty did foreshadow a flood of merchants and brigands pouring out of England into Asia. With such dizzying profits in the air, Drake's treaty with Babu sent shivers of excitement up the spines of the investors, and would-be imitators lined up to follow Drake's lead. In view of the effect the treaty seems likely to have had on the merchants of London, culminating in the formation of the East India Company two decades later, Drake's agreement with Babu was quite possibly the single most lasting achievement of his voyage, more far-reaching in its ramifications even that his lordly haul of stolen Spanish silver and gold that had the Spanish ambassador demanding the pirate's head.

Like Drake, these spice seekers were seldom chary of robust methods. A spice ship represented a fortune afloat, and from a strictly commercial point of view it was considerably cheaper and easier to plunder returning ships than make the long and dangerous voyage for oneself. Galleons and caravels returning from the Indies ran a gauntlet of pirates and raiders, lurking in the Atlantic to deprive the exhausted and disease-depleted crews of their precious cargoes. One such haul was witnessed by Samuel Pepys in November 1665, when as surveyor-victualer to the Royal Navy he inspected two captured Dutch East Indiamen. On board he saw "the greatest wealth lie in confusion that a

Sir Francis Drake arrives at Ternate. Although many of the cloves he acquired were thrown overboard when his ship ran aground, the remainder still brought a handsome return to those who had invested in his expedition. From Levinus Hulsius, *Voyages* (Frankfurt, 1603)

man can see in the world—pepper scatter[ed] through every chink, you trod upon it; and in cloves and nutmegs, I walked above the knees—whole rooms full . . . as noble a sight as ever I saw in my life."

By now, however, this was a token victory for the English, since their own outposts in the Spice Islands had long since gone the way of the Portuguese before them. One English merchant in the Moluccas reported that the Dutch "grew starke madde" at having to share the proceeds from the Moluccas' cloves and nutmeg. Accordingly, in February 1623, the staff of the English factory on the central Moluccan island of Ambon was rounded up, tortured, and killed. Their fate had been foreshadowed a few years earlier by the destruction of the English outpost on the nutmeg island of Run, which was then denuded of its trees for good measure. The "crying business of Amboyna" prompted an outburst of pamphlets, anti-Dutch tirades, and even a play by John Dryden (*Amboyna*—admittedly, not one of his better works; Sir Walter Scott considered it "beneath criticism"), its jingoistic huff periodically recycled ever since. The affair was finally tidied up with the signature of the Treaty of Breda at the conclusion of the second Anglo-Dutch war of 1665–1667. The English renounced their claims in the Moluccas in

Dutch soldiers torturing English traders on Ambon during the infamous "Amboyna Massacre" of 1623. At stake was a share of the lucrative trade in the Moluccas' nutmegs, cloves, and mace. From *The Emblem of Ingratitude* (London, 1672)

return for acknowledgment of their sovereignty over an island they had seized from the Dutch, the (then) altogether less spicy New Amsterdam, better known by the victors' name of New York.*

In the longer term, however, such seizures and horse trading, while spectacular, were unsustainable. There was more to be made from trade than plunder—a distinction that those at the sharp end of the spice trade would not perhaps have recognized—and by now the lion's share of that trade was in Dutch hands. After several decades of mercurial, spasmodic English forays in the first half of the 1600s, but without any consistent investment from London, by the middle of the century the Dutch had emerged as the uncontested masters of the spice trade. They had achieved what the Portuguese had sought in vain: dominance in

---

*The connection has long been a source of confusion for the unwary and fodder for a good deal of sensationalist historicizing, none of which should be taken too seriously. There was little more to the swap of the two islands than belated recognition of facts on the ground. At the time of the treaty's signing the English had already occupied Manhattan and the Dutch had taken Run. The matter was not much more complicated than that.

the trade in pepper and cinnamon and a near-total monopoly in cloves, nutmeg, and mace.

Under the auspices of the Dutch East India Company, or VOC, the problems that beset the trade were gradually ironed out. The bandit capitalism of the early days evolved into a more recognizably modern and permanent system. The market-disrupting cycle of gluts and short-ages was succeeded by a ruthlessly efficient monopoly. The catastrophic losses of life and shipping along the African coasts were reduced to a sustainable level. Much of the risk was taken out of the business. Whereas the finances of Portugal's Estado da India had never made the leap out of medievalism, hamstrung by clumsy royal monopolies and endemic corruption, the annual fleets setting off from the Zuider Zee were backed by the full panoply of joint-stock companies, shareholders, and boards of directors. In time the East India companies of the Dutch and their English rivals grew into the armies and administrators of for-mal imperialism.

Such were, very briefly, the bloody, briny flavors of the Spice Age. But if the discoverers marked the beginning of a new era, so too they marked an end, for even their efforts formed part of a grand tradition. In his opening stanza Camões claimed that da Gama and his Christian spice seekers had ventured into "seas never sailed before," but in fact the spice routes had been navigated for centuries, albeit not by Euro-peans, or at least not very many of them. As tends to be the way with pioneers, even the discoverers had precedents. Asia's spices had been familiar in Europe long before Europeans were familiar in Asia— because someone, or rather various someones, had been to get them. Besides the disconcerting Moors who accosted his envoy on the beach, da Gama had the deflating experience of finding Italian merchants active along the Malabar Coast—some selling their services to Muslim rulers—and there had been others before. In this sense the discoverers' achievements, however epic, were essentially achievements of scale. Neither the voyages nor the tremendous, transforming appetite that inspired them emerged from thin air. When da Gama and his contem-poraries raised anchor, spice was a taste that had already launched a thousand ships.

Had any of the protagonists in this vast and ancient quest been asked why this was so, some would have offered, if pressed, much the same functional answer as that pointed out by modern historians: profit. The reputation of fabulous riches clung so closely to spices that some peo-

ple, as we shall see, considered them tarnished by the association.
(Columbus himself was deeply embarrassed by the potential imputa-
tion of grubby, worldly motives to his quest, and he was accordingly at
pains to find some way of justifying the enterprise in terms of the spiritually worthy spin-offs: to retake the Holy Sepulchre, to finance a new
crusade, to convert the heathen.) But when it came to explaining why
spices were worth a fortune, if the medieval spice trader were asked *why*
they were valuable and why so sought after, he would have given
answers that seem less intelligible to the modern historian than such
reassuringly material arguments. In this regard the charms of spices
admit no easy explanation, nor would our forebears have found it much
easier. Indeed, part of their attraction—and the source of much of their
value—was simply that they were inexplicable. Before Columbus and
company remapped the world, spices carried a freight that we, in an age
of satellites and global positioning systems, can barely imagine.
Emerging from the fabulous obscurity of the East, they were arrivals
from another world. For spices, so it was believed, grew in Paradise.

That this was so was something more than a pious fiction. It was, in
fact, something close to gospel truth, an article of faith since the early
years of the Christian religion. One of many highly intelligent and educated believers was Peter Damian (1007–1072), an Italian Doctor of
the Church, saint, hermit, and ascetic in whose turbulent life the great
issues of the eleventh century, somewhat in spite of himself, converged.
In his hermitage at Fonte Avellana, in a bleak wilderness of rocks and
crags in the central Apennines, he dreamed of that gentle place where,
by the fount of eternal life,

> *Harsh winter and torrid summer never rage.*
> *An eternal spring puts forth the purple flowers of roses.*
> *Lilies shine white, and the crocus red, exuding balsam.*
> *The meadows are verdant, the crops sprout,*
> *Streams of honey flow, exhaling spice and aromatic wine.*
> *Fruits hang suspended, never to fall from the flowering groves.*

That Paradise smelled of spices was, for Damian, something more
than a passing fancy. His words and spiced imagery alike were lifted
directly from *The Apocalypse of Peter,* an early Christian work, now discarded as apocryphal but widely read in the Middle Ages. Damian himself returned to the theme in a series of letters to his friend and fellow
cleric Saint Hugh (1024–1109), abbot of the great Benedictine

monastery of Cluny in France, at the time the intellectual and spiritual center of Western Christendom. To Damian, the shelter of Cluny's cloister was a "Paradise watered by the rivers of the four Evangelists . . . a garden of delights sprouting the manifold loveliness of roses and lilies, sweetly smelling of honeyed fragrances and spices."

The belief in spices' unearthly origins is crucial to understanding their charm—and their value. For if Paradise and its spices were fair, so the world in which Damian lived was, so far as he was concerned, irredeemably foul. Among his other works is *The Book of Gomorrah,* one of the bleakest visions of humanity ever penned. In Damian's eyes the entire race was mired in baseness, its sole, slender hope a Church that was itself sunk in moral squalor and loathsome homosexuality. The priesthood was addicted to every variant of rampant lust, wracked by "the befouling cancer of sodomy." Bishoprics were bought and sold, lecherous priests openly took wives and handed on their living to their bastard offspring, and a corrupt and venal papacy was despised and disregarded by the secular powers. From his retreat in the wilderness Damian looked out on a world populated by a race of degenerate Yahoos. Paradise seemed a long way away.

Yet its aromas were there, as it were, right under his nose. Spices were a taste of Paradise in a world submerged in filth; they were far more than mere foodstuffs. And this reputation endured even as knowledge of the wider world expanded and travelers penetrated, sluggishly, into some of the dark spaces on the map. Jean, Sire de Joinville (ca. 1224–1317) provided a fairly typical explanation of the spices' arrival from the East. Long before and after Joinville's day, Egypt was the prime intermediary between the Near and Far East and as such Europe's prime supplier of spice. After the capture of the crusader army in 1250, Joinville was held in an Egyptian dungeon as a prisoner of the sultan, awaiting the payment of a hefty ransom. Though he had seen the Nile carry off the bloated bodies of his companions, decimated by plague after the Battle of al-Mansurah, he was prepared to believe in the river's unearthly origins, that it might carry more pleasant flotsam:

Before the river enters Egypt, the people who are so accustomed cast their nets in the river in the evening; and when morning comes, they find in their nets those goods sold by weight that they bring to this land, that is, ginger, rhubarb, aloes wood, and cinna-

mon. And it is said that these things come from the terrestrial
Paradise; for the wind blows down the dead wood in this country,
and the merchants here sell us the dead wood that falls in the
river.

This from someone who, unlike the overwhelming majority of Europeans, had wet his feet in its waters.

Yet Joinville's account was something more than a fabulous yarn
spun by a returning traveler out to dazzle the folks back home. Judged
by the standards of the day, his passed for relatively informed opinion;
he had, moreover, a willing audience, many of whom would have seen it
as impious to believe otherwise. For although no one had been there,
few doubted the existence of the terrestrial Paradise from where,
according to an ancient tradition, some of the fruits of a lost Eden still
trickled through to a fallen humanity: "Whatever fragrant or beautiful
thing that comes to us is from that place," said Saint Avitus of Vienne
(ca. 490–518). That spices grew in Eden's garden of delights was no
more than the literal truth, inasmuch as the vocabulary for delights and
spices was one and the same. The connection was explained by Saint
Isidore of Seville (ca. 560–636) in what was possibly early medieval
Christendom's single most influential description of the East and the
terrestrial Paradise: "Paradise . . . is called in Hebrew 'Eden,' which is
translated into our own language as *Deliciae,* the place of luxury or
delight [equally, the exotic delights and dainties themselves]. Joined
together, this makes 'Garden of Delights'; for it is planted with every
type of wood and fruit-bearing tree, including the Tree of Life. There is
neither cold nor heat but eternal spring." Unfortunately for humanity,
however, this Paradise was hedged in with "flames like swords, and a
wall of fire reaching almost to the sky."

As Joinville appreciated, with such barriers separating supply and
demand, the exact means of that transfer were necessarily obscure, and
the source of much speculation. According to the Book of Genesis, in
Eden was the fountain that "went up from the earth, and watered the
whole face of the ground." Translated into medieval cosmography, biblical exegesis held that this fountain was the source of the Nile,
Euphrates, Tigris, and Phison (or, to some, the Ganges). Saint Augustine of Hippo (354–430) concluded that the rivers circumvented the
flames by passing underground before reemerging. It was via these
rivers that spices arrived.

A silver spice plate with a scene from Genesis; English, ca. 1567–1573. In medieval and early modern times spices were commonly served in a range of vessels and dishes, often of exquisite craftsmanship. Besides displaying spices they also announced the wealth and taste of the owner.

Thus, when Joinville looked on the waters of the Nile and came up with his colorful explanation of its harvest, he was merely reconciling biblical truth to what he had seen with his own eyes. By unknown means and ferried by unknown hands, on streams flowing from another world, spices arrived from a place known only from Bible and fable, washing up in the souks of Cairo and Alexandria and thence to the markets of Europe like so much cosmic driftwood.

Or, perhaps more to the point, like gold dust. For mystery meant profitability. In a stroke of medieval marketing genius, there was even a spice that took its name from its purported origins, the grains of paradise that appear in spicers' account books from the thirteenth century on. In medieval times grains of paradise, or simply "grains," cost more than the black pepper of India. Sharp to the taste and now confined to specialty stores, the spice is in fact the fruit of *Aframomum melegueta* (also *Aframomum granum-paradisi*), a native of West Africa, where it was purchased by Portuguese traders on their voyages down around the continent's western bulge or else freighted by caravan across the Sahara, along the gold and slave routes of Timbuktoo. By the time the "grains" arrived in Europe their credentials were burnished and their origins forgotten. Paradise made for as plausible an origin as any other.

That spices have all but lost their luster in the twenty-first century is in large measure because much of the mystery has gone out of the trade and the places where they grow. Paradise survives not as a place but as a symbol. Yet for centuries spices and Paradise were inseparable, joined together in a relationship whose durability was guaranteed by the fact that it could not be disproved. The few known facts added up to a baffling puzzle that invited colorful explanations. Hardly anyone involved in the trade knew who or what lay before the last transaction, and much the same held true all along the spice routes. None but the first few handlers of these transactions had any idea where their goods originated; few had any idea where they were bound; and none could view the system in its entirety. Trade was a piecemeal business, passed on from one middleman to another. Perhaps the greatest wonder of the system is that it existed at all.

For between harvest and consumption Europe's spices traveled a long and fragile thread. The spice routes mazed across the map like the wanderings of a black ant, crisscrossing seas and deserts, now appearing, then abruptly vanishing and reappearing, forking and branching with the rise and fall of cities and empires, outbreaks of war, and fluctuating demand. When the visiting king and queen of Scotland celebrated the Feast of the Assumption at Woodstock in 1256 with no less than fifty pounds each of ginger, pepper, and cinnamon, four pounds of cloves, two pounds each of nutmeg and mace, and two pounds of galangal,* their seasonings had traveled journeys the diners could only guess at, acquiring an air of glamour and otherworldliness that we can imagine only with difficulty.

No spices were more traveled or more exotic than the cloves, nutmeg, and mace of the Moluccas. Served to the visiting monarchs in a glass of spiced wine, all that can be known with any degree of certainty is their origin. After harvest in the nutmeg groves of the Bandas or in

---

*Galangal is the root of *Alpinia officinarum,* a native of eastern Asia related to ginger, with a similar though slightly more astringent taste. Still popular in Thai cuisine, it was widely used in Europe in the Middle Ages.

the shadow of the volcanic cones of Ternate and Tidore, next, most likely, they were stowed on one of the outriggers that still flit between the islands of the archipelago. Alternatively, they may have been acquired by Chinese traders known to have visited the Moluccas from the thirteenth century onward. Moving west past Sulawesi, Borneo, and Java, through the Strait of Malacca, they were shipped to India and the spice marts of Malabar. Next, Arab dhows conveyed them across the Indian Ocean to the Persian Gulf or the Red Sea. At any one of a number of ancient ports—Basra, Jiddah, Muscat, or Aqaba—the spices were transferred onto one of the huge caravans that fanned out across the deserts to the markets of Arabia and on to Alexandria and the Levant.

Only in Mediterranean waters did the spices come at last into European hands. By the turn of the millennium, they crop up in the records of cities spread around its shores: Marseilles, Barcelona, Ragusa. Some spices arrived via Byzantium and the Black Sea, following the Danube to eastern and central Europe, but the greatest volume of traffic passed through Alexandria and the Levant to Italy. From Italy a number of routes led north over the Alpine passes toward France and Germany. Alternatively—which was both safer and faster—Venetian or Genoese galleys freighted spices out of the Mediterranean, through the Strait of Gibraltar, and up and around the Iberian peninsula before docking in view of the Gothic spire of Saint Paul's Cathedral. From a Thameside wharf they were transferred into the store of a London merchant—as likely to have been Italian, Flemish, or German as English—then into and out of a royal spicer's cupboard before finally ending their long journey in the royal stomach.

If such was the system, however faintly we discern it, contemporaries saw it more faintly still—a fact that did not stifle but rather stimulated the imagination. It was a romance writer's stock in trade that spices perfumed the air of the more beautiful dreamworlds that are such a feature of medieval literature. In a Castilian version of *The Romance of Alexander* written around the middle of the thirteenth century, galangal, cinnamon, ginger, cloves, and zedoary* waft through the air of the dreamscape. Much like Coleridge transported to the sunny ice caves of Xanadu, the anonymous author of *Mum and the Sothsegger* left behind

---

*Zedoary is an aromatic tuberous root of one of several species of *Curcuma,* related to ginger and turmeric. It was widely used in medieval medicines and cuisine.

the gray and grinding poverty of the fourteenth-century English countryside for a vision of a blissful, better land, where the Golden Age
endured in all its spicy abundance and lushness. The fantasyland of *The
Romance of the Rose,* among the most widely read and emulated poems of
the age, is similarly rose-tinted and spice-scented. In evoking these
fairer climes spices were as much a poetic convention as pearly teeth
and snowy breasts, chivalrous knights, and damsels in distress.

While poets and mystics were generally content to perfume the air of
their Paradise with spices and leave it at that, others made more concerted efforts to map the fabulous locales where the spices grew. This
was, necessarily, a highly creative enterprise. Since all reports of Paradise and spices alike arrived secondhand, the medieval imagination
was free to run riot. Though nothing could be confirmed (or, more to
the point, disproved), what was generally agreed was that spices came
from a topsy-turvy world where the normal rules of European life did
not apply. They were securely lodged in the same world of marvels and
misshapen prodigies that writhe across the portals of Europe's Roman-
esque churches or scamper and cavort across its manuscripts. An illu-
mination in a fourteenth-century manuscript in the Bibliothèque
Nationale in Paris has a team of swarthy Indians in loincloths harvesting pepper in wicker baskets while a European merchant samples the
crop; so far at least the botanical details are not far removed from the
reality. Nearby, however, a gaggle of dog-headed Indians haggle over
the harvest, men with faces set in their chests gambol among the
bushes, and other men hop around on a single, stout foot.

In its mix of half-accurate detail and wild distortion, this was a fairly
representative example of European visions of the East. But how seriously were such depictions meant to be taken? There is a risk, in considering these and similar visions, that our own modern credulity
outstrips the medieval. Evidently, some of the more fabulous tales of
the Indies and their spices were never meant to be taken wholly seriously; they are a notoriously unreliable guide to informed opinion and
a trap for the unwary. In the fantastic Asia of such illuminations we are,
manifestly, in a not-Europe. But while the tone of such depictions is
often playful or didactic, what is clear is that they derived their force
from their very invertedness. And spices were, for their creators, a
means to that end. It is precisely through this fictive inversion that we,
however dimly, can sense how extraordinary spices were in fact. Like
the dog-headed men and man-devouring Amazons with which they

were paired, spices were as ordinary in the imagined Indies as they were exceptional in Europe; that they were commonplace in medieval fantasies was because they were extraordinary in reality.

Retrospectively, of course, it is a little easier to extract fact from fantasy, but in medieval times the lines were more blurred. It is precisely this sense of a world turned upside down and inside out that animates the genre of the more or less fictional traveler's tales that appear from roughly the thirteenth century on. Many were parodies, such as the Brother Cipolla of *The Decameron,* with his trip to Liarland ("where I found a great many friars") and Parsnip, India, with its amazing flying feathers. Of these the most celebrated, and in every sense the spiciest, was the *Itinerarium* conventionally attributed to one Sir John Mandeville, a suitably chivalric-sounding pseudonym of an anonymous, probably French author. First circulated in various versions and translations between 1356 and 1366, along with the other by now stock features of the marvelous Eastern landscape—Gog and Magog, Prester John, the Great Khan and his Asian Utopia—spices are one of the hallmarks of his fantastic tableaux. Ginger, cloves, cinnamon, nutmeg, and mace grew in Java "more plentyfoulisch than in any other contree," a land that had "many tymes overcomen the Grete Cane of Cathaye in bataylle." Here, perhaps, is a grain of fact, a vague awareness of Javanese traders shuttling spices west from the Moluccas; so much the author might have learned from Marco Polo. But the force and the point—for Mandeville (or whoever) wrote not to inform but to amaze—is of the extraordinary become prosaic. Read on, and there are ox-worshiping Cynocephales, corpse-eating savages, and gems engendered from the tears of Adam and Eve. Such was the world where the spices grew. Along with dragons and mountains of gold, they were one of its distinguishing features.

Mandeville's account must have raised a knowing chuckle among the merchants, who, even now, knew better. And there were plenty who did know better. Odoric of Pordenone, a Franciscan friar who traveled through India, Southeast Asia, and China from roughly 1316 to 1330, reported having met "people in plenty" in Venice who had been in China. At much the same time, the Tunisian traveler Ibn Battuta saw Genoese merchants in India and China. But though the merchants did the legwork, it was the Mandevilles who set the tone. (Or perhaps this is to underestimate the savvy of the spice dealers, who, after all, had an interest in making bankable publicity for their exotic wares: "Thus men feign, to make things deer and of great price," as a thirteenth-century Franciscan monk said of the wilder myths concerning the origins of cinnamon.) Such accurate information about the spices as did make it through was either kept a close secret or else recast in brighter colors.

Or, alternatively, it was discarded as nonsense. Tellingly, Mandeville's account proved vastly more popular than a far more sober and factual authority on the Indies and their spices, the *Travels* of Marco Polo. Published a generation or so before Mandeville, Polo's book met with widespread suspicion. Despite Rustichello's best efforts (Rustichello being the professional romance writer with whom Polo shared a prison cell in Genoa, thanks to whose ability to spot a best-seller the *Travels* exist), the Venetian's unadorned account of Asia, with its straightforward, real-world qualities, was in some respects harder to credit than the fiction. In his straightforward businessman's manner Polo claimed to have sailed past lands where spices were commonplace, growing on real trees, harvested by real people, harvested in quantities that Europeans could not fathom. He claimed that the city of Kinsai (Hangchow), with its twelve thousand stone bridges and hundred-mile circumference, received one hundred times as much pepper as the whole of Christendom, "and more too." In his matter-of-fact tone, this was a little too much to swallow. It was somehow easier to place the Indies and their spices among the dog-heads and the floating islands. So extraordinary were spices that even the truth seemed fabulous.

And so it remained until the sixteenth century, when at last the discoverers chipped away at the great edifices of medieval ignorance and fantasy, dragging the realms of spice and gold into the prosaic light of day, into the unromantic focus of the profiteer and venture capitalist. The great Spice Age, the apex of the appetite, was also the age that killed off their mystery.

Ironically, the individual who did more than any other to draw spices out of fantasy into cold fact was himself one of the most avid consumers of medieval legends of spice and gold. This is perhaps Columbus's most remarkable achievement, for in respect of Eastern fables he bears, as has already been noted, more than a passing resemblance to Don Quixote, who so overcharged his fancy with the wooings, battles, and enchantments of Palmerin of England and Amadis of Gaul that he quite lost his grip on reality. But whereas Quixote's dreams sprouted from novels of chivalry and romance, Columbus's schemes were founded—and sold—on sources that presented themselves, however capriciously, as impeccably factual. The surviving remnants of his library in the Biblioteca Colombiana in Seville include several of the books from which he drew his ideas, among them the early-fifteenth-century *Imago Mundi* of Pierre d'Ailly (1350–1420) and the *Historia Rerum* of Pope Pius II (ruled 1458–1464), each laced with descriptions of the fabulous, spicy wonders of the East. There too is Columbus's copy of Polo's *Travels,* the margins crammed with the admiral's comments on each and every mention of gold, silver, precious stones, silk, ginger, pepper, musk, cloves, camphor, aloes, brazilwood, sandalwood, and cinnamon. Dipping into and out of these books, taking what he liked and disregarding what did not suit, spicing Polo's figures and distances with the vivid hues of the others, Columbus constructed the fabulous mental geography that, quite contrary to his expectations, succeeded in revolutionizing geography in an altogether different direction. When he sailed west, he quite genuinely believed he was sailing to Paradise. If he succeeded in reaching the place where the spices grew, he would, ipso facto, have arrived.

And to his dying day he believed that he had been but a hairsbreadth from getting there. He went to his grave not impoverished, as is often imagined, but unenlightened. Writing on the troubled progress of his third voyage in the autumn of 1498, charged with chronic mismanagement of the infant colony of Hispaniola, whose disgruntled settlers were now in open rebellion against his command, Columbus assured his patrons that he had been no more than a day's sailing from the earthly Paradise. At the time it seemed reasonable enough, at least to Columbus. Not only his reading told him so, but also the evidence of his own eyes. As he sailed around the top of South America, standing on deck in the waters off Trinidad, the Pole Star arced in the sky above him and the world seemed to spin off its usual axis. Columbus had the overwhelming, disconcerting impression that the ship was climbing, sailing up the incline to Paradise. (By this time Columbus had concluded that the world was pear-shaped, with the heights of Paradise perched on a protuberance shaped like a woman's nipple.) The Caribbean season was balmy and mild like an eternal spring: yet more evidence. Buckets were lowered over the side, and it was found that the ship, though still out of sight of land, was sailing in freshwater—the outflow, surely, of one of the four rivers flowing from the heights of Paradise. Columbus knew he had been, at most, only a short sail from the realms of spice and gold.

In the days of disgrace and humiliation that lay ahead, chained belowdecks, ignominiously sent back to Spain with his settlers in open revolt, it was a galling thought. But as Columbus's jailers and the increasingly impatient King Ferdinand were beginning to realize, he was adrift in a sea of delusion. The sweet water through which he had sailed was in fact the enormous outflow of the Orinoco; the people he met were not prelapsarian residents of the terrestrial Paradise but all-too-earthly Caribs. Even the translators of biblical languages that Columbus had had the foresight to bring along were of no use in deciphering their unintelligible clicks and grunts.*

But then Columbus always had been a dreamer; it was the quality that simultaneously made him great and, as far as some of his contemporaries were concerned, absurd. Even now there were harder heads that were beginning to see America for what it was, yet in his defense, Columbus's assumptions, his wildest surmises, seem a good deal stranger now than then. Given his premises and the mental universe of the medieval cosmographer, to seek the Kingdom of Sheba beyond the mangroves and jungled fringes of what is now the Dominican Republic was not, at the time, so quixotic. After all, the Bible said that Sheba's kingdom lay somewhere to the east—or west, if you went far enough—and was it not the biblical truth that Sheba had brought spices to Jerusalem? "There came no more such abundance of spices, as these, which the Queene of Sheba gave to King Solomon." And there were many people who were willing to push the notion of the unearthly origins of spice further still. Plenty of spices found their way into the medieval Heaven: according to a deep-seated assumption of medieval theology, God, Christ, the Virgin and saints, the holy and royal dead commonly smelled of spices. These were ideas and practices that were themselves inheritances from a much older, pagan past. Thousands of years before Columbus set off on his spice odyssey, it was not only Heaven and Paradise that smelled of spices, but the gods themselves.

Yet for the disappointed king this was of little interest—it was too recherché, too elevated by far. Short of cash and greedy for more, Ferdinand was not amused by his admiral's flights of fancy. And who can

---

*He took along a converted Jew who spoke Hebrew, Arabic, and "Chaldee" (Persian).

blame him? Columbus had promised earthly gold and spice but instead delivered meandering reworkings of old myths and fairy tales. With every year he seemed to be losing an already shaky grip on reality; he was becoming a crank. More galling still, between letters from his dreamy admiral Ferdinand was receiving altogether more down-to-earth missives from his Portuguese son-in-law, from whose boasting pamphlets of spiced Indian triumphs the booksellers were turning a tidy profit.

But if the Admiral of the Ocean Sea ended up sailing down spice routes of the imagination and discovering a new continent by a happy accident, these were not the only leads he might have followed. For if his fancy eventually led him far from reality, far out of this world, others took more earthy associations of spice for inspiration. To many of his contemporaries, spices were anything but paradisal, not so much on account of their origins as due to the uses to which they were put. Here the associations, above and beyond the pungent smell of Mammon, concerned very much more body than spirit. To those of less visionary inclinations than Columbus, it was not Paradise that spices evoked so much as Babylon.

Half a millennium after Columbus labored in vain, only vestiges of the former magnetism of spice remain: the twin poles of attraction and repulsion. But if the aura has long since faded, the continuing interest of the subject lies precisely in the complexity, the contradictory quality of the mixture: of sweetness and astringency; of hunger laced with misgivings; of recommendations and recipes hedged about with reservations. These were, moreover, tensions that even in Columbus's day had coexisted for centuries. Long before he set off on his optimistic blunder, there were others who pursued not only the Indies and their spices but also the paradises and Sirens that hovered about them, and others who decried them with equal vigor. This was an appetite of far greater antiquity than even Columbus could imagine and pregnant with greater ambiguities than he would admit.

II

PALATE

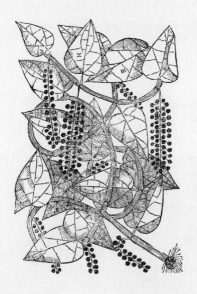

THE PEPPER PLANT
Acosta, *Tractado de las drogas* (Burgos, 1578)

CHAPTER 2

●

ANCIENT APPETITES

The beautiful vessels, the masterpieces of the Greeks, stir white
foam on the Periyar River . . . arriving with gold and departing
with pepper.

—*The Lay of the Anklet,* a Tamil poem of ca. A.D. 200

THE AROMANAUTS

From 11 to 8 B.C., the Romans' largest military camp in the land they
knew as Germania stood on a well-defended site by the banks of the
Lippe River, near the present-day town of Oberaden. Today the region
lies in the middle of the huge industrial sprawl of the Ruhr Valley, but
when the Romans arrived this was a wasteland dividing the barbarian
and civilized worlds. Behind were fields and towns; ahead, bogs and
forests. It was to push that division outward that the Romans were
here, and this, after three years of fighting, they did. The fearsome
tribesmen of the Sugambri were ground down, relocated, or put to the
sword. The legions moved on to new wars and new frontiers. The camp
on the Lippe was abandoned and left to an all but total obscurity, unin-
terrupted but for a brief flurry of interest some two thousand years later
with the visit of a team of German archaeologists. Picking through the
kitchen scrap heap, they found olive pits, coriander seeds, and black
pepper.

That the centurions hankered for a little variation from the dreary
German diet of roasted meat and porridge is no great surprise. In fact,
they were far from alone in enjoying their exotic seasonings, even in the
outermost bogs and forests of the barbarian north. In England a century
or so after Christ, soldiers stationed at the fort of Vindolanda regularly

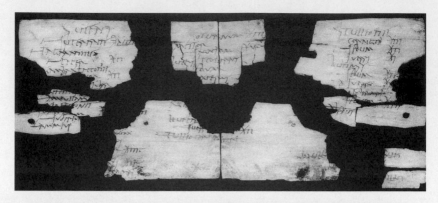

Roman accounting. A writing tablet from the fort of Vindolanda, south of Hadrian's Wall, dating from the first or second century A.D. Several tablets record the soldiers' expenditure on pepper.

seasoned their meals with Indian pepper as they peered over the battlements of Hadrian's Wall at the Caledonians; some of the inscribed wooden tablets recording their purchases still survive. Such concrete evidence confirms a fact that many Roman writers mention but that in the absence of physical evidence seemed barely credible: that before the time of Christ, a traffic in spices stretched across the Indian Ocean, from far beyond the easternmost reaches of imperial power, north and west across Europe to the outer reaches of the Roman world. And therein lay the roots of a culinary tradition that would endure long after the legions had crumbled and Rome itself lay in ruins.

The Romans were not the first Europeans to eat pepper, but they were the first to do so with any regularity. Locally produced seasonings had been used in the Mediterranean world since at least the time of the ancient Syrian civilization of Mari, late in the third millennium B.C., where inscriptions on clay tablets record the use of cumin and coriander to flavor beer. When Rome was still a village, Greek cooks knew a host of different seasonings. Cumin, sesame, coriander, oregano, and saffron are all mentioned in the Greek New Comedy of the fourth and third centuries B.C., but as yet no Eastern spices. It was not that the spices were unknown or that no one had yet thought to eat them, but rather that their exorbitant cost rendered them too precious for consumption by all but the very wealthy. There is a fragment by the Attic poet

Antiphanes dating from the fourth century B.C.: "If a man should bring home some pepper he's bought, they propose a motion that he be tortured as a spy"—from which not much can be extracted other than a vague allusion to a high cost. Another fragment contains a recipe for an appetizer of pepper, salad leaf, sedge (a grassy flowering herb), and Egyptian perfume. The philosopher Theophrastus (ca. 372–ca. 287 B.C.) knew pepper, but the context makes it clear that the spice was still the concern of the apothecary, not the cook.

Three centuries later, pepper was still an elite taste among the Greeks. According to Plutarch, one admirer was the Athenian tyrant Aristion, who was happy to feast even as his subjects starved. When a Roman army besieged Athens in 86 B.C., the cost of wheat soared to 1,000 drachmas the bushel, whereupon the chief priestess of the city approached the tyrant to beg for one twelfth of a bushel of wheat. Callously, he sent her a pound of pepper instead.

All that would change with the Romans. That a Roman soldier could share the taste even in the outer reaches of empire depended on one of Rome's more stupefying technical achievements, and it marks the moment when the spice trade between Europe and Asia first emerges into clear view. More than 1,500 years before Vasco da Gama sailed his three small caravels to India, the Romans had done the same, but in bigger vessels and on a much grander scale. And as with da Gama after them, a strong aroma of spice hung over their exploits.

By the time of the geographer Strabo (ca. 63 B.C.–ca. A.D. 24), writing a few decades before the legions decamped from the Lippe, a fleet numbering some 120 ships set off annually for the year-long round-trip to India. The outlines of their journey are described in the document known as the *Periplus,* a pilot's guide to sailing in the Indian Ocean. Written by an anonymous Greek-speaking sailor sometime in the first century A.D., the *Periplus* describes each step of the journey, identifying which harbors to stop in and which goods to acquire. His readers were the long-distance traders and trampers who serviced the ports and markets in what he calls the Erythraean Sea, by which he meant the huge expanse of water encompassing both the Red Sea and the Persian Gulf and Indian Ocean beyond.

There were two main trade routes within this vast expanse of water, each beginning at one of several ports along the Egyptian shore of the Red Sea. The first dropped down the African coast as far south as Mozambique, calling at the ports and trading stations that received products from the hinterland: ivory, incense, skins, slaves, ebony, exotic animals, and gold. The second and longer voyage, and the conduit by which Rome obtained its spices, turned east across the ocean to India. The ships that sailed it were some of the behemoths of ancient navigation, immense oceanworthy freighters displacing up to one thousand tons. One writer compared an Indian freighter to "a small universe in itself . . . equivalent to several ships of other nations." On board were crews of marines to protect the valuable cargoes from the pirates who plagued the waters until modern times. Picking their way south through the reefs and rocks of the Red Sea, the fleet fanned out at the Bab el Mandeb, the bottleneck where Africa and the Arabian Peninsula converge. Some made their last landfall on the southern tip of the Arabian Peninsula, near present-day Aden—the same place where the India-bound steamers of the Raj would stop for coal, telegraphs, and water some two thousand years later. Others sailed on south to Cape Guardafui, Africa's easternmost point, where the horn juts east into the Indian Ocean. In ancient times, the cape took its name from the traffic that paused here: the Cape of Spices. At this point the ships on the Africa route turned south and the India-bound vessels turned their prows east.

According to the *Periplus,* the next stage of the journey was pioneered by a Greek sailor by the name of Hippalus. In the age of sail all navigation in the Indian Ocean was—to some extent still is— overshadowed by the annual cycle of the monsoon. From May through August, the summer monsoon blows hard and wet out of the southwest, unpredictably and occasionally furiously. By late August, the blustery squalls weaken into stiff breezes and the occasional storm. By September, the summer winds splutter and falter, forgetting their outbursts and fading into indecisive squalls and calms.

Next comes a complete transformation. From November through March, the winter monsoon wafts unfaltering dry, balmy zephyrs from the northeast, as reliable and regular as any trade wind. With the right timing, outward or inward bound, ships were guaranteed a following wind in the starboard quarter. To Hippalus went the credit for recognizing this annual pattern, thereby unlocking the secret of navigating in the Indian Ocean. Armed with his insight, the Romans sailed across the belly of the ocean to India, bustling over in anything from twenty to forty days. While still out to sea, they were warned of the imminent approach of land by the swarms of red-eyed sea snakes that welled up around the hull, a mariner's guide in these waters to this day. Soon thereafter a blue-green blur lifted out of the sea, the cordillera of the Western Ghats.

The Romans called at any one of nineteen ports in which, in the words of the *Periplus,* "great ships sail . . . due to the vast quantities of pepper and *malabathron.*"* In return for manufactured goods such as glassware and works of art, tin, and Mediterranean coral—much prized in India for its imputed magical properties—and above all bullion, Rome's traders brought back ivory, pearls, tortoiseshell, diamonds, onyx, agate, crystal, amethyst, opal, beryl, sapphire, ruby, turquoise, garnet, bloodstone, emerald, and carnelian. There were silks transhipped from China, parrots for a senator's menagerie, and tigers, rhinoceroses, and elephants destined for public slaughter in the arena. There were spices from the north, costus† and nard from the Himalayan foothills, and still others arriving from further east (including, quite possibly, Moluccan cloves and nutmeg, although there are questions over their identification in Rome before the fourth century A.D.). But it was pepper that was Malabar's chief attraction.

Rome's spice traders were pointed in the right direction by less celebrated forerunners. Before the Romans arrived there were Greeks; and someone, presumably, had shown the Greeks the way. Tales of India had filtered west since the time of Herodotus, and Greek travelers had known the land route to the north of India from at least the time of the conquests of Alexander the Great. In 325 B.C., Alexander's Admiral Nearchus sailed from the Indus back up the Persian Gulf and up the Euphrates to Babylon. Around 302 B.C., one of Alexander's successors apparently sponsored two voyages from the Euphrates to India and its spices. However, the first hard evidence of any European involvement in regular seaborne trade with the spice-bearing south of the subcontinent dates from the time of the Greco-Egyptian dynasty of the Ptolemies (305–30 B.C.). Successors to the Egyptian fragment of Alexander's empire, the Ptolemies had sporadic commercial exchanges with India, though these exchanges were probably in Arab (and Indian?) hands. Ptolemy II (ruled 285–246 B.C.) exchanged ambassadors with the

*Malabathron is cinnamon leaf, sometimes called "Indian leaf," prized on account of its potent aromatic oil. It is the leaf of one of several relatives of cinnamon native to India.

†Costus is the aromatic root of *Sassurea lappa,* indigenous to Kashmir, from which is extracted a powerful oil widely used in ancient perfumes and unguents.

Maurya emperors Chandragupta II (ruled ca. 321–ca. 297 B.C.) and
Aśoka (ruled ca. 274–ca. 232 B.C.). Back in Egypt, his triumphal procession of 271–270 B.C. featured Indian women, oxen, and marbles.

According to the geographer Strabo, the first European to attempt to
establish serious commercial contacts with India was a certain Eudoxus
of Cyzicus, an entrepreneurial Greek who made the acquaintance of an
Indian shipwrecked somewhere on the shores of the Red Sea. Around
120 B.C., Eudoxus was in Alexandria when the regime's coast guards
brought a half-dead Indian sailor to the court of Ptolemy Euergetes II.
Most likely the castaway came from the Dravidian south of the continent or possibly even Ceylon, since by this stage an interpreter for one
of the northern languages could have been found without too much difficulty. Before long the enigmatic arrival acquired a sufficient command of Greek to interest Eudoxus in the possibility of going to India
himself.

Armed with firsthand knowledge of Indian waters, Eudoxus made
two trips to India to buy spices and other Eastern luxuries, returning on
each occasion with a rich haul of exotica, much to the delight of the
king, who promptly requisitioned the lot. Frustrated, and anticipating
an idea that would captivate the geographers of medieval Europe, he
attempted to circumvent the problem by circumnavigating Africa. On
the first attempt he made it no further than modern Morocco, where his
crew mutinied and he was forced to turn back. Undeterred, he set out a
second time, taking with him seeds to sow crops and some dancing girls
to keep his crew amenable. Having sailed west beyond the Strait of
Gibraltar, neither Eudoxus nor the dancing girls were ever heard from
again, but he deserves at least a mention in any history of navigation, for
his is the first name in a tradition that culminates with Vasco da Gama.*

Whereas history records Eudoxus as a flamboyant failure, Rome's
approach to the problem of reaching India and its riches was, character-
istically, a good deal more effective. Following the defeat and suicide of
Cleopatra, the last of the Greco-Egyptian dynasty of the Ptolemies, the
emperor Augustus annexed Egypt to the empire in 30 B.C., thereby

---

*A better parallel—for Eudoxus never reached his destination, or at least never lived to tell
the tale—might be with the Vivaldi brothers of Genoa, who in A.D. 1291 sailed west beyond
Gibraltar "that they might go by sea to the ports of India," never to be heard from again. In the
following years, several expeditions were sent to find them, to no avail. It was perhaps with the
Vivaldis in mind that Dante wrote of the "mad flight" of Ulysses, who likewise—in Dante's
version—disappeared over the western horizon without a trace (*Inferno,* 26.125).

granting Roman merchants direct access to the Red Sea. Flushed with the spoils of empire and with an emergent class of the Roman megarich demanding new and more exotic luxuries, Roman merchants now had the incentive, opportunity, and wherewithal to establish themselves as a serious presence in Indian Ocean trade.

They wasted no time and spared no means. Within a decade of Egypt's conquest a bustling traffic was under way. New ports were constructed on the Red Sea shore, and wells were dug along the caravan routes crossing the desert from the Nile to the coast. Most likely the impulse for this expansion came from competition with Eastern powers already established in the trade, among them the commercial empire of the Nabataeans, an Arabian people that had grown rich on the ancient caravan traffic from Arabia and beyond—the splendid ruins of Petra the most visible reminder of their wealth. Further south, the Romans faced competition from the trading powers of the Hadhramaut, successors to the trade and caravan routes once traveled, if the Bible is to be believed, by the queen of Sheba. No sooner had Egypt been subjugated than an army under the command of the prefect of Egypt was dispatched to sack ports along the Arabian coasts. The likely incentive for the expedition was much the same as had earlier spurred Eudoxus and would remain a perennial catalyst of the spice trade for the best part of another two millennia: the desire to circumvent—in this case, to rub out—the middleman. This obscure expedition was apparently the first war launched by a European power for the sake of the lucrative Eastern traffic, but it would not be the last.

With the way to India now wide-open to Roman shipping, East and West began to develop a clearer image of each other than had ever been possible. Roman emperors regularly received Indian ambassadors. Augustus apparently exhibited a tiger in 13 or 11 B.C. For their part, the Indians were evidently reasonably familiar with Rome and impressed by what they saw: at Ara, India, there is an inscription of King Kanishka in which he refers to himself as "Caesar." Contacts were deepening, yet from the distance of Rome, India still appeared as a hazy mix of fact and fantasy, as in Apuleius's (ca. A.D. 124–ca. 170) description:

The Indians are a people of great population and vast territories situated far to our east, by Ocean's ebb, where the stars first rise at the ends of the earth, beyond the learned Egyptians and the superstitious Jews, Nabataean merchants and flowing-robed Parthians, past the Ituraeans* with their meager crops and the Arabs rich in perfumes—wherefore I do not so much wonder at the Indians' mountains of ivory, harvests of pepper, stockpiles of cinnamon, tempered iron, mines of silver and smelted streams of gold: nor the Ganges, the greatest of all rivers and the king of the waters of the Dawn, running in a hundred streams . . .

The merchants who went there knew better, but it was not in their interest to be too forthcoming about what they saw—one reason, perhaps, why aside from the unadorned listing of ports and products in the *Periplus* no firsthand account is extant. Surviving Indian sources describe the foreigners' trading stations and warehouses as "residences of limitless wealth." There are references to Western converts to Buddhism and Greek mercenaries in the employ of Indian rulers. An Indian poet writes of his ruler's taste for Greek wine. Greek carpenters built a palace for an Indian king. At Muziris, the principal entrepôt on the coast, the Romans erected a temple to the emperor Augustus: an act of pious patriotism, perhaps, or a reminder of the long arm of the metropole. Its ruins lie somewhere under the modern town of Cranganore, on the banks of a river sprung from a maze of backwaters by which the pepper arrived, via porter, buffalo, and barge, from harvest further inland. Ancient Tamil poets describe Muziris as a scene of heaving activity: a town that "offers toddy as if it were water to those who come to pour there the goods from the mountains and those from the sea, to those who bring ashore in the lagoon boats the 'gifts' of gold brought by the ships, and to those who crowd the port in the turmoil created by the sacks of pepper piled up in the houses." Visiting Malabar today, it is easy to imagine that the scene that greeted the Romans cannot have changed much since antiquity. In the spice quarters of Malabar the tourist still sees the same scenes of pulsating energy: haggling merchants and a harbor crowded with boats from the backwaters unloading their cargo of spices. The occasional buffalo pushes its way through the crowd while porters scurry to and from the warehouses, bent double under sacks of cardamom and pepper.

With the right timing the return leg was a sleepier affair than the outward journey. Once the spices had been bought and loaded onto the

*A people in northeast Palestine.

ships, nothing remained for the Romans but to wait for the monsoon winds to shift in their favor and, sailors being sailors, knock back the toddy like water. With the gentle northeasters of the winter monsoon in their sails, Rome's spice fleets retraced their route eastward across the ocean, then north up the Red Sea. The cargoes were unloaded on the Egyptian coast, then transferred onto caravans that angled back across the desert to the Nile. During the course of one such crossing a returnee from the Indian voyage carved graffiti that may still be read on the walls of the Wadi Menih: "C. Numidius Eros made this in the 38th year of Caesar's [Augustus's] rule, returning from India in the month of Pamenoth." In modern terms the year was 2 B.C., the month of February or March, precisely the time when the fleets were expected back on the winds of the winter monsoon.

Having made landfall in Egypt, the sailors were back among the familiar sights and sounds of the Roman world. When the caravans reached the Nile, their cargo was loaded onto barges and freighted downstream to Alexandria, the chief port of the delta, where the spices were transferred onto a bulk freighter. The run from Alexandria to Rome was the home stretch, the most heavily trafficked trade route of the ancient world. Apart from supplying Rome with its pepper, this was the route by which the Egyptian grain arrived and kept the plebs quiescent. A few weeks' sailing brought the pepper to Rome's great port at Ostia at the mouth of the Tiber. From here it was shipped upriver for distribution and sale in the city's "Perfumers' Quarter," the *vicus unguentarius.*

Between harvest in Malabar and consumption in Rome, the pepper had come a distance, as the crow flies, of well over five thousand miles; considerably more once the twists of the long and winding journey are taken into account, down around the great dogleg of Arabia, shipped and reshipped from buffalo to barge and from ship to caravan. This was, by some distance, the longest trade route of the ancient world. Yet in Rome itself only the faintest of traces remain of the heroic efforts that went into getting the pepper from harvest to consumption. In the time of the emperor Trajan (ruled A.D. 98–117), spices, collectively known as the *pipera,* or peppers, were sold in a market built into the flank of the Quirinal Hill, of which several walls and arches are still standing. Until the end of the Middle Ages, the memory of the spices once sold here endured in the name of the ancient road still visible from the Via IV Novembre, like many other ancient names corrupted via the medium of medieval Latin but easily recognizable as the Via Biberatica. Further along the Forum are the remains of the *horrea piperataria,* the spice stores constructed by the emperor Domitian in A.D. 92. By Domitian's day the inflow of Eastern spices had become so great that a new store was needed over an older and by now inadequate portico dating from the reign of Nero (A.D. 54–68). Here the city's pepper and other spices were kept in a convenient central location, right in the heart of the ancient city. Two thousand years on, and the assiduous visitor can still see the remains of Domitian's pepper warehouse, now no more than a few crumbling, shin-high walls and unimpressive piles of rubble, disappearing beneath the sprawling ruin of the basilica of Constantine. They are, frankly, not much to look at, yet if there were such a thing, they would merit a mark on the culinary map of Europe. For the ruins of the *horrea* mark a beginning of sorts, as the oldest visible reminder of the serious advent of Eastern spices in European cuisine, the beachhead from which spices went on to conquer the palates of the Western world.

In the centuries that followed the construction of the spice stores, Rome's energies waxed and waned; the empire contracted, was overrun by barbarians, and finally collapsed. The volume of traffic and consumption that fueled the transoceanic spice trade would not be seen again for more than a thousand years. Yet both the taste and the traffic endured. When Rome faltered, the Arabs took over, and the Indian Ocean became a Muslim lake, home to the seaborne civilization that gave rise to the tales of Sinbad and his voyages to the magical realms of spice, giant birds and monsters, genii and gold. Spices were acquiring the romantic, glamorous freight they have carried down to the present day. And although the flow of spices into Europe slowed to a trickle and at times all but disappeared, it never quite stopped. The pepper left behind in Germany by a Roman soldier is the first faint spoor of an ancient tradition, perhaps the oldest continuous link between Asia and Europe and one that has survived, battered but intact, ever since.

OF SPICED PARROT
AND STUFFED DORMICE

Long-life spiced honey wine, given to people on a journey: put ground pepper with skimmed honey in a small container for

spiced wine, and when it is the time for drinking, mix some of the
honey with the wine. It is suggested to add a little wine to the
honey mixture, so the honey flows more freely.

—APICIUS, *De re coquinaria*

The vast wealth and reach that Rome acquired in the first century B.C.
transformed the classical idea of spices and the uses to which they were
put. Though even in Roman times cuisine was only one of the many
uses of spices—and even that not always the most important—one
result of the direct trade with India was that costs plummeted, with the
result that spices entered the diet more frequently. A revolution in the
way spices were used and viewed was under way.

The first world empire, Rome also boasted the first global cuisine.
By the time of Pliny the Elder (A.D. 23–79), Rome's cosmopolitan
tastes had reached such a pitch that he talks of the flavors of Egypt,
Crete, Cyrene, and India appearing in Roman kitchens. Even now there
were dissenters: Plutarch (ca. A.D. 46–ca. 119) writes that even in his
day there were some who had not acquired the taste, but they were,
apparently, a minority. Pepper in particular attained widespread familiarity, with contemporary literary sources taking familiarity with the
spice for granted. A schoolboy's textbook featured a talking pig by the
name of M. Grunnius ("Grunter") Corocotta, who obligingly asks to be
well cooked with pepper, nuts, and honey. Archaeology reinforces the
impression of a widespread taste. Silver pepper pots (*piperatoria*) dating
from the early imperial period onward have been found practically all
over the Roman world: at Pompeii; to the south in Corfinium and Mur-
muro in Sicily; at Nicolaevo in Bulgaria; at Cahors, Arles-Trinquetaille,
and Saint-Maur-de-Glanfeuil in France.

Neither the silverware nor its contents were for everyone, as numerous literary references make clear. In *The Golden Ass* by Apuleius, the
scabrous tale of the hero Lucius's adventures when transformed from
human to ass and back again, pepper is referred to as a "choice delicacy," fit for a banquet. While still in asinine form, Lucius amazes his
owners by eschewing hay and tucking into the sort of food that an ass
would be least likely to eat, namely meats seasoned with laser (another
costly seasoning), fish cooked in some exotic sauce, and fattened birds
in pepper. The epigrammatist Martial (ca. A.D. 38–103) writes of pepper in a quintessentially aristocratic pairing of wild boar, generous
Falernian—the most prized and expensive vintage of the Romans—

and "mysterious garum," a highly esteemed fish sauce. Martial balks at the expense, complaining that his cook has used up a "huge mound of pepper." "I have a more modest hunger," complains the penniless poet.

For the more solvent, pepper's air of exclusivity made the spice an ideal gift. It was customary to distribute pepper at the great midwinter festival of the Saturnalia—a ritual not unlike Christmas gift giving, whereby favors could be curried, debts acknowledged, and generosity displayed.* Martial writes of an influential Sabine lawyer's largesse: three half-pounds of incense and pepper along with hampers from all over the Mediterranean filled with Libyan figs and Tuscan sausages. One Saturnalia, Martial himself received some pepper, although this was a lesser gift than he had hoped for. A stingy patron's generosity had dried up:

> You used to send me a pound of silver; now it's down to half a pound,
> But of pepper. Sextus: my pepper doesn't cost me quite so much.

Yet pepper was no trifle: though it may have been widespread, this did not make it commonplace. In a satire addressed to an indolent student, Persius (A.D. 34–62) writes of pepper belonging in a "wealthy larder," along with hams, gifts from fat Umbrians, and tokens of gratitude from clients—in other words, not the sort of thing a poor scholar ought to be feeding himself, such as lentil soup and porridge. Martial implies that what was out of a workingman's reach fell within the budget of the cook-employing classes:

> So that bland beets, a workman's lunch, actually taste of something,
> How often the cook turns to wine and pepper!

Elsewhere, he advised pepper served with figpecker, a small bird esteemed by the Roman gourmet:

> When by chance a shining, waxy, broad-loined figpecker comes your way,
> If you have any taste, add pepper.

Martial reserved a special bile for stinginess, a failing for which he lambasts a certain Lupus, whose gift of a "farm" amounted to less than a window box "that an ant could eat in a single day":

---

*Saturnalia and Christmas may well have still more in common, in that the fourth-century Church seems to have appropriated the date for the celebration of its own festival of Christmas—a shrewd undercutting (or co-opting) of the opposition.

> *In which you might find no vegetable*
> *Other than Cosmus's leaf and uncooked pepper,*
> *Where you couldn't lie a cucumber straight,*
> *Nor a snake stretch itself out.* *

When in due course Martial found himself without a patron—unremarkably, perhaps, given his propensity to bite the hands that fed him—he fretted whether his latest publication would end up as scrap, used as a "cowl" to wrap fried tuna, incense, or pepper, the equivalent of finding one's book remaindered. (The custom survives in the Middle East and the Caucasus, where spices are still sold in cones of newspaper.) Robert Herrick (1591–1674) borrowed the notion for a book of his own:

> *Thy injur'd Leaves serve well,*
> *To make loose gowns for Mackerel,*
> *Or see the Grocers in a trice,*
> *Make hoods of thee to serve out Spice.*

It was also Martial who started a long tradition of figurative use of spice, concerning a light-fingered dinner guest more light-fingered or "peppery-handed" than Autolycus, patron of thieves. The conceit has survived in European languages in one form or another ever since, as in Sir Andrew Aguecheek's challenge to Viola in *Twelfth Night:* "I warrant there's vinegar and pepper in't." Or the *OED*'s complaint of a misused servant: "My master pepered my ars with well good speed."

As with its figurative uses, so it was at the table, where pepper apparently served much the same role as it does today, as a more or less universal seasoning. As for spices' other culinary applications, reliable information is in short supply. The one significant exception is the cookbook known by the unspectacular title of *De re coquinaria,* or *Cookbook,* the sole example of the genre to have survived from antiquity. Both the author and the date of composition are unknown, although traditionally it has been ascribed to a certain Apicius, a legendary gourmand of the first century A.D. The version we have has passed through the hands of a compiler who rewrote the book in his late Latin of the fourth or fifth centuries. Most commentators tentatively date the original to the second century A.D.

---

*Cosmus was a famous parfumier, whom Martial lampoons elsewhere for his superexclusive cinnamon scents. His "leaf" is probably malabathron, or cinnamon leaf.

On the evidence of Apicius, it would seem that the Romans liked it hot. *De re coquinaria* is as suffused with spices as, say, a more modern Italian cookbook is with olive oil. Pepper alone appears in 349 of the book's 468 recipes. Spices are used to enliven vegetables, fish, meats, wine, and desserts. The very first recipe is for a "spiced wine surprise," followed by a traveler's honey-spiced wine. There are spiced salts "for many purposes," including one mix for "digestion, and to move the bowels," the latter including white and black pepper, thyme, ginger, mint, cumin, celery seed, parsley, oregano, arugula, saffron, bay leaf, and dill. The mix is described as "extremely mild, more than you would think."

Mixtures such as these were evidently added after cooking, and many recipes end with the directive to "sprinkle on pepper and serve"—no great change there. To modern eyes the most striking use of spices is in a huge variety of sauces, both hot and cold, either cooked as an integral part of the dish or added after cooking. There was a sharp sauce to cut fat, made of cumin, ginger, rue, cooking soda, dates, pepper, honey, vinegar, and *liquamen,* a fermented fish sauce much loved by the Romans. A digestive sauce helped the meat go down with the sharp-sweet combination of pepper, cardamom, cumin, dried mint, honey, *liquamen,* vinegar, and various other aromatics. There was a green sauce of pepper, cumin, caraway, spikenard,* "all types of mixed green herbs," dates, honey, vinegar, wine, *garum,* and oil. Another, served cold with poultry, consisted of pepper, lovage, celery seeds, mint, myrtle berries or raisins, honey, wine, vinegar, oil, and *garum.* Some sauces were more complicated, using spices with all manner of trussed and embellished meats: kid, lamb, suckling pig, venison, boar, beef, duck, goose, and chicken. There was even dormouse stuffed with pepper and nuts—presumably a fiddly operation. There was a peppery sauce for "high" (literally "goatish") birds, by which the author meant not putrid but gamey. To subvert lettuce's flatulent properties, Apicius suggests a pepper sauce of vinegar, fish sauce, cumin, ginger, rue, dates, pepper, and honey.

While most of Apicius's seasonings grew within the empire, the Eastern spices occupied a prominent place in his spice rack: most conspicuously, ginger, cardamom, and of course pepper. There is a learned debate on the possibility of others; some have speculated whether clove

---

*Spikenard, *Nardostachys jatamansi,* a scented grass from which an aromatic oil is extracted, is native to northern India.

and nutmeg lie hidden under unfamiliar names. One notable absentee is cinnamon. Apart from a solitary reference in Pliny's *Natural History* to a recipe for cinnamon-spiced wine,* in Roman times the spice appears to have been reserved for more elevated purposes.

The Roman table, then, was apparently not so bizarre as some have been willing to believe. *De re coquinaria* offers the same discordant mix of the strange and the familiar as one finds with so many other aspects of Roman civilization. Minus exotica such as parrot, flamingo, and dormice, there is much here that would not be out of place on the average twenty-first-century table; in recent years several editions of the work adapted to the modern kitchen have appeared. Many of his seasonings can still be found in any well-stocked spice cupboard, and even the fermented fish sauces that revolted some early commentators were probably not so far removed from Vietnamese or Thai fish sauces, or for that matter the pungent anchovy relish much loved by English gents in the age of Queen Victoria. His spiced wines are not at all dissimilar to the mulled wines and vermouths still around today, and some of the spiced sauces are startlingly reminiscent of the pungent and sharp sauces enjoyed by the European nobility through medieval times and beyond. It would seem that the art of the sauce has been a perennial feature of elite cuisine, from Apicius's day down to our own.

Even the notion of peppered desserts is not as odd as it might at first sight appear. To round off a meal, Apicius suggests a variety of spiced desserts such as a peppered wheat-flour fritter with honey or a confection of dates, almonds, and pine nuts baked with honey and a little pepper. The pepper is still used to add tang to sweet confections such as *panforte,* now a specialty of Siena but once widespread through medieval Europe. Were it possible to trace the ancestry of this Italian dessert, the path would lead, I suspect, back to ancient Rome.

SPICE FOR TRIMALCHIO

If Atticus feasts in style, he is considered very grand.

—JUVENAL, *Satires*

---

*In his lost work *On Drunkenness* Aristotle claimed that wine spiced with cinnamon was less intoxicating.

> One course of a Roman meal would lay us very low, probably, and
> strip our palates for many days of even the crudest perceptions
> of flavor. —M. F. K. FISHER, *Serve It Forth*

Familiar is not, however, how most modern readers have seen Apicius.
In the last few centuries, his book has provoked more bafflement than
admiration, particularly in the matter of spice. "Perhaps the craving for
excessive flavouring is an olfactory delirium, a pathological case, as yet
unfathomed like the excessive craving for liquor, and, being a problem
for the medical fraternity, it is only of secondary importance to gastronomy"—such was the verdict of one of his nineteenth-century editors.
And this opinion is fairly representative of the received wisdom on
Roman food. Until very recently, the ancient Roman meal was generally considered on a par with other notoriously lurid displays served up
for public consumption, along the lines of gladiatorial bloodbaths and
public crucifixions: harsh and brutal, a subject more for revulsion than
for emulation or serious study. Apicius's cookbook in particular is regularly cited as proof of rampant excess in the kitchen, nowhere more than
in the taste for overpowering, palate-stripping seasonings.

Well, maybe. But it is a confident judge who reaches a verdict on
the cuisine of an entire civilization on the basis of one cookbook, and
in fact there are good reasons to read Apicius with due caution. The
physiology of the human palate has not evolved appreciably in the last
two millennia, and it is likely that the Romans no more regularly
seared their mouths with spices than we do. Nowhere does Apicius
give quantities for his recipes, so we know that the end result was
spicy, but we don't know *how* spicy. Doubtless if a recipe for an Indian
curry were transcribed in the same manner, it would provoke similar
confusion among those for whom Indian food is as alien as Roman food
is to us.

In any case, it is more than a little naive to read the text simply as a
practical cookbook, since the nominal author of the book was himself a
figure of some notoriety. According to a version of events circulating in
the first century A.D., Apicius supposedly ate his way through a vast
fortune before finding himself down to his last 10 million sesterces: still
a healthy bank balance but not enough for this gourmand, who took
poison rather than face life on a limited budget. To the satirist Juvenal
(ca. A.D. 55–ca. 127) his name was mud. Christians were still more
prejudiced: to the Church Father Tertullian (ca. A.D. 155–ca. 220) Api-

cius's greed was legendary, contributing an adjective of his own for his trademark seasonings; to Apollinaris Sidonius (ca. 430–ca. 490), "Apician" was another word for "glutton." The notoriously debauched and luxurious emperor Elagabalus (ruled A.D. 218–222) is recorded as having had a high regard for his works, a detail the author of *The Augustan History* slipped in as mutually revealing and damning. There was, in short, nothing neutral about Apicius; his name carried none of the comforting, homely associations of a Fannie Farmer or Delia Smith. In any case, the contents of the cookbook that bears his name were of practical interest to only a relatively narrow segment of Roman society. Most of the population of the empire lived at or not far above the subsistence level, and on the grounds of cost alone Apicius's more celebrated recipes—boiled, spiced flamingo, for instance—were out of reach of the vast majority.

Which was, in all likelihood, precisely the point. For like flamingos, spices were an expensive taste. Only pepper was reasonably available to a sizable share of the population, and even pepper, as we have seen, carried an air of exclusivity. In his *Natural History* Pliny gives a list of spice prices that were probably fixed by the state. Black pepper was the cheapest at 4 denarii the pound, white pepper nearly double that at 7. A pound of ginger cost 6 denarii, the same quantity of cassia anything from 5 to 50. By far the most expensive were various grades of cinnamon oil, in mixed form ranging from 35 to 300 denarii the pound, in pure form a whopping 1,000 to 1,500. At this time a citizen soldier earned a wage of 225 denarii per annum, and a little later a free day laborer could earn about 2 denarii per diem. In the days of the early empire, a pound of black pepper, the cheapest and most available spice, would buy forty pounds of wheat, representing in the order of a few days' wages for a member of the "working class." A pound of the finest cinnamon oil would cost a centurion up to six years' work.

They at least would not have been pouring on the spice with a heavy hand. And even for those with the money, there is plenty of evidence that Romans knew when their food was overspiced. The irony of the now traditional images of Roman food as an exercise in baroque excess is that they were in large part the product not of Rome's enthusiasm for bingeing but of its reticence, the credit for which is due to Christian polemicists, who were virtually obliged to portray Rome as a vast, gluttonous sink; culinary history, like any other form of history, is written by the winners. But in fact a great deal of Roman writing on food is

couched in the sort of language we might associate more with Zen minimalism than with a Lucullan banquet. In his eleventh satire Juvenal
lays out the criteria of the morally blameless meal: modest, rustic, and
homegrown, it will not break the bank. The service is simple and unaffected, without any indecent floor shows. A bracing reading of epic
poetry is entertainment enough. One of the letters of Pliny the Younger
reproaches his friend Septicius Clarus, who repeatedly scorned invita-
tions to simple meals of lettuce, snails, and wheat cakes chez Pliny for
the flashy delights of oysters, sow's innards, sea urchins, and Spanish
dancing girls (can we blame him?). In Pliny's opinion the ideal meal
should be "as elegant as it is frugal."

In this respect Pliny was far from alone—particularly, it would
seem, in respect of seasonings and spices. The comedies of Plautus
(ca. 254–184 B.C.) and Terence (ca. 195–ca. 159 B.C.) are sprinkled
through with references to seasonings (*condimenta*), one of their stock
characters the boastful cook who can reel off all the exotic flavors at his
disposal: Cilician saffron, Egyptian coriander, Ethiopian cumin, and,
most tempting of all, silphium of Cyrene. This North African aromatic, ultimately harvested to extinction, turned Roman gourmets
weak at the knees.* There was even a musical comedy on the topic. And
when the seasonings were overdone, Romans were capable of expressing
themselves with a forcefulness that makes even the most hostile restaurant review seem a model of restraint. In Plautus's *Pseudolus,* first produced in 191 B.C., a pimp by the name of Ballio goes to hire a cook
from the "Cooks' Forum" (or "crooks' forum," as the tightfisted Ballio
calls it). Through his preening chef, Plautus has fun at the expense of
all the trendy cooks who employ all the latest spices and "celestial seasonings," the names of which are pure fantasy: *cepolendrum, maccidem,
secaptidem, cicamalindrum, hapalocopide, cataractria.* Some of these mock
Greco-Latin pastiches sound vaguely menacing: *secaptidem,* for instance,
sounds like something that cuts or slashes through you (from *secare,* to
cut or sever), and the unappetizing *cataractria* evokes a waterfall, a
portcullis, a sluice, or a type of seabird. For such mockery of novelty for
novelty's sake to get a laugh, the culinary scene must already have been
reasonably diverse and sophisticated. (The inflated language of Plautus's cook often comes to mind when I'm looking over the menu of a

---

*By the middle of the first century A.D., Nero could acquire just one specimen, apparently
the last. Thus to his many crimes must be added an extinction.

fashionable new restaurant.) Trying to justify his high fee, the cook declares of his rivals that "they don't season with condiments, but with screech-owls, that devour the guests' innards alive."

Which is not, in so many words, the sort of language one would expect of a culture accustomed to drowning out its flavors with over-powering, palate-stripping seasonings. And in fact there is a perfectly reasonable explanation of Rome's apparent addiction to spices, one that has more to do with the social than the strictly practical purpose of cookery. In Rome no more than in any other developed culture can one explain habits of cooking merely in terms of function, any more than other fashions such as dress or language can be accounted for in such narrowly utilitarian terms. Historically, people have eaten spices not simply because they taste good but also, and sometimes more impor-tantly, because they look good. "Tell me what you eat and I will tell you what you are," wrote Brillat-Savarin. For most of their history spices spoke unequivocally of taste, distinction, and wealth.

For a wealthy Roman the dinner table (technically, the couch, the dining table being a medieval innovation) was one of the most effective stages on which he could display his sophistication and liberality. Public or semipublic events such as banquets offered the perfect oppor-tunity for flaunting it (the cost and flamboyance of a dish were a procla-mation of opulence and generosity). At his banquets the emperor Elagabalus mixed together jewels, apples, and flowers, tossing out as much food from the window as was served to his guests. He "loved to hear the prices of the food served at his table exaggerated, claiming it was an appetizer for the banquet." He fed foie gras to his dogs, served truffles in place of pepper and ground pearls on the fish, and dished up gold-encrusted peas.

Elagabalus was an extreme and indeed a pathological case, yet his appetites exemplified an ingrained tendency of Roman society. Romans of a certain class generally took an uncomplicated attitude to the rela-tionship between wealth and happiness, an ethos well summarized by Apuleius: "Truly blessed—doubly blessed!—are those that trample gems and jewelry underfoot." A single adjective, *beatus,* sufficed for both wealth and happiness. To those inclined to agree, display at the table was nothing less than a social imperative. Only the poor or miserly patron stinted in his hospitality, at the expense of influence and regard, whether in his own eyes or those of the client's. Juvenal's fifth satire is addressed to the contemptible client who accepts second-rate hospitality and a miserly meal of fish bloated on Tiber sewage, "like some public buffoon." Even the host's satirically sentient lobster disdains such contemptible guests.

For those keen to avoid such a fate, whether a host out to impress or a client on the receiving end, spices were a godsend. They were expensive and exotic, not far behind the gems Elagabalus tossed from his window. Elagabalus himself perfumed his swimming pool with spices. They were the ideal accoutrements of the flashy gourmands who, in Juvenal's words,

> *scour air, sea and land for tasty morsels,*
> *and cost is never an object; pry more closely, and you find*
> *the more they spend, the greater their pleasure.*

It was doubly impressive that spices were, in nutritional terms, superfluous: prime examples of what Lucan (A.D. 39–65) saw as "what luxury, frenzied by an inane love of display has sought out throughout the entire globe, unbidden by hunger." The Romans certainly did not invent gastronomic snobbery, but they raised it to a high art. Athenaeus (ca. A.D. 200–?) dedicated a book to the subject, *The Deipnosophists* or *Banquet of the Learned,* a fifteen-book marathon of recherché commentary on matters gastronomic through the course of a nightlong banquet.

In social terms, then, the cost of spices was less a liability than an asset. They were, moreover, ideally suited for the equally ancient inclination to pretentiousness. One of the *Satires* of Horace (65–8 B.C.) mocks an absurdly affected banquet hosted by a certain Nasidienus Rufus, who waxes lyrical over the dinner he serves. For the appetizer there is wild boar "captured while a gentle south wind was blowing." Pepper—the white variety is *de rigueur*—features in one of the main courses, a dish of lamprey served in a sauce of live shrimp, described by the host in language worthy of a modern gourmet magazine. His lamprey,

he said, was caught while still pregnant; had it been taken later, the flesh would have been inferior. These are the ingredients of the sauce: extra-virgin olive oil from Venafrum; fish sauce from Spain; a five-year-old wine, but Italian-grown, and added during the cooking—if you add it after the cooking a Chian vintage suits best—white pepper, not without a little vinegar, made from fermented wines from Lesbos. I was the one who first pointed out that you should boil arugula and bitter elecampane* in the sauce; whereas Curtillus prefers sea urchins, unwashed.

For Nasidienus it was apparently the sheer difficulty of obtaining ingredients that counted. Elagabalus refused to eat fish while at the coast, yet insisted on it when he found himself far inland. The emperor's insistence on novelty could take a sadistic turn:

> By way of entertainment he used to propose to his guests that they should invent new sauces for seasoning the food, and he would offer a great prize to him whose sauce he liked, even giving him a silk robe, which was at that time regarded as a rarity and an honor. If, however, he disliked the sauce, he would order that its creator would have to keep eating it until he came up with a better one.

But it is a character from fiction that is most closely identified with the Roman penchant for culinary exuberance. The *Cena Trimalchionis,* or Trimalchio's banquet, is a mid-first-century work by Petronius (?–ca. A.D. 66), bon vivant, courtier, and style consultant to the emperor Nero—a position that presumably left him well informed on the subject of lavish dinners. The action of the *Cena* revolves around a dinner laid on by Trimalchio, a fabulously wealthy parvenu who has made a pile from speculative voyages—exactly, as it happens, the milieu of the India trader. (Similarly engorged characters reappear many centuries later, in the time of the Dutch and English East India companies.) Trimalchio's guests are treated, if this is the *mot juste,* to a banquet of toe-curling vulgarity. The meal is part theatrical stunt show, part gastronomic marathon. There is a daunting variety of courses, the only common element a stress on the exotic, the unexpected, and the bizarre. One guest tries the bear meat and "practically spews her guts out." Another, impressed, whispers to his neighbor that everything— even the pepper!—is homegrown (without a greenhouse, a botanical impossibility). If you want hen's milk, Trimalchio can get it. He orders mushroom spawn from India and serves boar stuffed with live birds that fly out when the boar is cut open. There are dormice seasoned with honey and smoking sausages resting on a silver grill above "coals" of plums and pomegranates. A slave brings in a basket containing a

---

*Also known as "horse-heal," a perennial herb prized for its bitter, aromatic leaves.

wooden hen atop a pile of eggs, at which point Trimalchio wonders out loud if the eggs are half cooked. The narrator tries to crack an egg and finds it made of pastry. He is about to toss it aside, imagining that there is nothing but a half-formed embryo inside, when he fishes about within and pulls out a figpecker swimming in peppered egg yolk.

The spices, evidently, were in keeping with the flashy and expensive display. Another dish, borne in by four slaves, consists of heaped plump fowls topped with sows' bellies. Perched at the apex is a hare to which wings are attached in imitation of Pegasus, the winged steed of myth—the effect not unlike a broiler hen trussed up as Superman. Live fishes flop about this pile of flesh in a slew of peppered wine sauce. The spicy sauce is little better than the bear meat, but then a display of taste was never the host's intention.

Thanks in no small measure to the brilliance of Petronius's creation, the lurid hues of Trimalchio's debauch continue to shape modern images of the Roman meal. But as Trimalchio's unfortunate guest is at pains to point out, to many Romans this was all a bit much. A powerful purist aesthetic ran through Roman culture, indeed was basic to a cherished if increasingly tarnished self-image until the final days of the empire. Viewed in this light, not merely spices but for that matter all seasonings were superfluous, luxurious, and even harmful fripperies. The correct purpose of food was nutrition; all else was vanity. Cicero (106–43 B.C.) was of the opinion that the best spice for his dinner was—or should be—hunger. He even claimed that he preferred the smell of earth to that of saffron. In his *Tusculan Disputations* he relates the salutary tale of the visit to Sparta of Dionysius, tyrant of Syracuse, a town famous in antiquity for the quality and sophistication of its cooks. Spartan food was equally stereotypical, but to the other extreme. This was, in short, an encounter made to order for edification: the archetypal rich sybarite meets the dour ascetics, famed for their renunciation of all pleasure. On being served a stodgy black broth, Dionysius complained that the meal was not to his taste, whereupon the Spartan cook put the visitor in his place. "Small wonder," replied the cook, "for the *condimenta* are lacking." "And what *condimenta* are they?" asked the visitor, obligingly walking into the trap. "Honest toil in hunting, sweat, a run to the Eurotas [the local stream], hunger, and thirst" was the tart response, "for with these things the Spartans season their feasts."

Self-evidently, the message of such exemplary incidents ran deeper than a straightforward declaration of personal preferences. To Romans such as Cicero, how and what you ate were issues of the utmost ethical importance. Diet was a yardstick of, and in some sense shaped, moral worth. It was Brillat-Savarin's point inverted: you were what you ate. And what a shocking contrast present indulgence formed with the rugged heroes of the past! Historians and satirists never tired of contrasting contemporary debauch with ancient virtue. Manius Curius Dentatus, conqueror of Pyrrhus, is reported to have cooked his own vegetables. The emperor Augustus, according to Suetonius, liked his dinner plain and unaffected; the Stoic Cato declared that he ate meat only so as to be strong enough to fight for the state. The past was tough, frugal, and pristine; the present, luxurious and bloated.

In this sorry tale of decline, the cook naturally deserved special mention. The historian Livy (59 B.C.–A.D. 17) went so far as to date the onset of Roman decadence to the time when the cook rose above his station: "And it was then that the cook, who had formerly the status of the lowest kind of slave, first acquired prestige, and what had once been servitude came to be thought of as an art." There were even sumptuary laws passed in an effort to regulate the culture of excess. Julius Caesar (ca. 100–44 B.C.) once ordered brigades of food police to the market to look for forbidden delicacies and sent his soldiers into private homes to check whether the state's edicts were being violated at the banqueting couch.

That spices and luxuries fell foul of this vision of Rome's character and its past was all but inevitable. Like the pearls that came back in the holds of the same India ships (another favorite target of the moralists), when it came to foreign contamination spices stuck out like a sore thumb. The satirist Persius (A.D. 34–62) was honoring an old tradition when he blamed "learned Greeks" for corrupting even that most homely, Catonian symbol of Roman authenticity, a farmhand's porridge, with their highfalutin ideas, greasy sauces, dates, and pepper. In Dryden's splendid translation:

> We never knew this vain Expence, before
> Th' effeminated Grecians brought it o're:
> Now Toys and Trifles from their Athens come;
> And Dates and Pepper have unsinnew'd Rome.

Thus it was that spices entered a discourse of decadence and decline: piquant symbols of corruption and degeneracy, the flavors of a lascivious Eastern Other. And if any confirmation of the truth of the assertion were required, one needed only to look to the rough vigor of the barbarians, who were, at least for edifying, literary purposes, not the type to flavor their meals with expensive and luxurious seasonings. Before leading her troops on the slaughter of the effete Roman colonists of Britain, the Briton queen Boadicea reminded her troops of their superiority, drawing particular attention to the culinary divide. Dainty eaters made weak fighters. In the account of the historian Dio Cassius (ca. 150–235), "We ought not to term these Romans 'men,' who bathe in warm water, eat artificial dainties, drink unmixed wine, anoint themselves with myrrh, sleep on soft couches with young boys for bedfellows—boys past their prime—and are enslaved to a lyre player—a bad one!"*

Charges such as these easily dovetailed with more material concerns. To a Roman moralist, the waste entailed by fine and expensive foodstuffs was not just that they were needless, but that the money flowed out to foreigners. The Romans had little they could trade in return for the Indians' spice, with the exception of the empire's coinage of near-pure gold and silver—the reason why today a number of Indian museums boast some excellent collections of Roman coins. To date some seven thousand gold and silver coins have been found in India, representing, presumably, a fraction of a much larger total. The high-quality denarii and aurei were so esteemed that some Indian rulers even went so far as to mint imitations of their own.

Yet Rome's coins were as sorely missed in Rome as they were sought after in India. The consequence of the largely cash basis of the India trade was, to some, a disastrous outpouring of the empire's finite currency reserves, provoking a debate about a national balance-of-payments crisis and marking the debut of an economic bogeyman that would survive and flourish into the age of mercantilism and beyond. In the days of the early empire, fretting over what the historian Tacitus called "spendthrift table luxuries" attained the significance of a question of national importance. In A.D. 22 the emperor Tiberius lectured the Senate that the habit of luxury and the appetite for Eastern exotica had provoked a hemorrhage of Rome's money "to alien or hostile countries." Buying imported goods was nothing less than "subversion of the state," and few of his distinguished audience were blameless. (One and a half millennia later, the English would encounter the identical problem, finding no market for their heavy woolen goods in the sweltering

---

*A reference to Nero.

tropics. Only in the age of industrialization was the flow of gold and silver from Europe into Asia reversed.) Pliny the Elder complained that India swallowed up the colossal sum of 50 million sesterces per annum—all for the sake of pepper and other "effeminate" Eastern fripperies. India and its luxuries were turning Rome into a city of wimps.

Presumably the traders who made their fortune from India felt differently, but the moralists had a ready riposte for them as well. What better illustration of the lunacy of living for money and the stomach than the long and perilous journey to India? In Horace's first *Epistle* the merchant trading out of India appears as an iconic figure, a symbol of the pursuit of profit taken to perverse extremes, regardless of the risks and the cost to one's personal life: a character he elsewhere calls "a beggar amid wealth." Like the corporate workaholics of the twenty-first century, the India merchant of the first epitomized the cost of soul-destroying materialism and overwork:

> You rush, a tireless merchant, to furthest India,
> Fleeing poverty across the sea, through rocks and flames . . .

Poverty is a lesser risk to the well-being of the soul than the rocks and flames Horace imagines in the Indian Ocean. The risks and costs of wealth outweigh the rewards. Horace, having none of it, will buck the world's trend of getting and spending for the simple pleasures of Stoic philosophy.

For those inclined to agree, India and its pepper became almost paradigmatic. In the early imperial period, pepper served as a convenient symbol for the satirists, much in the way that junk bonds came to epitomize the greed of the 1980s. Persius claims that only sheer greed (*avaritia*) could account for the appetite for pepper, driving a trader to take the newly arrived spice from the camel's back without even giving the thirsty beast a drink. In Dryden's translation:

> Nature is ever various in her Frame:
> Each has a different Will; and few the same:
> The greedy Merchants, led by lucre, run
> To the parch'd Indies, and the rising Sun;
> From thence hot Pepper, and rich Drugs they bear,
> Bart'ring for Spices their Italian ware.

Persius's fellow satirist Juvenal likewise saw in the spice trade all the risks and delusions of wealth. He claimed that a merchant with a cargo of pepper would cast off beneath an inky sky in the teeth of a tempest—"It's only a summer storm!" he declares—and for his folly be pitched overboard and swallowed by the waves, still clutching his purse between his teeth as he gasps his last breath. Where we might see heroic endeavor, many Romans were more inclined to see greed and lunacy. To Pliny the Elder—who, being a former naval commander, might have been inclined to admire this sort of enterprise more than most—the voyage to India was no more than a grubby quest for loot, "and so India is brought near by a lust for gain."

So it was that spices failed the moralists' checklist of acceptability on all counts. They were expensive, enfeebling, Eastern, effeminizing. And as if this were not enough, they lacked any evident nutritional value, their sole apparent function being to stimulate the appetite into new excesses of gluttony. Pliny drew these themes together while affecting an air of lofty contempt for the taste for pepper then sweeping the empire. The spice never stuck to Romans' ribs but merely tickled their palates:

> It is remarkable that its [pepper's] use has come into such favor: for with some foods it is their sweetness that is appealing, others have an inviting appearance, but neither the berry nor the fruit of pepper* has anything to recommend it. The sole pleasing quality is its pungency—and for the sake of this we go to India! Who was the first person who wanted to try it on his food, or who in his craving for an appetite was not content simply to go hungry?

It must have been galling for Pliny that his fellow Romans apparently paid him little attention, yet his complaint would ring down the ages—enduring, in fact, until our own day. Modern historians are less prone to make the same connection between luxury and decline, yet much ink has been spilled on the question of Rome's balance of payments with India, although it would seem that the surviving economic data are too fragmentary or too biased to reveal whether or to what extent the spice trade was in fact harmful to the Roman economy. In any case, the murky reality is arguably less important than the perception, which was crystalline. Even the equation of spicy Eastern luxury and Roman enfeeblement has rung some bells. E. H. Warmington, one of the authorities on Rome's trade with India, worked himself into a

---

*Apparently a reference to white and black pepper.

flap in suggesting that "India with its manifold supplies of precious stones, perfumes and spices . . . contributed a very large proportion towards satisfying the luxurious inclinations of a Rome which had lost most of its ancient morality, and helped to increase certain tendencies which led to the downfall of the western Roman Empire."

The merits of the case need not detain us. More interesting is the moralizing thrust, which forms one of the central themes of the history of spice from the days of imperial Rome practically to our own day. All of these themes would in due course resurface—often, ironically enough, in the form of Christian polemics directed at the decadent empire. As spices were sought after, so too were they seen as an insidious cancer eating away at Rome's personal and public vigor. (How the eastern half of the empire, which survived until 1453, was any less dissolute or less addicted to Eastern luxury than the western half is unclear. With its access to the trans-Eurasian caravan routes, there were more, not fewer, spices in Byzantium.) In this view it was not the barbarians or even the lead pipes but all that spice that caused the fall of Rome.

DECLINE, FALL, SURVIVAL

The pepper tree grows in India, on the flanks of Caucasus. Seen from the ground, its leaves resemble those of the juniper. The forests are guarded by serpents, and when the pepper is ripe the inhabitants of that region set them on fire. The serpents flee the fire, which blackens the pepper. For pepper is white by nature, although it has several fruits. The immature variety is called long pepper; what is untouched by the fire is white pepper; and the pepper that has a rough and wrinkled skin gets both its color and its name from the heat of the fire.

—SAINT ISIDORE OF SEVILLE (ca. 560–636), *Etymologiae*

Even as Rome weakened and fell, the demand for spices endured, but at a vastly reduced level. It is often claimed that the barbarians who conquered the empire had no taste for the refinements of life, but this is far from being the case. In fact, an eager appetite for spice survived in those isolated corners of Europe where trade and civilization outlasted the

Roman collapse. Contrary to the stereotypes, ancient and modern, the barbarians themselves were hugely interested in the luxuries long enjoyed by Romans, not least their spices. Europe's chief obstacle was finding the means to pay.

Even Christians acquired the taste—though Christians, as we shall see, had as many if not more reasons to be as wary of spice as the most stoic Roman. Once Christianity became the official religion of the empire, senior churchmen had access to the *cursus publicus,* or government post, the imperial network of inns and warehouses supplying food, transport, and accommodation to all senior officials traveling on state business. A warrant granting access to the *cursus* survives from A.D. 314, addressed to three bishops en route to a church council at Arles. When they arrived at an inn along the route, the bishops could expect to be supplied with lodging, horses, carriages, bread, oil, chicken, eggs, vegetables, beef, pigs, sheep, lamb, geese, pheasants, *garum,* cumin, dates, almonds, salt, vinegar, and honey, along with an impressive array of spices: pepper, cloves, cinnamon, spikenard, costus, and mastic.

Warrants such as this one could be presented at any of the inns on the empire's vast network of highways. Since the document stipulated that the bearer was entitled to demand his provisions without delay, it would seem that the well-heeled traveler could expect to find spices even outside the major centers. The state made similarly spiced provision for bishops en route to the great council at Nicaea. Evidently the exigencies of Church business overrode any qualms the bishops may have had about the mortification of the flesh.

Junketing bishops aside, plenty of other Romans knew spices in an age of decline. Trade continued. In 337, Constantine received an embassy from the Indians, "who live near the rising sun," and a little later his nephew Julian the Apostate received emissaries from various Indian nations, Sri Lanka, and a mysterious island off the west coast of India, possibly the Maldives. An imperial edict of the western emperor Honorius describes the bustling commercial life of Arles in 418: "All the famous products of the rich Orient, of perfumed Arabia and delicate Assyria, of fertile Africa, fair Spain, and brave Gaul, abound here so profusely that one might think the various marvels of the world were indigenous in its soil. . . . It unites all the enjoyments of life and all the facilities of trade"—this less than a decade after successive tides of barbarian hordes had swept through Gaul and reduced its major cities to ashes. It is not until late in the fifth century that the very last Roman coins found in India finally peter out.

In these centuries, pepper in particular was still familiar as a food-stuff, at least to a certain class. The Gallic poet Ausonius (ca. 310–ca. 395) mentions pepper in an epigram entitled "On Food," and around 350 Rutilius Taurus Aemilianus Palladius makes numerous references to pepper and other spices in his *Opus Agriculturae.* He used the spice when making vinegar and flavored cheese, mixed with thyme. To Palla-dius "pepper" was practically synonymous with "condiment." Even in the calamitous fifth century, when frontiers collapsed and barbarians swarmed across the empire, the grammarian and philosopher Macro-bius could assume familiarity with the spice. In one of the dialogues of his *Saturnalia,* Caecina Albinus has a question for his learned friend: "Tell me, please, Disarius, why mustard and pepper, if applied to the skin, penetrate it and make a sore, but, when eaten, they do no harm to the substance of the belly?"

At first glance, references such as these suggest that little had changed since the heyday of the trade in the days of the early empire. Yet the continued availability of spices concealed more subtle and enduring shifts. For one, their cost had soared. In Pliny's day, when the trade was at its zenith, pepper cost only 1/250 to 1/280 the price of gold by weight; by 301 the ratio had slipped to 1/90. Finds of Roman coins in India begin diminishing in frequency after the reign of Cara-calla (211–217). The disappearing currency and the price hike alike had much to do with the fraying of the empire's eastern periphery. Through the turbulent years of the third century, the empire suffered one disaster after another along its eastern borders, rendering the east-ern traffic hazardous and ultimately all but impossible. The Red Sea lit-toral passed under the control of the Blemmyes, a hostile African tribe, and Rome's direct route to India was cut. Trade passed into the hands of Arab middlemen, which is where it would remain until after Vasco da Gama sailed around Africa to India.

New means of supply entailed new perceptions. Now that no more Roman fleets sailed to India on the monsoon, the spice lands once familiar to Horace's "tireless merchant" slipped off the horizons of European spice traders into medieval realms of fantasy and the unknown. The Indies retreated beyond what the medievalist Jacques Le Goff has called a "dreamlike horizon," and there they would stay until the Age of Discovery. Saint Jerome (ca. 347–419/420) knew of merchants who, on leaving the Red Sea and entering the Indian Ocean,

> arrive in India after nearly an entire year, at the River Ganges (which Holy Scripture names as Phison), which flows around the entire land of Evila, and is said to bear many types of spices from the fountain of Paradise. Here are found carbuncles, emeralds, and shining pearls, for which desire burns in the breasts of noble women; and mountains of gold, which it is impossible for men to approach, because of gryphons, dragons, and huge-bodied monsters: so that it might be disclosed to us what type of guards avarice has.

This mingling of ignorance and a pious wariness would set the tone for the next thousand years.

As Rome frayed before it fell, when the barbarians finally arrived at the gates they found the spice trade greatly reduced from its glory days of the first and second centuries. Their impact on the long-distance luxury trade was mixed. On the one hand, the barbarians shattered the prosperity and order on which trade depended; on the other, they inherited the taste. The Gothic invaders who overran the dismembered Western empire took particularly to the Romans' pepper. In 408, Alaric, king of the Goths, besieged the city of Rome into submission, and the terrified Senate sent out envoys to negotiate a humiliating ransom. In return for their lives and a lifting of the siege, Alaric agreed to accept 5,000 pounds of gold, 30,000 pieces of silver, 4,000 robes of silk, 3,000 pieces of fine scarlet cloth, and 3,000 pounds of pepper—a revealing comment on the relative values of these luxuries. The conspicuous prosperity of the Roman cities acted like a magnet for the roving Germanic armies, drawing them like so many flies to a carcass. In this sense the moralists who detected in Rome's luxurious ways the harbingers of decline were, after all, onto something.

Yet if spices accompanied Rome on its long road to ruin, they were not wholly unmarked by the experience. During the last centuries of empire the very idea of spice ripened into something at once richer and more obscure than the *pipera* and *condimenta* of imperial Rome. The word *species* was now first employed as an umbrella term signifying a great many high-value, readily transferable, and generally low-volume goods, as distinct from the ordinary or bulk items of commerce. Along with an implication of high cost, the word conveyed a sense of extraor-

dinariness, of special distinction. Run-of-the-mill or homegrown flavorings did not qualify. Alongside pepper, cloves, cinnamon, and nutmeg, there were pearls, fine linens, and cottons, silks from China, and
the purple dye once reserved for senators and emperors but now worn
by bishops. The *species* included other rare and expensive goods such as
panther skins, leopards, lions, ivory from Africa, furs transhipped from
Parthia and Babylon, chattering parrots from India and Africa, lapis
lazuli from Afghanistan, and tortoiseshell from the tropics. There too
were all the legendary gemstones of the Indies: "hyacinth stone," beryl,
bloodstone, carnelian, sardonyx, diamonds, and emeralds. More salient
than function or botany, cost was what made a spice a spice. In the marketplace as in the mind, spices came surrounded by riches and exotica.

This lush medley of associations was transferred directly from the
world of late Rome to its conquerors. Emerging from the forests and
the steppes, the barbarians had no word of their own for the goods they
coveted and so adopted the terminology of the vanquished. The sixth-
century laws of the Franks, Visigoths, and Alamanni all mention a *spi-
carium,* a warehouse where high-value goods were stored. By this route
the word entered the ferment of Late Latin and Germanic dialects that
in turn evolved into today's Romance languages. Hence, in short, the
terminology that persists into the third millennium, at root unchanged
since late antiquity: Spanish *especia,* Portuguese *especiaria,* French *épice,*
Italian *spezia.* As the barbarians borrowed, so they burnished. In these
centuries of breakdown and isolation, spices' air of mystery intensified.
In Visigothic Spain, Isidore of Seville was willing to believe that the
pepper plant was guarded by serpents that were put to flight by har-
vesters setting the undergrowth ablaze, from which the peppercorns
acquired their distinctive black and wrinkled appearance. Isidore's version of how pepper got its color was endlessly recycled until well into
the sixteenth century. Spices continued to flow into Europe, but their
origins were now firmly lodged in the realm of the fantastic.

It was, of course, precisely this mix of mystery and cost that helps
explain why they were so special. Luxury may have been a deadly sin,
but it was also a marker of status. For this reason spices were often
included with official correspondence, a practice that endured late into
the Middle Ages. On several occasions spices helped lubricate Rome's
humiliating embassies to the barbarians. In 449, an emissary to Attila
the Hun from the emperor Theodosius II (ruled A.D. 408–450) presented Indian gems and pepper to one of Attila's subject queens—

doubtless the barbarian diet benefited from a little spice. In 595, a praetor in the service of the Byzantine emperor Mauricius (ruled A.D. 582–602) sent gifts of pepper, cinnamon leaf, costus, and cassia to the Avar chieftain Chajan, the barbarian professing himself delighted with the gift.

While such ceremonial uses of spices are relatively well documented, information on their culinary applications is in short supply. Somehow the image of the bloodthirsty Hun savoring a perfect blend of exotic flavors does not ring true. Attila the Hun, for example, used Eastern luxuries to pay off his various subject chiefs, but even at banquets he insisted on the traditional steppe diet of grilled flesh. Historians are now chary of the expression "Dark Ages," but in a gastronomical sense the implied slight seems fully deserved. Along with all the other refinements of life, cookery suffered from the fall of empire. Brillat-Savarin's vision of an age of "fierce mouths and scorched gullets" seems, on the whole, justified.

In what had been Roman Gaul, the Frankish dynasty of the Merovingians (476–750) certainly ate spices, but apparently—this judgment on the basis of extremely few sources—with less sophistication. The poet Fortunatus of Poitiers (ca. 540–ca. 600) portrays the women of Merovingian Gaul as having a taste for the refined novelties of cooking (the men were another matter). The few recipes to have survived from the period are crude versions of Roman archetypes. One of the very few culinary sources from this period is a treatise on dietetics by Anthimus, ambassador of Theodoric, king of the Ostrogoths in Italy from 493 to 526. Anthimus knew ginger, cloves, and pepper, though spices appear far less frequently in his recipes than in the *De re coquinaria* of Apicius, on which they are otherwise modeled. As with his Roman prototype, if he knew cinnamon, he didn't eat it. But with the other spices he had a heavy hand. For a piece of beef to be braised or roasted, he recommended no fewer than fifty peppercorns, further spiced with cloves, costus, and spikenard. Reading Anthimus, one does not have the impression of being in the presence of a gourmet. He is at pains to stress that his main concern is with health—whether and how food is good for you, how to cook it so as to avoid any harmful consequences—and not, apparently, with the creation of a particular taste.

Most references of these centuries betray a similar bias toward practicality over pleasure. Yet if the early Middle Ages offered precious little evidence of an epicurean culture, there was certainly plenty of enthusiasm for spice. The contemporary cookbook by the splendidly titled "Vinidarius, the Illustrious Man" assumes spices' ready availability. Written in either the fifth or the sixth century, it now survives in a single manuscript copied in the eighth century, now housed in the Bibliothèque Nationale in Paris. The manuscript begins with a summary of spices "that you ought to have at home so that nothing is lacking for seasonings." Along with a range of locally available aromatics, pepper, ginger, cloves, and cardamom are regarded as indispensable.

The spice-loving Apicius, too, remained in vogue. The text of *De re coquinaria* survives through two manuscripts dating from the middle of the ninth century, one written at Tours, the other at the German monastery of Fulda. Assuming that these ancient cookbooks were not recopied for purely antiquarian interest, spices must have been at least reasonably familiar and available, at least to the wealthy. Via these two writers the Roman kitchen lived on in a strange half life in the halls of the early medieval nobility. Indeed, in one sense both Anthimus and Vinidarius represented an advance on Roman times, since they were aware of the clove, a spice apparently unknown to Apicius. That they were was due to the efforts of unknown others, the crews and merchants of the Arab dhows, Malay outriggers, and Chinese junks pushing east, many thousands of miles away, to the five tiny volcanic islands where the spice grew. By such obscure means the clove appeared in European cuisine the best part of a millennium before any European source makes mention of the Moluccas.

These cookbooks aside, the next few centuries offer extremely lean pickings for the culinary historian. Taio, bishop of Zaragoza (?–651), makes a passing reference to sumptuous banquets sprinkled with the exquisite aromas of sweet-smelling spices. At much the same time, the Frankish collection of diplomatic form letters known as the "Formulary of Marculphus" mentions a variety of spices that could apparently be eaten in the former Roman province of Gaul. Along with more solid fare such as piglets, chickens, and eggs, legates on official business were granted access to pepper, cinnamon, dates, almonds, pistachios, salt, and oil, all of which could be supplied by the remnants of the Roman *cursus publicus*. Assuming that the document is something more than a nostalgic fantasy, its spices are an astonishing testament to the survival of Roman institutions in an age of collapse.

But by the standards of early medieval Europe, Merovingian Gaul was a bright spot. It comes as a greater surprise to find spices across the

English Channel at much the same time, when Saint Egbert (ca. 639–729), a Northumbrian monk and archbishop of York, knew some exotic recipes with pepper, all suffixed with a description of their medical utility. He sounds like a dangerous host to have dinner with: his chapter on "foxes, birds, horses and wild beasts that may be eaten" features an alarming recipe that served as a remedy for fever and diarrhea. He advised emmer groats mixed with pepper to heal sores of the mouth. In Italy around 643, Jonas of Bobbio wrote of pepper and nard arriving from India. In Visigothic Spain, Isidore knew all the major spices, although in all these cases it is unclear whether they were used for what we might regard as gastronomic so much as dietetic or medical purposes.

As medieval demand was slowly easing itself into the channels it would follow for another thousand years, so too with supply. In the early centuries of the Middle Ages, Europe's immediate sources of spice were the Byzantine and Jewish traders who even now remained in contact with the East. From the fifth century onward, references crop up to the "Syrian"—that is, Byzantine—merchants in most of the Mediterranean's major ports. Their commercial networks stretched from Trebizond on the Black Sea to Barcelona, penetrating as far inland as Paris, Orléans, and Lyon. When the Burgundian King Guntram (ca. 535–592) visited Orléans, he was greeted by its merchants in Syrian, Latin, and Hebrew—the languages of commerce in sixth-century France. Eastward, Byzantine traders reached at least as far as Sri Lanka. Even in the sixth century, the Byzantine state maintained a customs official at Clysma on the Gulf of Suez, who made yearly trips to India. Cosmas Indicopleustes, a Greek-Egyptian monk who traveled to India sometime around 550, tells the tale of a Byzantine merchant who was able to indulge in a little one-upmanship with a Persian trader at the court of a Ceylonese king, not long before Cosmas's own day. Thanks to the superior quality of his coinage, the Byzantine succeeded in convincing the Ceylonese that he was the emissary of a king far greater than his Persian rival's. (A similar yarn was told in the first century by Pliny the Elder of a tax collector blown from Arabia to Ceylon, where he was likewise saved by the quality of the coin in his pocket.) Thanks to his solid gold nomismas, the Byzantine was rewarded with a trip around the city on an elephant's back, to the accompaniment of drums and fanfaronade, leaving the Persian "deeply chagrined at what had occurred."

The rise of Islam would put an end to voyages such as this and send the Byzantine long-distance trade into a terminal decline. The following century, the armies of Mohammed exploded outward from Arabia, seizing within a few short decades all the ancient routes and markets of North Africa and the Levant. Islam's expansion in maritime and commercial terms was scarcely less dazzling. Within a century the great Islamic merchants had established themselves along the spice routes of both land and sea, from Malabar in India as far west as Morocco.* By camel and dhow, traders and mariners fanned out east even to China and the Moluccas. By the eighth century, Arab traders had their own commercial enclave in Canton; as early as 414, the Chinese pilgrim Fa-hsien had reported the presence of many Arab-speaking merchants in Sri Lanka. Where there were spices there were Muslims. The supply of spices to Europe became, several Jewish merchants excepted, an Islamic concern.

Under the new management the spice trade of the Indian Ocean flourished as never before. Even in the Mediterranean religion was a porous barrier to commerce. The Hellenic city of Alexandria continued to flourish under Arab rule, and Byzantium remained in communication with the spice routes right up to its final capture by the Ottomans in 1453. Caravans bearing Eastern luxuries snaked across the deserts of Central Asia, Persia, and Arabia, transferring their goods into Byzantine hands at any one of a number of the empire's Black Sea ports. To the south, Byzantine merchants bought spices from Muslim merchants at entrepôts in Anatolia or the Levant.

In return for such high-value goods as early medieval Europe could muster—furs and amber from the Baltics; slaves, timber, and metals from the Alps and the Balkans—Jewish and Byzantine intermediaries ferried spices and other luxuries back west. By the sixth century their chief westward conduit flowed through the ports of Byzantium's remaining Italian possessions, via the head of the Adriatic and the Po Valley. (Ravenna and its tributary towns remained Byzantine possessions until the middle of the eighth century.) Slightly to the north, Venice was still at this stage little more than a cluster of settlements on the islands of the lagoon, whose residents scraped out a meager existence from salt and fishing. As unpromising as their watery circum-

---

*A token though highly symbolic statement of Arab supremacy was the use of timber from a Greek ship wrecked in the Red Sea in the roof of the Ka'bah in Mecca—where, presumably, it remains.

stances must have seemed, their location would, in due course, grant
them an unrivaled entrée into the trade. In the happy coincidence of
geography, politics and appetite were the key to the traffic that would
enrich the Venetians for the best part of a thousand years.

Unfortunately, the evidence is too fragmentary to say how substantial that traffic was. We do know that early in the eighth century spices
were arriving in Lombardy in sufficient volume that King Liutprand
(ruled A.D. 712–744) could grant one of his officials a salary of one gold
solidus (½ of a pound), one pound of oil, one pound of *garum,* and two
ounces of pepper. In Germany, Frisian traders bought spices and silks at
Mainz. In northwest France in 716, King Chilperic II granted the
monks of Corbie monastery a toll exemption on an annual allowance of
thirty pounds of pepper, two of cloves, five of cinnamon, and two of
spikenard, along with other Eastern or Near Eastern imports such as
almonds, chickpeas, rice, and pistachios, all of which they acquired at
faraway Marseilles. Chilperic's ruling was a renewal of older concessions
by Chlotar III (ruled 657–673) and Childeric II (ruled 673–675). The
context suggests that these were intended more for the monks' diet
than for their medicine cabinet. It seems reasonable to assume that the
monks were not alone in enjoying their flavors.

At much the same time as the monks of Corbie received their
exemption, spices started cropping up around Europe in the context of
commercial transactions. Given a chronic shortage of trustworthy
specie and the absence of a standardized coinage from one region to the
next, spices had the supreme merit of being accepted everywhere, a sort
of universal currency. There are records of serfs buying their freedom
with a payment of pepper, and the spice was commonly used as rent
payment. During the reign of Charlemagne the church of San Fidis in
Genoa received rent in the form of one pound of pepper, a custom that
lingered on as long as any other tradition of spice. As late as 1937, the
king of England received rent from the mayor of Launceston consisting
of a hundred shillings and one pound of pepper—the mayor might
have reflected that this particular rent ceiling had proved very much to
his financial advantage. When Prince Charles crossed the River Tamar
in 1973 to take symbolic possession of the Duchy of Cornwall, his
tribute included a pound of pepper. According to the *OED,* a token
pepper rent remained a form of payment until the end of the nineteenth
century.

However, what was token by the nineteenth century was, in the ninth, anything but ordinary. By the time they arrived in Europe, spices were so wildly expensive and rare as to prohibit consumption for all but a tiny few, as some writers are at pains to point out. In 535, Senator Cassiodorus (ca. 490–ca. 585) penned a letter to a minor official in the service of Theodahad, the Gothic ruler of Italy, insisting that he perform various duties in equipping the army and seek with all due assiduousness "such spices as befit the royal table." Even more than in Trimalchio's day, spices were the preserve of privilege—and one of its markers.

They were not, evidently, a plebeian pleasure. In a *Life* of Pope Gregory the Great (ruled 590–604) attributed to a ninth-century biographer known as John the Deacon, there is an intriguing reference to the redistribution of the goods that the Church received as rent. On the first day of the month, the pope would make a public appearance outside Saint Peter's, where he would distribute grain, wine, vegetables, cheese, lard, fish, and oil to the poor who gathered for alms. The more fortunate nobles received spices (*pigmenta*) and other luxury goods "so that the Church should be thought of as nothing other than a repository for all." To modern eyes, Gregory's deliberate lack of evenhandedness might seem a slightly odd way of getting the point across, but the gesture was quite in keeping with the strict hierarchies of medieval society—and spices, like nobles, belonged at the top. If the anecdote does not date from Gregory's time, it at least reveals the assumptions a Roman deacon might have harbored in the ninth century.

As the conditions of life steadily deteriorated, the force of such statements could only increase. Around the time of the breakup of Charlemagne's empire in the ninth century, a monk or scribe prepared a "form letter" from a bishop to his ruler, begging to be excused from attending a council on account of illness. The request is sweetened with spices, among various other exclusive goods, described self-deprecatingly as "trifling but exotic little gifts from over the sea, such as I believe befit the honor of your divine piety." Cinnamon, galangal, cloves, mastic, and pepper are all recommended gifts, complementing a dark green cloth, date palms and their fruits, figs, pomegranates, an ivory comb, vermilion, parrots, and "a very long spike of a sea-fish" (a narwhal spike?). As with the papal offering, the clear implication is that spices were apt for nobility: the one was closely identified with the other.

They were grouped among the trappings of wealth and power, and therein, as ever, lay much of their attraction.

It would be misleading, however, to suggest that spices' exclusivity was accepted by all with the same relish as that evidenced by kings and nobles. Their air of luxury was restated in a more morally loaded manner in a riddle of Saint Aldhelm (ca. 639–709), a relative of King Ine of Wessex (ruled 688–726) and friend of Aldfrith, king of Northumbria (ruled 685–704). With his royal connections Aldhelm could have eaten as well as anyone else in early medieval England, but he seems to have been unimpressed by the experience, judging by one of his riddles:

> I am black on the outside, clad in a wrinkled cover,
> Yet within I bear a burning marrow.
> I season delicacies, the banquets of kings, and the luxuries of the table,
> Both the sauces and the tenderized meats of the kitchen.
> But you will find in me no quality of any worth,
> Unless your bowels have been rattled by my gleaming marrow.

The answer to the riddle, needless to say, is pepper.

That Aldhelm looked on spices with a jaundiced eye is not surprising. His disdain for the comforts of life was legendary: he was in the habit of reciting the entire Psalter up to his neck in a barrel of ice-cold water. The more remarkable fact is that he knew them at all. For his was an age when towns and cities had all but disappeared; when the greater part of the population never moved more than ten miles from their native villages; when brigands and raiders roamed the roads and seas, descending on the few residual pockets of urban life with terrifying fury; when even neighboring lands must have seemed scarcely less fantastic to most Europeans than distant India. The mere fact of the presence of pepper in Dark Age Europe is a source of wonder. Though fragmented and at times barely visible, the spice trade remained a ligature between parts of the earth that had only the faintest inkling of the others' existence.

◑

The reputation of spices as luxuries confined to kings and great noblemen would begin to change, at glacier pace, only as the millennium drew to a close. After a flurry of references around the time of Charlemagne, followed by a near century of silence, the trade returned to western Europe on a more solid basis toward the end of the ninth century.

Driving this increased consumption was a slow stirring of Europe's economy and the steady growth of its population. The revival of the metallurgy and textile industries in central and western Europe and the opening of silver mines in Germany's Harz Mountains went some way to remedying a chronic shortage of the precious metals needed to pay for high-value imports from the East. Increased surpluses in the hands of an emergent landowning class—kings and local strongmen, bishops and monasteries—brought with them a new level of demand for luxuries and the trappings of wealth.

Meeting this demand brought about one of the pivotal developments in European history. Through trade and travel Europe was exposed to a wider world from which it had been effectively isolated for centuries; and where goods and money flowed, books, people, and ideas followed. Exotic and expensive luxuries were, after piety and war, the chief expenses of the aristocracy. The trade that supplied them sparked a whole "complex of activities"—economic, political, geographic, and technical—whose effects are still with us. Slowly, surely, Western Christendom developed from a sheltered, isolated backwater into an increasingly confident, assertive culture.

In the memorable phrase of Richard Southern, this was the heroic age of trade, when success could bring riches and ennoblement but failure meant death or slavery. All travel was perilous, but none more so than the international luxury trade. Outside the isolated centers where urban life was once more beginning to stir, the countryside was often utterly lawless; feeble central authorities struggled with local lords to make their writ run beyond their city walls. Further afield, traders risked all manner of predation. In the ninth and tenth centuries, bandits still roamed the Alps and attacked the passes. In 953 the emperor Otto I sent an emissary to the caliph of Cordoba, his mission to enlist the latter's support in suppressing the Saracen marauders who controlled the Alpine passes, the jugular of the luxury trade. Their depredations could be spectacular: one of their most illustrious victims was Abbot Mayeul of Cluny, captured and ransomed at the cost of a thousand pounds of Cluny's silver. Nor were the seas any safer. At the end of the tenth century, the Mediterranean was, for Christians, hostile waters. Sicily, Sardinia, Corsica, and Malta were all in Muslim hands. Pirates preyed on all the shipping they could seize. There was no common law to arbitrate disputes, and all redress came from force or reprisals in kind.

Yet all these perils notwithstanding, there was an international network that managed to distribute spices from the Moluccas to England. Its hub was the northern Italian town of Pavia, the ancient capital of Lombardy. A text describing the situation at the start of the tenth century lists the levies and duties payable by merchants passing through the town, foremost among whom were the "many rich Venetian merchants" who used to go there each year. Each of their merchants visiting the city was obliged to pay the master of the king's treasury an annual tax of one pound each of pepper, cinnamon, galangal, and ginger. (To his wife they had to pay one ivory comb and a mirror and 20 gold solidi, plus 1 denarius of Pavia.) Also in the city were English merchants, who in reparation for past troubles — the English seem to have acquired a reputation for hooliganism early — paid compensation every three years of fifty pounds of silver, mirrors, and weapons, plus two big greyhounds fitted with silver collars.

The merchants who supplied such luxuries remain shadowy in the extreme. The great Belgian scholar Henri Pirenne was probably correct in arguing that in this age of fragmentation the Jews were uniquely well placed to cross, and profit from, the divide between early medieval Christendom and Islam. Apparently no one ranged further afield than the loose alliance of Jewish merchants known as the Rhadanites. Their name appears, tantalizingly, in the *Book of Routes* composed around 850 by Ibn Khordabeh, director of posts to the caliph of Baghdad. The postmaster outlines a network of trade routes that reached from Gaul to China — at a time when the Christians, in Ibn Khordabeh's words, could "not even put a plank on the water." In the ninth century, Muslim armies and raiders sacked Arles and Marseilles; in 846, they ravaged Saint Peter's Basilica. In such adverse circumstances Charlemagne and his Frankish nobles apparently relied on Jewish intermediaries for their Eastern luxuries, and it was doubtless his need for that trade that explains Charlemagne's tolerance for the Jews, a sharp contrast to the persecution and forced conversions they had endured under the earlier dynasty of the Merovingians.

By the end of the ninth century, however, the Italians were beginning to outpace all their competitors. With access to the iron and timber of the north, the Italo-Byzantine cities of Amalfi, Gaeta, Salerno, and Venice had the goods needed by the Islamic powers; in Constantinople they had a ready portal to the East. The Venetians were still nominally subjects of Byzantium, and since 813 they had claimed a monopoly on all Byzantine trade, the foundation for their absolute primacy in the centuries ahead. They dealt with the competition by fair means and foul. One of the oldest surviving decrees of the Venetian Senate forbade Jews from traveling in Venetian ships. On land, their merchants ranged far and wide. As Saint Gerald of Aurillac passed through the outskirts of Pavia around the year 894, he was accosted by a group of Venetian merchants who tried to interest him in their spices and fabric, both of which they had acquired in Constantinople. If Venice did not yet quite hold the gorgeous East in fee, it certainly had an early foothold in the trade.

Thanks to the efforts of these obscure, far-flung traders, spices began to return to Europe in volumes not witnessed since the days of the Roman Empire. And as consumption of spices picked up, so too other traditions began to reappear. The old strain of their seductive, decadent luxury resurfaced with new vigor. A history of Charlemagne's reign relates the tale of a corrupt and worldly bishop, one telling proof of his decadence being his predilection for rich dishes seasoned with "all manner of various spices" and other "incitements to gluttony"—the sort of lavish feast, the author adds, as was never prepared for the austere and virtuous Charlemagne.

The salutary contrast between the high-living, spice-quaffing simoniac and the plain-eating emperor is pure *romanitas*. History was repeating itself: a millennium after Rome had first sent its fleets to India and its moralizers had fretted whether spices were corroding its once steely ethics, the same concerns were resurfacing. Just as medieval Europe lived in the long shadow cast by Rome, drawing its water from still-functioning aqueducts and traveling its worn but still-workable roads, conducting its diplomacy and theology in Rome's language, so with its cuisine. The mingled fascination and revulsion spices provoked, the intertwining of taste and distaste, wound back in time as far as the Caesars.

CHAPTER 3

●

MEDIEVAL EUROPE

In the meadow there is a tree, very fair to look upon.
Its roots are of ginger and galangal, the shoots of zedoary.
Its flowers are three pieces of mace, and the bark,
    sweet-smelling cinnamon.
The fruit is the tasty clove, and of cubebs there is no lack. *

—"The Land of Cockayne," an anonymous (Irish?)
poem of the early thirteenth century

THE FLAVORS OF COCKAYNE

The medieval mystic dreamed of spices in Paradise; the gourmand, in
Cockayne. Indeed, for the true gourmand, Cockayne *was* Paradise. For
as Paradise soothed and delighted the weary spirit, so Cockayne was
tailor-made for the empty or, for that matter, the merely greedy stomach. Here the only virtues were gluttony, leisure, and pleasure, the only
vices exertion and care. Doing nothing earned a salary, work was penal-
ized, women were rewarded for sleeping around. A decent fart earned
half a crown. Even in church the truest form of worship was to stuff
oneself. Conveniently, the church itself was edible, its walls made of
pastry, fish, and meat and buttressed with puddings. There were rivers
"great and fine," flowing not with water—a rarity in Cockayne—but
with "oile, milk, hony and wine."
   Yet for all this food there was not a single cook in the place, for the

---

*Cubeb, or "tailed" pepper, *Piper cubeba,* is a pepper look-alike native to the Indonesian
archipelago, popular in medieval times as a seasoning, medicine, and aphrodisiac.

meals in Cockayne were at once ready-made yet delectable—a combination, evidently, as arresting then as now. Supper walked, flew, ran, or swam up to the plate. The larks obligingly delivered themselves, pre-spiced, to hungry mouths:

> *The larks, already cooked,*
> *Fly down to men's mouths,*
> *Seasoned in the pot most excellently,*
> *Powdered with cloves and cinnamon.*

Being a product of the medieval imagination, that there was a smell of spices to Cockayne's miraculously self-serving larks was all but inevitable. Nor did the spices end there. One of the abbey's wells was filled with spiced wine, another with a healing mixture of spices. The walls of the live-in gingerbread houses were nailed with cloves. In the garden grew the vegetable kingdom's equivalent of the philosopher's stone, an all-in-one spice tree, with roots of ginger and galangal, shoots of zedoary, flowers of mace, bark of cinnamon, and fruit of cloves. In one version of the poem, "Ginger and nutmeg, all one can eat / are what they use to pave the street." Even the dogs shat nutmegs.

All in all, in all of its many versions in the various European vernaculars, Cockayne was a very spicy place. In the tongue-in-cheek judgment of one author, such attractions as the abundance of spices and the precooked larks made Cockayne not only comparable to Paradise but better: "Though Paradise is merry and bright / Cockayne is far the fairer sight." The sizable share of medieval Europeans for whom an empty stomach was a daily concern would probably have been inclined to agree.

Satirical fantasy it may be, yet the various visions of Cockayne that survive suggest something of the depth of the medieval fixation with spices. They were objects of extraordinary charm and appeal, so enticing that they did not seem out of place among the pleasures of a dream. It was, moreover, a dream that cooks labored hard to turn into reality, for spices featured as conspicuously in the real-world smoke and grime of the medieval kitchen and hall as they did in the make-believe landscape of Cockayne. Other foodstuffs have at one time or another held a similar grip on the imagination—coffee, tea, sugar, and chocolate—yet all were, in comparison, passing fads. None accumulated a comparable body of myth and lore nor carried quite the same social clout.

When the glutton's paradise of Cockayne took shape, spices had already held a grip on the European imagination for centuries and would do so for centuries yet.

It is often claimed that spices returned to European cuisine with the crusaders, but this, we have seen, is manifestly not the case. They had never left. The first and most enduring taste, and throughout the Middle Ages far and away the most important spice, was pepper. In 946, there was a pepper sauce—poisoned, in this case—on the table of King Louis IV (ruled 936–954) of France. By the turn of the millennium, the spice was established as a regular feature of the noble and monastic diets. In 984, the monks of Tulle paid three pounds of pepper to their brothers of Aurillac to celebrate the feast day of their patron, Saint Gerald. At the Swiss abbey of Saint Gall the spice was sufficiently familiar that the monks nicknamed one of their number "Peppercorn" on account of his prickly personality.

Though spices were by now a taste shared by the elites across Europe, supply was a largely Italian affair. By the closing years of the millennium, traders from several Italian maritime republics were energetically expanding their presence in the Muslim Levant, led, as they were five hundred years later, by the Venetians. To safeguard their vulnerable position abroad, Doge Pietro II Orseolo (ruled 991–1009) negotiated commercial treaties with the Muslim North African powers. Even so, the trade remained a risky business, liable to periodic incarcerations, seizures of goods, and shipwreck. At the turn of the millennium, the Saxon chronicler Thietmar of Merseburg wrote of the loss of four Venetian ships crammed with many different spices.* At this point the Venetians still shared the trade with merchants from Salerno, Gaeta, and Amalfi—the dominance of the republic still lay in the future. In 996, a traveler to Cairo counted 160 merchants from Amalfi alone; in Syria, there were hundreds of others from Bari and Sicily.

From Mediterranean ports spices were dispersed over the Alps and across the breadth of Christendom. In 973, Ibn Jaqub, a Jewish merchant from Andalucia, was astonished to find Indian spices for sale at the German town of Mainz. Under King Aethelred II "The Unready" (ruled 978–1013, 1014–1016), German merchants in London paid

---

*The incident brings Shakespeare's fretful Antonio to mind: the "dangerous rocks / Which touching but my gentle vessel's side / Would scatter all her spices on the stream, / Enrobe the roaring waters with my silks": *The Merchant of Venice,* 1.1.33.

their customs duties in pepper. In England spices were a sufficiently common feature of the commercial scene to find their way into a school textbook, a set of translation exercises written around 1005 by Aelfric, abbot of Eynsham, in Oxfordshire. Spices feature as part of the cargo of a merchant returning from across the sea, among his silks, gems, gold, oil, wine, ivory, metals, glass, and sulfur: a detail to fire a bored school-boy's imagination but one that he—or the abbot—must at the very least have recognized.

By such means the absence of pepper was becoming more notewor-thy than its presence, at least for a certain class. Toward the middle of the century, the Italian Cardinal-Bishop Peter Damian wrote of a blas-phemer who sprinkled his chicken with pepper "as is customary." At the century's close, Ademar III, viscount of Limoges, hosted a visit by Duke William IX of Aquitaine, only to find his larder bare of pepper "for the count's sauces"—with such an exalted visitor in the house, an intolerable situation. Ademar sent his seneschal to a neighbor, who showed him great mounds of pepper piled on the floor, so that it had to be shoveled out "like acorns for pigs."

The same William was the first of the Provençal troubadours, a Fal-staffian character of prodigious appetites who on account of his riotous living managed the rare feat of being both excommunicated and going on crusade. His poem "I'll do a song, since I'm dozing" tells of a ménage-à-trois in the castle of two noble ladies who waylaid him one summer's day as he rode through the Auvergne. Mistaking him for a mute and so unable to tell of their escapades, nor write of them—William's literacy was a rarity among the nobility—they kept him at their pleasure for a week, in which time the lusty count bedded them 188 times, primed for this Herculean effort by "a lordly meal" of two fat capons, white bread, good wine, "and the pepper laid on thick." "I nearly broke my tool and burst my harness. . . . I can't express the remorse that overtook me."

By now pepper was well on the way to being considered obligatory, a highly visible and highly esteemed hallmark of the nobility. Yet if spices were becoming more familiar with every year, it was a familiarity that rested on a network of trade and travel that few could have com-prehended. The reality was scarcely less wonderful than the fantasies of Paradise and Cockayne. A Rhineland nobleman in the eleventh century could order furs from Siberia, spices and silks from Byzantium and the Islamic world beyond, pepper from India, ginger from China, and nutmeg and clove from the Moluccas. Individuals such as Nahray ibn Nissim, a Tunisian Jew settled in Egypt, were dealing in products as diverse as Spanish tin and coral, Moroccan antimony, Eastern spices, Armenian cloths, rhubarb from Tibet, and spikenard from Nepal. By this stage the trading guild known as the Karimis, a group of Jewish spice merchants based in Cairo, had their agents scattered across the Old World, from China in the east to Mali in the west.

Thus when Pope Urban II proclaimed the First Crusade at Clermont in 1095, both the taste for spices and the trade that fed it were already on a firm footing. When the crusaders made their bloody entry into the markets of the Levant and looked bedazzled at the spices and other Eastern exotica, they knew exactly what they were seeing. Religious zeal aside, this was a prospect that made crusading as attractive to the body as it was beneficial to the spirit.

In another sense the Crusades did transform the way spices were used and acquired in the West. The establishment of a foothold in the Levant helped drive a great quickening of economic life. New industries brought new spending power, and the demand for Eastern luxuries grew steadily. The chief movers and profiteers remained much the same as they had been four centuries earlier: chiefly, the Italian maritime republics, joined now by Barcelona, Marseilles, and Ragusa. By nature inclined more to commerce than to crusading, the Italians had initially heard the call to holy war with diffidence, but they soon changed their tune when the Franks seized towns and fortresses along the Levantine coast and, for a time, Jerusalem itself. Shortly after the First Crusade, Genoa, Pisa, and Venice all sent fleets to the East, where, in return for providing naval transport and protection, they extracted commercial concessions in several of the captured towns and seized what shipping they could lay their hands on. A Venetian squadron cruising off Ascalon in 1123 seized a rich Egyptian merchant fleet, plundering a fortune's worth of pepper, cinnamon, and other spices. They meant to continue as they had begun. For the first time since the fall of Rome, European merchants had a substantial presence at one end of the ancient caravan routes.

Although the crusaders' most spectacular conquests were soon whittled down and their enclaves pushed into the sea, the deepening and broadening of a commercial presence in the Levant marked a shift of enduring significance. Midway through the twelfth century, the earlier trickle of Eastern luxuries had become something approaching a flood.

Early in the twelfth century, Anselm of Laon could write of pepper as a traveler's "necessity," to be carried on a journey along with cheese, bread, candles, "and other such things." In the 1170s, William Fitzstephen saw spices in the markets of London, a town that though blighted by "the immoderate drinking of fools and the frequency of fires" had cosmopolitan appetites:

> *Gold from Arabia, from Sabaea spice*
> *And incense; from the Scythians arms of steel*
> *Well-tempered; oil from the rich groves of palm*
> *That spring from the fat lands of Babylon;*
> *Fine gems from Nile, from China crimson silks;*
> *French wines; and sable, vair, and miniver*
> *From the far lands where Russ and Norseman dwell.*

Around this time guilds of spicers and pepperers began to crop up across the major towns of Europe. The *speciarius* became an increasingly common figure on the urban scene; by the thirteenth century he was part of the mercantile establishment. In Oxford in 1264, the shop of one William the Spicer was burned by boisterous students. In London, the Company of the Grocers is still in existence, having grown out of the older guild of the Pepperers; their coat of arms has nine cloves at its center. Guilds such as these were the remote ancestors of the supermarkets of the twenty-first century.

There, however, the similarity ends. For the medieval spicer's products, though increasingly familiar, were anything but prosaic. The secrets of the spice routes would not be revealed to European savants for centuries, and even today only the outlines are clear. From India spices flowed west along two broad routes, each heavily trafficked since ancient times. The first followed the western shore of the subcontinent north to Gujarat, passing Ormuz at the mouth of the Persian Gulf, and north to Basra, the port from which Sinbad set off on his adventures. Here caravans took the spices north and west, through Persia and Armenia to Trebizond on the Black Sea. Alternatively, they charted a more southerly course, snaking out along the valleys of the Tigris and Euphrates, via the oasis towns of the Syrian desert to marketplaces in the Levant. Many of these spices that came via the Persian Gulf ended up in Constantinople. What was not consumed within the Byzantine empire was then reshipped to other destinations as far away as Scandinavia and the Baltic.

The second main spice route from India followed the path once taken by Rome's fleets, now largely in Arab hands. From Malabar the spices were ferried across the Indian Ocean, around the Horn of Africa, and north up the Red Sea. Some were unloaded at the Red Sea port of Jiddah, then proceeded by caravan to Levantine outlets via Mecca and Medina. What did not pass overland followed the old Roman route to the western shores of the Red Sea, where the cargoes were carried overland to the Nile and then shipped downriver for taxing, sale, and reshipment in Cairo before finally reaching the Mediterranean at Alexandria.

By the end of the tenth century, it was by this second, Egyptian route that most of Europe's spices arrived. The reason was political, in the form of the decline of centralized power in Mesopotamia and the emergence, in Egypt's Fatimid dynasty (969–1171), of a strong and wealthy commercial rival. Like the Romans, the Fatimids encouraged trade by maintaining naval patrols in the Mediterranean and Red Seas. They offered reliable guarantees for the security of merchants, native and foreign alike. Cairo was then embarking on the period of its greatest commercial splendor, drawing commerce, merchants, and travelers like filings to a magnet. Alexandria regained the position it had occupied in classical antiquity as Europe's chief point of access to the exotic goods of the East.

Like the Romans, Alexandria's Fatimid masters did not have to look hard for buyers. When the Spanish rabbi Benjamin of Tudela called at Alexandria in the 1160s, he found a Babel of all the major western European nations, with Italians rubbing shoulders with Catalans, Frenchmen, Englishmen, and Germans. In an age of religious wars theirs was a somewhat anomalous position, yet they succeeded by and large in maintaining the commercial relations on which the flow of spice into Europe depended. The Egyptians needed customs duties, and the Europeans were willing to run the risk of the occasional extortionate or even murderous ruler for the sake of the profits at stake, secure in the knowledge that any unexpected price hikes could be passed on to the captive European market.

But if trade could be profitable, it could also be perilous, for body and soul alike. Not until the twelfth century did the Church accept trade as a respectable occupation, and even then misgivings endured. No trade provoked more distrust than the long-distance trade in luxuries, as much on account of the goods themselves as what getting them entailed. Dealing with the Infidel only made matters worse. The dexterity of the Venetians in particular scandalized more zealous believers, contributing to their reputation as avaricious merchants but tepid Christians. In 1322, the pope excommunicated many leading citizens of Venice for their dealings with the Muslim powers, and for a time a papal ban succeeded in disrupting trade with Egypt. However, even papal sanctions could not halt so much as redirect the traffic—the Venetians simply went elsewhere. The Armenian port of Lajazzo became a new conduit to the West, and for a time Europeans paid a little more for their spice. Shortly thereafter, the Venetians were back in Egypt as if nothing had changed.

The trade and traders alike had an undeniable glamour. For if the risks were great, the profits were colossal. Success in the spice trade conferred vast fortunes and, particularly in the early and central Middle Ages, the rise to ennoblement. The merchants and financiers who established themselves in the traffic were the Rockefellers of their day, such as the Venetian Romano Mairano, who, emerging from relatively humble beginnings and having already made and lost one fortune, financed a cargo of lumber to Alexandria in the 1170s with a loan from the Doge Sebastiano Ziani. The cargo returned a profit sufficient to repay his creditor (in pepper), leaving enough for Mairano to set up a trading network of his own that stretched from Venice to Alexandria, Syria, and Palestine. Such were the risks involved that the valuable cargoes were not entrusted to lumbering, beamy cogs, the workhorses of medieval maritime commerce, but to oared galleys swift enough to outrun any pursuer, leased out by the state to the highest bidder. If the rowers were too slow, there were marines to act as the defense of last resort.

With the growth of the traffic there came a slow but decisive shift in the way spices were viewed in Europe. No longer were spices reserved for a tiny few. Medieval cooks dreamed up hundreds of different applications, leaving practically no type of food free of spice. There were rich and spicy sauces for meat and fish, based on an almost limitless number of combinations of cloves, nutmeg, cinnamon, mace, pepper, and other spices, ground and mixed in with a host of locally grown herbs and aromatics. To follow there were desserts such as frumenty, a sweet porridge of wheat boiled in milk and spices, and sugary confections of spices and dried fruits, washed down with spiced wine and ale. Though there were significant variations in cooking from one place to another and changes over time, with one or another spice falling into and out of fashion, the spicy tenor of medieval cooking remained a constant.

Thus if the mental world of medieval Europe was provincial, its palate was globalized. The aroma of spice was all-pervasive. In cookbooks of the day spices feature in more than half the recipes, often more than three quarters. Not until modern times, with the advent of air travel and the bulk refrigerated freighter, an age in which Costa Rican bananas are sold in Moscow and Argentine beef in Bangkok, has there been such dependency on foods grown on the other side of the earth. Long before there was world cuisine there were spices.

SALT, MAGGOTS, AND ROT?

These spices played, alas! A great role in the appalling stews in which our forebears took such delight.... They understood nothing of the refinements of the culinary art.

—A. FRANKLIN, *La Vie privée d'autrefois,* 1889

While for the vast majority of medieval Europeans the dreamworlds of Cockayne and Paradise were where the spices stayed, a fortunate few translated their imagined spiciness into reality. Medieval cookbooks and accounts are commonly as suffused with spices as the fantasy. The early-fourteenth-century kitchen of Jeanne d'Evreux, the widow of King Charles IV of France, boasted a small tonnage of cauldrons great and small, solid iron pots, pans, spits, and roasters, offset by an equally heavyweight assembly of spices. Jeanne's pantry found room for no less than 6 pounds of pepper, 13½ pounds of cinnamon, 5 pounds of grains of paradise, 3½ pounds of cloves, 1¼ pounds of saffron, ½ pound of long pepper, a small quantity of mace, and a colossal 23½ pounds of ginger.

By the standards of the day the widowed queen's spice stockpile was impressive but by no means exceptional. In England less than a hundred years later the household of Humphrey Stafford, duke of Buckingham, ate its way through a similarly imposing mountain of seasonings. In twelve months, Humphrey and his family, guests, and retainers devoured no less than 316 pounds of pepper, 194 pounds of ginger, and various other spices, translating into a daily average of around two pounds of spices per day. The account books of the medieval nobility tell of a consumption that looks less like a taste than an addiction. Why this gargantuan appetite for spice, and how on earth did they get through it?

Traditionally, historians have resorted to a straightforward explanation: that old and indestructible myth that medieval Europe had a problem with rancid and rotting meat and that the spices were there to cover other, less appealing tastes. The notion apparently originated with eighteenth-century scholars who looked with horror at the cuisine of their forebears. Like many myths, this does contain a kernel of truth. On the one hand, it is true that, lacking refrigeration, meat and fish were liable to corruption, and food poisoning was a recognized if poorly understood risk. Standards of hygiene could be lackadaisical, as suggested by an ordinance of England's Henry VIII forbidding the kitchen scullions "to goe naked or in garments of such vilenesse as they now doe." The cook of *The Canterbury Tales* has in his shop "many a flye loos"; his repeatedly heated and reheated "Jack of Dover" pies sound like a recipe for botulism. His disease-dealing dishes called down on his head many a poisoned customer's curse.

The threat was particularly acute with fish, above all in summer. In a famous letter the cleric Peter of Blois (ca. 1130–1203) complains that even at the court of England's King Henry II the fish was often served four days old: "Yet all this corruption and stench will not reduce the price [of the fish] one penny; for the servants couldn't care less whether the guests fall sick and die, so that their lord's tables are served with a multitude of dishes. We who sit at meat must fill our bellies with carrion and become graves, so to speak, for various corpses."

Against such perils spices were, it is true, a remedy. It is also true that at least some Europeans knew that spices could defuse the risks of old foodstuffs and extend their shelf life. In the medical theory of the day, this preservative effect was explained in terms of the purported physical properties of spices, corruption being understood as an excess of moisture counteracted by the supposedly "heating" and "drying" spices; "fiery" salt was believed to do much the same. The dietetic concerns of the medieval cook are suggested by "The Tale of the Four Offices" by the French poet Eustache Deschamps (ca. 1346–ca. 1406), the four offices in question being the kitchen, cellar, bakery, and saucery, the latter by this time a standard feature of the larger medieval household. Deschamps's poem is framed as a mock-rhetorical encounter in which each of the offices is endowed with the gift of speech so as to attack the others and proclaim its own superior worth. When it is the saucery's turn, it claims that not only do spices smell good, they "expel the stench and smell of many meats," preserving and "rectifying" the meat while aiding digestion. The saucery continues:

> *Your flesh will go off,*
> *When it is not cooked in sauce.*
> *Whoever keeps meat two days,*
> *Will find it has a big smell,*
> *Followed by flies and vermin.*

Absent the "all-surpassing spices," the act of eating would be a perilous business. "Many would be in grave peril and at risk of death."

Similar claims can be found with less hyperbole elsewhere. The *Trésor de Evonime* of 1555 contains a recipe for an essence made of ground nutmeg, clove, cinnamon, and ginger, used for keeping "any meat, fish and all food . . . from all corruption with their [the spices'] good aroma and taste." This was not always done with the consumers' knowledge. John Garland, an English scholar resident at the University of Paris in the early thirteenth century, writes of the cooks who pass off meats "unwholesomely seasoned with sauces and garlic" to "simple servants of scholars"—a scam still flourishing in some of the less salubrious curry houses of the world.

These sources suggest that the traditional view of spices as instruments of concealment has at least some merit. And while medieval rhetoric was seldom without exaggeration, it loses all its force if its claims were simply invented. It is telling that when the kitchen of Deschamps's poem responds, it chooses not to dispute the substance of the saucery's claims, but rather their seriousness.

What the kitchen does point out is that the saucery, like many a food historian since, greatly overstates the threat of decomposition. Though the problem of old meat and fish was real, it was the exception, not the rule: not all the meat and fish consumed in the Middle Ages was rotten. Indeed, since most products were grown locally, it is likely that much medieval food was in fact fresher than food today. (In this connection it is worth recalling that spices went out of vogue long before refrigeration was invented.) Moreover, the argument is at odds with the economic reality. The issue of decomposing ingredients was of least concern to those in a position to afford spices, particularly noble or royal households. Spices were expensive, and those with the money would generally have had enough to acquire at least half-decent meat at a fraction of the cost of spices. Why waste good, expensive spices on poor, cheap meat? Rotting ingredients were a more serious concern for the poor, and the poor lacked the money to buy spices in the first place.

Medieval Europeans were no more hardened to the taste of putrid meat and fish than we are. The risk of unsafe ingredients was not taken lightly, and by the later Middle Ages municipal authorities across Europe were taking steps to crack down on sellers of bad meat and fish with harsh penalties. In comparison, the modern health inspector is a toothless creature. The pillory was primarily a punishment for crimes committed in the marketplace. In Oxford in 1356, the chancellor of the university was granted jurisdiction over the market, with authority to remove "all flesh and fish that shall be found to be putrid, unclean, vicious or otherwise unfit." In 1366, one John Russell of Billingsgate was prosecuted for selling thirty-seven pigeons deemed "putrid, rotten, stinking and abominable," for which offense he was sentenced to a spell in the pillory while the offending pigeons were burned beneath him. Offended customers — and interested passersby — had the opportunity to rearrange his guilty features with any filth or stones at hand — hardly the sort of response one would expect from a culture that was indifferent to the wholesomeness of its dinner. Anyone willing to believe that medieval Europe lived on a diet of spiced and rancid meat has never tried to cover the taste of advanced decomposition with spices.

There were, however, other flavors that spices helped surmount. The offending taste was not of putrefaction but of salt, as mentioned earlier. In the winter months fresh meat was at a premium for the simple reason that there was nothing to feed the animals. Medieval Europe lacked most of the high-yielding grass and root crops that are today used to feed herds through the winter and enable a year-round supply of fresh meat — the turnip, for instance, was still considered a garden vegetable. (The beauty of the pig, so to speak, and the main reason behind its importance to the medieval diet, was that unlike sheep or cows it could be left to fend for itself, foraging on chestnuts and waste, whether in town or country; but even for pigs there was not enough food to go around through the lean months.) Only the largest and wealthiest households had either the pasture to keep their herds alive or the storage space to put aside sufficient hay to see them through the winter.

For all those who lacked this luxury, as soon as the frosts moved in and the pasture died off, a good proportion of the herd had to be slaughtered. Traditionally, the seasonal killing was set for Martinmas, or November 11 — for which reason the Anglo-Saxon name for November was "Blood Month." What could not be eaten within a few days had to be salted down, with the result that most if not all of the meat eaten from November through spring was dry, chewy, and salty, requiring soaking and prolonged cooking to alleviate the taste. As winter dragged on, the tedium became, by all accounts, unbearable. In Rabelais's second book, Pantagruel and his companions are utterly fed up with the salty repetitiveness of the winter diet, one of their number, Caralim, professing himself quite "knocked out of shape" by the experience. The one good word Rabelais can find for salted meat is that it worked up a fearsome thirst, the better to throw down the wine.

At least in theory, there were ways around this problem, but in practice the food for one third of the year suffered from an unrelenting lack of variety. Most of the herbs and vegetables available in summer had yet to germinate, and many of the staples of the modern diet—tomatoes, potatoes, pumpkins, corn—were still undiscovered across the Atlantic. Several long-lived staples—onions, beans, garlic, leeks, and turnips—were available, but an already limited selection was further narrowed by cultural and class bias. Fruits were seen as "moist" and "cool," for which reason the sources advise that they should never be eaten raw. With extremely rare exceptions, carrots, kale, lettuce, and cabbage are entirely absent from the surviving cookbooks, the reasons being misguided medical belief and snobbery.* This is not to say that vegetables were never eaten—they were—but that they were looked down on as food for the poor and animals, unfit for a nobleman. To eat meat was an expression of superior class, whereas to eat vegetables was to join the ranks of gruel-munching churls (or monks). With nobility came land, and with land came meat, whether salted or fresh.

To the constraints of climate and class, religion added another. The

*The insistence of modern doctors on the healthfulness of a diet rich in fruits and vegetables would have startled an ancient or medieval physician. Throughout the medieval period pears, apples, peaches, and other moist fruits were viewed with suspicion as "meates that breed ill bloud," in the words of one sixteenth-century authority. For the same reason, long after its introduction from the Americas the juicy tomato was viewed as dangerous, ripe with the seeds of madness. In Italian the eggplant retains an echo of its erstwhile unhealthy reputation in its name *melanzana*, "unwholesome apple."

dietary restrictions of fast days and Lent further narrowed an already limited selection. Even salted meat was off limits for the forty days of Lent, Fridays, and the other fast days on the religious calendar—in all, nearly half the days of the year. At the start of the thirteenth century, the Twelfth Ecumenical Council decreed no fewer than two hundred fast days in total, which put fish on the menu (and gave a huge boost to the fishing industry) but provided little respite from the salt. Particularly for those living inland, all the fish that could not be supplied by local rivers, lakes, and ponds came heavily salted: herrings pickled in brine; codfish flattened, salted, and dried hard like strips of yellowy leather. Lent was a far more severe form of abstinence than it is today, a fact that accounts for the glee expressed when it ended, most famously in the gluttonous riot depicted by Brueghel in his famous *Carnival and Lent.* Such was the monotony of the season that Eustache Deschamps could flirt with sacrilege, writing of the "stinking herrings, rotten sea-fish . . . A curse on Lent, and blessings on Carnival!" One poor fifteenth-century scholar complained, "You will not believe how weary I am of fish, and how much I wish that flesh were come in again, for I have eaten nothing but salted fish this Lent."

In the modern West, secularization, greenhouses, and cold storage have brought variety to the tedium of the Lenten fast. In the Middle Ages, for those with the means, one escape was spice. If salt and a deadening lack of variety were the constraints facing the medieval cook, spices were the great opportunity, a means of enlivening a drab and numbingly repetitive diet. What the sixteenth-century Portuguese botanist and physician Garcia d'Orta said of ginger applied to all the major Eastern spices: "On our days of fish it gives us flavor." This the medieval cook did with a dazzling inventiveness. Far from being an age of culinary primitivism, such was the cooks' ingenuity that the "lean" dishes of Lent could be scarcely less appetizing or diverse than meat dishes. Spices helped make a feast of the fast.

They were used with practically every type of meat, fish, or vegetable, from the start to the end of the meal. Over and above material necessity, the delight in spices for their own sake—oftentimes with unsalted meat—is unmistakable. Their role was to offset and enhance contrasting flavors, making each taste better—like an espresso before bitter chocolate. The effect was perhaps not wholly dissimilar to the mingling of sweet and sour, pungent and fresh, such as can still be found in dishes of Persian and Moroccan cuisine—many of which are,

in fact, medieval survivors. The twelfth-century encyclopedist Honorius of Autun claimed that people ate spices such as pepper to prepare
the palate so that wine would taste sweeter afterward.

The most important role of spices was in a huge variety of piquant
sauces, perhaps the single most distinctive feature of medieval European cuisine. In his fifteenth-century *Boke of Nurture,* John Russell,
usher and marshal to Humphrey, duke of Gloucester, noted that "the
function of the sauce is to whet the appetite"—a more refined purpose,
in other words, than a simple exercise in damage limitation. Sauces
came in many flavors and colors: blue, white, black, pink, red, yellow,
and green. They accompanied a huge variety of foodstuffs, both homegrown and exotic—practically anything that moved or swam. Russell
mentions spiced sauces for swan, peacock, beef, goose, pheasant, partridge, curlew, thrush, sparrow, woodcock, bustard, heron, lapwing,
snipe, beaver, porpoise, seal, conger, pike, mackerel, ling, whiting, herring, perch, roach, cod, whale, and minnow, among others.

Not unlike the major Indian spice mixes still in use today, medieval
European sauces tended to be built around a few basic templates that
admitted infinite personal variation. Most tended to have one spicy
"note" standing out foremost, with dozens of variations on the theme.
Every cook was expected to have the basic repertoire at his disposal to
make his employer "glad and mery," as Russell phrased it. Of the various sauces, one of the oldest and most popular was black pepper sauce,
in which the sharpness of pepper was offset by bread crumbs and vinegar. There was a hotter variant called *poivre chaut,* hot pepper, and
another called *poivre aigret,* sour pepper, with verjuice and wild apples.
Taillevent, cook and equerry to the French kings Philip VI, Charles V,
and Charles VI, gives a recipe for a green sauce for fish comprising ginger, parsley, bread crumbs, and vinegar. Another perennial favorite,
often served with roasted poultry, known as galantyne, was made from
bread crumbs, ginger, galangal, sugar, claret, and vinegar. Some took
their names from the meat they accompanied, such as the "boar's tail"
mentioned by a fourteenth-century householder of Paris, based on
cloves, ginger, verjuice, wine, vinegar, and various other spices. One of
the most popular sauces across the breadth of medieval Europe was
camelyne, so called for its tawny camel color, the keynotes of which
were cinnamon, vinegar, garlic, and ginger, mixed with bread crumbs
and occasionally raisins. (The name was doubly apt, for much of the

cinnamon so consumed would have done time on a camel's back while in transit through Arabia.)

The usefulness of spices did not end with the main course. It was customary to round off the meal with an after-dinner "dainty" of fruit, nuts, and various spiced confections. When dinner is finished, the valets of Chrétien de Troyes's twelfth-century *Perceval* bring in "very costly" dates, figs, and nutmegs. In the early-thirteenth-century romance *Cristal et Claire* the meal is followed by dates, figs, nutmeg, "cloves and pomegranates . . . and ginger of Alexandria." When Sir Gawain is entertained at a fabulous castle en route to meet the Green Knight, he is served the same after-dinner treats.

Typically, these after-dinner spices were candied with sugar and fruit, like the Provençal *orengat,* fine slices of orange left to soak in sugar syrup for a week or so before being boiled in water, sweetened with honey, and finally cooked with ginger. The convention endured well beyond the medieval period, the candied and jellied fruits served today its direct descendants. Another survivor is gingerbread, which takes its name from the Middle English "gingembras," originally a composition of ginger and other spices. The modern "bread" bears little resemblance to the original, which was more of a stodgy paste.

Spices were, if anything, still more in demand in medieval wine and ale. The custom, like so many others, was shared with the Romans. In one of his sermons Saint Peter Chrysologos, archbishop of Ravenna (ca. 400–450), refers to the custom of smearing leather wine flasks with fragrant spices "in order to keep the taste of the wine preserved." What apparently began as a necessity in due course became an acquired taste. The mid-fourth-century writer Palladius refers with relish to the use of cassia, ginger, and pepper in wine, according to a recipe preserved among the Cretans and given them, so tradition had it, by the oracle of Delphi. The Roman statesman and monk Cassiodorus (ca. 490–ca. 583) drank his wine mixed with honey and pepper. In Gregory of Tours's late-sixth-century *History of the Franks,* one Frankish thug offers another a glass of spiced wine after dinner, shortly before swords are drawn and blood is spilled.

The methods of preparing spiced wine remained much the same throughout the Middle Ages. The basic technique was to mix and grind a variety of spices, which were then added to the wine, red or white, which was then sweetened with sugar or honey and finally filtered through a bag, bladder, or cloth. The latter was known as "Hippocrates's sleeve," hence the wine's name, "hippocras." A late-fourteenth-century book of household management gives the following instructions:

> To make powdered hippocras, take a quarter of very fine cinnamon selected by tasting it, and half a quarter of fine flour of cinnamon, an ounce of selected string ginger (*gingembre de mesche*), fine and white, and an ounce of grain [of paradise], a sixth of nutmegs and galangal together, and grind them all together. And when you would make your hippocras, take a good half ounce of this powder and two quarters of sugar and mix them with a quart of wine, by Paris measure.

This basic template admitted almost infinite variation. Hippocras could also be made with cloves and nutmeg; another variant called for mace and cardamom. Clarry was much the same as hippocras, the chief difference (though not necessarily) being the use of honey in place of sugar.

As with sauces and sweets, then, spices vastly expanded the drinker's possibilities. But if spices were the means of invention, necessity was the mother. To a far greater extent than with solid foods, their use was dictated by a need to preserve against corruption, or at least cover its taste. It is suggestive that when medieval writers turn to the topic of wine, the emphasis tends to be as much on results as on taste. Taken neat, medieval wine could be a harrowing experience, and the problem of foul wine was sufficiently common to inspire all kinds of complaints, as with the man-strangling "hard, green and faithless" wines of the poet Guiot de Vaucresson. In the poem "Dispute Between Wine and Water," composed sometime in the fourteenth century, the best the anonymous author can say of Gascon wine is that it does better than it tastes, "satisfying without doing harm." Geoffroi de Waterford said of the variety known as vernache that it "tickles without hurting"—faint praise indeed. Several centuries earlier in England, Peter of Blois began a still-flourishing tradition of French complaints about the quality of the wine drunk in England. If Peter is to be believed, the wine consumed at the court of King Henry II tasted like paint stripper: it was "sour or musty; muddy, greasy, rancid, reeking of pitch and quite flat. I have witnessed occasions when such dregs were served to noblemen, they had to sift it through clenched teeth and with their eyes shut, with trembling and grimacing, rather than just drink it." But even in France there were similar problems. The Burgundian poet Jean Molinet (1435–1507) borrowed some of the starkest lines from scripture to evoke the full nastiness of those vinegared wines that he could only imagine came from Gomorrah, that left him crying in repentance and calling on God for mercy: "Thou hast made us to drink the wine of astonishment."

While there is a good deal of exaggeration in these descriptions, by the same token they point to an underlying truth. Expectations were low, a problem stemming, ultimately, from the barrels in which wine was shipped and stored. Even if the wine survived shipping and storage in a reasonable condition in the barrel—a big "if," as barrels were often poorly sealed—the contents began to oxidize as soon as the barrel was tapped, rapidly acquiring a powerfully unpleasant taste, variously described as bitter, musty, smoky, ropy, or cloudy. To get the wine at its best, the contents of the barrel had to be drunk within the space of a few days—fine for feasts and binges but less than ideal for all but the largest or most alcoholic of households.

Failing that, old wine quickly turned so acid as to scour even the hardened medieval palate. Records from England's royal account books tell of the royal cellarers disposing of their spoiled stocks either by pouring them down the drain or—a gesture of dubious largesse—by giving them away to the poor.* But such drastic measures represented a serious loss of capital. A better alternative was to drink the wine young. Though young wines were considered very much better than old, they were themselves none too gentle on the palate, being naturally harsh and sour. Eustache Deschamps complained that one year's green vintage was sharper than spears, slashing razors, and stabbing needles: "I piss a hundred times night and day, yet I'm constipated nearly to death." So the trick was in the timing: finding the happy medium between too young and too old, too sour and too musty. In effect, the medieval wine drinker was caught between two evils and faced an unenviable trade-off. In his poem "Battle of the Wines," Henri d'Andeli relates the difficulty of finding wines for even the king's table

---

*In England this generally meant Ireland or some other neighbor. In 1374, despite a general shortage of wine and a ban on its export from England, the king made an exception for a certain Thomas White of Great Yarmouth, a wine merchant who found himself in possession of twenty casks of spoiled Gascon wine. His wine was so noxious that not even the London poor would buy it, so he was granted the right to send it to the less discriminating drinkers of Scotland and Norway instead.

that are not either "too yellow" or "greener than a cow's horn"; yet all others are "not worth an egg." (Though even these were preferable to beer, which he left to the ignorant Flemings and English.) Compounding the problem was the fact that the stronger and harsher the wine, the longer it was likely to last. Hence one common medieval formula for "good drinking now," which made perfect sense then but sounds self-contradictory today, was "strong and harsh and drinking well." It may have burned on the way down, but it was at least likely to last and was at least less caustic than a more "mature" vintage.

By taking the sting out of a young, astringent wine, defusing a barrel "on the turn," or else suppressing the full malevolence of a vintage that was destined never to be anything other than horrible, spices made the wine drinker's life a little less painful. As far as the medical authorities were concerned, this virtuous trinity of benefits was capped off by a fourth, in the form of potent healing properties. Writing of the popular clove-flavored wine known as *gariofilatum,* John of Trevisa summarized the attractions of the spices: "The virtue of the spices and herbs changes and amends the wine, imparting thereto a singular virtue, rendering it both healthy and pleasant at the same time . . . for the virtue of the spices preserves and keeps wines that would otherwise soon go off."

With the advent of the technology of the bottle and cork in the sixteenth century, the need for spices in wine was abruptly less pressing. Winemaking techniques and the quality of the end result improved. Yet of all of spices' uses in the medieval world, spiced wines were perhaps the most enduring, long outlasting the Middle Ages. Samuel Pepys (1633–1703) enjoyed an occasional glass of hippocras; it even gets a mention in *Der Rosenkavalier.* Neither clarry nor hippocras has ever quite disappeared, ultimately evolving into the vermouth, glögg, and mulled wine of today—still one of the best ways of dealing with a red on the turn, short of pouring it down the sink.

Spiced ale, on the other hand, has gone the way of the crossbow and the codpiece. In the Middle Ages, ale really was good for you— comparatively speaking. It was certainly better than the available water, an observation traditionally credited to Saint Arnulphus, bishop of Soissons and abbot of the Benedictine foundation of Oudenbourg, who died in 1087. Arnulphus is the patron saint of brewers, an acknowledgment of his realization that heavy ale drinkers were less afflicted by epidemics than were the rest of the population. Particularly in Europe's densely crowded towns, with their poor drainage and rudimentary public hygiene, untreated water was a daily reality and an extremely effective vector of infection. Though the effect of contaminated water was only dimly appreciated, the medical theory of the day added intellectual respectability to the wariness of water, classing it as wet and cooling and therefore potentially inimical to the body's natural balance of moderate warmth and moisture. (It was most likely the probable physical consequences of drinking untreated water that explain the severity of a diet of bread and water, often handed out to errant monks as punishment or adopted willingly as a form of penitence: given the intestinal upsets likely to result, this was truly, in the words of the prophet Isaiah, the bread of adversity and the water of affliction.) Given that the ale drinker was exposed to fewer microbiological nasties, Arnulphus's bias against water made perfect sense.

The upshot was that ale was consumed in prodigious quantities. In twelve months during 1452 and 1453, the household of Humphrey Stafford, duke of Buckingham, whom we met above galloping through the spices, consumed more than 40,000 gallons of ale, a daily average of about one gallon per staff member. A few years earlier the more modestly run household of Dame Alice de Bryene in Suffolk had maintained the same girth-stretching rate of consumption. Since its manufacture called for only the most rudimentary technology and ingredients, ale was within the reach of all but the very poor. In England at the start of the fourteenth century, ale cost approximately one sixth as much as wine and was often provided to day laborers as part of their rations. It was, moreover, a crucial source of carbohydrates. In the middle of the sixteenth century, Johann Brettschneider said that "some subsist more on this drink than they do on food."

Ale's shortcoming, like wine's, was its very short shelf life. Its optimum age was around five days, after which time it rapidly deteriorated, turning "ropy" or "smoky," whereafter it turned undrinkable and occasionally even injurious. (Beer, on the other hand, is made with hops, which contain a natural preservative. Hopped beer is mentioned in a document from the abbey of Saint-Denis dated to 768; however, its consumption did not take off in continental Europe until roughly the thirteenth century. Its acceptance in Britain dates from the fifteenth century.) Old ale could be truly foul: Saint Louis found the drink so noisome that he took it during Lent as a form of penance. Peter of Blois called it a "scurvy drink, sulfurous liquor"—had not Christ elected to turn water into wine, not beer? The sixteenth-century medical writer Andrew Borde was merely stating the obvious when he insisted that ale should be drunk "fresshe and cleare. . . . Sowre ale, and dead ale, and ale the whiche doth stande a tylte, is good for no man."

This was where spices came, yet again, to the rescue. The medieval popularity of the nutmeg owed much to ale's perishability: as the clove and cinnamon were to wine, so the nutmeg was to ale—the context of Chaucer's reference to "notemuge to putte in ale." Here too, the medieval palate seems to have developed a virtue out of necessity, acquiring a taste for spiced ale to the point that the addition of spice became expected, even preferred; the spice was used "wheither it [the ale] be moyste [fresh] or stale," as Chaucer puts it. Further down the social scale, ale laced with spice could even be regarded as a poor man's delicacy. When Chaucer's "joly lovere" Absalom pays court to the miller's wife, he sends her spiced wine, mead, and ale—little good though it did him. Some of these spiced ales survived until relatively recently, such as "Stingo," a variety of pepper-flavored beer popular in London in the eighteenth century. Russian writers of the nineteenth century mention *shiten'*, a spiced mead flavored with cardamom and nutmeg.

Much as occurred in the wine trade, advances in hygiene and technology eventually rendered spices redundant, as better preservation and sterilization took the harmful bacteria, and so the spice, out of ale drinking. The invisible and unavoidable action of bacteria was not, however, the only threat to ale that spices had to counter. Other problems with the ale were man-made, the culprits being the taverns and alewives who produced perhaps the bulk of the ale consumed outside the great households. The alewife's profession was not, to put it mildly, renowned for its integrity. (Along with prostitution, this was, incidentally, one of the very few economic opportunities open to women in the Middle Ages.) The thirteenth-century German monk Caesarius of Heisterbach included the tale of the honest alewife among his collection of miracles. So outstandingly repugnant were some of the alewives' home brews that they inspired a whole subgenre of poetry, the "good gossips" tradition. Nor was the law any gentler with the unscrupulous alewife than with the monk or satirist. Towns of any size appointed officials responsible for performing spot checks on ale and enforcing harsh penalties on offenders. In London in 1364, one Alice Causton was obliged to "play Bo Peep through a pillory" for tampering with her ale;

others did worse (and received worse) for selling bad ale—befouling the national drink, after all, was not to be taken lightly. Even the Church had something to say on the issue. In Ludlow church in Shropshire parishioners were either warned or gratified by a carving of an alewife in Hell, condemned to eternal torment among claw-footed devils.

But while such laws and warnings may have sent the occasional shiver down an unscrupulous alewife's spine, their sheer proliferation suggests that laws on ale quality were regularly flouted. In this world if not in the next, spices were a more dependable ally of the ale drinker than the authorities, the pillory, or even, it would seem, the threat of perdition. Just how desperately they were needed can be gauged from John Skelton's *The Tunnyng of Elynour Rummynge,* a poem composed early in the sixteenth century and perhaps based on a real alewife of the same name, recorded to have lived at Leatherhead in 1525. Skelton's heroine had come up with an ingenious way of accelerating the production of her home brew—by letting her chickens run in the "mash-fat," the vat where the malt and the water were mixed. Worse, they roosted

> *Straight over the ale-joust,*
> *And dung, when it comes,*
> *Drops right in the ale . . .*

There were worse tastes for spices to counter than salt and sourness.

THE REGICIDAL LAMPREY
AND THE DEADLY BEAVER

> The first thing is to know and recognize the complexion and nature of all things that are suitable to eat, and of him who eats them.
> —ALDOBRANDINO OF SIENA (thirteenth century),
> *Le Régime du corps*

> If the dish is hot, mix it with another cold one; if it is wet, join it with its opposite.
> —AVICENNA (ca. 980–1037), *Canon of Medicine*

Alas for poor King Henry. Though he arrived in Lyons-la-Forêt (Normandy) in the autumn of 1135 sound in body and mind, he left there a corpse, all on account of an ill-advised meal. In the words of Henry of Huntingdon, author of *Historia Anglorum,* or *History of the English:* "When he came to Saint-Denis in the forest of Lyons, he ate the flesh of lampreys, which always made him ill, though he always loved them. When a doctor forbade him to eat the dish, the king did not take this salutary advice. . . . So this meal brought on a most destructive humor and violently stimulated similar symptoms, producing a deadly chill in his aged body, and a sudden and extreme convulsion." Within a few days he was dead, and his kingdom was at war.

Seldom can a poor menu selection have mattered more, at least in the chronicler's version of events. The ensuing wrangle took the better part of two decades to sort out: "When King Henry died . . . the peace and harmony of the kingdom were buried with him," as a contemporary put it. With his son and heir dead in the disaster of the White Ship, drowned in the English Channel, Henry had proclaimed his daughter Matilda next in line to the throne, but his nephew Stephen and the Norman nobility were not so sure. Overlooking his sworn oath of loyalty, Stephen made a rival claim for the crown, resulting in a civil war that ended only with his death and the accession of the young King Henry II in 1154. If only the first Henry had listened to his physician—or read his cookbooks.

At the time, they amounted to much the same thing. In the modern bookstore the contents of the food section can typically be divided into three categories: the practical, the dietetic, and the whimsical. During the Middle Ages the whimsical—by which I refer to travel, history, and essays on gastronomy—did not exist, and between the first two there was no clear distinction. Cooking *was* dietetics. The concern of the medieval food writer was as much in maintaining or restoring health as with creating an aesthetic effect. Cooking was considered more a medical science than an art. (There is a distant echo of this past in the modern term "recipe," which originates with the medical precepts of the Salernitan school, the most widely read medical textbooks of the Middle Ages. These were written as a series of formulae beginning with the Latin injunction "*Recipe,*" that is, "Take . . .") In the opinion of Andrew Borde, author of *The Dyetary* and *Breviary of Helthe,* both published in 1547, "A good cook is half a physician, for the chief physic (the counsel of a physician except) doth come from the kitchen." Once this fact is appreciated, much of the mystery of medieval cooking is abruptly explained. Were it possible to beam one of today's celebrity chefs back to the court of Henry I, the king would find his or her best-sellers bland, bizarre, and more than a little dangerous, bound to finish him off even faster than a surfeit of prohibited lamprey.

The medieval overlap of cuisine and health is particularly significant to understanding the taste for spices. (The European taste for coffee and tea likewise began on doctors' orders, as it were.) Medical theory held that all foods diverging from the temperate ideal risked causing a humoral imbalance; that is, illness. Many a death caused by natural causes or some unknown agency was attributed to food provoking a supposed disruption of the humors—as was the case, in all likelihood, with Henry's death-dealing lamprey. Writing early in the sixth century, Anthimus claimed to have witnessed two peasants brought near death by eating turtledoves, birds believed to be replete with melancholy humors, resulting in an alarming outbreak of diarrhea and "vomiting that constricted part of the face." Aldobrandino of Siena claimed that foods he classed as cold and moist, such as fruit, brains, and oily fish, were "viscous . . . producing abomination."

With such dire warnings ringing in the diner's ears, the spiced dishes that were such a feature of medieval cuisine made a good deal of medical sense. It was all a question of striking the right balance. There was nothing new in this notion; indeed, its sheer antiquity guaranteed its authority. From Hippocrates onward all the major medical writers of antiquity cite various spicy recipes, many of which reappear, sometimes changed little if at all, in the cooking of the Middle Ages. Even the cookbook of Apicius, the foremost document of the Roman delight in the belly, pragmatically counsels a dose of spiced salts "for the digestion" and to ward off "all diseases and the plague and all types of cold." Sanctioned by the wisdom of the ancients—if wisdom it was—spices were believed to heal, mitigate, and rectify as much as they delighted.

Underlying this faith—for medieval medicine had a great deal more to do with belief than empiricism—was an acute suspicion of many foods now regarded as eminently nutritional. Food frequently took the blame for all the far more deadly but as yet inexplicable and invisible killers such as salmonella, cholera, pneumonia, typhus, and tuberculosis. According to medieval medical theory, many foods required modification before they could be eaten safely, the supposedly heating and drying properties of spices being seen as a form of compensation, their primary duty being to rectify the otherwise harmful properties of the food. If the premise was not scientific, the methods were. Writing in the 1330s, the Milanese physician Maino de Maineri claimed that spiced sauces could counterbalance the effects of "intemperate" food-stuffs. His *Opusculum de Saporibus*—"A Medieval Sauce-Book" was Lynn Thorndike's apt translation—begins with a summary of meats, fish, and fowl, setting out a classification system by which to judge their place on the spectra of hot through cold and dry through wet, with the appropriate sauce tailored accordingly. Depending on their classification, some otherwise problematic foods could be rectified with spices, the potentially dangerous effect of one canceling out that of the other. Pork was generally seen as cool and moist by nature, apt to generate phlegmatic humors, and therefore amenable to spices. Beef, in contrast, was dry and cold, suitable for spicing but requiring some wetting as well.

The corollary of the same was that there was an equal though opposite danger from foods occupying the hot and dry end of the spectrum. Like all creatures, wildfowl were held to take after their element, being regarded as warm and a little on the dry side—all that flying around in the dry, hot air—from which it followed that they had to be seasoned accordingly. One common remedy was the addition of a compensatory "cool and moist" pea puree. For the same reason birds were apparently seldom eaten with spices, at least not without some countervailing "cooling."

Some foodstuffs were more dangerous than others. Lamb was widely regarded as dangerously warm and moist, for which reason it was never popular. One of the most problematic meats was beaver tail, widely classified as fish and therefore much sought after by certain monastic communities for fish days.* Like fish, it was judged to be "a very delicate dish," for which reason the medieval diner apparently never ate his beaver *au naturel*. It was not gastronomy so much as dietetics in Edward Topsell's mind when he advised how to get one's beaver done right: "The manner of their dressing is, first roasting, and afterward seething in an open pot, that so the evil vapours may go away, and some in pot-

---

*Eating barnacle goose, believed by some to be neither fish nor fowl, was another way around the rules.

tage made with Saffron; other with Ginger, and many with Brine; it is certain that the tail and forefeet taste very sweet, from whence came the proverbe, that sweet is that fish, which is not fish at all."

But it was not the fishy beaver so much as real fishes that caused the greatest concern. Taking after their cool and moist native element, they were held to be likely to nourish bitter humors, considerations that made them particularly amenable to spicing. According to Maino de Maineri, the porpoise was a "bestial" fish, cold and wet, calling for a particularly sharp, hot pepper sauce. It was likewise with King Henry's regicidal lamprey, classed as cold and moist and as such highly dangerous. Though throughout the Middle Ages it was an esteemed and luxurious dish, lamprey was apparently never eaten without amending, or not without the fear of dire consequences. (One of the ironies of Henry's fate is that he was, his exit aside, a monarch with a keen interest in medicine.) For this reason it was customary to kill lampreys by drowning them in wine, classed as warm and drying, after which they were invariably cooked by the heating and drying method of roasting, then spiced. According to Laurence Andrew, author of *The Noble Lyfe and Natures of Man* of 1521, lamprey "must be soaked in good wine with herbs and spices, or else it is very dangerous to eat, for it has many venomous humours, and is evil to digest." Similar concerns dictated the preparation of oysters, mussels, cockles, scallops, eels, and congers, classed as wetter and colder still.

King Henry's death was, then, a particularly dramatic illustration of a broader orthodoxy: you were what you ate. Complicating the issue still further was the consideration that it was not just the qualities inherent in the food but the adjudged qualities of the diner as well that had to be taken into account. Like diseases, individual variations were accounted for in terms of one's natural humoral balance or "complexion," as determined on the basis of a number of outward signs such as eyes, temper, voice, laughter, urine, or coloring (whence, very obviously, the modern use of the term *complexion*). Diet had to be tailored accordingly, as with Jack Sprat's celebrated diagnosis: he could eat no fat and his wife no lean, his natural disposition being on the wet side, hers on the dry. An early-fifteenth-century handbook of health summarized the physician's belief that "a man should choose meat and drink according to his complexion: if he is of a hot complexion he should use hot meats in moderation, and if the bodily heat augments and is inflamed by a surfeit of overly strong meat and drink, or by any other happenstance, then contrary meat and drink are more helpful to his health." Melancholics were to avoid cold and dry beef, for it would only aggravate their condition. So, too, it was possible to alleviate one's natural predisposition by means of the appropriate diet. Falstaff said of Prince Henry that through drinking sufficient Spanish sack he had so heated the "cold blood he did naturally inherit of his father" that he did become "very hot and valiant." Hence the old soldier's claim: "If I had a thousand sons, the first humane principle I would teach them should be to forswear thin potations and to addict themselves to sack."

What sack did for Harry, spices did more powerfully. For those whose complexions inclined to cool or melancholy, the risk of illness could be mitigated or neutralized. A patient with a cold, dry complexion should be given spices (hot) and meat (wet), whereas a "hot" individual should avoid them, for they would merely aggravate a predisposition to choleric humors. Erasmus (ca. 1469–1536) attributed the endemic plague and "deadly sweating fever" in England partly to the national addiction to seasonings, "in which the people take an uncommon delight." These considerations varied with age as well as nation. An old, cold, and dry man could benefit from a little meat "lightly flavored with sweet spices, such as cinnamon, ginger and others that are suitable." On the other hand: "The use of pepper is of no good to sanguine or choleric men, since pepper dissolves and dries the blood . . . ultimately breeding measles and other full evil sickness and evils." The trick of finding the right balance varied according to age, the aging process being seen as a progressive cooling down and drying up of the organism—the reason why spices are continually recommended for "old folkes" but cautioned against for the young. As the widely read, pseudo-Aristotelian *Secretum Secretorum* puts it, "For young men, an abundant, moist diet, to old men, moderate diet and hot."

Reaching such judgments was, needless to say, a subjective business. A certain degree of objectivity was at least possible with the final variable, it being an article of faith that certain foods should be eaten at certain times of the year and avoided at others. Hot weather called for cool food and vice versa. It followed that spices should be used only moderately or not at all in the hot summer months; the cold and wet winter, on the other hand, was the season for hot, dry foods, such as birds and roasted and spiced meats. The Venerable Bede advised cloves and pepper for the winter months but none in the summer. He had it on the authority of Hippocrates that pepper and warm sauces could counteract the phlegm of the season. On cold days a cup of spiced wine was not only warming but healthy, the perfect excuse to indulge—"With Wines and Spice the Winter may be bolder," in the words of the Elizabethan poet Sir John Harrington. (Another source of heat recommended for the winter was sex; summer was the season of chastity.) The risk of catching a wintry affliction was redoubled by the Lenten diet of fish, in a season ever prone to engendering wet and cool diseases. The impression of the unmitigated spiciness of medieval cuisine can largely be attributed to the highly spiced seasonings developed to offset (and relieve the tedium of) the cold, fishy season of Lent.

Medically, of course, the greater part of this was nonsense. (Though who are we to laugh? Modern dietary fads can be just as bizarre—and we have fewer excuses for our gullibility.) But if the foundations of medieval dietetics rested less on verifiable proofs than on inherited belief, from the practitioner's point of view the supreme merit of humoral theory—and one reason for its durability—lay in its flexibility to fit any situation: retrospectively, any disease could be "explained."

In wealthier households, the task of juggling these considerations fell to the *speciarius,* or spicer. Occupying a role midway between pharmacist and in-house health consultant, the spicer was considered an indispensable employee. In 1317, the household of the French king found room (or cash) for only four officers of his chamber: a barber, a tailor, a taster, and a spicer. Charged with both acquiring and then supervising supply, his main duties were the acquisition, composition, and prescription of the appropriate drugs and seasonings. In conjunction with the physician and cook—arrangements varied from one time and place to another—he was there to ensure the suitability of dinner, taking into account both the diner's constitution and the different courses on offer at any given meal as well as their proportions, qualities, and quantities. Among the most important of his tasks was the preparation of the after-dinner spices that were such a conspicuous feature of medieval cuisine. Occupying a place somewhere between dessert and medicine, these were regarded as healthy pleasures, the idea being that the warming and heating spices helped digest or "cook" a meal in the stomach, suppressing the stomach's tendency to generate wet and cold humors. The household of King Edward IV had an "Office of Greate

Spycerye" charged with delivering sugar and spice to the "Office of Confectionarye" for the preparation of highly sweetened after-dinner spices. It was doubtless a diagnosis of a cold, wet stomach that explains an entry in the account books of the Avignon papacy in 1340, recording the pontiff's consumption of a whopping thirty-two pounds of ginger, a remedy for the pain in his belly.

Few medieval Europeans, as we shall see, could afford to eat (or indulge their hypochondria) on such a grand scale. For those who could, the reputed physiological effects of spices were an important determinant of how and when food was prepared—and a reminder that medieval food was not as overwhelmingly or as uniformly spicy as later ages have tended to imagine. Fear of the consequences of overdoing it were very real. In wealthy households the physician would often stand behind the head of the household and ensure that things did not get out of hand. During his brief stint as governor of the island of Barataria, Sancho Panza is tormented by a comically finicky physician who stands behind him as he eats, rejecting every dish but for the wafer cakes and a few thin slices of quince. He considers the fruits too cold and wet, and even the hot spices are inappropriate:

> My chief duty is to attend on his [Sancho's] meals and feasts, and to let him eat in my opinion what is suitable for him, and to keep from him what I think will be harmful, and injurious to his stomach; and therefore I ordered the plate of fruit to be removed on account of its excessive moistness, and that other dish likewise, as being too hot and containing many spices that aggravate thirst; and he who drinks a lot kills and consumes the radical moisture wherein the life force resides.

This was parody, but even Sancho was no more credulous than the well informed. But if getting the balance right was deadly serious, what of the quality of the end result? How spicy was it? Some old preconceptions can easily be dispensed with. The medical context argues strongly against the familiar images of medieval cuisine as an over-spiced, pungent welter of competing flavors. One reason why people have been so willing to accept the received wisdom on medieval cuisine—besides the fact that it makes for a good story—is that medieval cookbooks seldom stipulate quantities, leaving them up to the cook's discretion. But any immoderation modern readers detect therein is of the reader's making.

Moreover, moderation with spices made economic sense as well as medical. As we have seen, spices were expensive and so were not to be thrown around without good reason. In middling households they were kept under lock and key in a special hutch. The accounts of some noble households and monasteries detail a very modest expenditure. In England in the fifteenth century, the pepper consumed in the household of Dame Alice de Bryene averaged out at about one teaspoon per person per week; cinnamon at a paltry 2½ ounces per year. A fourteenth-century Parisian book of household management advises the following quantities of spice for a dinner for forty people: 1 pound of ginger, ½ pound of cinnamon, ¼ pound of clove, ⅛ pound of long pepper, ⅛ pound of galangal, and ⅛ pound of mace. These are impressive though not swamping quantities—less than half an ounce of ginger per person is less than one would use in a mild Indian curry, and even this was spread over several courses. Furthermore, all of these spices were staler than we know them, having spent at least a year in transit from harvest in Asia; nor were they sealed in airtight containers, as they are today.

At least some medieval cooks were well aware of the need for balance in cooking, as much for aesthetic as for medical reasons. Cookbooks constantly stressed the need to offset one ingredient with another, stipulating which spices went with which foods. One English recipe specifically cautions against overspicing the dish: "Add ground mace, cinnamon and cubebs, take care it is not too hot." John Russell, whom we met above advising would-be cooks to know their repertoire, warns darkly that in the endless search for new combinations, cooks' "nice excess . . . of life will make an ending." The fifteenth-century Italian culinary manuscript known as the Neapolitan collection advises discretion with spices, one recipe stipulating a moderate five or six cloves for a standard serving. This is not the voice of an age of anesthetized palates and cast-iron guts.

But if the medieval diner was not quite the bone-tossing oaf of Hollywood legend, it does not follow that medieval cookery was all that delicate or refined—we should not go looking for modern gastronomes dressed in medieval clothes. "Gastronomy" was not yet the word (at least in Europe), nor did it make much sense before the end of the seventeenth century. For while the medieval cook may not exactly have smothered all other flavors with spice, there can be little doubt that at times he laid it on thick. The Franklin of *The Canterbury Tales,* a middling landowner, was something of a gourmand—"Epicurus' own son"—with a taste for spicy sauces. He liked his food hot and had a temper to match:

> Woe to his cook, if his sauce was not
> Pungent and sharp, and all his utensils at the ready.

And when the fifteenth-century *Book of Vices and Virtues* weighed the merits of a meal, the terms of the question were whether the sauces had been sharp enough.

No aspect of the past vanishes so completely as its tastes. Perhaps the best that can be said is that though some liked food hot, some did not. And notwithstanding the doctors' abundant caution, there can be little doubt that on occasion spices were used with a heavy hand, for reasons that apparently had very little to do with taste. The Middle Ages were, after all, an age that developed elaborate public rituals in which machismo could be publicly paraded and tested. If manliness could be paraded and strutted on mock fields of battle, why not at the table? For characters such as the Franklin, a hale and hearty stomach was a declaration of sanguinity; toughness of guts was more of a manly virtue (and certainly more of an asset) than now. As the English writer Robert Burton (1576–1640) put matters, "As much valour is to be found in feasting as in fighting, and some of our city captains and carpet knights* will make this good, and prove it." After all, similar instincts are alive and well in our own day. At the start of the third millennium, the market offers a variety of scorching chili sauces, suggestively if not always appetizingly trademarked: Liquid Lucifer, Dave's Insanity Sauce, Blair's Sudden Death Sauce, Psycho Bitch on Fire, and Rectal Revenge ("particularly effective on in-laws"). Since a drop or two benumbs the palate, it seems a reasonable assumption that the appeal of these products is not culinary, at least not in the conventional sense of the term. It is more about seeing than tasting.

But at this point we are heading into different realms of appetite, which is where we must go if we are to fully account for the attraction of spices. We need to look beyond the table, beyond even the dictates of medicine and cuisine, to the equally powerful and perennial demands of society.

---

*A "knight" whose deeds of valor were all performed indoors, in a carpeted room; or, quite possibly, on the carpet.

KEEPING UP WITH THE PERCYS

Nobility is judged by the costliness of the table,
And taste gratified by the greater expense.
>—JOHN OF HAUTEVILLE, *Archithrenius*, ca. 1190

Let not your table be rustic if you are to be counted rich.
>—ANONYMOUS, *Modus cenandi*, ca. 1400

For a young crusader setting off to win his spurs, it was imperative that the catering should rise to the occasion. The scene was the house of Prince Henrique of Portugal, the occasion Christmas Eve 1414. Better known in the English-speaking world as "Henry the Navigator" (because he sent others to navigate), Henrique was about to set off to attack the Moroccan town of Ceuta. Before this first step in his and Portugal's imperialist career, he was determined to show himself as generous a host as he was valiant a knight. Noblemen, bishops, family— anyone who was anyone was invited, and supplies were ordered in from all corners of the kingdom. There were opulent silk cloths, wax for hundreds of candles, torches "in such a number that it would be impossible to count," barrels of the finest wines, sugared confections, all sorts of meats, fresh and preserved fruits. Rounding off this extravagant display was a lavish selection of spices. Why go Moor killing on an empty stomach?

At the time Henrique's catering arrangements seemed very much more impressive than they do now. The details are taken from *Account of the Capture of Ceuta,* written around 1450 by King Afonso V's Chronicler Royal, Gomes Eanes de Zurara. Unencumbered by the modern historian's qualms about objectivity, Zurara's job was to present Henrique in as regal a manner as possible: the flower of chivalry, an exemplary knight and nobleman. Hence the lengthy description of the Christmas Eve feast, notwithstanding the menu's complete and utter irrelevance to the ostensible topic of the work, the capture of Ceuta. Hence, too, the exacting catalogue of Henrique's largesse: the prince had to be seen to be rich—and generous. On account of their high cost and exclusivity, spices, along with the other costly luxuries listed by Zurara, were the ideal means to that end.

It is no coincidence that the rise of the spice trade toward the end of the first millennium coincided with the reemergence of the European nobility, a nascent class with surpluses to spend and social needs to meet. Just as in Roman times, much of the appeal of spices was not so much that they tasted good as the fact that they *looked* good. Along with the other luxuries with which they are almost invariably grouped—pearls, gems, furs, tapestries, and mirrors—spices fulfilled a need for display, for conspicuous consumption. Spices' attraction was not so much that they were necessary, but that they were *un*necessary: money on a plate.

At the table—as indeed anywhere else—the medieval nobleman was unconstrained by a sense of modesty. This is to put it very mildly. To live the life of a medieval monarch, nobleman, or higher clergy required being seen to live that life. Wealth was something to be paraded, with its purposes as well as pleasures. As Max Weber (1864–1920) said of a later age, luxury was "a means of social self-assertion." And what was true of the various other trappings of wealth flaunted by the medieval nobility—the number of retainers, the architecture, the jewelry, the dress, the halls bedecked with rich tapestries—held equally true at the table. At the semipublic event of the feast, the flavor or any imagined salutary effects of the food were no more esteemed than its sheer cost or superfluity.

The food, in not so many words, proclaimed the man. (Whereas noblewomen were less frequently in a position to dispense largesse. Their birth and station had to be advertised by means of other, less material refinements.) Accordingly, an elaborate ceremonial developed around the rituals of the table. In the noble or royal household, the after-dinner spices were typically served on gold or silver spice plates, often highly prized works of exquisite craftsmanship. In England in 1459, one well-born merchant owned one such plate "well gilt like a double rose, with my master's helmet in the middle, surrounded by red roses of my master's arms." So heavy was the baggage of class that the desserts they carried—"dainties"—took their name from the Latin *dignitas,* conveying a sense of honor, station, and bearing. From the head of the table the host would dispense his dainties as he saw fit, yet another means of signaling honor and precedence. If the situation and rank of the guests and hosts demanded, the quantities could be immense. When he hosted the emperor Charles IV at Valence in May 1365, the Avignon pope Urban treated his guests to a stupendous 150 pounds' worth of spices.

Likewise during the main part of the meal, when many a spiced dish was intended more to be seen than savored. At the marriage of Charles the Bold of Burgundy (1433–1477), six models of ships were mounted on the main table, one for each of the duke's territories. These in turn were orbited by sixteen smaller vessels, each trailing still smaller craft brimming with spices and candied fruits. On a more modest scale, around the year 1400 the Parisian merchant Jacques Duché had a walk-in gingerbread house constructed, its walls inlaid with precious stones and spices.

Cost, convenience, and aura all suited spices to the medieval penchant for courtly playfulness, as exemplified by the exotic food fight staged by Albizzo da Fiore, podesta of Padua, in 1214. For his guests' enjoyment he constructed a "Court of Solace and Mirth," at the center of which stood an allegorical castle of love, defended by a dozen of the noblest and fairest ladies and besieged with mock ferocity by selected noblemen. The battlements were of sable and furs, precious cloths, ermine, and brocades of Baghdad, which the besiegers assaulted with an extravagant arsenal of apples, dates, nutmeg, tarts, pears, quince, roses, lilies, violets, rose water, pomegranates, cardamom, cinnamon, cloves, "and all manner of flowers or spices that are fragrant to smell or fair to see." All went swimmingly until the Venetian guests took their contention for the ladies' honor a little too seriously, wrecking the party when they started a brawl with the Paduans—all in all, a very medieval mix: stage-managed gallantry and whimsy, offended honor, spice, and blood.

The limits to such occasions of spiced largesse were set only by the budget of the host or his imagination. A poem by Juan Manuel of Castile (1282–1348) tells of the weakness of the Moorish king of Seville for indulging the many whims of his wife, Rramayquia. When she protested at the heat of the Andalusian climate, he had the hills around Córdoba planted with almond trees, so the blossoms would remind her of snow. Still unsatisfied, she envied the bucolic life of a brick-making peasant woman (mawkish nostalgia for the honest virtues of the peasant life was another common pastime), whereupon her husband had a lake filled with rose water, cinnamon, ginger, cloves, musk, and "all conceivable good spices and sweet odors," so she could make bricks of fragrant mud amid the aromas to which she was accustomed—all this without leaving the comfort of her palace.

For more day-to-day purposes, the spiced sauces of the medieval kitchen were an opportunity for more affordable opulence. Medieval

cooks were forever in search of new combinations, driven in large measure by what one critic described as their employers' "vainglory in
rehearsing how they are fed, how many varieties of dishes they eat, and
how inventively they are dressed." As John Gower (ca. 1330–1408)
punned in an untranslatable line, rich and expensive sauces were a
social law for the rich and powerful.* Just as game and wildfowl were
the nobleman's meat, the yield of his fields and forests, kept off limits
to others by draconian laws against poaching and trespass, the rare and
expensive spices were his trademark seasonings, a signpost of his class.†
In the words of the Dutch author Jacob van Maerlant (ca. 1225–ca.
1291), they were the particular food of distinguished, worldly people.

The message, though essentially a very blunt one, was amenable to a
thousand different permutations and reiterations. One of the many rituals of medieval life to which spices were ideally suited was the gift giving that accompanied formal correspondence and diplomacy. Between
1294 and 1303, Pope Boniface VIII was regularly presented with spices
by ambassadors and sovereigns. Early in the twelfth century, the Venetians offered a gift of fifty pounds of pepper per annum to Emperor
Henry V. An early-thirteenth-century church ceremonial records that
the Jews of Rome marked the accession of a new pope with a gift of pepper and cinnamon—though this is likely to have been less a sponta-
neous offering than a form of tribute. Like the best diplomatic gifts,
they were bound to impress. In May 1290, envoys from England's King
Edward I sailed on board a "great ship" from Yarmouth to Norway,
their mission to arrange the marriage of Edward's son to Margaret, "the
Maid of Norway" and rightful heir to the crown of Scotland. Along
with the standard provisions for crew and envoys—including beer,
wine, whale meat, beans, stockfish, nuts, flour, and so forth—the dynas-
tic dealings were lubricated with ample supplies of sugar, pepper, ginger, zedoary, rice, figs, raisins, and gingerbread.‡

While there was no mistaking the bottom line of such abundance, it
would be misleading to reduce spices' cachet to a simple economic
measure. Much of their charm derived from a sense of mystery and
glamour, an intensely evocative effect of Utopian opulence. They were a

---

*The pun relies on the Latin homonym for "law" and "sauce" (*ius*).

†Consumption of wildfowl was another badge of noble status.

‡A similar custom was observed in the East as well: emissaries from the Great Khan to Pope
Benedict XII left Beijing in the middle of the fourteenth century bearing gifts of silk, precious
stones, camphor, musk, and spices.

totem of what the great Dutch medievalist Johan Huizinga called the "more beautiful life" for which the medieval nobility continually hankered, in its rituals, its tapestries, or the dreamy make-believe of its literature.

Which is where, at the distance of half a millennium, in a culture less disposed to public culinary exuberance, we can best sense their effect. For literary purposes, spices meant nobility. In the anonymous Middle English poem known as "The Debate of the Body and the Soul," the ghost of a "haughty knight" reflects on the trappings of his proud and vainglorious life, not the least of which are the "fragrant spices sweet to smell," prominent among the castles and towers, pages and palfreys, hounds, falcons, and noble steeds, chambers and stately halls. Spices serve a similar purpose in Jehan Maillart's early-fourteenth-century *Roman du comte d'Anjou,* in which a young countess tells the sorry tale of her banishment from home and family on account of her father's incestuous passion. The heroine is pursued by one trial after another, forced to conceal her noble ancestry and live incognito off the kindness of strangers, all the while pining for the life of comfort and ease she knew in her father's castle. At one point in her wanderings she is offered a piece of bread by an old peasant woman, but finding it black, hard, and moldy, she breaks down and, abandoning her disguise, recites the delights she knew at her father's table, for which she has an encyclopedic memory.* The peasant is subjected to a catalogue of all manner of delectable fish and fowl, including capons, peacocks, swan, partridge, pheasants, hare, venison, rabbits, boar, congers, cod, mullets, bream, lampreys, eels, and sole, all served with the appropriate spicy sauce: black pepper sauce, green sauce with ginger, tawny brown with cinnamon and cloves. These are followed by confections such as spiced apples and pastries, washed down with spiced and precious wines from all over France, over which the gruel-chomping churl—and well-born readers—presumably shed a salty tear.

In the real world, however, spices were generally put to more prosaic purposes. And while this instinct to display was common to the European nobility and senior clergy, they found their most exuberant

---

*As spices and meat were noble foodstuffs, so black bread was regarded as a correlate of peasantry. The hierarchies of bread existed even within a single loaf. The English expression "upper crust" dates from medieval times, when the quality of bread served in the hall varied according to rank. On account of medieval baking techniques, the best bread came from the top of the loaf and so was served to the "best" people.

expression at the apex of that society: namely, at court. Royal superiority may have been divinely sanctioned, but still the message had to be hammered home. Along with an increasingly elaborate courtly etiquette, architecture, and art, a royal meal was propaganda on a plate (or, more accurately, a trencher). When Henry II descended on Lincoln to celebrate Christmas in 1157, he demanded sixty pounds of pepper from the local grocers for his feast. This they were unable to cope with and sent to London for extra supplies.

Given the scale of their appetites, the royal family and the court were a large part of the market for spice for all of the medieval period; in London, possibly the lion's share until late in the era. When Edward I returned to London from the wars in Wales at the end of the thirteenth century, his officers spent more than £1,775 on spices out of a total expenditure on luxuries of just under £10,000—a staggering sum, even taking into account that many of his "spices" included items such as oranges and sugar. To put the figure into perspective, his spice expenditure was about the same as the total annual income of an earl, of whom there were about a dozen in the kingdom. Such regal appetites ensured that the office of supplying the king's "wardrobe" with spices was highly sought after by medieval merchants. The risks, however, could be great: in 1301, Edward I owed the Genoese merchant Antonio Pessagno the staggering sum of £1,030 for spices alone.

Pessagno's compatriots could afford to be more sanguine. The riches that flowed from the trade in Eastern luxuries routed through Genoa's ports and factories on the Black Sea and Constantinople helped transform the physical fabric of Genoa from the twelfth century; much of the wealth that built the cathedral of San Lorenzo came from this traffic. It was therefore wholly natural that the poet known as the Anonymous of Genoa, a contemporary of Dante, could celebrate spices as symbols of civic pride and affluence. In a poem addressed to a citizen of Brescia arriving from Venice, he points to the rich spices, the shops and stalls crammed with Eastern luxuries, symbols of Genoa's commercial and imperial greatness: "More pepper, ginger, nutmeg and merchandise . . . than in any other great city."

In the medieval as in the modern world, however, the ultimate in ostentation was not to boast, display, or dispense but to discard. Early in the fifteenth century, the lord mayor of London curried the favor of his king (and debtor) Henry V by publicly burning the king's IOUs in a fire of cinnamon and cloves: a fragrant twist on the medieval pyre of the vanities. The king was impressed: "Never king had such a subject," murmured a grateful Henry. This spiced incineration of debtors' notes seems to have been something of a convention. When Charles V visited his creditor Jakob Fugger in Augsburg in 1530, the banker threw a promissory note into the stove with a bunch of cinnamon. Given the emperor's chronic money troubles, the cinnamon was worth more than the note.

But of course the situation of a mayor, a king, a Fugger, or an emperor was scarcely representative of the population as a whole. With spices as with any other luxury, the instinct for ostentation could be gratified by only a very few. The celebrated spiciness of medieval cuisine holds true only for those with the money. For the poor the attractions of spices were, for the most part, strictly academic.

Researching the diet of the medieval poor is a frustrating business. By their very nature, most of the relevant sources are heavily biased in favor of the wealthy, the nobility, the Church, and royalty, and even these speak less of day-to-day consumption than of special occasions such as weddings, feasts, and coronations. Yet these sources represent only a relatively small segment of the population. By a crude estimate, for the greater part of the Middle Ages the clergy or nobility made up about 1 percent of the population, and about 5 percent of the population lived in towns. The remainder was the rural and generally poor peasantry. At the start of the thirteenth century, a majority of the population of western Europe was to some extent unfree, tied in some sense to land and lord.

For these, cost alone ensured that spices remained out of reach. This was particularly true of the fine Eastern spices: the cinnamon, cloves, nutmeg, and mace that are so liberally sprinkled through the cookbooks. Like any other books, cookbooks were for the rich, though occasionally they make a nod to the diet of the masses. The fourteenth-century English *Modus cenandi* suggests a pepper sauce for wild goose; birds of lesser quality are seasoned with salt alone and served to diners of lower station. One English culinary manuscript gives details for the preparation of three variants of hippocras, specifying different quantities of spice according to rank and budget: *pro rege, pro domino,* and, with the least spice of all, *pro populo.* A rare exception to the generally upper-class tenor of medieval cookery books is the mid-fifteenth-century *Liber*

cure cocorum, written for those who could afford to practice only eco-
nomical "petecure," literally "small cooking."* The preface outlines the
principles of cooking on a budget: "This craft is set forth for poor men,
that may not have spicery as they would like." The history of cooking is
the history of class cooking.

Though spices became a more familiar presence over time, the essentials of the situation remained unchanged throughout the Middle Ages.
The data are sporadic, but the picture is clear. In England in 1284, a
pound of mace cost 4 s. 7 d., a sum that could also buy three sheep—a
whopping outlay for even the better-off peasantry. At much the same
time, a pound of nutmeg would buy half a cow. In London at the start
of the third millennium, the best places to shop for spice tend to be in
the poorer, immigrant areas of the city, whereas seven hundred years
ago it was the exact reverse, with the business addresses of London's
grocers and spicers concentrated in the (then) well-off areas of the City.
Spice could be bought from a number of retailers in the wealthy
parishes of Saint Pancras, Saint Benet's Sherehog, Milk Street, and Saint
Mary-le-Bow; but no spicer saw fit to set up shop in the poorer area of
Farringdon. Spices went where the money was.

And where the money was not, spices occupied much the same position as they had in the age of Bede: out of reach but not out of mind.
When the poor did eat spices, they did so sparingly or at someone else's
expense—at public feasts, for example, or, for those attached to a noble
household, as leftovers from the high table. For the medieval poor,
spices were seen primarily as rent payments and medicines, and as seasonings only rarely, if at all.

Medieval poverty was seasoned with more run-of-the-mill flavors.
For the majority the only seasonings on the menu were garlic, garden
herbs, and salt, and for some even salt was out of reach. Chaucer
describes the situation of a "poor widow" who shared a cottage with her
two daughters, Chanticleer the cock and his hens, three pigs, three
cows, and Malle the sheep. No "piquant sauces" for her, and "no dainty
morsel ever passed through her throat." Her calories came from "many
a slender meal" based on the staples of milk, brown bread, bacon, and
occasionally an egg or two. However, even Chaucer's skinny widow was
better off than the wretched peasantry described by his contemporary
William Langland (ca. 1330–ca. 1400). His Piers Plowman has "no

*From the Old French *petite queuerie.*

penny" to buy "pullets, nor geese nor pigs"; the most he can afford is two green cheeses, curds, cream, an oatcake, two loaves made of beans, and bran. Yet even Piers was one rung up the ladder from the truly destitute who did not have enough to quiet the sobbing of their children "in their craving for food": "A farthing's worth of mussels were a feast for such folk." Starvation was a frequent visitor to medieval Europe, as much the result of dreadful communications and transport as poor harvests and pests, and most peasants would have experienced at least one serious famine in their lifetime. Here and there in the sources there are references to cannibalism and even disinterring of the dead so they might be eaten. One modern scholar has argued that the frenzied millennialism of the sixteenth century can in part be attributed to hallucinations and trepidation arising from a life spent in a cycle of famine and subsistence, constantly overshadowed by the very real risk of starvation.

Although standards varied widely, it is fair to say that the diet of the majority of the population ranged from meager to adequate for the entirety of the Middle Ages. The greater part of the peasantry lived at or not far above subsistence level, acutely vulnerable to fluctuations in cost and climate, getting by (or not) on a diet built around staples such as cabbage, beans, turnips, onions, ale, and above all bread. The latter was commonly black, impure, and made from oats or rye; in hard times, it was made from bean flour or even straw. Wine was an occasional luxury. Meat and especially fowl were exorbitantly expensive. The henpecked husband of the anonymous English medieval poem of the same title dares not so much as ask his bossy wife for meat:

> *If I ask of our dame flesh,*
> *She breaks my head with a dish.*

The only alternative supplies were illegally obtained from the king's forest, poached at the risk of one's limbs or life.

In households such as these, on the rare occasions when there was money to spare, it was spent on foods that were more likely to stick to the ribs than spices. That fact would not change in its essentials until the Middle Ages were a distant memory.

The exception, at least by the late medieval period, was pepper. Thanks to the success of the Venetians and their competitors in ferrying an ever increasing volume of the spice from Alexandria and the Levant to Europe, in real terms the cost fell steadily but surely through the Middle Ages. In England in the middle of the twelfth century, the cost of a pound of pepper ranged from 7 d. to 8 d., the equivalent of a week's wages for a laborer in the king's vineyards in Herefordshire (and therefore marginally more expensive in real terms than it had been in Roman times). Fifty years later, the price was down, at least in real terms, though one pound was still worth around four days' work. Over the next three centuries, the price continued to fall, though not without occasional spikes caused by crises in the money supply or by political turmoil along what was an extremely long and sensitive supply line. The price soared in the middle of the fourteenth century, then steadily fell back again. In England in 1400, one day's work by a skilled craftsman would buy half a pound of pepper—roughly half the cost of two centuries earlier. The spice was expensive but well within the means of the better-off peasantry.

Uniquely, pepper had made the transition from luxury to costly necessity. Such was the importance of the spice that in London in 1411 the authorities intervened to keep the price down, Parliament calling on the king to step in and protect the consumer from the perceived rapacity of the London grocers and resident Italian merchants.* Moved by the appeal, the king set a price ceiling of 20 d. a pound. By the time the *Mary Rose* sank in 1545, pepper was accessible to a common seaman earning a wage of 7 d. a week: when their corpses were raised some four hundred years later, most were found to have owned a small bag of pepper.

In the growing availability of the spice to an ever-larger swathe of the population is the first glimpse of a profound shift in perceptions. For intriguingly, pepper's accessibility to the common sort seems to have caused a loss of interest on the part of the nobility. Much as vegetables carried the stigma of commonness in the eyes of a meat-eating nobility, so too pepper gradually lost its air of exclusivity. As the spice became progressively more affordable and less exotic, the nobility turned its nose up at pepper and began to hunt around for more exclusive flavors. The trend is clearly reflected in the cookbooks. In the twelfth century, pepper had been deemed fit for a king: in the *Urbanus* or *Civilized Man* of Daniel of Beccles, a courtier of England's King Henry II, the spice features in numerous recipes, for poultry, meats, fish, beer, and wine; it is in fact the only Eastern spice mentioned by

---

*It would seem unjustly so: disruptions further down the spice routes were more to blame, for the Venetians had themselves paid a high price at Alexandria.

name. Pepper is likewise the sole Eastern spice mentioned in the earliest surviving accounts of an English noble household resident in London and Windsor in the late twelfth century. On trips to the capital they bought pepper, cumin, saffron, sugar, fish, meat, eggs, wine, flour, and apples.

Two centuries later, their well-born descendants looked down on pepper as irremediably déclassé. In *The Forme of Cury* written for King Richard II around 1390, pepper features in a mere 9 percent of the recipes. It was much the same on the Continent, the spice barely featuring in the early-fourteenth-century Italian *Liber de coquina,* another upper-class production. More revealing still is the gradual disappearance of pepper from successive editions of the French cookbook known as *The Viandier,* published in many editions in the fourteenth century and thereafter, traditionally attributed to Taillevant, cook and equerry to Kings Philip VI, Charles V, and Charles VI. Over time the amount of pepper decreases, as it is gradually superseded by other spices that carried a greater social cachet, such as grains of paradise and cardamom.

What is most striking about pepper's slow fall from grace is that it ran precisely counter to economic developments. The period when pepper went out of vogue, beginning around the middle of the fourteenth century, was exactly the moment when pepper imports to Europe reached unprecedented levels. From 1394 to 1405, pepper cargoes formed about 75 percent of all Venetian imports of spices. However, it was not the kings and nobles but the next few rungs down the social ladder that were paying for new palaces along the Grand Canal. The main consumers were the wealthy peasantry and the emergent bourgeoisie. In the mid-fourteenth-century *Livre des mestiers* pepper is the only spice that features in the shopping list of a bourgeois householder in Bruges. The accounts of the Bonis brothers, spicers at Montauban in the same period, tell a similar story of diet mirroring class. Pepper, mustard, and garlic are the seasonings sold by the mustard maker, a poor man's spicer. Likewise, the lower nobility, merchants, and prosperous bourgeois bought pepper, often with smaller purchases of ginger, saffron, and cinnamon. Artisans and peasants, on the other hand, bought pepper and nothing else.

An economic change, in not so many words, had social implications: tastes mirrored class. Occasionally pepper's fall from grace is made explicit. As early as the beginning of the fourteenth century, pepper appears in an anonymous poem as an ingredient of a "common sauce" of sage, salt, wine, pepper, garlic, and parsley. A little later it is dismissed as a poor man's spice in the *Thesaurus pauperum* or *Treasure House of the Poor* of Pedro Hispano, later Pope John XXI (ca. 1215–1277), whose reign was famously and abruptly curtailed by the collapse of a Vatican ceiling. And as the trade grew, so too grew the stigma. A medical treatise of the Salernitan school dating from the fifteenth century dismissed pepper as the "seasoning of rustics," fit only for the lowly beans and peas of peasants.

But pepper's fate was the exception, not the rule. If the other, finer spices did not form part of the peasantry's diet, this did not make them any less attractive. For just as the nobility esteemed spices as a highly visible expression of superior birth and wealth, so too the message of spices as a glittering correlate of the better life lost none of its potency for those on the receiving end. Viewed from the other side, spices were doubly desirable for being the privilege of the "great and the good"; which is to say that those barriers themselves contributed in no small part to spices' allure. Like beggars clustered outside a restaurant window, the medieval poor could only look on and drool as the well-off spiced their meat. What Montaigne (1533–1592) said of sumptuary laws applied equally to the still more unyielding laws of the market: "To declare that only princes may eat turbot and wear velvet and gold braid, forbidding them to the people, what is that but enhancing such things and making everyone want to have them?"

Those who could not afford spices, on the other hand, were inclined to view the issue less analytically. For those outside the charmed circle the line between admiration and resentment was a fine one. During Wat Tyler's Peasant Revolt of 1381, the rebel priest John Ball, self-styled "Bishop of the People," harangued the crowd of rebels in Canterbury before marching on London. In Jean Froissart's (ca. 1333–ca. 1405) version of events, Ball asks of his feudal overlords:

> Are we not descended from the same parents, Adam and Eve? And what can they show or what reason can they give why they should be more masters than ourselves? They are clothed in velvet and rich stuffs ornamented in ermine and other furs while we are forced to wear poor clothing. They have wines and spices and fine bread while we have only rye and refuse of the straw and when we drink it must be water. They have handsome manors . . . while we must brave the wind and rain in our labors in the field.

Burning the Savoy and sending their overlords scurrying for safety would not change the situation one iota. Someone more resigned to the situation than Ball, but like him one of the many who found himself on the wrong side of those insuperable barriers, was the Kentish hero of the medieval English poem "London Lickpenny." Visiting London from the country, he was overwhelmed by the street scene that greeted him in the capital:

Into London I set off;
Of all the land it bears the prize.
"Hot peascods!" someone cried—"Cherries on the branch!"
One called me over to buy some spice: pepper and saffron they offered me,
cloves, grains of Paradise . . . but for the lack of the money I could not
avail me.

The culture's objects of desire may have changed, but not the impulse. The unattainable glitter and glamour along Bond Street or Madison Avenue continue to inspire much the same sentiment in the cash-strapped visitor—or, for that matter, the impoverished writer.

III

BODY

THE NUTMEG PLANT
Acosta, *Tractado de las drogas* (Burgos, 1578)

CHAPTER 4

○

THE SPICE OF LIFE

They pulled out his bowels, and they stretched forth his feet,
They embalmed his body with spices so sweet.
—ANONYMOUS, "The Duke of Grafton," ca. 1694

Sleep in thy peace, while we with spice perfume thee,
And Cedar wash thee, that no times consume thee.
—ROBERT HERRICK (1591–1674), "Dirge upon the Death
of the Right Valiant Lord, Bernard Stuart"

THE PHARAOH'S NOSE

The first known consumer of pepper on whom we can hang a name did not use his spice to season his dinner, for he was long past any pleasures of the flesh. He was, in fact, a corpse: the royal skin and bones of Ramses II, arguably the greatest of Egypt's pharaohs, up whose large, bent nose a couple of peppercorns were inserted not long after his death on July 12, 1224 B.C.

The upper reaches of the pharaoh's nose mark the beginning, for the time being, of one of the most important chapters in the history of spice. Long after Ramses' day, many other illustrious corpses went to a spicy grave. In 565, the Byzantine poet Corippus recorded the embalming of the emperor Justinian with balsam, myrrh, and honey, whereupon "a hundred other spices and wondrous unguents were borne in, preserving the holy body for all eternity." In *Pericles,* a play based on a novel of late antiquity, Shakespeare described the burial of Thaisa:

> *Shrouded in cloth of state, balm'd and entreasur'd*
> *With full bags of spices!*

A generation later the English poet Robert Herrick expressed the sentiment that to be buried with his Anthea would be spice enough: "For my Embalming (Sweetest) there will be / No Spices wanting, when I'm laid by thee." For the better part of three millennia they were, for those with the cash, an integral part of dying.

As tends to be the way with spices, the origins of the custom are a matter for guesswork and speculation. In the case of Ramses, the contents of his nose are known only thanks to the efforts of researchers at the Musée de l'Homme in Paris, where his mummy, or what was left of it, spent the winter of 1975–1976. The mummy had been sent to Paris in collaboration with the Cairo Museum, its home for the last hundred or so years, where it had lain in a glass box, looking for all the world like a large, leathery locust, slowly decaying under the humid breath of tourists and nibbled by borers. The last century had been harder on Ramses than the previous thirty-two, which time he had spent in no fewer than three graves, enduring repeated robberies and relocations within several decades of his death. These were indignities the Egyptians viewed with the utmost horror (grave-robbing Egyptians excepted), and elaborate precautions were taken to prevent their occurrence by means of secrecy and sorcery. Shortly after the pharaoh's death, a team of priests and embalmers set about preparing the body for burial, accompanied by prayers for the future and curses against any malefactor so bold as to lift a hand against the royal cadaver. It was during this time that the pepper was inserted up the pharaoh's nose, where it was sealed in place with plugs of an unidentified resinous substance. And there it remained, hidden and forgotten, swimming into view only with the benefit of X-ray examination, its identity confirmed after an exhaustive process of elimination of native African species some three millennia after its harvest somewhere in the tropical south of India.

How it got there, or who had brought it, is unknowable. The most tantalizing possibility is that there was even then a direct traffic between Indians and Egyptians. More likely, the spice was shuttled from one obscure market to another, ferried west by an assortment of traders whose names and origins are now wholly lost to history. That the pepper came from India is certain; the rest is pure surmise.

But while the presence of the pepper came as a shock, that the Egyptians should have seen fit to insert it up the nose of a dead king should not. (Researchers also found traces of the spice in his abdominal cavity.)

Slowing or killing the bacteria that cause decomposition, spices seem
custom-made for the quintessentially Egyptian custom of mummification. In an age without the benefits of formaldehyde or arterial embalming, let alone the refrigerated morgue, spices played the crucial role of
keeping a corpse fresh and presentable when otherwise it would soon
have putrefied.

There was a good deal more to the Egyptians' legendary attentiveness
to the mortal remains than a desire for preservation for preservation's
sake. According to Egyptian belief, death was not so much the end as a
transition. As they understood matters, the priests and embalmers
charged with mummifying the pharaoh's body were preserving a home
to which the pharaoh's immortal *ka,* or life principle, could return.
Though the Egyptians held that the *ka* was immortal, they also believed
that even after death it still needed a physical frame if it was not to wan-
der aimlessly through the afterlife: an everlasting, living death far more
horrible than the death of the body. Hence, in short, the extraordinary
importance the Egyptians attached to preserving the mortal remains,
and hence the colossal energies they expended on building houses and
cities for their dead. The raison d'être of mummification—and the best
explanation of the preservative pepper—was to guarantee the pharaoh's
eternal life. As the sacred formulae put it, to keep the body from the
smell of corruption was to keep the dead free of the "sweat of Seth":
death's stamp. It was in all likelihood the supreme metaphysical importance of this end that accounts for the Egyptians' extraordinary efforts
to obtain a spice all the way from India.

Before there was pepper, other substances did a similar job. Ramses'
pepper was apparently grafted into the mortician's repertoire by a
process of analogy with gums, aromatics, and resins available closer to
home. The use of myrrh, balsam, and bdellium* is documented from
the early third millennium B.C. When Howard Carter examined the
mummy of Tutankhamen, interred almost exactly a century earlier
than Ramses, he found that the corpse had been treated with coriander
and resins. When the Greek traveler Herodotus passed through Egypt
in the fifth century B.C., he found three grades of mummification on
offer, the most expensive version of which used a variety of spices, the
names of which Herodotus either was ignorant of or omitted to note.

*Bdellium is a gum resin that oozes from one of several shrubs of the genus *Commiphora.*
The dried product resembles impure myrrh.

The only Eastern spice he mentions by name is cassia. But this, he tells us, was for the rich. The poor made do with simply eviscerating and desiccating the body, leaving the dry Egyptian climate to do the rest.

The Egyptians were not alone in sending their dead to an aromatic grave. Although customs varied from one time and place to another, spices, resins, flowers, and aromatics were used by all the major cultures of antiquity, whether the body was mummified, buried, or incinerated.* A Phoenician inscription on a sarcophagus in Byblos states that the dead person "lies in myrrh and bdellium." In the *Iliad* Aphrodite rescues Paris from death and returns him smelling of balm and incense. Later the same goddess anoints the dead Hector with rose-scented oil. The dead Israelite King Asa, slain by a disease of the feet, was incinerated in a fragrant pyre:

> And Asa slept with his fathers, and died in the one and fortieth year of his reign. And they buried him in his own sepulchres, which he had made for himself in the city of David, and laid him in the bed which was filled with sweet odours and divers kinds of spices prepared by the apothecaries' art: and they made a very great burning for him.

While perfuming the body in one form or another was common to the ancient Mediterranean, it is the Romans whose use of spices is best documented. To Tacitus (ca. A.D. 56–ca. 120) the practice of spicing the dead was a recent and un-Roman import—he sniffs at a "custom of foreign kings"—yet by his day it was reasonably widespread. Cinnamon in particular was a regular feature of burials; apart from a solitary reference to spiced wine in Pliny's *Natural History,* there is no sign that the Romans ate the spice. On the demise of the dictator Sulla in 79 B.C., after a slow and hideous death caused by worms devouring his flesh, an effigy of cinnamon was constructed in his image. "It is said that the women contributed such a vast bulk of spices for the interment that, aside from what was carried on two hundred and ten litters, there was enough to make a large figure of Sulla, and that an image of a lictor [staff bearer] was molded from expensive frankincense and cinnamon."

At this time the attractiveness of spices apparently had more to do with their aroma than any preservative effect. By the time of Christ the prevailing custom among the Romans was incineration. The more fra-

---

*The Mayans used allspice in embalming.

grant the send-off, the better. The epigrammatist Martial (ca. A.D. 38–103) writes of a patron all set to expire, with his bier prepared with cassia and cinnamon at the ready, only to recover at the last minute, thereby denying the poet a promised inheritance. By the end of the second century, it was customary to cremate the dead emperor "with every perfume and incense on earth." The body of the dead emperor was set on a bier in a large wooden tower, a little like a lighthouse, erected on the Field of Mars. "The whole structure easily catches fire and burns without difficulty because of the large amount of dry wood and aromatic spices which are piled high inside." The rite was a conscious reenactment of the spiced inferno of the phoenix, that fabulous bird of sun, spice, and eternal life that according to myth died and was reborn in a pyre of cinnamon. In the case of imperial deaths the symbolism was echoed more literally still by the release from the burning pyre of an eagle, soaring up to heaven with the dead emperor's soul in tow.*

There was a good deal more to these aromatic obsequies than merely aesthetic considerations. To Romans cinnamon in particular not only smelled of sanctity but sanctified. These sacral associations were apparently understood quite literally. Burned with or applied to a corpse, the spice was believed to play a redemptive role—just as it did with the mythic death and rebirth of the phoenix. There is a poem by Sidonius (ca. 430–ca. 490 B.C.) in which the phoenix is captured by Dionysos and brought back to Greece from India, fretting that without cinnamon he will be unable to be reborn in his fiery holocaust. Elsewhere the same poet calls the spice "resurrecting," the "cinnamon that brings life while dying." In this sense the sweet smell represented the triumph of life over death, symbolizing if not actually conferring immortality. Death smelled of corruption, but infinity, like the deathless gods and phoenix themselves, smelled divine—and spicy.

Yet however theologically charged the symbolism, social concerns, as tends to be the way with spices, lurked not far beneath the surface. When Herod the Great was buried, he was seen off with a procession of five hundred freedmen and a vast quantity of aromatics. When Nero's consort, Poppaea, died from a kick he dealt to her stomach—according to the historian Suetonius they had a row after he came home late from the races—her body was cremated on a colossal pyre of cinnamon. His

---

*In respect of its fire and aromatics the event was apparently not dissimilar to the perfumed royal cremations practiced to this day in Bali.

near contemporary Pliny had it on good authority that Arabia did not produce so large a quantity of cinnamon and cassia in one year as went up in smoke in a single day for her funeral rites. Her send-off was as much an economic as a theological statement.

For the poor, on the other hand, a spiced burial was probably not an option. It is probably no coincidence that memorials of spiced deaths tended to occur with the grand personage, particularly the emperor. Saint Augustine (354–430) writes of the custom as a rich man's privilege. A satire by Persius (A.D. 34–62) features a rich man fretting that if he should die without leaving as much money as he might have to his heir, the latter, disappointed by a paltry inheritance, will consign his bones to the tomb without perfume, content to use weak or insufficient cinnamon on the pyre and second-rate, adulterated cassia. Among truly wealthy Romans even a prized pet merited a send-off with cinnamon. The poet Statius (ca. A.D. 45–96) writes mock-seriously of the sweet smells accompanying the obsequies of a pampered parrot, punning on the spicy death of the phoenix:

> . . . *his ashes redolent of Assyrian cardamom,*
> *His slender feathers exhaling Arabian incense*
> *And Sicanian saffron; he will ascend the perfumed pyre,*
> *A happier Phoenix, unburdened by wearisome age.*

However, the most famous spiced corpse of them all was not a rich Roman but a poor subject of Roman Judaea. According to the gospels of Luke and John, the body of Jesus was wrapped in linen and anointed with spices, "as the manner of the Jews is to bury."

The spiced entombing of Christ was, of course, the most influential precedent of all. In the Christian epoch many followed where he had led. Among the early Christians there was a preference for embalming over cremation, though there are signs that this was a direction in which pagan Romans were already moving. (Before the Turin shroud was shown to be a medieval fake, some argued that its image might have been made by the embalming spices leaching into the cloth.) What more Christian exit than to be buried in the manner of the Messiah? The acts of Peter and Andrew, composed early in the Christian era but later discarded as apocryphal, record similar ends for the two apostles. When Saint Luxorius was martyred in Sardinia during the persecutions of the emperor Diocletian, his followers buried him with hymns, torches, and the embalmers' sweet spices. To spice the dead was to make them Christlike.

Yet such an eminent precedent notwithstanding, that Christians should have embraced embalming and spices so wholeheartedly is surprising. In the eyes of the Church fathers spices had a problematic past, redolent of paganism and vain luxury—they were, after all, no less luxurious on a corpse than as condiments. Saint Augustine writes approvingly that his mother spurned an expensive burial with spices. The more polemical Tertullian (ca. 155–ca. 220) noted that pagans were in the habit of offering spices to their gods, for which reason Christians who used them for solace at funerals were aiding and abetting idolatry. The Christian apologist Lactantius (ca. 240–320) agreed, seeing the spiced funeral as a pagan hangover hidden in Christian guise. Favoring dead flesh was not easily reconciled with the notion that the flesh was dross. Augustine asked, "What does it avail if the corpse has cinnamon and spices, wrapped in precious linens?" In the testament of Ephraim the Syrian, purportedly composed shortly before the saint's death around 375, he stipulates, "Lay me not with sweet spices: for this honor avails me not." His reasoning was apparently more practical than spiritual: "What can goodly odor profit to the dead who cannot perceive it?"

But eminent as these authorities were, there were other and apparently more compelling considerations. Most early Christians seem to have been more inclined to accord the embalming of the dead the status of a sacred duty. Some early Christians clung to a literal belief in the imminent physical resurrection of the body, from which it followed that preserving the soon-to-be-resurrected body was a task of the utmost importance. In his encyclopedic history of Christian ritual, the great French Benedictine scholar Edmund Martène (1654–1739) cites the cases of martyrs whose bodies were gathered by other Christians, then spiced and buried in the manner of Christ. But whereas Christians were inclined to take the greatest possible care of the mortal remains, from the perspective of those doing the martyring, to deprive their victims of a Christian burial was to inflict a double death. When Saint Calepodius was martyred in an uprising in the time of Pope Calixtus I sometime in the early decades of the third century, the Prefect Maximus threatened to take the body away from the "little women" who hoped to embalm his body with aromatics and destroy it utterly, so depriving the martyr of both life and afterlife.

In this sense spices, as among earlier cultures, kept the Christian dead alive—when the last trump sounded and the graves were emptied, it would pay to be in good shape. The rule is proved by the exception, an occasion when failure to spice the body brought deliverance. The *Dialogues* of Pope Gregory the Great, who reigned from 590 to 604, relate the strange tale of a certain Stephen, an eminent person who died while on a business trip to Constantinople in the sixth century. His soul was promptly dispatched to Hades, where he was brought before the infernal judge, who thereupon declared—such is the lineage of the knocking-at-the-pearly-gates joke—that there had been a case of mistaken identity, his infernal minions having brought him the wrong Stephen: it was his neighbor, Stephen the blacksmith, that he was after. Fortunately for the other Stephen, back on Earth no spicer had been found in the meantime to eviscerate and spice the corpse, and so the mistake could still be rectified. Stephen's soul was sent back to his still-intact body and that of the blacksmith dragged down in his place.

Certain myths inherited from outside Christian tradition also lent themselves to Christian adaptation, none more so than the ancient myth of the phoenix. In the bird's cinnamon-scented resurrection there were obvious affinities with Christian belief, for which reason the phoenix was a popular subject of Christian poetry and art in late antiquity.* It was perhaps with the phoenix in mind that cinnamon was used in burials and in the aromatic anointing oil, the chrism, with which the dead were occasionally anointed. The ancient belief in a pleasant aroma as marking the triumph of life over death had apparently survived more or less intact, an impression reinforced by archaeology. During a sojourn in Rome during the pontificate of Paul III in the mid-sixteenth century, the Spanish scholar Andrés Laguna witnessed the opening of an early Christian mausoleum exposed during construction work for a side chapel in the new basilica of Saint Paul. Inside the builders found a type of cinnamon Laguna knew as red or mountain cinnamon, terms by which the Iberians of the day referred to the inferior coarse cinnamon of the Malabar Coast. The tomb containing the spice housed the remains of the empress Maria, the wife of the emperor Honorius, ruler of the western half of the Roman Empire from 395 to 423, her body easily identified by a golden necklace bearing her name. Also among

*The phoenix was, moreover, a common motif on early Christian sarcophagi. It is possible that the motif and spice were commonly paired in the grave as in literature.

the grave goods were thirty different cosmetics and unguents, which, Laguna remarked, had retained their sweet odor, "as though they had been mixed only yesterday."

Christian or pagan, the Romans ultimately owed these customs to the Egyptians, just as Rome's Germanic conquerors acquired them from the Romans. In what had once been the Roman province of Gaul, the Frankish dynasty of the Merovingians (476–750) apparently made regular use of spices and embalming. Gregory of Tours (538/9–594/5) writes of the saintly Queen Radegunda being embalmed with spices, and thereafter the custom remained a feature of royal burials. In treating the body after death, the real intention was not lifelike preservation, as sought after by the Egyptians—indeed, the increasingly rudimentary techniques of embalming were not up to the task. The appeal probably had much to do with the odor of sanctity that by now was a commonplace of the religiosity of medieval Christendom, the spices being seen as proof of God's favor, symbolic evidence of special status. To lie among spices was to lie in the odor of the saints.

Such scarce evidence as has survived suggests that the spices were now employed more for their supposed redemptive potency than for any preservative effect. A sixth-century Merovingian coffin unearthed in Alsace contained two cloves inside a little golden box. Since the cloves were not in contact with the corpse, they were clearly not there to preserve or for that matter to deodorize. Midway through the eleventh century, Jotsaud, disciple and hagiographer of Saint Odilo, abbot of Cluny, wrote an extraordinary lament on his patron's passing, in which he describes the transfigurative powers of his deathbed of "mystical spices":

> *Beloved Odilo, now fair and blushing,*
> *With a steady tread follows in Christ's footsteps.*
> *A flowery, snowy couch is borne forth for him,*
> *Covered with lofty cedar, and adorned with fragrant cyprus:*
> *Sprinkled with violets, strewn with lilies.*
> *Behold him adorned with flowery roses,*
> *Looking on the various plants with glad eyes.*
> *Balsams are there, and many aromas are ground,*
> *Nard and myrrh shine palely, and strong cinnamon burns. . . .*
> *There are a thousand spices, their several odors intermingle,*
> *The savor of nectar fills even to highest heaven.*

The following verse sees Odilo transferred to eternal life:

Availing himself of these delights, Odilo is made new again.

The force, in not so many words, was metaphysical, even magical—a sentiment a Roman, or for that matter an Egyptian, would have found quite familiar.

By Jotsaud's day, however, the desire to preserve the worldly remains was becoming increasingly hard to reconcile with dogma. By the central Middle Ages, Church doctrine hardened in its view that the body was worthless, mere dross sloughed off by the immortal soul. Yet the custom of spicing the dead endured, apparently for more pragmatic reasons. Perfuming the dead was by now an essentially social rite. Here too spices fulfilled a need, offering several attractions over more primitive methods, not the least of which must have been the aesthetic one of concealing the smell of a decaying corpse. Europe's only homegrown preservatives were salt, wine, and vinegar; failing that, the body was simply boiled, as befell Archbishop Reginald of Cologne in 1167, who died on a trip through the high Alps, far from any spicer. Lacking the necessary equipment and unable to get the body home without it putrefying, his followers had no choice but to "cook" the bishop in boiling water. But this was a very inadequate method and left the corpse in bad shape, mere bones and bishop stock (and required, presumably, a large cauldron).

On purely pragmatic grounds, spices represented a far more attractive and practical option. Around the turn of the millennium, cinnamon and pepper in particular were a regular feature of noble burials. When the emperor Otto I died at Merseburg in 973, he was seasoned with spices, as the formula put it, then taken to Magdeburg to be buried. Often the sources are explicit that the incentive was simply to enable transport of the corpse from one place to another or to counteract the heat of the season. When Saint Wicbert died in 962, the monks of the abbey of Gembloux, "fearing lest the heat of the summer should cause harm to the holy body," removed and buried his entrails, sprinkling salt and various fragrant spices on the body, "which can repel the putrefaction or the decay of the body." Like Wicbert, senior prelates, nobles, and kings frequently wanted to be buried in their home chapels or in an abbey or monastery they had founded, requiring preservation for a last, posthumous journey. One who failed to make it back was King Charles the Bald (823–877), who had the misfortune to die while

returning from an expedition to Italy, hundreds of miles from the royal
abbey of Saint-Denis, the traditional burial ground of the French kings.
His companions eviscerated the body and carried out what sounds like
a fairly agricultural attempt to embalm the body with wine and
unspecified aromatics, but in spite of their best efforts, by the time the
funeral cortege arrived at Nantua the king smelled so bad that he had
to be buried on the spot.

More fortunate was the crusader King Baldwin I, the Frankish king
of Jerusalem, the account of whose death in 1118 suggests the extraordinary importance the medieval nobleman attached to the correct treatment of his earthly remains. Sensing his end draw near while on an
expedition in Egypt, Baldwin implored his entourage to take him back
to Jerusalem, where he could lie alongside his brother. His fellow crusaders objected, pointing out the difficulties: the weight of his corpse,
the distance to travel, the unbearable heat of the Egyptian summer.
Alarmed, Baldwin pressed the point, describing the procedure he
wished them to follow in minute detail. First they were to slice open
his stomach with a sword, remove his entrails, and thoroughly salt his
insides. The body was then to be rolled in carpet or cowhide. But the
knights were still squeamish. Finally Baldwin entrusted the task to his
cook, the loyal Addon, making him swear by the love he held for him
that he would diligently carry out the task of his gutting, specifying
that he was not to overlook his eyes, nose, ears, and mouth, which
should all be "seasoned with balsam and spices." True to his vow,
Addon carried out the task entrusted him, and Baldwin's body made it
back to Jerusalem more or less in one piece, leaving only his entrails to
lie in infidel ground.

As Baldwin was at pains to point out, the honors due medieval
nobility extended into the grave. Even posthumously, the medieval
nobleman or senior prelate was concerned with keeping up appearances. In death as in life, spices suited noble instincts. They were a last
opportunity to show the nobleman as belonging to a class apart, as
though death were not quite the leveler that it was for lesser mortals.
Moreover, as Baldwin was doubtless well aware, his spiced obsequies
echoed those of the paragon of paladins and exemplary crusader, the
dead and double-crossed Roland. The eleventh-century poem of
Charlemagne's invasion of Spain, *Chanson de Roland,* tells of the hero's
last stand in the pass of Roncevaux, where he is betrayed and hopelessly
outnumbered by infidels, whereupon he blows his own brains out by

blasting too hard on his horn and dies. The bodies of Roland and two
other noble companions are returned to Charlemagne, who orders them
washed in spices and wine. The fictional Roland's real-life suzerain,
Charlemagne, was similarly spiced after his death in 814 and buried in
the cathedral of Aachen. His body was perfumed and seated in a golden
chair, dressed with a diadem and gold chain, armed with a gold sword
and carrying a golden gospel in his hands and knees, "and they filled
the tomb with perfumes, spices, balsam and musk and treasures."

Though few could afford to go out in such style, Charlemagne's burial typified the aspirations of the class he headed: the twin imperative of
piety—buried with a Bible in his hand—and luxury, in the form of
gold and spices.* Thus, although the theological significance of the
mortal remains had been downgraded, the need to demonstrate status
remained as pressing as ever and so too the usefulness of spices to that
end. If anything, the social and indeed the political imperative
increased over time. It is probably no coincidence that the demand for
more effective and more luxurious materials in the form of the Eastern
spices coincides with the reemergence of the nobility as a distinct class
around the tenth century. With its steady emergence as a class apart,
acutely conscious of its dignity and identity, the nobility relentlessly
sought to advertise its superior status in ritual, not least the rituals of
death. Many of the consumers whose demand was a major impetus for
the revival of the trade, and the vast broadening of Europe's intellectual
and physical horizons, were already dead.

As Charlemagne's and Baldwin's deaths suggest, that demand was
felt most acutely at the pinnacle of society. Most particular on this
point were the kings of France, whose bodies were put on posthumous
display in the abbey of Saint-Denis, an opportunity for a last parade of
magnificence after the body had been washed with wine, vinegar, and
spices. The ritual gave the dead monarch's subjects a last chance to render homage, or to see for themselves that he was dead. In 1307, the
body of Edward I of England lay embalmed and displayed on a bier for
four months, by the end of which period he presumably required some
potent deodorants. Whereas Nelson came back from Trafalgar in a barrel of brandy, the dead King Henry V "was embalmed and dressed with
rich spicery and ointments . . . shut fast in a chest and carried down to

---

*Similar treatment was presumably given to the body of the eleventh-century Spanish hero
El Cid, which remained on display in an ivory chair in the monastery of San Pedro de Cardeña
for a decade before burial.

Rouen, where a dirge and mass were said for him, with the most solemnity that might be ordained and done in Holy Church."

As with any other conspicuous royal ritual, the expense could be huge and the king's credit—he was, after all, a corpse—doubtful. When King Edward I lay dying at Lanercost Abbey in 1307, the apothecaries supplying the court readied a supply of spices and incense for the imminent embalming. Their bill (a big one) was apparently not paid, since the following year the widow of one of the king's spicers lodged a petition, pointing out that her late husband was still owed a near-identical sum by the deceased king.

Over time, however, the costs of embalming came down. By the fourteenth century, spices were becoming more readily available, and the once royal custom was increasingly mimicked by the lesser nobility. The final entry in the account books of Robert d'Artois, a nobleman of the Pas-de-Calais, records the purchase in 1317 of two pounds of powdered ginger, cinnamon, and cloves for the corpse (at a cost of sixteen sous). By the fifteenth century, it was not unheard of for criminals' heads, once they had been removed by the royal executioner, to be preserved and exhibited *pour encourager les autres.* Typically the severed head was parboiled and seasoned, though apparently with cheaper aromatics such as cumin. Owing to the exceptional circumstances, slightly better treatment was given to the head of Thomas More, severed by order of Henry VIII and cooked in water before being set on a spike on London Bridge. There it stayed for a month before being taken down to make room for new arrivals and returned to More's daughter. In the words of Thomas Stapleton, one of More's early biographers, "Margaret Roper [More's daughter] . . . as long as she lived kept the head with the greatest reverence, carefully preserving it by means of spices, and to this day it remains in the custody of one of his relatives." Stapleton was writing in the Armada year of 1588. At some stage not long afterward, More's family deposited his head in Saint Dunstan's church in Canterbury, where it was seen, still in reasonable condition, when the vault was opened in 1837; and there, presumably, it still remains. If and when the vault is reopened, it will be possible to see how well Margaret's spices did the job.

Odd as the idea might seem, then, from the ancient world and through the Middle Ages spices smelled not only of other worlds but of worlds to come. In some unrecoverable sense, just as the wealthy dead smelled of spices, so spices smelled of death. The overlap was particu-

larly pronounced in Latin, since the vocabulary was the same. To prepare a corpse for burial was literally to "season" or "spice" it, *condire,*
whence *condimentum,* or seasoning. Moreover, the materials used on the
embalmed were standard kitchen seasonings. We have seen that when
Baldwin I died he entrusted the treatment of his body to his cook;
when Henry I died in Normandy in 1135, his butcher was given the
job of dealing with the corpse and getting it back to Reading Abbey
more or less in one piece. In Roman times, the dual meanings and purpose of spice were material for a sort of gallows humor. In his defense of
vegetarianism, the historian Plutarch compared the gourmet's habit of
eating his meats and fishes spiced and seasoned with wine and vinegar
to eating an embalmed corpse. Martial regarded cinnamon and cassia as
"redolent of funerals." He accuses a certain Zoilus of filching the grave
goods: "Shameless Zoilus! Give back from your grubby pockets the
unguents, cassia and myrrh, redolent of funerals, and the half-cremated
frankincense that you filched right from the pyre itself, along with the
cinnamon you snatched from the Stygian couch. Your grimy hands
learned their wickedness from your feet—since you were once a runaway slave, small wonder you're a thief!"

This whiff of the grave was, for that matter, an association that
applied not only to spices but to all perfumes; there was a hint of
formaldehyde in the air, as it were. In another epigram Martial complains that a dinner host gave his guests a decent perfume but no food:

> *The perfume you gave your guests yesterday was, I admit,*
> *a good one; but you didn't serve them anything to eat.*
> *To smell good and go hungry—very droll.*
> *He who does not eat but smells good, Fabullus,*
> *Seems like a dead man to me.*

ABBOT EBERHARD'S COMPLAINT

The apothecaries keep preserved and Alexandrian ginger, such
as befit cold complexions.

—JOHN GARLAND, ca. 1180–ca. 1252

The millennium was new, but Abbot Eberhard was old. Old, weary,
and ill. In the depths of an icy Bavarian winter, he languished in his cell

in the ancient abbey of Tegernsee, his insides grumbling, his head spinning, his limbs feeble. He had tried all the herbs and potions of the monastery's resident doctor, but to no avail. There was nowhere to turn but to a local noblewoman, a patron of the monastery, for help. His letter conveys something of the spicy, rugged flavor of medieval medicine:

> As my infirmities are perilous, because I am forever frail, I beseech you to send me the ingredients for a healing potion, including some nutritive cloves with other spices, such as are necessary for this remedy. Indicate in writing how this potion should be taken, and with what precautions I should follow, and whether I will vomit it out from above, or expel it from below. If I am restored to health, know that I am hereafter your dedicated servant, for the simple reason that I am still alive. And if you would be so good, please send some deer kidneys or something of the sort, because chewing on the toughness of lean meat with my teeth, for they are worn, gives me nothing but pain. Wherefore, if possible, that the potion should come before Lent, I beseech you.

The effectiveness of the cure and whether he received his shipment before Lent are unrecorded.

As Eberhard's letter attests, spices were used to preserve living bodies as well as dead—or, as in Eberhard's case, bodies somewhere between the two. In the medieval mind spices and medicines were effectively one and the same. Not all drugs were spices, but all spices were drugs. The identity was reflected in vocabulary: the Late Latin term for spices (*pigmenta*) was practically synonymous with medicines, and so it remained through the Middle Ages. Apothecary and spicer were effectively one and the same: "one who has at hand for sale aromatic spices and all manner of things needful in medicine," in the words of a fourteenth-century manuscript at Chartres Cathedral. The apothecary took his name from the Greek term for a warehouse where high-value goods such as spices were stored. Even today one Italian word for pharmacist is *speziale*. He is the direct descendant of the medieval spicer (*speciarius*), whose wares were among the most sought after and esteemed medicines of the age.

Without appreciating the medicinal freight that spices carried, the European appetite for spice is simply unintelligible. They came recommended by the authorities in an apparently limitless number of permutations, a hodgepodge of inheritances that survived from antiquity and far outlasted the Middle Ages. A work compiled at the watershed of those two epochs, the fifth-century *Syriac Book of Medicines*, illustrates the sheer variety of the medical applications of spice and the quasi-religious faith in their efficacy. Pepper alone is prescribed for a bewildering array of illnesses: to be poured into the ears for earache and paralysis; for sore joints and excretory organs; for abscesses of the mouth and pustules in the throat; for general debility, blackening, and nubbing of the teeth; for cancer of the mouth, toothache, gangrene, and stinking secretions; for a lost voice or a frog in the throat; for coughing up pus; for lung diseases; mixed with jackal fat for chest and internal pains; as a soporific; for heart disease and a weak stomach; for constipation and sunburn; for sleeplessness, insect bites, "bad burps," and poor digestion; for a cold stomach, shivers, and worms; for a hard liver, a sore liver, wind, and dysentery; for jaundice, hard spleen, loose bowels, dropsy, hernias, and a general "evil condition." None of these prescriptions, to my knowledge, has been shown to have the slightest basis in medical fact. But the fact that these prescriptions would not have done the least bit of good did not stop physicians from elaborating endless variations on the theme. Viewed over the longer term, the history of medicine is more a matter of faith than proof, and spices are no exception. The uses to which they were put were seemingly limited only by the ingenuity of the doctors.

For an age commonly supposed to be shut within its own narrow horizons, when evidence of European involvement in the spice trade is practically nil and Europeans' knowledge of Asia not much better, the frequency with which spices crop up in the medical texts of the early Middle Ages is nothing less than astonishing. Saint Benedict Crispus, the early-eighth-century bishop of Milan, wrote several medical poems featuring Eastern spices. For an arthritic hip he advised cloves, pepper, and cinnamon, "which long serves against the plague." For angina he suggested pepper. A generation later Saint Egbert, archbishop of York, prescribed the spice to cure sores of the mouth. Theodore of Tarsus, archbishop of Canterbury from 669 to 690, claimed that pepper mixed with the gallbladder of a hare could mitigate the pain of dysentery. The Northumbrian scholar Alcuin (ca. 735–804) claimed that spices were as effective a defense against pestilence as the writings of the Church fathers were a bulwark against heresy, and his compatriot the Venerable Bede said of cassia and cinnamon that they were "very effective in curing disorders of the guts." It seems a safe assumption that the medical use of spices was the single most important reason for the survival of the long-distance luxury trade through the dark years of the early Middle Ages. Which is to say that the survival of Europe's contacts with the wider world owed much to its demand for spicy drugs.

The potency of their reputation emerges most clearly from the institutions that kept the best records through this age of fragmentation and collapse, the monasteries. Before the turn of the millennium, most references occur in a medical context. In the ninth century, a priest named Grimlaic wrote matter-of-factly of doctors who were accustomed to compose their medicines from various spices. Around the same time a plan of the Swiss Benedictine monastery of Saint Gall featured a cupboard for storing spices (*armarium pigmentorum*) attached to the doctor's quarters, its role to complement the locally grown herbs supplied by the garden. A history of the same monastery written not long after mentioned a doctor named Notker, "singularly learned in spices and antidotes." In a contemporary book of medicines from the monastery, pepper is the single most frequently recommended medicine.

Among the monasteries the spicy flavor of Saint Gall's medicine cabinet was now the rule. To the west in Burgundy, a monk of the great monastery of Cluny boasted of the infirmary in which "rarely or never will there be lacking pepper, cinnamon, ginger, and other roots that are health-giving, so there will always be at the ready what is needed for the patient, whether he is seized sometime by a sudden fever or, if it suits, so a spiced wine can be prepared for him."

Given the limits of the physician's mental horizons and his still more limited understanding of illness, it is perhaps no great wonder that these inexplicable arrivals from the East should have been regarded as medicines of extraordinary force. There was a certain consistency in countering the unknowable with the inexplicable. Moreover, theirs was a reputation that was readily converted into social capital, for which reason many of the references to spices concern healing gifts accompanying correspondence or sweeteners to lubricate diplomatic dealings. In the works of Jotsaud, companion to Saint Odilo, fifth abbot of Cluny, there is a scene early in the new millennium at the court of the Holy Roman Emperor Henry II, where the host honors his distinguished guest with "an extremely valuable glass vessel of the Alexandrian type, with ground spices inside." Glass and spices alike had arrived from Alexandria, presumably, via Italian merchants. The emperor instructed two young monks accompanying the saintly Odilo to take it to him "for the sake of his bodily health." But the incident ended unhappily. In their curiosity the two young monks squabbled to see who would carry it, and the glass slipped and broke.

From the emperor's perspective, dispensing spices was as magnanimous as it was healing. Wealthy prelates could return the favor, as did Saint Mayeul, Odilo's immediate predecessor as abbot of Cluny. While traveling in Germany, the abbot's company received a delegation on behalf of a sick count, asking for a little of the food served to the blessed Mayeul, who responded with a little bread with almonds, fragrant spices, and prayer. The count immediately started to feel better, ate his spiced bread, and within a few days was well enough to go to the saint and thank him in person.

In tales of such supernatural intercessions, there lies a revealing paradox. For with their faith in the miraculous powers of the holy man or woman, the *vitae,* or Lives of Saints, are naturally inclined to credit cures to supernatural agency; yet they are for precisely this reason especially suggestive of the esteem in which spices were held. It is a recurrent motif of the *vitae* to find the miracle-working saint having no need of spices, much to the astonishment and chagrin of the spice-reliant doctors. The plot is repeated time and time again, the holy man or woman healing an illness that has defeated even the spices of the *pigmentarius.* One such tale in Bede's *Ecclesiastical History* tells of a young man afflicted with a hideous, deforming tumor of the eyelid that threatened to rob him of his eyesight. After the doctors had tried but failed to heal it with poultices of spices, finally, when all hope was lost, his eye was saved by the relics of the saintly Father Cuthbert.

The faith that informed such tales, religious and medicinal alike, is not to be doubted. For if the authors sought to convince and convert others, their ability to do so relied on the readers believing in spices as firmly as they believed in miracles. A little more than a century before Bede's day, when Gregory of Tours sought a metaphor for divine intercession, he could think of none more apt than theriac, a legendary mix of herbs and spices reported to have saved the life of Mithridates VI, a king of Pontus in northern Anatolia who died in 63 B.C.* A hypochondriac, Mithridates took this secret mix every day, and so effective did it prove that when he tried to poison himself his most potent toxins were utterly nullified, and in the end he had to ask a Gallic mercenary to fin-

*The origin, incidentally, of the modern "treacle."

ish him off. Shortly after being elected to the see of Tours in 572, Gregory was laid low by acute dysentery, with fever and aches spreading from his stomach through his body. The mere thought of food filled him with horror, and he was unable to digest what he was able to force down. He rapidly weakened. He and his doctors abandoned all hope of life, and preparations were made for his funeral.

One last remedy remained. In Gregory's words:

> Despairing of my chances, I called the specialist Armentarius, and I said to him: "You have employed every trick of your art, already you have tried the strength of all spices, but the things of this life are of no avail to him who is about to die. There remains one thing that I might do: that I proffer you a great theriac. Get some dust from the holy tomb of Saint Martin, and then make for me a potion. If this does no good, then all hope of recovery must be abandoned." Thereupon, a deacon being sent to the tomb of the blessed Leader, he took some of the sanctified dust, and they gave it to me to drink. No sooner had I drained it than thereupon the pain subsided—I received health from the tomb. Which then was of such great benefit to me, that though I drank it at the third hour of the day, at the sixth hour of the same day I went to dinner in full health.

The effect of such anecdotes, and dozens like them, depended almost wholly on the reputation of spices as the most potent of medicines; when even they are of no avail, only divine intervention will work.

The medical profession, however, could not bank on miracles, or at least did not like to admit as much. With time doctors developed an increasingly elaborate system to explain and justify a heavy reliance on spices. Just as the High Middle Ages were the golden age of the spice trade, so they were the golden age of spiced medicine. Around the turn of the millennium, the traditional leeching and superstition that had for so long set the tone of European medicine came gradually to be supplemented, if not yet quite supplanted, by a new degree of pharmacological sophistication. Europe was home to a great blossoming of medical studies, in some respects preceding but dramatically catalyzed by an infusion of Arab science introduced by the violent medium of the Crusades.

The new learning was led and exemplified by the medical school of Salerno, first recorded as a center of learning in the tenth century. The

Salernitan school was in many ways the conduit between Europe and the far more advanced science of the Muslim world. Via the Arabs, the scholars, doctors, and translators of Salerno restored to Europe a knowledge of the doctors of antiquity and diffused it far and wide across the breadth of Christendom. The quasi-supernatural reputation of spices was now enshrined as impeccably scientific. They are typically conspicuous in the natural history of the German abbess Hildegard of Bingen (1098–1179), who advised pepper for pleurisy and the splenetic individual, galangal for heartburn and stinking breath, cinnamon for tertian and quartian fever, and sore guts and lungs. To the encyclopedist Vincent of Beauvais (ca. 1190–1264) cinnamon and pepper were panaceas, and much the same was said at one time or another of all the Eastern spices. The Catalan *Libre del coch* of one Mestre Robert recommended a distillation of chicken and spices as "so healthful a thing that it will transform a man from life to death." There was scarcely an illness spices were not believed to cure, besides a great many illnesses that, we now know, never existed: such nightmarish visions of the medieval physician as hard spleen, the furious and exalting bile, or distempered brain.

Ultimately, this reputation rested on theoretical foundations built long before in Greece and Rome that, we have seen, laid down the ground rules of medieval dietetics. It was a starting premise of humoral theory that all things, animate or inanimate, combined the four elemental qualities of heat, cold, dry, and wet. Applied to the human body, the elements manifested themselves in four humors, which in turn found physical expression in the four internal liquids of blood, phlegm, yellow bile, and black bile. The sanguine humor, corresponding to the air, combined warmth and moistness; the phlegmatic was watery, cool, and moist; fiery choler, warm and dry; and earthy melancholy mixed coldness and dryness. In antiquity the most celebrated exponent of humoral medicine was the Greco-Roman Galen, doctor to emperors in the second century A.D. and throughout the Middle Ages the physician's gospel truth and lodestar.

According to the Galenic system it was above all the balance of the humors that determined the body's condition, the ideal state being a correct balance of all four. An acute disequilibrium of humors expressed itself as illness. The naturally phlegmatic individual, or the individual suffering from phlegmatic illness, was considered cold and moist; to be

Magellan's expedition reached the Moluccas, where the clove tree thrives. Here it is given due prominence in one of the earliest editions of Pigafetta's account of Magellan's circum-navigation, *Le Voyage et navigation faict par les Espaignolz es Isles de Mollucque* (Paris, ca. 1526). (Courtesy of the Beinecke Rare Book and Manuscript Library)

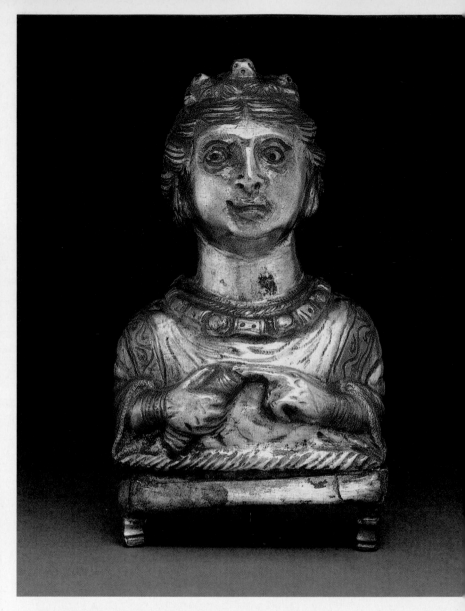

An outstanding example of a Roman pepper-pot, made of silver and gold, in the form of an empress or a grand matron of the late imperial period. The base is fitted with a disk that could be opened or shut for sprinkling or refilling. This is one of four such pepperpots buried in a treasure cache in the fifth century at Hoxne, Suffolk, shortly before the Roman armies abandoned Britain.

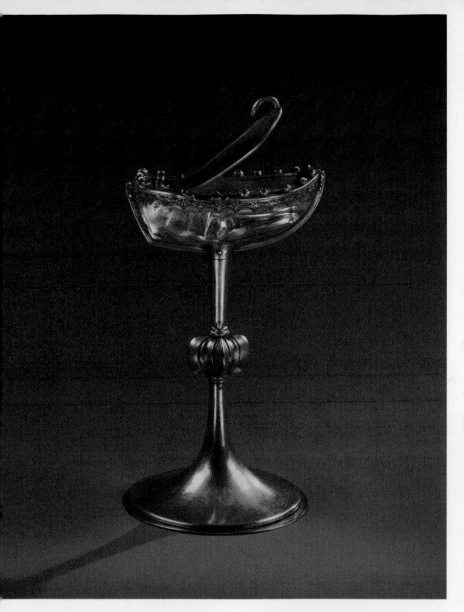

A superb example of a medieval *nef*: a marriage of function, craftsmanship, display, medicine, and taste. *Nefs* such as this one, made in Paris in the mid-thirteenth century, were typically used as spice vessels and salt-cellars, generally fashioned in the form of a ship. Here the healing power of the spices is complemented by a variety of other, quasi-magical defenses against illness. The figure of a serpent on the lid was believed to sweat in the presence of poison. The vessel itself is made of rock crystal and set on a gold stand, embedded with pearls, rubies, and emeralds, all substances reputed to have healing or apotropaic properties.

(The Metropolitan Museum of Art, The Cloisters Collection, 1983 [1983.434]. Photograph © The Metropolitan Museum of Art)

The burial of a king. In medieval times the preservation and display of the royal cadaver was a highly symbolic, final ritual of kingship. In France, treatment of the royal body was almost a fetish. Spices, wine, and vinegar were commonly used to preserve and deodorize the dead monarch.

(Westminster Abbey Library. Litlyngton Missal 1383-4 f. 224^r. Photograph © Dean and Chapter of Westminster)

A German pomander of the early seventeenth century. Pomanders came in all shapes and sizes, typically fastening with a clasp, enabling the user to insert fragrant substances within as a portable defense against "bad air." With time pomanders became purely decorative.

(Courtesy of the Trustees of the Victoria and Albert Museum. Photograph © V&A Images)

Pepper is harvested (above) before being presented to the king (below). A fanciful depiction from the *Livre des merveilles du monde,* an early-fifteenth-century collection of eastern travelers' accounts. (Photographs courtesy of the Bibliothèque Nationale, Paris)

Malabar today: Pepper farmers punt the new
crop along a backwater. (Author's photograph)

Tidore then: The Dutch seize control of the Moluccas. Hulsius's
Voyages (Frankfurt, 1612)
(Courtesy of the Beinecke Rare Book and Manuscript Library)

Tidore today: The view from Ternate harbor (Author's photograph)

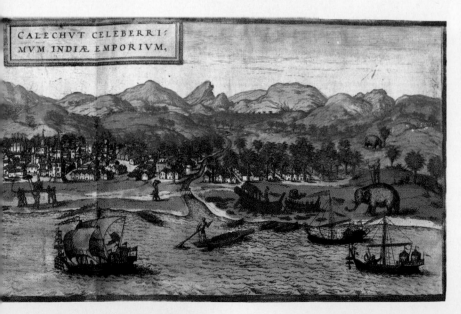

A view of Calicut in the time of the Portuguese. When da Gama arrived, Calicut was the principal port of the Malabar Coast. Georg Braun and Franz Hogenber, *Civitates orbis terrarum* (Cologne, 1572)   (Courtesy of the Beinecke Rare Book and Manuscript Library)

A pair of Jewish spice boxes for the Havdalah ceremony marking the end of the Sabbath. The example on the left was made in thirteenth-century Spain, the oldest surviving example. The box on the right is possibly of Dutch origin, dating from the seventeenth century. The design of spice boxes commonly imitated the architecture of the town where they were made.
(Courtesy of the Trustees of the Victoria and Albert Museum. Photograph © V&A Images)

A censer in the shape of a town, possibly the Heavenly Jerusalem. English, twelfth century. In the Middle Ages cinnamon was a frequent addition to incense, and spices were commonly burned on special religious occasions.
(Courtesy of the British Museum. Photograph © The Trustees of the British Museum)

choleric was to be hot and dry. Too much black bile generated the cold and dry temper. A cold—the name itself is an echo of older beliefs—was caused by the onset of cool and wet humors. Fever was generally interpreted as a surfeit of hot and dry. Even moods and mental state were determined by humors—for which reason until well into the eighteenth century the word suggested any state of mind, not necessarily the comic.

Though medically way off-beam, Galenic medicine at least had the merit of a fundamental consistency. As illness was a form of disequilibrium, so a cure called for restoration of the original balance. The system was scientific inasmuch as prescription followed from diagnosis, the doctor's task being first to determine the nature of the complaint and then to come up with the countervailing treatment. As the great Persian physician Avicenna (980–1037) put it in his *Canon,* perhaps the single most famous book in the history of medicine:

> Having treated of the conservation of health, I am going to speak
>   of the healing of illness,
> and that is summarized in a single rule: counter the bad with its
>   opposite.
> The sickness due to heat is treated with cold; it is the reverse if the
>   illness comes from cold.
> If it originates from the wet, it is treated by the dry, and the con-
>   verse.

Via the physicians of medieval Islam, Europe inherited the identical framework, and in the medical schools of Salerno, then Bologna, Montpellier, Paris, and Padua, the best medical minds of the day subjected these basic rules to centuries of scholastic, syllogistic, and disputatious embellishments and reworkings. (Avicenna's *Canon* was taught in Europe's medical schools until the seventeenth century.) As Chaucer says of his "Doctour of Phisik":

> *He knew the course of every malady,*
> *Whether it was hot, cold, moist or dry,*
> *And where they were engendered, and by which humor.*
> *He was a very perfect practitioner. . . .*

It was in the capacity of safeguarding a healthy equilibrium or restoring a disrupted balance that spices entered the picture. Considered as powerfully heating and drying (for the most part), they were the drugs of choice for all illnesses classed as cool, wet, or both.* Like illnesses, drugs were classified according to degrees of heat, cold, wetness, or dryness, on a scale of zero to four, and most spices appeared at the hot and dry end of the spectrum. For this reason Avicenna includes spices among the healthfully heating defenses against melancholy.† (Others were sugar, egg yolks, coral, pearls, wine, gold, and silk.) Cinnamon was typically classed as hot in the fourth degree, dry in the second. Nutmeg was hot and dry in the second; and so on. These gradations were essentially a matter of tradition and intuition; medical writers waged arcane debates on precise qualification. Nor was there any single or unifying dietetic theory from one place to another. But while practitioners might have disagreed on the details, the broader grouping of spices as heating and drying holds good across the entirety of the medieval period.

So potent were spices that the authorities never failed to advise due caution. The *Regimen sanitatis salernitanum,* or *Salernitan Guide to Health,* a book of health tips written in verse form and translated into all major European languages, held that one nutmeg is good, two bad, and three deadly. One of the areas for which spices are most commonly cited is the stomach, believed to be particularly prone to cold and wet afflictions—a belief that goes a long way toward accounting for the medieval taste for spiced sauces. The stomach was conceptualized as a form of cauldron heated by the liver, digestion being understood as the final phase of the cooking process. It was simple logic that if the cauldron was to stay hot and functioning, cold substances were inimical and heating ones were good. A typical and authoritative instance of this thinking is provided by Galen in an account of a diagnosis of the Roman emperor Marcus Aurelius (121–180). The emperor had overdone it at a banquet and paid for it afterward as the excess of food was converted into phlegm. As the cold and moist phlegm reduced his body temperature, a fever ensued and he was unable to digest his foods, his stomach being too moist and wet. A cool, wet affliction called for a heating and drying remedy, so Galen prescribed the emperor a thin, dry, and acidulous Sabine wine with some heating and drying pepper.

And so into the Middle Ages. The eleventh-century Byzantine

---

*The odd ones out were ginger and galangal, which, being classed as hot and wet, were generally prescribed for illnesses of a cold and dry nature.

†When tobacco was introduced to Europe, physicians initially classed it as "warming," for which reason it was prescribed for "moist" lungs.

emperor Michael VII used nutmeg to comfort his stomach from surfeit of wetness. Writing around 1450, John of Burgundy likewise advised nutmeg for gastric chills, advising his readers to "eat a nutmeg in the morning, for the voiding of wind from the stomach, the liver and the guts: it is good for people recovering from an illness." Water, classed as cold and wet, was considered a particular risk. In the sixteenth century, the father of the botanist Gaspard Bauhin (1560–1624) claimed he had been brought to the brink of death by water, saved only by a timely reheating of his stomach. Taken gravely ill while harvesting herbs in the Apennines—too much drinking from an icy mountain stream— he effected a last-minute and semimiraculous cure with four nutmegs.

Other afflictions admitted of no remedy, but they could at least be mitigated. Old people were considered particularly susceptible to ill- nesses of a cool nature, the aging process being seen as a progressive diminution of "inner heat," a gradual cooling down and drying out, fading completely with death. Old age, it followed, could be delayed or at least offset by some warming spices. The Franciscan monk and poly- math Roger Bacon (ca. 1220–1292) recommended a mixture of viper's flesh, cloves, nutmeg, and mace to delay the onset of old age. In his ambitiously titled *On the Preservation of Youth and Slowing of Old Age,* Arnau de Vilanova (?–1311) advised an "Electuary of Life," composed of licorice root, nutmeg, and galangal. The medical texts of the Middle Ages are replete with dozens of similar illusory cures.

But that the underlying faith was misplaced did not harm spices' reputation. There was, it is true, the occasional serendipitous success among the myriad—and often harmful—misses. But it would be naive in the extreme to transpose the empiricist assumptions of modern medicine back to a time where they do not belong. Faith in spices far outstripped any proof. Spices even had a role to play in veterinary med- icine. The Spanish Franciscan Juan Gil de Zamora (ca. 1240–ca. 1320) claimed that a rheumy falcon could be cured with a mix of ground amber, ginger, and pepper; a mix of cloves, cinnamon, ginger, pepper, cumin, salt, and aloes would cure a goshawk of a headache, though this was presumably a tricky diagnosis to make. In 1353, Pope Innocent VI bought spices to perk up the pining papal parrot: for an Indian bird, an Indian remedy.

Other illnesses were less natural. The nobility of both the ancient and medieval worlds shared a fixation with poisoning, and the hand of a poi- soner was frequently sought where only poor hygiene and bacteria were

to blame: the poisoned mushroom alleged to have killed the emperor
Claudius may have been just the wrong mushroom, just as the deadly
melons reputed to have done away with Pope Paul II in the middle of
the fifteenth century were probably no more substantial than a physician's best guess. With such terrors and suspicions so firmly rooted in
the consciousness, antidotes were a constant presence in the shops of
medieval *speciarius,* and the literature was correspondingly hefty. Since
poisons were generally believed to kill by cooling the organism to the
point of death, from the earliest times spices came recommended as the
most potent of antidotes.* Theophrastus refers to pepper as heating and
for that reason an antidote to hemlock, which was believed to kill by
cooling from the toes up. A fragment of the Attic poet Euboulos refers
to pepper in conjunction with Cnidus-bay berry, another staple antidote. Pepper was recommended against hemlock by Theodulfus, bishop
of Orléans (ca. 760–821), who served the spice at the court of Charlemagne. In the hugely influential *De materia medica* Dioscorides (ca. A.D.
77) recommends ginger if someone slipped a toxin into dinner.

But the most important work on the subject, and one that guaranteed spices' position on the shelf, was Galen's *Concerning Antidotes.* In
his capacity as physician to Marcus Aurelius, Galen had supplied the
hypochondriac philosopher-emperor with a daily dose of cinnamon and
other lauded "antidotes"—the more expensive, the better. Galen testi-
fies that during the reign of Severus toward the close of the second century it was hard for the emperor to get a good stash of cinnamon.
Imperial stocks of the spice dated back to the time of Trajan—a sign,
perhaps, that even then the Roman trade with India was drying up.

Yet while these and many other spiced prescriptions were sanctioned
by the weight of tradition, not all of the attractions of spice were so
intellectually respectable. The protoscientific framework of Galenic
medicine easily shaded into magic; indeed, the exact division between
the two cannot always be so easily distinguished. Even in the most sober
medical textbooks many spiced recipes were pure superstition. Late in
the thirteenth century, Arnald de Vilanova referred to the enchantments
of the "old wives of Salerno," who gave three peppercorns to women to
suck during childbirth, with the proviso that they should never chew
them—presumably a somewhat delicate operation during the pains of

---

*Other treatments were "unicorn horn" and magic knives that were believed to change
color when used to cut contaminated food.

labor. Even Galen, who so prided himself on his systems and authorities, was not above using magic numbers and combinations. For colic, he advised dried cicadas with three, five, or seven grains of pepper. Sometimes spices were esteemed purely on account of an exotic reputation. Among the *Acts* of Saint Francis of Paola (1416–1507) is an account of the illness of Loysius de Paladinis de Lecia, the royal auditor of Calabria, who in 1447 suffered a mysterious illness of thirty-three days, at which point his wife, Donna Catharinella, sent a servant to beseech the holy man's intercession. His advice was to bake two loaves of bread, sprinkle each with ground pepper, cinnamon, cloves, and ginger, then place one loaf on the patient's back and the other on his stomach.

Uncertain as to whether she should follow the saint's advice, Catharinella asked for a second, medical opinion, but the doctors disagreed, so she did nothing. The patient did not improve. Sending another messenger to Francis for more prayers, she was reprimanded, the saint being miraculously aware that his advice had not been followed. Chastened, the fickle noblewoman now did as she had first been told, thereby curing her husband and confirming the miraculous powers of the holy man.

By the standards of medieval medicine Don Loysius got off rather lightly. One of the more enduring strains in traditional medicine to which spices were particularly well suited was the notion of cure by shock treatment. Galen himself was a great believer in jolting the patient out of his illness. For an attack of epilepsy he recommended a draught of gladiator's blood; for hydrophobia he suggested throwing the patient into a pond. Prescriptions likewise often lay a heavy emphasis on the rare, costly, exotic, and revolting. Galen's *The Healing Art,* one of his most widely read works during the Middle Ages, gives a peasant's remedy for headache, consisting of a poultice of earthworms and pepper, ground together, mixed in vinegar, and held on one side of the head. *The Syriac Book of Medicines* advises a mix of pepper, myrrh, and dog excrement for the treatment of jaundice. One thousand years later the naturalist Edward Topsell (1572–1625) advised a mixture of hedgehog and pepper for the colic: "Ten sprigs of Lawrel, seven grains of Pepper, and of Opopanax as big as a Pease, the Skin of the ribs of a Hedge-hog, dried and beaten and cast three cups of Water and warmed, so being drunk of one that hath the Colick, and let rest, he shall be in perfect health."

Even the most respectable authorities were seldom free of this sort of thing, and even those who could afford better were willing to try the most disgusting remedies. Marcellus Empiricus, doctor to Theodosius the Elder (347–395), gave a remedy attributed to an old African woman that was "efficacious beyond human hope," comprising ashes of burnt deer horn, nine grains of white pepper, myrrh, and an African snail pounded into the mix while still alive and then ground into a cup of vintage Falernian, the finest wine of the Romans. The potion, he suggested, should be drunk while facing east.

From a vague belief in the effectiveness of a sharp shock, it was but a short step to the doctrine of no gain without pain; the if-it-hurts-it's-good-for-you school of thought, alive and well until very recent times. This impulse is the only explanation I can think of for the regularity with which spices were applied to the parts that apparently needed them the least, such as the nose, anus, and genitals. Juan Gil de Zamora (1240–ca. 1320) prescribed pepper for various ailments of the anus, the idea being that a sufficient quantity of the spice would somehow burn off the affliction. In *The Book of Secrets,* attributed to Albertus Magnus (ca. 1200–1280), pepper and powdered lynx are recommended for piles and "growing out of flesh around the buttocks." Gout was commonly treated with the direct application of spices in the hope that the pricking, burning effect of the spices would drive out the disease.

If such treatments did not heal, they presumably distracted, and they were probably less uncomfortable or less harmful than various treatments intended for the brain, a part of the body seen as particularly prone to wet and cold humors. Juan Gil de Zamora prescribed pepper and cinnamon for epileptics, gout, madmen, rheumatics, and vertigo—all of which he classed as originating from cold, wet diseases of the brain. The methods of getting the spices to the affected organ could be truly gruesome. Since the nose was often viewed as the most direct route, spices were often simply thrust up the nostrils. The early Portuguese *Crónica de D. Dinis,* king from 1279 to 1325, tells the story of the unfortunate Uraca Vaz, one of the handmaidens of Queen Isabel, who from time to time suffered from what the *Crónica* vaguely describes as "very bad pains," possibly epileptic fits. Whenever she had one of these attacks, she was tied hand and foot—this being the only way of securing her—"and they flung ground pepper up her nose." (To no avail. The unfortunate handmaiden was cured only by the intervention of the saintly queen, who placed her hands on her head and body and cured her by making the sign of the cross.)

Remedies such as Uraca's may have hurt, but most of them would not have done any lasting damage. Given the risks involved, however, the consistency with which spices were applied to the eyes is nothing less than astonishing. Pepper salves appear in Greek medical manuscripts of the fifth century, mixed with copper, saffron, opium, lead, and calamine. Pedro Hispano, later Pope John XXI (ca. 1215–1277), author of one of the most widely consulted medical works of the Middle Ages, *Universal Diets and Particular Diets,* claimed that "pepper is good for dimmed eyes." For "dimness of the eyes" the early-eleventh-century Anglo-Saxon manuscript known as *The Herbarium of Apuleius* suggests, obscurely but alarmingly, a poultice made of ground celandine,* honey, pepper, and wine, with the direction "to smear the eyes inwardly." The thinking seems to have been that just as bleeding drew off ill humors from the blood, so provoking tears drained off the ill humors of the eye, warming and drying the wet and runny eye of superfluous fluid. More likely they simply caused unnecessary damage. The accumulated authority of medical tradition overruled observation.

But it was animals, being unable to express their feelings on the subject, who probably suffered the most. At the turn of the twentieth century a traditional Malay remedy for an elephant having trouble with its vision was to rub pepper in the poor beast's eyes. Juan Gil de Zamora recommends sprinkling pepper up a goshawk's beak if it suffers from clouding of the eyes; another prescription called for cloves. As late as the seventeenth century, it was still customary for falconers to pepper their hawks after a day in the fields. The Elizabethan naturalist Edward Topsell suggested that horses suffering from "bloud-shotten eyes" could be treated with a poultice of ground cloves, rose water, malmsey wine, and fennel water rubbed into the eyes.

Given the likelihood of extreme pain or even permanent damage that was likely to ensue, carrying off such hocus-pocus required a certain chutzpah on the part of the exponent, gullibility on the part of the audience, or both. And indeed much of the act is best classed as performance art, relying heavily on a degree of mystification and bedazzlement in which, not least, the costliness and rarity of the spices were seen not so much as liabilities as assets, whether in the eyes of a wealthy patient or a practitioner: if it costs more, it must be better. This was an

---

*Celandine is a small flowering plant that produces a thick yellow juice long considered a remedy for poor eyesight.

instinct physicians were naturally keen to cultivate. John of Gaddesden, physician to England's King Edward II (1284–1327), freely confessed his interest in getting a good fee, referring to secret remedies of his own that he divulged only when the price was right. Gilles Corbeil (1140–ca. 1220), physician to King Philip Augustus (1165–1223), unblushingly advised doctors to tailor fees and medicines alike to their patients' financial health: if the patient was wealthy, "then the medical man should come down with a heavy hand," prescribing only the rarest and most expensive spices.

By and large, however, the public's chief concern with quackery was not whether the spices worked but whether—that perennial bane of the spice trade—they had been adulterated. In seventh-century Spain, Isidore of Seville knew traders who added shavings of silver to their pepper so as to increase the weight—a telling aside on relative values. Such frauds only grew with time, yet the profusion of laws against adulteration suggests a widespread and persistent problem, in spite of ferocious penalties. At Nuremberg, spicers convicted of falsifying their wares were liable to be buried alive. The Old French poet known as the Spicer of Troyes, author of the romance *Contrefait de Renard,* written from 1319 to 1322, freely admits the cynicism of his profession. Having once been destined for a career in the Church, he was expelled for bigamy, an experience that left him, somewhat unfairly, a lifelong misogynist. Though he clearly regarded his new profession as more honorable than any other, even the spicer admits that his colleagues are prone to substituting cheap, local ingredients for the rare and expensive spices, lying through their teeth over the counter:

> *"This comes from far across the sea,*
> *I had it sought at great expense,*
> *Since it grows not in this land.*
> *This one comes from Armenia,*
> *And this from Romania,*
> *That from Acre, and that from Nîmes."* . . .
> *And the whole lot grows in his garden!*

Often the spicer and physician worked hand in glove to milk the patient. Chaucer's "Doctour of Phisik" had reached a mutually profitable arrangement with the apothecaries who supplied him with expensive spices, each filling the other's pockets at the client's expense:

He had his apothecaries at the ready
To send him drugs and electuaries,
Each working to profit the other.

It would be misleading, however, to suggest that such schemes and frauds were entirely lost on a credulous public. A well-deserved reputation for trickery did not endear either physicians or spicers to their customers. In the thirteenth century, the town council of Avignon had statutes forbidding collusion between spicers and doctors in the fraudulent prescription of expensive ingredients. Corruption was believed to come with the job—indeed, it was almost part of the job description. In the late fifteenth century, Don Rodrigo Sánchez de Arévalo, bishop of Zamora, defined the apothecary as the person who adulterates and falsifies the spices. In *Piers Plowman,* the character of Liar finds refuge with the Spicemongers, "for he knew the tricks of their trade, and their merchandise too."

But that the spicer was the object of such contempt was precisely because he was regarded as indispensable—the force of such denunciations rested on skepticism not of the spices but of the spicer. The author of the poem known as the "Simonie" or "Poem on the Evil Times of Edward II" berates "false fisiciens that helpen men to die," convincing an anxious wife that her husband is as good as dead unless she pays him a half a pound to buy spices: "dear at the price of a leek, for all he achieves." The poorer the victim, the more grievous the con.

For what was true of the table was equally true of medicine. The best-known medieval medicines, and the lion's share of the spices, belonged to the rich. As with cuisine, the most popular and affordable medicinal spice was pepper: a budget antimelancholic. Pepper features among the wares of a "poor herbalist" described by the thirteenth-century wandering poet Rutebeuf, hawking his meager wares outside a church door in a shabby, badly stitched cloak and serving a clientele that was, presumably, no better off than he was. The poor man's theriac, according to Arnald de Vilanova, was garlic. By the twelfth century, the herb-spice class differential seems to have been something of a cliché. John of Salisbury (ca. 1110–1180) cites "an old proverb" that obtained "among courtiers and physicians everywhere":

In return for words we use mountain herbs;
For things of value, spices and drugs.

A verse attributed to Saint Isidore—for even pharmacy has its poetry—nicely captures the intermingling of potency and exclusiveness that was such a large part of their appeal:

> *Aromas that Arabian altars and Indus breathe,*
> *That the waves of the Ionian sea have borne:*
> *Cinnamon, myrrh, Indian leaf and cassia,*
> *Balsam, incense, calamus, saffron of Anatolia:*
> *These are found in the spice-stores of great kings,*
> *And the house overflowing with riches.*
> *We poor people make do with the simple herbs of the fields,*
> *That the low valleys and high passes bear.*

The irony is that in terms of medical efficacy the poor were not much worse off, if at all, than the rich: the peasant was probably better served by his garlic and herbs than a monarch treated with costly theriacs of exotic spices and powdered gemstones. But in terms of their appeal, the point is irrelevant. Spices were an elite luxury, no more run-of-the-mill than Hollywood clinics for detox and Botox—and this was, of course, a large part of the attraction. For being out of reach they were all the more to be coveted.

POX, PESTILENCE, AND POMANDERS

Take Storax Calamita, Ireos, Mastike of eche two partes, Cloves, Maces, Nutmigs, Cinamon, Saffron, of eche one parte amber the fifth of one parte, muske the tenth of one parte, mingle all together and make a fumigation.

And of these powders ye may make little balles of Pomanders, to beare about with you at all times.

—J. GOUEROT, *The Regiment of Life*, 1606

Having survived the terrible pestilence of 1603, when the pox carried off some twenty-five thousand of his fellow Londoners, corpses rotted in the streets, and those who could fled for their lives, John Donne (1572–1631) knew the terrors of the plague firsthand. Hunting around for an elegant conceit to please his new patron, Lucy, countess of Bedford, he settled on a medical metaphor. She must have been delighted with his elegant promise:

> *In recompense I would show future times*
> *What you were, and teach them to'urge towards such.*
> *Verse embalmes vertue; and Tombs, or Thrones of rimes,*
> *Preserve fraile transitory fame, as much*
> *As spice doth bodies from corrupt aires touch.*

A simile as medically well founded as it was poetically elegant, this was just the sort of thing a countess and patron of poets liked to hear. For that spices protected bodies was as much an article of medical belief as the claim of immortality was a Jacobean poet's convention.

Like Donne's patron, Lucy, "corrupt air" has retreated into the footnotes, but at the time it represented the medical orthodoxy, the key to the final and perhaps single most important aspect of spices' medicinal reputation. Odors, airs, and vapors occupied a central place in ancient and medieval medical thought, and continued to do so until the nineteenth century. Helpless to explain the agencies of infection, ignorant of the existence of microbes and bacilli, doctors looked to the invisible air around them to account for the apparently random and utterly terrifying outbreaks of disease that suddenly appeared and then disappeared with no apparent cause. A capitulary of Charlemagne writes of plagues provoked by an "imbalance of the air." Shakespeare's John of Gaunt speaks of a "devouring pestilence [that] hangs in the air," and Dante writes of plague-wracked Aegina, "when the air was so charged with corruption." A medieval physician of Valencia, writing to his two sons in Toulouse in 1315, argued that bad air was still more harmful and infectious than corrupt food and drink. As fanciful as the idea may strike us—for while it is true that the vectors of disease are occasionally carried within the air, the air itself is harmless—the belief seemed to make a good deal of sense. In lieu of any visible proof of infection, blighting miasmas and gases, the baleful influence of ill winds, and noisome exhalations from the earth stood in for pathogens and bacteria, which would remain unseen and unknowable until the advent of the microscope.*

---

*Galen was nearer the mark in attributing the outbreak of summer fevers to poisonous vapors rising from swamps, although it was not the air itself but the mosquitoes flying through it that were responsible for the illness. One legacy is that malaria derives its name from the Latin for "bad air."

Prescriptions followed naturally from the premise. If bad air brought disease, it was reasonable to imagine that good air offered some form of protection: a pleasant aroma was a healing aroma. In the Old Testament Aaron averts a plague sent by Yahweh by setting up an incense burner, much as the Thebans burn incense when the pestilence ravages Thebes at the beginning of Sophocles' *Oedipus Rex.* Plutarch claimed that physicians brought relief from pestilence by burning a fire, especially if fragrant substances were added. At the Greek town of Callipolis there survives an inscription from the second or third century A.D., recording the sacrifice of burned offerings of meat and spices to the "gods below the earth" and the Clarian Apollo, "the warder-off of plague." As the god held responsible for visitations of plague (it was Apollo whose death-dealing arrows struck down the Greeks at the start of the *Iliad*), Apollo was the natural recipient of such an offering. To offer spices was to please the god responsible for the illness and in so doing—or so it was hoped—to avert it.

With the emergence of the scientific study of medicine, the gods were removed from the equation (by and large), but the spices remained. In the medical schools of ancient Greece and Rome the effects of their aromas were systematized and related, however fancifully, to empirical observation. By the fourth century B.C., suppliers of spices were sufficiently familiar figures that the comedian Alexis (ca. 375–ca. 275 B.C.) could write a comedy entitled *The Apothecary,* whose character combined the roles of druggist, herbalist, and spice merchant. Such was the interest in smells that Theophrastus (ca. 371–ca. 287 B.C.) dedicated a work to the topic, *On Odors,* in which many of the spices appear for the first time as the subject of sustained philosophical inquiry. Aromatic fumigation had attained the status of medical fact.

Where Greek medicine led, many others followed.* Credence in the virtues of spices was apparently worldwide, long outlasting antiquity. In T'ang China cloves were used for "driving off evils" and "getting rid of evil things." In India the Uzbek polymath al-Biruni (973–1048) witnessed the use of cloves against smallpox, which the Indians took for an airborne malaise arriving from the land of Lanka across the sea:

---

*The similarities between ancient Indian and Greek medicine have been the cause of much speculation: Was there an early transmission of ideas, or did the faith in aromatic medicines emerge independently in East and West?

The Hindus who are the neighbours of those regions believe that the small-pox is a wind blowing from the island of Lanka towards the continent to carry off souls. According to one report, some men warn people beforehand of the blowing of this wind, and can exactly tell at what times it will reach the different parts of the country. After the small-pox has broken out, they recognise from certain signs whether it is virulent or not. Against the virulent small-pox they use a method of treatment by which they destroy only one single limb of the body, but do not kill. They use as medicine cloves, which they give to the patient to drink, together with gold-dust; and, besides, the males tie the cloves, which are similar to date-kernels, to their necks. If these precautions are taken, perhaps nine people out of ten will be proof against this malady.

Apart from what looks like a garbled account of inoculation—generally credited to China, around 1200 A.D., but not used in the West before the early eighteenth century—his account is a fairly representative diagnosis: an airborne illness called for an aromatic prescription.

While many illnesses arrived from the sky, no visitation of malign air was more deadly than the bubonic plague, or Black Death. Broadly, there were three main schools of thought about the causes of and remedies for the plague, none of which was necessarily incompatible with the others. Some looked to God's wrath at the sins of humanity, while others looked to the comets and stars, a baleful alignment of the planets. A third group looked to the malignant vapors and odors borne "by a rotten and corrupt ayre by a hidden and secret propetie which it hath." First documented in Europe in the reign of the emperor Justinian, the plague returned with terrifying unpredictability, most devastatingly in the pandemic of 1348–1350, when it carried off some 30 percent of Europe's population, and up to 50 percent in some of the cities. Though this was far and away the most deadly outbreak, the plague returned regularly until the eighteenth century. In London there were more than a dozen outbreaks in the sixteenth century alone.

While doctors agreed no more then than now on the best course of action—far from it—aromas and spices were conspicuous in the countermeasures. Those lacking the cash for spices fumigated their houses by burning fragrant woods or garden plants such as rosemary, violet,

juniper, lavender, marjoram, oregano, and sage.* One budget option
was the nosegay, generally a bundle of herbs or flowers. (Hence the
"pocket full of posies" of the nursery rhyme; "Ah-tshoo! Ah-tshoo! / We
all fall down" is a reference to the sneezing that accompanied the first
onset of the disease, the falling down the sequel.) According to popular
belief, the smell did not necessarily have to be pleasant to be effective,
merely potent enough to ward off miasma. Onions were a perennial
favorite of the English—they were buried in the ground in an infected
neighborhood so as to soak up the disease—along with other still more
eye-watering substances. Some people burned shoes, some hung old
socks under their noses; still others dangled over cesspits so as to enve-
lope themselves in a sheltering stench.

Among the savants, however, and for those with the cash, the preference was for less noxious odors. (In *Gulliver's Travels* Swift mocks the
Yahoos' penchant for treating their illnesses with shit and urine.) The
potency and durability of their aromas, their exoticism and cost, all recommended spices, as did the enthusiastic testimony of survivors. John
of Eschenden, a fellow of Merton College, Oxford, and a survivor of the
Black Death, claimed that a powder of cinnamon, aloes, myrrh, saffron,
mace, and cloves had seen him through the time when Oxford's narrow
streets were clogged with the bodies of the dead. More than a hundred
years later, the exact same confection was recommended by Nicolaus de
Comitibus of Padua, a "marvellous medicine against the corruption to
the air in the time of pestilence which John of Oxford gives as tested by
all the medical men of England in the great mortality which prevailed
throughout the world in the year of grace 1348."

Spices also had the merit of aesthetic appeal, being sufficiently
strong and penetrating to exclude the odors of the medieval townscape,
which was, at the best of times, a malodorous place; at times the
crowded and filthy streets of the cramped medieval cities must have
smelled, to borrow a phrase from Melville, "like the left wing of the day
of judgment." London was notoriously mephitic: in 1275, the White
Friars who dwelt by the River Fleet in London complained to the king

---

*In the longer term reeds, herbs, and matting were liable to decompose and stink. Describ-
ing a typical English residence, Erasmus (who generally admired England and the English)
wrote of decomposing rushes covering twenty-year-old vomit, spit, and dribble of dogs and
men, old fish bones, "and other filth not to be named . . . in my opinion harmful to the human
body." Despite this domestic filth, he ascribed the plague to noxious winds and vapors admitted into the house by poorly sealed windows.

that the river's "putrid exhalations . . . overcame even the frankincense used in the services and had caused the death of many brethren." The public privy of Ludgate was reported to smell so vilely that it "rottith the stone wallys."

Over and above their purported salubriousness, spices had the supreme attractions of portability, power, and long life. According to Boccaccio, when the plague descended on Florence the inhabitants took to "carrying in their hands flowers or fragrant herbs or diverse sorts of spices, which they frequently raised to their noses." One of the most esteemed defenses was the pomander, from Old French *pome d'embre* or apple of amber, a lump of amber or ambergris aromatized with a mixture of spices so as "to be worne against foule stinkyng aire," as one authority phrased it. At the time of the great fourteenth-century outbreak of the Black Death, a pomander generally consisted of a soft, resinous substance—wax was the most common—bound together, studded, or sprinkled with spices, and enclosed within a portable metal or china container worn around the neck or attached to a belt or wrist. Simpler variants of the same were made from a hollowed-out piece of fruit. One popular seventeenth-century remedy was "a good Sivill Orenge stuck with cloves," long considered a defense against the pestilence but now downgraded to a folksy form of air freshener.

Beneath these prescriptions lurked memories of class and money. Only long after the end of the Middle Ages did spices—or, for that matter, oranges—become relatively accessible to all who wanted them. Before then, cost was a large part of their cachet. Gerard Bergens, author of *De pestis praeservatione,* published in Antwerp in 1587, suggests for the "altogether rich" a pomander of nutmeg, cloves, or aloes, to be carried on the person at all times. The wealthier one was, the greater opportunities to indulge and elaborate on one's hypochondria. Whenever she was exposed to public spaces, even in times free of disease, Queen Elizabeth I wore gloves of Spanish leather perfumed with rose water, sugar, and spices plus, for good measure, a pomander filled with the most expensive spices. Over time, pomanders were fashioned with ever increasing cost and ingenuity, to the point that by the twentieth century they had become purely ornamental, the vehicle for Fabergé's fancies.

But when bad air was thought to be a matter of life or death, such aesthetic considerations yielded second place to function. Coming as he did into regular contact with the sick, the medieval or early modern doctor relied particularly heavily on the pomander and its spiced variants. In times of pestilence, some doctors resorted to a medieval forerunner of the gas mask, in the form of a hood with a large "beak" filled with fragrant herbs and spice. Alternatively, spices could be used as a sort of internal fumigation. One authority advises anyone visiting a plague victim: "Let him hold in his mouth a peece of Mastic, Cinamon, Zedoarie, or Citron pill, or a Clove. Let him desire his sicke friend to speake with his face turned from him."

The irony, of course, is that the medical utility of such measures was nil. The array of aromatic defenses that Europeans erected against the plague was a medicinal Maginot Line: a huge effort on which vast resources, intellectual as much as economic, were lavished, but one that the rats, fleas, and bacilli simply went around. If spices were of some marginal benefit, it was not against the plague but in disinfecting food or, at a stretch, in supplying micronutrients to deficient diets.* It is, however, just as likely that spices were counterproductive, in that the generally unquestioning belief in their effectiveness diverted attention from the real causes of the disease. For while thinkers lavished their intellectual energies on building an airborne defense, they neglected such basics as sanitation, thereby rendering the lives of fleas, rats, microbes, and lice all the easier. One widely held belief was that washing opened the pores, supposedly rendering the body more prone to infection. Even such a rich person as Elizabeth I of England took a bath but once a month, "whether she need it or no."

It may be that spices had a still more directly detrimental impact. In an age of limited horizons, the most likely culprit for introducing to Europe the pandemic of 1348 was none other than the same long-distance trade that brought spice from the East. First documented in China in the 1320s, bubonic plague is caused by a bacterium transmitted by the bite of a flea that has drunk the blood of an infected black rat, *Rattus rattus*. Originally a native of Southeast Asia, the Asian rat was probably first introduced to Europe by the Romans' seaborne commerce with India: a Roman rat was found at a site in London's Fenchurch Street dating from the fourth century. (The brown or Norwegian rat, which does not carry the fleas that transmit the plague

---

*Studies suggest that they have a similar effect on the diet of the extremely poor in modern India.

bacillus, was not introduced into the greater part of western Europe before the eighteenth century. Its gradual supplanting of the black rat may explain the disappearance of the plague from Europe at much the same time.) *Rattus rattus* could not cross the deserts, but it could hitch a ride on the transoceanic pepper ships.

In the absence of other explanations the theory is a tempting one. Certainly it fits with the narrative of the Byzantine historian Procopius, a witness to the plague in the time of Justinian (483–565). He tells a tale of creeping doom, charting the inexorable spread of the disease from lower Egypt to Alexandria in 540, then north from Alexandria to Byzantium. With trading networks reaching out in all directions as far as India and ultimately China, these two cities were especially vulnerable to the importation of infection via ship and caravan. "This disease always started at the coast, and from there went up into the interior," wrote Procopius. With no understanding of how the disease was transmitted, let alone any quarantine, every freighter and galley shuttling from India to Egypt and from Alexandria to Byzantium was, potentially, a death ship.

The spice trade might conceivably have played a still more direct role in the great outbreak of the Black Death of 1348. From a very early date, the advent of the plague was attributed to galleys returning to Italy from the Black Sea, where they went to acquire Eastern luxuries at the terminus of the trans-Asian caravan routes. In the words of a Flemish chronicler:

> In January of the year 1348 three galleys put in at Genoa, driven by a fierce wind from the East, horribly infected and laden with a variety of spices and other valuable goods. When the inhabitants of Genoa learnt this, and saw how suddenly and irremediably they infected other people, they were driven forth from that port by burning arrows and divers engines of war; for no man dared touch them; nor was any man able to trade with them, for if he did he would be sure to die forthwith. Thus, they were scattered from port to port.

And so the plague was exported from one town to the next. Chroniclers across Europe relate the horrifying moment when a plague ship pulled into harbor bearing a dead and dying crew and their deadly cargo. In every port of Europe the tale unfolded with the same dreadful regularity. Everywhere, the arrivals were driven from the city, but by then it was too late. Thus was the long-distance trade the unwitting, indispensable accomplice of flea, bacillus, and rat. In a world of limited horizons there could scarcely have been a more effective way of spreading the disease.

CHAPTER 5

❶

THE SPICE OF LOVE

I have perfumed my bed with myrrh, aloes, and cinnamon.
Come, let us take our fill of love until the morning;
let us solace ourselves with love.

—Proverbs 7:17–18

"WHAN TENDRE YOUTHE HATH WEDDED STOUPYNG AGE"

Even before he caught his wife *in flagrante delicto* with his squire up a pear tree, January was anxious about the physical aspects of his marriage. Not that he would have admitted as much: though some forty years the senior of the two, January would boast to his friends of his still-rampant virility, declaring himself "nowhere grey but on my head," more than capable "to do all it befits a man to do." Before his marriage, he even fretted whether his young wife could withstand the sexual tornado that awaited her: "God willing you might endure my ardour: it is so sharp and keen—I fear you cannot bear it." She would be as putty in his hands.

His brother, on the other hand, had his misgivings, suggesting that it wasn't that easy for even the most sprightly husband: "The youngest man among us will have his work cut out to keep his wife to himself." Events would prove his pessimism, and not January's bravado, correct. Before long it came to pass that January unwittingly led May to clamber up a pear tree to her rendezvous with Damian:

> *Whereupon this Damian pulled up the smock,*
> *And in he thrust.*

So runs, in brief, the unhappy tale of January's misplaced bravado and subsequent cuckolding, the subject of Chaucer's *Merchant's Tale,* "Whan tendre youthe hath wedded stoupyng age." Given the period and the subject matter, it comes as no surprise to find a little spice lurking in the details. For all his braggart's confidence in his sexual prowess, January was not above seeking a little chemical assistance. And as fretful males had done for hundreds if not thousands of years, he turned to spices for a wedding-night boost. Following traditional formulae to increase his virility, January downed some spiced wines, followed by some sweetened mixes of spices known as "electuaries":

> *He drinks hippocras, clarry, and vernage**
> *Hot spices to kindle his lust,*
> *And many an electuary full fine,*
> *Such as the accursed monk, damned Constantine,*
> *Has written in his book,* De Coitu —
> *To eat them all he did not eschew.*

And presto! The spiced aphrodisiacs worked as the "cursed monk" had said they would, and though he stood on his grave's edge, the ancient January labored hard until the dawn. On the morrow, he sat up in bed and sang for joy, immensely satisfied with his performance, "as full of chatter as a spotted magpie." His wife, on the other hand, counted his efforts as "not worth a bean": for all her husband's spiced aphrodisiacs and exertions, she was more interested in Damian, his squire. She read his love letters in the privy; Damian sighed with longing. The encounter in the branches followed in due course.

While some of the features of January's troubled marriage were a little peculiar, there was nothing unusual about his methods (nor, according to Chaucer, the outcome). Spices were among the premier aphrodisiacs of the day, not least thanks to the author January turned to for his stimulants, "damned Constantine." More conventionally known as Constantine the African (ca. 1020–1087), Chaucer's "cursed monk" was in fact one of the major intellectual figures of the age, his work occupying a central place in the canon of medical studies in European universities until the end of the fifteenth century. Elsewhere Chaucer

---

*Strong spiced and sweetened wines.

mentions him as being on a par with Hippocrates and Galen, the two greatest medical authorities of classical antiquity.

Born in Carthage around 1020, Constantine chafed at the limited intellectual horizons of his hometown, abandoning it for Babylon, the premier seat of learning of the age. His curiosity led him to India, Egypt, and Ethiopia, before he finally returned home after thirty-nine years. His travels might be said to have broadened not only his own mind but that of Europe as a whole, for it was he who initiated the translation of Arabic philosophical and scientific texts into Latin, thereby reintroducing to Europe a rigor of method and inquiry forgotten since the fall of Rome. In all he translated some thirty-seven books from Arabic into Latin, including many translations of long-forgotten Greek originals. He was also credited with playing a part in the foundation of the famous medical school at Salerno, the first institution of its kind in Europe since ancient times. He was a profoundly influential figure. He died at the Benedictine monastery of Montecassino in 1087.

He was also, to use an anachronism, the preeminent sexologist of the age. His work *De coitu* (*On Sexual Intercourse*), the book consulted by January, might be termed the foremost sex handbook of the Middle Ages: three hundred years after Constantine's death, it was still the obvious choice, as Chaucer's late-fourteenth-century audience could evidently be taken to understand. There were plenty of other works January might have turned to, but this was, in its time, the major scientific work on the topic, covering all aspects of sexual health, albeit from a somewhat mechanical and wholly male perspective. (Historically speaking, much the same might be said of the overwhelming bulk of the literature on sex: the search for the perfect aphrodisiac has been, overwhelmingly, a masculine anxiety.) Admittedly, Constantine does not wholly omit what we might regard as more conventional seduction techniques: a peck on the cheek, holding hands, a look at the face, deep sighs, or "sucking the tongue" (this seems to be medieval Latin for "French kiss"). But if none of these does the trick, he has a host of spicy prescriptions.

Spices figure in practically every one of Constantine's remedies. For impotence he advises an electuary of ginger, pepper, galangal, cinnamon, and various herbs, to be taken sparingly after lunch and dinner. For a morning pep-up he recommends cloves steeped in milk. He has other spiced prescriptions to boost a flagging sex drive, a compound of galangal, cinnamon, cloves, long pepper, arugula, and carrot being rated as "the best there is."* He prescribes an electuary for those who suffer from impotence on account of a cold temperament; spices to strengthen the libido and augment semen, in both potency and volume. In light of his calling as a Benedictine monk, perhaps the most startling claim comes attached to a remedy for mild impotence, recommended for those in need of nothing more serious than a boost, consisting of chickpeas, ginger, cinnamon, honey, and various herbs. The learned monk writes that he has tried the recipe himself, and it comes "highly recommended." His spices get results: "I have put them to the test. . . . They act rapidly, with a gentle action."

Hence, with a nod and a wink, Chaucer's condemnation of the "cursed monk." Yet if Constantine's aphrodisiacal interests may have been a professional liability for a celibate monk, they were evidently not seen as such by the readers of his books, which were regularly published into the sixteenth century. But Chaucer (or January) could equally have picked any number of authors who made similar claims for spices, for this was a belief that long preceded and long outlasted Chaucer's day. And herein lay not the least of spices' attractions or, depending on one's perspective, a good reason for avoiding them altogether.

Why this was so admits of no simple answer. If there is a single, solid conclusion to be drawn from the deeply bizarre study of aphrodisiacs, it is that practically everything remotely edible has at some time or another been credited with sexually enhancing powers—and many inedible substances besides. Cost, rarity, exoticism, texture, odor, color, taste, or shape—all seem to play a part. At one time or another strychnine, arsenic, phosphorus, and cannabis have all enjoyed a certain vogue, though the last is now more commonly viewed as an anaphrodisiac, and strychnine and arsenic sound unwise. Moreover, claims of sexual enhancement vary radically with the social setting. Brillat-Savarin prized fish as an aphrodisiac of rare subtlety and potency; yet to the medieval cleric—if not necessarily Constantine—it was the cool and watery safeguard of his celibacy. I have read that a society of disgruntled women of eighteenth-century London once petitioned against the craze for coffee then sweeping the country on the grounds of the

---

*The carrot's suggestively phallic shape apparently accounts for its long-lasting reputation as an aphrodisiac.

allegedly enfeebling effect it had on their husbands; yet others have made the reverse claim. There have been thousands of vaunted aphrodisiacs. The law of probability suggests that it would be odd if spices did not appear among them from time to time.

Yet even by the standards of this pseudo science, spices were special. In the ancient and medieval consciousness spices and eroticism were inseparable, their purported effects spicing their reception at the table for thousands of years. That spices were sexy was an unchallenged nostrum of the medieval scientist, numbering among its advocates some of the founding fathers of the rationalist tradition in science and medicine, figures such as Aristotle, Hippocrates, Galen, and Avicenna: a "truth" less cosmic in its implications but perhaps more relevant to people's day-to-day existence than the no less certain fact that the sun revolves around the earth.

They were, moreover, the pick of the bunch. When Jean Auvray (ca. 1590–ca. 1633) wrote a paean to the charms of the humble rustic bowl—"for all time a precious relic in the temple of Venus"—he claimed that its libidinous effect outgunned even the other foremost aphrodisiacs of the day, which he listed as egg yolks, pine nuts, Spanish fly, truffles, badger, rooster, hare and beaver testicles, ginger, and the other Eastern spices.

Though Auvray spoke in jest—mocking, in fact, the nonsense the subject inspired—similarly grand claims concerning spices and ginger in particular had long been the medical orthodoxy. To the Franciscan encyclopedist Bartholomew the Englishman, writing early in the thirteenth century, the erotic effects of spices were part of the cosmic order, inextricably linked to and explicable in terms of the larger schema of medical science and astrology. The spicer was one of several libidinous professions born under the sign of Venus, along with singers, jewelers, music lovers, and tailors of women's clothing. According to a gloss attributed to the Catalan scholar Arnald de Vilanova, medieval Europe's appetite for exotic Eastern spices was fueled by an unholy marriage of lust and gluttony, the "corrupter of morals." The spice trade was driven not so much by the palate as by gullet and loins.

To point out the sexiness of spice was to state the obvious. When he berated the corrupt and debauched priesthood of tenth-century Italy, Ratherius of Verona (ca. 887–974) came close to tautology when he accused them of pampering their bloated bodies, slaking their unholy lust and recharging it with "libido-nourishing spices." There was, how-

ever, nothing inherently Christian about the association; it was merely
that Christians were viewing the sins of the flesh with a new and baleful intensity. The tradition and the medical reasoning that under-
pinned it were antique. When Pliny said of Augustus's daughter Julia
that she had made long pepper famous, he left it to his readers to do the
rest. No one could fail to connect Julia to the scandal of the age, when
the emperor's daughter had been exiled on account of an overactive sex
life: Caesar's daughter, like his wife, had to be above reproach. It was
moot whether she had made the spice famous—or had it been the other
way around?

Once the purported aphrodisiac properties of spice are appreciated,
much of the taste they aroused, and so too the corresponding distaste,
becomes abruptly more intelligible. Likewise with the context in which
they tend to appear. Spiced wines were a common feature of the
medieval wedding, and it is a reasonable surmise that there was more to
the combination of nuptials, wine, and spice than the desire to celebrate
in style. Spiced wine, or *piment,* was, according to the hymnographer
Marbode de Rennes (1035–1123), the voluptuary's drink of choice.
Alongside the cheerful bawdiness of its medieval predecessor, the modern Western wedding seems almost studiously prudish, notwithstanding the embarrassing telegrams or recollections of college exploits and
indiscretions. There was much unabashed mirth at, and little skirting
around, the impending consummation, the success or failure of which
was dutifully noted and, if appropriate, toasted. It fell to the cook as
well as the priest (and guests) to promote the union of both bodies and
souls. A medieval gloss on a collection of Roman recipes mentions that
bulbs were recommended for "those who seek the mouth of Venus" and
were for this reason served at weddings with pepper and pine nuts—
another traditional aphrodisiac. As late as the eighteenth century, it was
still the custom for English newlyweds to be served a "posset" immediately before retiring to the wedding bed: a mixture of wine, milk, egg
yolk, sugar, cinnamon, and nutmeg.*

Admittedly, the force of this sort of symbolism is notoriously elusive. It would be naive to imagine that each time a medieval spice eater
sat down to a drink of hippocras or a spicy electuary he anticipated,
eagerly or otherwise, the effects below the waistline, as though popping

---

*When Lady Macbeth returns from drugging the wine of Duncan's guards—she calls them
"surfeited grooms"—she boasts, "I have drugg'd their possets" (*Macbeth* 2.2.6).

Viagra with the ice cream. It would, however, be no less anachronistic to assume that spices could ever be unburdened of their ancient promise of fecundity. The point is made with characteristic bluntness by François Villon, the fast-living lyric genius of fifteenth-century France whose criminal excesses repeatedly landed him in prison—he was jailed for killing a priest—and whose poetic abilities got him out again. His *Testament* is written as a bequest in which, bidding farewell to Paris, friends, and life, Villon leaves his worldly goods to friends and enemies. To the "woodworker," the torturer who once interrogated the poet in the Châtelet, he leaves some ginger to perk up his love life:

> *I give the woodworker*
> *One hundred stems, heads and tails*
> *Of Saracen ginger,*
> *Not for coupling his boxes*
> *But getting arses under the sheets,*
> *Stitching sausages to thighs,*
> *So the milk surges up to the tits*
> *And the blood races down to the balls.*

The graphically black humor is typical of Villon: with a little spice, even a torturer might lighten up a little.

It was equally self-evident that for those whose erotic problem was not a lack but a surfeit of libido, spices should be avoided at all costs. Clerics in particular were well advised to steer clear—a theme we shall return to in a later chapter. In the *Registro di cucina* of Johannes Bockenhym, cook to the early-fifteenth-century Pope Martin V, there is a recipe for a mild and cooling omelette, recommended specifically for the lustful members of society and as such a conspicuous exception to the otherwise spicy tenor of the work: "Take beaten eggs and oranges, mix the juice of the oranges with eggs and sugar. Heat some oil in a pan and fry the egg and orange mix. . . . It will serve for scoundrels, parasites, flatterers, and whores."

For purely professional reasons it seems doubtful whether his intended audience would be so inclined. So tempting were spices that not all those who should have known better were able to resist, and clerics in particular spun off many a cautionary tale of those whose chastity had been undone by a spicy diet: the worldly abbot diverted from his dedications by his rich diet, his meditations "more of sauces than of Solomon"; or the monk who, succumbing to his appetite, was undone by the flames of impure lust. One such in its later permutations is the legend of Pope Joan, reputed to have occupied the fisherman's throne at some stage in the late ninth century. The earliest references to Joan by Marianus Scotus (ca. 1028–1086) and Sigebert of Gembloux (ca. 1030–1112) are sparse and almost certainly fantastical. Nevertheless, in the late Middle Ages the legend proved hugely popular and despite papal denunciations was embroidered upon by dozens of authors. Recently, there has been a revival of interest among the credulous, some of whom are willing to see Joan as a real person (though all years of the ninth century are in fact accounted for by male popes) and even reincarnated as a protofeminist.

Joan almost certainly did not exist; however, the real interest of the tale is the telling. And in this respect Joan can claim to be a protofeminist martyr, albeit a fictional one. For in the poetic versions of her life that crop up from the twelfth through the fifteenth centuries she is generally cast as impressively learned but ultimately, like all women, weak, lustful, and prone to overindulgence. The later writers concur that these feminine traits and in particular her weakness for spicy foods proved her undoing. Her tables were always laden with richly spiced dishes and flavors of the sensual Orient. One spiced meal too many, and this weak female, overcome with desire, fell into the arms of her (presumably startled) attendant. After nine months—in which time her increasingly ample girth went unnoticed among the well-fed cardinals—out popped a bouncing baby boy in the middle of a papal procession, whereupon the enraged populace turned on the impostor and stoned her to death. To this day papal processions avoid the alleyway in which this unsavory incident is said to have occurred, between San Vicente and the Colosseum, still lugubriously signposted as Vicolo della Papessa.

HOT STUFF

To make a Tarte that is a courage* to a man or woman: Take two Quinces and two or three Burre rootes, and a potaton, and pare your Potaton and scrape your rootes and put them in a quart of wine, and let them boyle till they be tender, and put in an ounce of Dates, and when they be boyled tender, draw them through a

*Here meaning potency or sexual vigor.

strainer, Wine and all, and then putte in the yolkes of eight Egges,
and the brains of three or four Cock Sparrowes and strain them
into the other and a little Rose water and mix them all with Suger,
Cynamon and Ginger, and Cloves and Mace, and put in a little
Swete butter.

—THOMAS DAWSON, *The good huswifes iewell,* 1610

Essentially, spices' erogenous reputation rested on the medical precepts
of the previous chapter. The tenets of humoral theory applied to sexual
as to any other branch of medicine. Like any other ailment, erotic dysfunction was seen as symptomatic of an imbalance: one or more of the
humors was out of kilter. Broadly, a loss of erotic interest or capacity
was viewed as symptomatic of excessive coldness. And as impotence
was frigid, so lust was hot—a thousand pop songs are the heirs to an
ancient tradition. The hot spices, as we have seen, were the heating
medicine par excellence—and therefore, quite logically, aphrodisiacs.

Sex drive, however, was only part of the equation. Fertility, on the
other hand, was generally regarded as a function of both heat *and* moisture. It followed that a hot substance increased libido, while perhaps
reducing the ability to deliver. Since fertile, fecund sperm and womb
alike were classed as hot *and* wet, it was simple logic that the best aphrodisiacs were both warm and moist. Hot and dry translated into potent
but possibly infertile. A diagram scribbled by a thirteenth-century
copyist in Hereford framed the issue in stark terms: the sanguine members of the monastery (hot and wet) were the most fertile and potent,
whereas the choleric (hot and dry) had a higher level of desire but less
capability. His fellow melancholics might as well abandon any thoughts
of love. Given that they were monks, this was probably just as well.

To summarize the tenets of sexual medicine as they applied at the
more lustful end of the spectrum: a warm and wet temperament meant
lots of sperm and a healthy level of desire; warm and dry translated into
less but more "fiery" sperm and more lasciviousness still.

Such, at least, were the outlines. As the hottest of heating drugs,
spices were an obvious choice for the first part of the equation.* Spices

---

*Another common sexual dysfunction amenable to endless speculation was premature ejac-
ulation. The Portuguese physician and botanist Garcia d'Orta suggested that opium, regarded
as extremely cooling, served to constrict the channels "along which the genital seed comes from
the brain," with the advantage that it slowed down men, by nature prone to orgasm earlier than
women, and helped facilitate simultaneous orgasm.

stood near or at the head of a very short shortlist, since substances reputed to impart bodily heat were strictly limited in number. From ancient Greece through to early modern Europe, the same foods were cited time after time, the ideal hot-wet combination for both potency and fertility being particularly rare. To Constantine the African, the top hot-and-wet sperm and libido boosters were pepper, pine nuts, egg yolks, warm meats, brain, and arugula.* Chickpeas were another perennial favorite. Centuries after Constantine, the French writers Nicolas Venette (1633–1698) and Paul Lacroix (1806–1884) were advising much the same formulae as suggested by Constantine. The latter advised a nightcap of ginger, pepper, rocket, Spanish fly, sugar, and skinks as a remedy for impotence.

Because of ginger's rare hot-wet classification, it was the most sought after of all the spices. There may be some substance to this reputation, for it is indeed true that ginger boosts circulation, and in this sense the spice may in a minor way stimulate erectile tissue. In her *History of Food* Maguelonne Toussaint-Samat cites the grisly case of Portuguese slavers in West Africa who fed ginger to the "studs" on their slave farms so as to increase their productivity. The same author suggests that it is perhaps on account of ginger's reputed aphrodisiac properties that the spice appears in the Islamic vision of Paradise. According to Sura 76 of the Koran, beautiful houris serve the virtuous martyrs "cups brimming with ginger-flavored wine from the fount of Selsabil."

Whereas ginger was regarded as a hot and wet all-rounder, boosting both sperm *and* desire, the other spices were generally classed as drier and accordingly more libidinous but less productive of sperm. One popular choice was the clove, situated midway along the spectrum of dryness and generally classified as less fiercely heating than pepper or cinnamon, for which reason it was commonly recommended to "favor the seed" of male and female alike. A Middle English guide to women's health suggests that three ounces of powdered cloves mixed with four egg yolks will make a woman conceive "if God wills," whether it is eaten or applied to the stomach. Pepper, on the other hand, was regarded as extremely hot and dry and therefore powerfully productive

---

*John Davenport (1789–1877) relates the salutary tale of an abbot whose monks suffered from that bane of medieval monastic life known as *accidia,* a combination of boredom, lassitude, and laziness conventionally but inadequately translated as "sloth." Hoping to stir them from their idleness, he fed them arugula, succeeding so well that they promptly abandoned the cloister for the brothel.

of erotic performance but liable to "dry up" the sperm. The seventeenth-century Nicolas Venette summarized its effect: "Pepper, by dissipating the superfluous humors . . . warms and dries the genital parts, which are naturally cold and humid, and thus procuring a uniform temperament it augments their power, which is in turn the cause of a more advantageous coction."

While the variations on these themes were limited only by the imagination, perhaps the best sense of their force is in the prolific warnings against overdoing them. The medical writers seldom fail to warn darkly of the effects of too much sex and spice. Too many spices could induce drying out, derangement, and even death. Something along these lines occurs in the twelfth-century romance *Cligès,* by Chrétien de Troyes. After the heroine is forced into a marriage against her will, her nurse, Thessala, prepares a spiced potion that so overheats her unwanted husband's libido and addles his brain that he suffers from erotic delusions. On his wedding night he is convinced he has consummated his marriage when in fact he has done nothing of the sort: "He is satisfied by a vain semblance, embracing, kissing and fondling nothing at all. . . . All his pains are of no avail. . . . He thinks that the fortress is won." Her virtue unsullied, the heroine is free to indulge in her hopeless love.

For a young or healthy man or woman, then, spices were so potent as to pose a health risk. For this reason Hildegard of Bingen (1098–1179) said of ginger that it was harmful if eaten by a man in good health and weight—an individual in whom, in other words, the humors were in balance, "because it makes him ignorant, stupid, tepid and lascivious." One version of *The Salernitan Guide to Health,* a medieval medical work of composite authorship, claims that unless the desire for lust-enhancing spices is held in check by the healthy precepts of the doctors, the human inclination to lechery and luxury will lead to permanent ill health as our systems overheat and slowly desiccate themselves to death.*

Viewed from the present day, it is difficult to appreciate that these were claims of the utmost academic respectability. Their respectability,

---

*A lesser risk of too much sex or heat was hair graying and loss, conditions attributed to dryness reaching the head and killing off the hair. Many a case of premature baldness could be attributed to (and consoled by?) a healthy virility: "I have found by experiment that fornication destroys the hair of the head, the eyebrows and the eyelashes," wrote the great Muslim philosopher-physician ar-Razi (Rhazes) (ca. 865–ca. 930).

moreover, was not eroded but rather grew with time: for the medieval physician there was no argument so clinching as antiquity. But while Galen and ancient Greek medicine provided the setting and the theoretical framework of sexual medicine, in medieval times a more immediate source of spices and prescriptions alike was the Muslim Near East and Spain. It was via the medium of Arabic that the teachings of Galen and for that matter serious scientific study of medicine as a whole were reintroduced to Europe, where, by the turn of the new millennium, they found a ready market. The medieval nobleman was as worried about the well-being of his loins as any other fretful male in history; probably, given the high mortality of his offspring and low fertility rates, he had more reason to be worried.* His fears, and the cash with which to assuage them, coincided with the revival of the spice trade and, to some unknowable extent, help explain it. For both spices and advice on how to use them, he looked east.

Led by Avicenna (Ibn Sina) (980–1037), the most famous scientist-philosopher of Islam, the teachings of the Arab writers laid down the outlines of sexual medicine that Europe would recycle down to modern times. It is one of the great paradoxes of the history of European thought that medieval Europe looked to its religious enemy for guidance in the fields of science, astrology, and philosophy. Building on Galenic foundations, Arab scientists added new recipes and spices, many of which, such as nutmeg, had apparently been unknown in Galen's day. In tenth-century Andalusia, Arib ibn Saïd al-Katib al-Qurtubi (918–980), doctor and secretary to the caliphs Abd ar-Rahman III and Alhakam II, laid out the theoretical basis of spices' heat and its effect on sexual health. These were, essentially, the principles summarized above. The author of several works on the topic, including *On the Generation of the Foetus* and *The Treatment of Pregnant Women and Newborns,* he attributed failure to conceive and the inability to maintain an erection alike to a loss of heat. The remedy he prescribes

---

*Private or public humiliation was another likely consequence of impotence. Impotence was a legal ground for divorce, and there are numerous records of neighbors and friends being called on to testify about the state of a couple's sex life. Doctors might be called to examine a man's genitalia and pronounce upon their adequacy, and men might even be expected to provide public proof of their capacity. A court record from fifteenth-century York records the report of a group of women who were called upon to witness a husband's unsuccessful efforts to copulate with his wife. When he was unable to do so, the women berated him "with one voice . . . because he presumed to take as a wife some young woman by defrauding her."

consists of a type of marmalade, ginger, pepper, pomegranate blossom, and eggs, to augment both sperm and potency.

Still more influential was his follower Ibn al-Jazzar (898–980), a Tunisian physician who was the immediate source of Constantine's prescriptions. He, too, enshrined ginger as the aphrodisiac of choice, ascribing to the spice an impressive versatility in several works on the topic: increasing sex drive and fertility, engendering more abundant sperm, making pleasure last longer. The latter in particular was a common claim of the Arab physician. Al-Tifashi, a thirteenth-century Cairene physician, recommended cinnamon, cloves, ginger, and cardamom, for "strength for coition . . . useful to anyone who manages to copulate twice running." Other spices played the supporting role of adequate substitutes. According to Ibn al-Jazzar, when there is no ginger at hand, black or white pepper can be used, though with an attendant risk of drying out. He credits ginger's relative galangal with producing an instantaneous erection.

Like those of all religions, Islamic authorities were capable of prudishness, but theirs was a climate vastly more suited to study and frank discussion of the topic than was found in the Christian West. In Ayyubid Syria, it was not beneath the dignity of Saladin's nephew to commission a treatise on the topic from Maimonides (1135–1204), incontestably the greatest Jewish scholar of the age. As Maimonides' preface explains, the sultan freely admitted that he was in need of a little more vim, the result of advancing age, emaciation, and the demands of his many concubines: "He reports, may the Lord preserve his power, that he desires to give up nothing of his habits in connection with sexual intercourse." Nominally, however, most Islamic works tend to promise results in terms of function and fertility as opposed to pleasure alone. (Though one wonders about *The Old Man's Rejuvenation in his Power of Copulation* by al-Tifashi.) And whereas Christianity actively discouraged inquiry, Islam provided a greater degree of religious sanction, perhaps a consequence of the greater demands of polygamy. The specter of demographic catastrophe remained a preoccupation of Arab thinkers from the Prophet's own day, a time of small nomadic tribes liable to annihilation or absorption in one of the endemic wars of the Arabian Peninsula, through Islam's expansion into an urban society based in the most populous cities in the world. Aphrodisiacs even enter into the *hadith,* or traditions attributed to sayings of the Prophet. According to the scholar al-Ghazali (1058–1111), when the Prophet

complained of impotence, the angel Gabriel recommended *harīsa,* a
mixture of porridge and meat seasoned with pepper.

Such frankness was unthinkable in the Christian West. Even as Maimonides penned advice for Saladin's nephew, in England clerics berated
Richard the Lionheart for his dalliance with Sodom (meaning, in this
case, not anal intercourse but masturbation or general debauchery).
Viewed from the West, over time the spiciness of Eastern sexual medicine had a dual effect. On the one hand, the Eastern origins and the
reputation of Arabic medicine provided Western scholars with the
intellectual cover for an interest they could otherwise justify only with
difficulty: Constantine's works were translations. And doubtless it was
largely on account of their reticence and reliance on Eastern sources
that they stuck to their Arabic models, many of which reappeared centuries later, changed little if at all, acknowledged or unacknowledged,
in the West. A concoction first credited to Youhanna ibn Massaouih
(Jean Mesué), a celebrated Baghdad doctor of the ninth century,
appears practically unchanged in the *Pharmacopée royale* of Moses Cha-
ras, published in France at the end of the seventeenth. This makes it
one of the most enduring, if not necessarily the most effective, prescriptions of all time.

Yet this reliance on the East had a paradoxical effect. In at least some
eyes the association poisoned spices and may even have helped fuel the
old myth of the lascivious Orient. It was perhaps inevitable that as
Asia's most visible exports, spices should have arrived trailing associations of the East where they grew. So, for instance, in John of
Hauteville's satirical twelfth-century poem *Archithrenius,* or *The Arch-
weeper,* it is both the Eastern origins and the erotic quality of spices that
single them out for condemnation. As the teary hero goes on his cheer-
less way to the abode of Gluttony, he meets with the belly worshippers
or *ventricolae,* who egg on their lasciviousness with a diet of hot seasonings, their greed driving them beyond the Meridian to seek the spices
of the Orient, ever searching for more novel delicacies from around the
world and condiments that nourish the libido. (What would the arch-
weeper have made of a curry house?) To some, spices could simply not
be separated from their sexual baggage. Two hundred years later, the
Carmelite Richard Lavynham, author of *A Litil Treatise on the Seven
Deadly Sins,* linked spices to those lechers guilty of "abusyon," by which
he meant sex for pleasure. The characteristics of such a sinner were a
diet of "hot meats and drinks . . . spices and medicines," the sole pur-

pose of which was to inflame the libido "more to perform lust than decent procreation, increasing the frailty of the flesh."

For the English clerical poet John Myrc, even the morally perfect were susceptible. In his poem *Instructions for Parish Priests,* written around 1450, he warns that the side effects of spiced electuaries were grievous and would "enforce . . . to lechery." Such was the erotic power of spices that, even if eaten with healing in mind, they might lead one into committing "that foul deed." In Myrc's eyes spices were doubly noxious, since both taste and smell provoked sins of the flesh, the latter leading even those who came forewarned into such venial sins as "rib-awdlry," "harlotry," and touching "woman's flesh or thy own":

> *Hast thou smelled anything to your liking,*
> *Meat, drink or spicery,*
> *That after you have sinned by?*

And while medieval Christians at times showed complete disdain for the study of medicine—it is something of a myth that the medieval monastery was a center of medical studies; more often, the Church actively discouraged inquiry—they did not need a Constantine or an Avicenna to tell them of spices' perils, for they knew as much on impeccable ecclesiastical authority. In his work *On the Customs of the Manichaeans,* Saint Augustine accuses his erstwhile coreligionists (Augustine had once been a Manichaean himself) of misunderstanding the true nature of spices' eroticizing contamination. Manichaean belief held that foods such as pepper and truffles contained within them a form of ritual pollution, whereas to orthodox Christians this was heretical nonsense. Spices' contamination resided not in any inherent or ritual effect—matter, being God-made, was innocent—but ensued from their fueling of the "sensual appetite." Those who ate "peppered truffles"—two aphrodisiacs in one—did not pollute themselves so much as goad themselves on to lust.

The practical conclusions that followed were self-evident. For the chaste, spices were out; cool and wet foods were in. To Christians concerned about the possible ramifications of such an incendiary diet, the polar opposite of foods such as truffles and pepper was a native Mediterranean aromatic known as agnus castus, *Vitex agnus-castus.* Classed as powerfully cold and dry, it was used by monks to incline their bodies and thoughts away from the flesh. Serapion, the hugely influential fourth-century monk and companion of the Egyptian hermit Saint

Antony, one of the founding fathers of Christian monasticism, dubbed the plant "monk's pepper," because, as one medieval authority phrased it, "it makes men as chaste as lambs." To this day the plant is known as "Monk's Pepper Tree."

Yet if the aphrodisiac reputation of spices long had the status of medical fact, it is equally true that their appeal also relied on a heavy dose of pure superstition. For a magical reputation an outré quality is often recommendation enough, and like other aphrodisiac staples such as rhino horn and tiger penis, spices long carried the freight of Eastern mystery, rarity, and a high price. This held good for as long as spices retained their air of mysteriousness. Philostratus of Tyre (ca. 170–ca. 245), the biographer of the miracle-working Apollonius of Tyana, wrote that "lovers especially are addicted to this art [of magic]; for since the disease from which they suffer renders them prone to delusions, so much so that they seek the counsel of old hags, it is small wonder, in my opinion, that they resort to these charlatans and pay attention to their quackery." What was true of the third century still applies in the twenty-first: "They will accept from the hags a magic girdle, and precious stones, some of which come from the depths of the earth, soil from the moon or stardust; and then they are given all the spices that are grown in India."

Other sexual magic involved greater risks. It has been a recurrent belief that the pricking action of particular ingredients can have a sympathetic effect, the best-known example being the blister-causing and myth-begetting cantharides, or Spanish fly, a favorite of the Marquis de Sade (on one occasion his stash was unwittingly consumed by some of his guests, who complained that they had been poisoned). The Greco-Roman author Aelian (ca. 170–ca. 235) writes of shepherds using black pepper to stimulate mating: "From the ensuing irritation the females of the herd cannot contain themselves, but go mad over the males." Something similar occurs in the *Satyricon* of Petronius Arbiter (?–66), where the shipwrecked Encolpius, seeking a remedy for impotence, is sodomized with a peppered leather dildo as punishment for killing a sacred goose of Priapus (the latter being the huge-phallused god of fertility, protector of vines and gardens, reputed to sodomize any thief unlucky enough to be taken in the act; Encolpius's fate was, however, a lesser punishment than the crucifixion stipulated by law). The Augustan poet Ovid (43 B.C.–A.D. 17) refers to an old wives' love remedy of pepper and biting nettle, which he dismisses as worthless—

prudently, it would seem—compared to his altogether more poetical methods of sweet-talking, flirting, and playing hard to get.

This unblushing acceptance of sex and aphrodisiacs vanished along with the world of pagan antiquity, but both the notion of stimulation through irritation and a sense of the potency of spices survived well into modern times. Paul Lacroix (1806–1884) cites a medieval recipe for effecting the return of a missing loved one: take a black chicken, sacrifice it "in the name of Jesus Christ," then pierce its heart with five cloves, repeating all the while "in the name of Jesus Christ . . . who suffered as you [the chicken] are suffering now," while making the sign of the cross with the spices. "So primed the returned will do whatever you desire." Often magic merged into more medically respectable beliefs. Eggs and testicles in particular were widely believed to have a powerful sympathetic effect. In a second work on the topic attributed to Constantine the African, the *Liber minor de coitu,* ginger and pepper are recommended in conjunction with calves' testicles, roosters' testicles—all manner of testicles, in fact—and other ingredients such as grapes, melon, and, another aphrodisiac staple before it became commonplace, the suggestively phallic banana.

By aphrodisiac standards even these are remarkably mild. Faith in the exotic tended to shade into faith in the out-and-out revolting, as was revealed in a curious witchcraft trial in the Danish town of Naestved in 1619. The accused, a young man, was charged with having taught a friend of his the trick of seducing a young woman with nutmeg. The idea was to eat an entire nutmeg and wait for it to reemerge at the other end, whereupon the semidigested nutmeg was grated into a glass of beer or wine, which was in turn administered to the unsuspecting object of the nutmeg crapper's affections. So primed, she was powerless to resist and likely, as the judge ruled, to do "whatever he might desire." She might even pay for the privilege. In the case in question the judge found that by such foul and insidious means the accused had robbed a young woman not only of her virtue but of the cash she had laid down for the unhappy experience.

And maybe, if victim and perpetrator so believed, something along those lines happened. Looking over the bulk of such remedies, however, the chief impression is not only how ineffective but how unpleasant they must have been. This is, perhaps, no great surprise, given the authorities' credentials: the authors are almost invariably male, often clerics, and women's enjoyment was seldom in their thoughts. But still more startling than the credulousness of a supposedly chaste monk is the survival of similar notions into more recent times. Pierre Pomet, chief druggist to Louis XIV, recommended that "a few Drops of the Oil [of pepper], in any proper Liniment, rub'd upon the *Perinœum* three or four Times will restore a lost Erection." This old-wifeish strain of sexual medicine endured long after the principles of Galenic medicine were in abeyance and humoral theory discredited; indeed, in some of the wilder publications on the topic it endures to this day—run a search on the Internet for "spice" and "erection" and see the results. The self-styled "aphrodisiologiste" Marcel Rouet, author of the idiosyncratic *Le Paradis sexuel des aphrodisiaques,* suggests that spices can be eaten, albeit only intermittently, with spectacular results: "A young man of twenty years whose organs, particularly the kidneys, have not had any problems, can use strong doses of spices one or two times a week without inconvenience for a prolonged erotic festival of several hours' duration." (An older gent with weaker kidneys is advised to use other, less explosive stimulants for the sake of his health.) Rouet cites the *Kama Sutra* as his authority that ground pepper can be applied directly to the penis before intercourse, in which event the lucky recipient of his spiced attentions will be entirely at the disposal of the owner of the peppered penis. His one concession is to rate it "much more practical" to substitute oil of pepper and allspice in place of the spice in its natural state. His suggestions involving chili pepper—"extremely erogenous for the woman"— are more eye-watering still. And if the chili fails to do the trick, a piece of ginger up the rectum will do just as well.

In a field distinguished by a general willingness to suspend reason and risk extreme discomfort, perhaps the best that can be said is that at some point a reputation becomes self-sustaining, for which reason to look too hard for explanations is to take the material too seriously; at times one wonders whether authors such as Rouet were motivated more by foolhardiness, naïveté, or a general ill will toward humanity. The rules lack rigor—and in at least one case a spice itself was at the receiving end of sexual magic. In the Moluccas, the home of the clove, mace, and nutmeg, *Homo sapiens* sought to return the favor, as it were, and impart a little of his own sexual vigor to the spices, in this case the clove. On the island of Ambon in the nineteenth century, the Dutch colonial administration had taken over the control of the clove plantations after several hundred years of brutal management by the Dutch East India Company. Plantation managers set Stakhanovite targets, enforcing them with ruthless efficiency. Here Baron van Hoëvell witnessed some strange goings-on in the clove groves: "In some parts of Amboyna, when the state of the clove plantation indicates that the crop is likely to be scanty, the men go naked to the plantations by night, and there seek to fertilise the trees precisely as they would impregnate women, while at the same time they call out for 'More cloves!' This is supposed to make the trees bear fruit more abundantly."

Perhaps the Moluccans' horticultural eccentricities were not so far removed from the beliefs and practices of the Europeans. From their perspective, what other than some magical force of attraction could account for the extraordinary magnetism the clove exerted over the merchants who sailed from the far side of the planet, scurvy-ridden and nearly dead, all for the sake of a spice?

SPICE GIRLS

Looke, and to morrow late, tell mee,
Whether both the India's of spice and Myne,
Be where thou lefst them, or lie here with mee.
—JOHN DONNE, "The Sun Rising," 1633

Not all of the amorous reputation of spices was as direct, or laid such stress on love's more physical aspects, as Villon's boast of the explosive effects of his ginger or doctors' claims of bolstering sperm and enhancing the libido. Like Donne chafing at the arrival of the daylight, not everyone has taken the spice-sex connection too literally. Spices have long held the promise of more subtle enchantments, often more figurative than real. At the start of *Moby-Dick,* Ishmael, mooching around a wintry New Bedford, sings the praises of the women of Salem, "where they tell me the young girls breathe such musk, their sailor sweethearts smell them miles off shore, as though they were drawing nigh the odorous Moluccas instead of the Puritanic sands." A fond hope, perhaps, but a common one. Oskar's lover in Günter Grass's *The Tin Drum* smells of cinnamon, cloves, and nutmeg, the scent of Christmas and cake spice. No object of desire ever suffered from the comparison.

For poets of all ages spices have served as powerfully evocative shorthand. It is a particularly enduring conceit that the truly desirable woman need not eat or apply them, for she smells of spice naturally. The seventeenth-century poet and voluptuary Robert Herrick was particularly fond of the idea. Anthea smelled of cinnamon:

> If I kisse Anthea's brest,
> There I smell the Phenix nest.

Anne, on the other hand, smelled of cloves:

> So smell these odours that do rise
> From out the wealthy spiceries:
> So smels the flowre of blooming Clove;
> or Roses smother'd in the stove {dried roses}.

Julia, trumping them all, smelled of all the spices:

> Breathe, Julia, breathe, and Ile protest,
>   Nay more, Ile deeply sweare,
> That all the Spices of the East
>   Are circumfused there.

So spicy was Julia that with one kiss she could infuse a wedding cake with a taste of spices:

> This day my Julia thou must make
> For Mistresse Bride, the wedding Cake:
> Knead but the Dow and it will be
> To paste of Almonds turn'd by thee:
> Or kisse it thou but once, or twice,
> And for the Bride-Cake ther'l be Spice.

Other poets saw a parallel in the astringency of the spices. Juan Ruiz (ca. 1283–ca. 1350), the rambunctious Castilian priest jailed by an archbishop of Toledo for his licentious life and writings, found in pepper an allegory for the hot and feisty short women he preferred over their tall sisters, whom he found frigid and aloof. Though cold on the outside, the short woman is blazing hot in love; in bed, she is comforting, fancy free, and cheerful, and good around the house besides:

> Though the grain of good pepper is small,
> It is hotter and spicier than a nutmeg;
> So a little woman, if she gives herself to love—
> There's no pleasure in the world she cannot give.

Tall or short, others turned to spice to evoke hidden, mysterious charms. "Consider her lips and realize / The joy of besieging that scarlet prize / Wherein all nectar and spices seem to be," as the Florentine-Pisan poet Fazio degli Uberti (ca. 1310–1367) had it.

The archetype to which many of these poets looked was, perhaps surprisingly, the Bible. In every sense the spiciest of its books is the Song of Songs, generally believed to have been composed in its present form in the fourth or third century B.C., though perhaps containing much older fragments. Cinnamon and cassia are recurrent features of its lushly amorous, spice-rich imagery:

> A garden enclosed is my sister, my spouse; a spring shut up, a fountain
>   sealed.
> Thy plants are an orchard of pomegranates, with pleasant fruits; cam-
>   phire, with spikenard,
> Spikenard and saffron; calamus and cinnamon, with all trees of frank-
>   incense; myrrh and aloes, with all the chief spices:
> A fountain of gardens, a well of loving waters, and streams from
>   Lebanon.

Love, in the Song, enters through both eyes and nose:

> His cheeks are like beds of spices, yielding fragrance . . .

And elsewhere:

> Thou hast ravished my heart, my sister, my spouse; thou hast ravished
> my heart with one of thine eyes, with one chain of thy neck. How fair is
> thy love, my sister, my spouse! How much better is thy love than wine!
> And the smell of thine ointments than all spices.

While the Song is far and away the most consistently spicy biblical book, the notion of scent and its seductions is a recurrent one. The harlot of Proverbs used cinnamon to lure the unwary young man into her bed "as a bird rushes into a snare." The oldest biblical text touching on the subject is the tale of queen of Sheba: "There came no more such abundance of spices as these which the Queen of Sheba gave to King Solomon."

Notwithstanding the brevity of the biblical account of Sheba, later poets tended to give her visit a romantic gloss—the Eastern queen arriving trailing all the gorgeous trappings of the splendid Orient. (Historians, on the other hand, have tended to see in the episode a

memory of trade routes and agreements with the Arabian Peninsula.)
One who smelled of Sheba's Sabaean spices was Quixote's Dulcinea, at
least in the knight-errant's imagination. When Sancho Panza returns
from his visit to his master's lady, Quixote asks whether he perceived
about her a certain "Sabaean odor, an aromatic fragrance." Sancho
replies that it was not so, but rather mannish or "butch," as though she
were dripping with sweat from overexertion. He must, concludes the
don, have been smelling himself.

Spices, needless to say, did not evoke an unwashed, goatish squire.
They were exotic, rich in mystique, their attraction as mysterious as it
was elusive of description, poetic shorthand for an exotic sensualism.
When Quixote imagined Dulcinea's Sabaean aromas or when Donne
compared his lover to the spiced Indies, the effect was to convey a sense
of alluring and distant promise; like Oberon returning from the fairies,
the beloved carried with her something of the oriental air—no ordinary Londoner savoring of Southwark and Stepney Marsh or a sweaty
Manchegan peasant reeking from her labors in the field.

Behind this long literary tradition, behind even the biblical texts,
lay more literal applications for spice, of which the most enduring and
ancient was perfume: poetry for the nose. When Eastern spices were
first used is a matter for speculation. Akkadian texts dating from
around 1200 B.C. refer to a "perfumeress" employing various aromatic
gums and resins, but it is unclear whether she would have known any
Eastern spices. It is clear, however, that each of the major Near Eastern
civilizations had a wide and sophisticated repertoire of perfumes onto
which spices, once they became available, could readily be grafted. In
ancient Egypt, perfumes utilizing various Near Eastern aromatics
played an important role in worship, which in turn drove a far-ranging
trade—a subject to which we shall return. The Ishmaelites who
bought Joseph from his brothers were en route to Egypt with an
unspecified range of spices: "They saw some Ishmaelites on their way
coming from Galaad, with their camels, carrying spices, and balm, and
myrrh to Egypt." By the time of the Egyptian Middle Kingdom
(1938–ca. 1600 B.C.), perfume was put to widespread secular uses. In
the British Museum there is a wall painting of a Theban tomb depict-
ing a feast, where the guests are attended by serving boys and girls
offering wreaths, bowls of wine, perfumes, and ointments. The inscription urges the guests to "celebrate the joyful day! Let sweet odors and

oils be placed for thy nostrils, Wreaths of lotus flowers for the limbs." It is all too much for one guest, who casually vomits over her shoulder.

By Greek times both techniques and the range of aromatic materials had broadened considerably. By Homer's day there was, moreover, a clear association of scent and sensualism. The oldest seduction scene in Western literature occurs in the *Iliad,* where Hera distracts her wandering husband with the aid of an irresistibly fragrant oil: "One breath of the scent in the bronze-floored house of Zeus and it filled heaven and earth." It worked to such effect that Zeus declared that "never before had such lust rushed in a flood over my heart, whether for a goddess or a mortal woman," proceeding to reel off a list of previous conquests.

However, the most consistently aromatic of the gods were none other than the gods of love themselves, Aphrodite and her son Eros, the limb loosener. In *The Republic* Plato argues that desire is stimulated by perfume—and I suspect that most lovers of fine perfume would agree; this at least is the message of the advertising. During his discussion on the nature of love in *The Symposium,* Plato credits the poet Agathon with the argument that Eros is attracted by sweet scents and flowers. But this was merely to put a philosopher's spin on an ancient belief, whereby scent was one of Aphrodite's hallmarks, her attractant and harbinger, if not a disembodied manifestation of love itself. In the Homeric *Hymn to Aphrodite,* the goddess appears shrouded by an irresistible fragrance as she wafts down from Olympus to her island of Cyprus and her perfumed altars. All the gods of the Greeks received perfumes among their offerings, but Aphrodite did more with it. In one myth Aphrodite gifted a ferryman with a perfume that rendered women utterly powerless to resist him. For a time he made hay, although, as tends to be the way with Greek myths, his gift proved his eventual undoing; after cuckolding one husband too many, he was caught in the act and killed.

It was the Greeks, too, who made aroma a feature of erotic verse. Archilochus (ca. 675–ca. 635 B.C.) wrote of courtesans who "with their hair and breasts covered in perfume would arouse the desire even in an ancient." In *Lysistrata* by Aristophanes (ca. 447–ca. 385 B.C.), the comedy of a sex strike by the women of Athens, Myrrhine (her name means "Little Myrtle") drives her frustrated husband wild with desire with the help of a fragrant ointment. The poet Antipater of Sidon expressed this close association of aroma and eroticism in his epitaph for his fellow

206

BODY

poet Anacreon (ca. 582–ca. 485 B.C.), known for his frivolous, drunken eroticism. Even dead, this famous seducer smelled good, as in Robin Skelton's translation:

> *This is Anacreon's grave. Here lie*
> *the shreds of his exuberant lust,*
> *but hints of perfume linger by*
> *his gravestone still, as if he must have chosen for*
> *his last retreat*
> *a place perpetually on heat.*

That this was something more than a theological or literary conceit is suggested by the fact that perfumes and spices were widely employed at fertility rites and weddings. At the midsummer festival of the Adonia, fennel seeds were grown in small flower beds known as the "gardens of Adonis," so named in honor of the dead mortal loved by Aphrodite, accompanied by drinking and unbridled sexual excess. In Aristophanes' *Clouds,* Strepsiades recalls his wife's perfume as she came to her wedding bed, when she "positively oozed perfume and saffron, not to mention sex, money, sex, overeating, and, well, sex."

When the Eastern spices arrived, they slotted right in. They were certainly there by the fourth century, when Theophrastus, who wrote an entire book on the subject of perfumes, says that the necessary aromatics came from either India or Arabia, mentioning cassia, cinnamon, and cardamom by name. Other ingredients were nearer to hand, such as balsam of Mecca, storax,* saffron, marjoram, and myrrh. There was still a good deal of confusion as to their origins, but this only added to their appeal: Theophrastus thought his cardamom came from Persia, though he says that some were of the opinion that it came from India, along with the other spices. Cinnamon in particular stood out as superlative. The Middle Comedy poet Antiphanes mentions a perfumer by the name of Peron in his *Anteia,* composed ca. 380–370 B.C. Peron was known for his cinnamon:

> *I left him trying Peron's unguents,*
> *Bent on mixing nards and cinnamons for your scent.*

---

*Storax is the aromatic resin obtained from the shrub *Styrax officinalis,* native to eastern Europe and Asia Minor. It was widely used in ancient incense.

A few years later Aristotle warned that the "dryness" of perfumes risked causing premature grayness: "Why do those who use perfumes have gray hair sooner? Is it because perfume, through the spices in it, has a drying quality, wherefore the users of perfume become parched? For parching makes people more gray. For whether grayness is a drying up of the hair or a deficiency in heat, certain it is that dryness withers."

No one seems to have listened, although a few shared Aristotle's misgivings. Middle Comedy poets were fond of mocking young men with an excessive fondness for fragrances, eager for the latest products. Aristophanes' lost play *Daetales* featured two brothers, one a sophisticate from the city with a big selection of the latest imported perfumes, the other a yokel who has heard of none of them. Egypt in particular was renowned for its scents, many of which found their way to the Athenian *myropoleion,* a part of the market dedicated to the purpose. Besides Peron's cinnamon formula, several of their brand names survive, among them Psagda and Megallus, each named after a celebrated parfumier.

Imitators and inheritors of the Greeks in so many other respects, the Romans likewise lost their heads over perfume, with the difference that the erotic associations were, if anything, more heavily accentuated. Plutarch, who disapproved of this sort of thing, regarded perfumes as "an effeminate, emasculating luxury which has absolutely no real use. Yet, although it is of such nature, it has depraved not only all women, but also the greater part of men, so that they will not even sleep with their own wives unless they come to bed reeking of myrrh and scented powders." Too much perfume was seen as tawdry. In a comedy by Plautus (ca. 254–184 B.C.) one courtesan asks another, "Do you really want to go around with those common prostitutes, the friends of jail-birds, dripping with ginger grass oil?"

Like the Greeks and Egyptians before them, the Romans were inventive in the uses they found for their perfumes. In Nero's Golden House there was a scented dining room, the roof of which rained down roses and scented water. They followed the Greeks in branding and marketing the choicest blends with appropriately exotic names. Pliny mentions one choice perfume grandiloquently known as "The Royal Unguent of the Kings of Parthia," a suitably regal mix of many exotic and expensive ingredients, some of which defy identification, but including cinnamon, cardamom, cassia, calamus, ginger grass, saffron, marjoram, and honey. While variety, rarity, and the obscurity of the aromatics meant cachet, there was agreement that cinnamon was the pick of the bunch. In poetry the spice commonly appears as a paragon of the sublime, as in the lament of a grieving widow for the "cinnamon smell" of her dead husband's "ambrosial body." Plautus's comedy *Casina—Cinnamon*—takes its title from the object of an old man's extramarital longings, which are betrayed by the smell of her perfumes. The aged procuress of his *Curculio* waxes lyrical in and over her cups: "My beauty of Bacchus! You're old, but then so am I, and how badly I need you! Compared with you, every other essence is bilge water! You are my myrrh, my cinnamon, my ointment of roses, my saffron, my cassia, my rarest of perfumes! Where you are poured is where I want to be buried."

As a rule, the associations of spice and perfume tended toward the erotic. Nowhere is this clearer than in Apuleius's *Metamorphoses* or *The Golden Ass,* the bawdy tale of Lucius's adventures in human and asinine form. At some point in his adventures trapped in the body of an ass, the perpetually sex-starved hero sleeps with a beautiful noblewoman. Though initially reluctant to commit a bestial act, after a few drinks he is unable to withstand the desire brought on by plenty of good wine and the "inflammatory scent" of the woman's oil of balsam. Earlier, while still in human form, he is drawn into a passionate affair with a witch's serving maid, powerless to resist her jiggling buttocks and cinnamon-scented breath. But even cinnamon had its limits. To Lucius, who admired nothing about women as much as their hair, not even a liberal dose of cinnamon could rescue a bald woman: "If you were to take even the most outstandingly beautiful woman, cut off the hair from the head and so deprive the face of its natural setting: well, even if she were cast down from heaven, even if she were Venus herself, accompanied by all the Graces and with every Cupid in attendance and girded with her famous belt of love, blazing with cinnamon and dripping in balsam—if she were bald, she couldn't please even her own devoted slave."

In part, the esteem in which spices were held boiled down to a question of technique. Ancient perfumes and unguents were a good deal weaker than their modern equivalents, there being no way of isolating the powerful essential oils that enable modern perfumes to pack such a punch, based on alcohol, synthetic chemicals, and essential oils isolated by the process of distillation. In their place, the ancient perfumer obtained his perfumes by soaking aromatics in fat or oil, which was then gently heated (maceration) or left to sit unheated (enfleurage). The end product was commonly worn on clothes and hair or, alternatively, poured onto a brazier and burned (the modern word itself derives from the Latin *per fumum,* "through the smoke"). Spices had the added attraction of unrivaled potency and durability, for which reason they were critical ingredients for the perfumer, and they remained so until the equation was transformed with the invention of distillation and then the advent of the chemical age.

This is, of course, just the sort of tidy, functional explanation that historians like: spices were necessary, ergo fashionable. But in Roman eyes—or noses—the matter was more complicated. Not the least of spices' attractions were their godly associations. Cinnamon in particular came with a heavy freight of fable and religion and was reputed to grow in quasimythical lands of gods and monsters. A Roman audience, steeped in the literature of Homer and Virgil, could not escape the parallel with the ambrosial aroma of their gods and heroes, for whom fragrance was a hallmark of more-than-mortal status. In *The Iliad,* the dead heroes Patroclus and Hector are anointed with fragrant ointments, and the Venus of Ovid's *Metamorphoses* likewise makes Aeneas immortal by applying a perfume: "She anointed his body with the heavenly perfume." An ambrosial substance was by definition deathless, for that was what the word meant, from the Greek *am-brotos,* "immortal."

As angels have wings and saints haloes, so the pagan gods of love had cinnamon. In *The Aeneid,* the distinguishing characteristic of Venus's divinity is her perfumed hair, wafting ambrosial aromas. To Apuleius, the erogenous trinity of Venus, Cupid, and the Great Goddess Isis all smell of all the perfumes of Arabia. When Cupid visits Psyche invisibly by night, his identity is betrayed by the smell of his "cinnamon-fragrant curls."

While few educated Romans would confess to a literal belief in their myths, in this respect, at least, faith translated into practice. For in the matter of scent and its seductions mortals aped immortals. In life as in myth, scent was a weapon of seduction. As she is about to meet her lover, Plautus's courtesan Erotium gives orders to "spread the couches and burn the perfumes" as "a lover's enticement." When the penniless and love-struck poet Catullus cannot afford to offer his friend a proper meal, "his purse being full of cobwebs," he offers compensation by way of an exquisitely attractive perfume:

For I will give you a perfume,
That the very Venuses and Cupids gave my girl;
When you smell it, you will beg the gods,
Fabullus, to make you all nose.

On account of their propitious overtones, perfumes were conventionally burned at weddings. When Catullus despairs that Lesbia will not
marry him, he laments that she will never be led by her father to the
house fragrant with Assyrian odors but he must make do with her
furtive nighttime gifts.

As was ever the case with spices, this erotic-mythic resonance translated into social capital. Then as now, perfume was an important fashion
accoutrement with all the social fallout that entailed; in a fashion-
conscious town like Rome, its exotic quality, rarity, and cost were not so
much liabilities as recommendations. The most expensive, spiced perfumes were the most socially charged. Just as style, innovation, and
ostentation recommended spices to wealthy Romans, so too their countrymen had a flair for eloquent and generally censorial commentary on
any form of modish affectation. And there was none more eloquent than
the sardonic and chronically penniless epigrammatist Martial.

Along with a handful of other writers such as Proust and Baudelaire,
Martial was acutely sensitive to smell. He was particularly scornful of
vain and unnecessary luxury, a vice of which he saw expensive perfume
as a prime example. To Martial, artificial scent was another form of pre-
tension, vanity, and worthless artifice. If cinnamon was the most poetic
and mystical of all the spices, so too it came loaded with opprobrium,
for the simple reason that it was the most expensive. Pliny quotes the
prices of the various grades of cinnamon oil, in mixed form ranging
from 35 to 300 denarii the pound, in a pure form a whopping 1,000 to
1,500: six years' wages for a centurion. It was the smell of money evap-
orating—which was, depending on where one stood, either a good or a
bad thing. One of Martial's targets who favors the spice is a prissy and
affected "pretty boy" by the name of Cotilus. He minces about Rome
singing all the latest hits from Egypt and Spain; he curls his hair just so
and trips off all the latest gossip. Typical of such a vain and flighty
lightweight, he reeks permanently of balsam and cinnamon—to Martial's mind, "a trashy article." Honoring a virile tradition dating back
to Socrates, who disdained any masculine odor not acquired in the

gymnasium, Martial affects a lofty disdain for all scent as unworthy of a real man:

> *Because you are always fragrant*
> *With the leaden boxes of Niceros,*
> *Tarred with cassia and cinnamon from the nest of the proud Phoenix,*
> *You laugh at us, Coracinus, since we smell of nothing:*
> *I would rather smell of nothing than smell good.*

Nor was perfume any better on a woman. Among the clients of a celebrated parfumier named Cosmus was a certain Gellia:

> *Wherever you go, you'd think Cosmus was on the move*
> *And that the cinnamon oil was pouring from a shaken flask.*
> *Don't take pleasure in exotic trifles, Gellia.*
> *You're aware, I suppose, that my dog could smell as good.*

The implication being that Gellia is a bit of a dog herself.

Even to Martial, however, not all scent was modish excess. His gripe was not with spice or perfume as such, but with overdoing it. Even he was not immune to their charms. One of his most beautiful and tender poems compares the perfume of his boy's morning kisses to saffron and Cosmus's perfumes. He is not inclined to buy silks and cinnamon-leaf scent for his girl, he says elsewhere, but he would like her to be worthy of them all the same. The problem with spices was their cost and artifice; the real deal needed no embroidering. It was a familiar complaint of the Roman erotic poet: homegrown and unadorned is best.

For those who disagreed, the essential techniques of Roman perfumery endured into the Middle Ages. By the turn of the millennium, perfume's possibilities were vastly improved with the slow revival of the Eastern trade and the steady influx of Arab science and know-how. Distillation, acquired from the Arabs, enabled the extraction of flower essences, thereby beefing up the new perfumery and reducing its reliance on stronger gums, resins, and spices. Even so, a Roman would have recognized most of the ingredients and their social purposes alike. In medieval times, perfumes were commonly made on a base of oil or animal fats, with the addition of wine, spices, and aromatics. The same qualities recommended spices as before; and the more exotic the ingredients, the greater the cachet. The Spanish Franciscan Juan Gil de Zamora (ca. 1240–ca. 1320) writes of the use of fat from exotic animals such as leopards and camels with wine and cinnamon. The fat was first cut away from the flesh, then cooked in wine, then taken off the heat and left overnight. On the following day, more wine was added; then the mixture was ground, stirred, and left to sit awhile, then finally reheated with seven exotic oils. At the final stage, various fruits such as plums were added, along with the old staples of Greek and Roman perfumery, primarily cinnamon and cassia. He gives a formula for a medieval prototype of the underarm deodorant, advising a timely application of cinnamon, cloves, and wine to counter a stinking armpit.

Bad breath was another medieval affliction amenable to a little spice. Jean de Meun (ca. 1240–ca. 1305), author of the second part of the *Roman de la rose,* advised a woman with bad breath never to speak to others on an empty stomach: "If possible, she should keep her mouth away from people's noses." In the eleventh century Peter Damian—the same, remember, who compared Cluny to a garden of spices and who imagined their perfumes wafting through Paradise—refers to the wives of noblemen who "carnally" chewed spices so as to freshen their breath; whereas the only things they should be chewing on, in Damian's opinion, were their psalms and prayers, "so you might have a sweet odor in the sight of God." Still less happily, Chaucer's Absalom chewed cardamom before his disastrous attempt to seduce the Miller's Wife.

Here too, as with perfumes, some regarded the trick as just that, the genuinely savory woman having no need of artificial enhancement. Such seems to have been the thinking of England's King Henry VII as he looked through the courts of Europe for a new wife in 1505. He sent three trusted gentlemen to make an assessment of one candidate, the young queen of Naples, specifying that they were "to note the colours of her hair," "specially to note her complexion," "to mark whether there appear any hair about her lips or not," "to mark her breasts and paps, whether they be big or small"; and so on and so forth. The breath of his potential queen was of some importance to Henry, his instructions requiring that his ambassadors "approach as near to her mouth as they honestly may, to the intent that they may feel the condition of her breath, whether it be sweet or not, and to mark at every time when they speak with her if they feel a savour of spices, rose water, or musk by the breath of her mouth or not."

The ambassadors reported back satisfactorily: "We have approached as nigh unto her visage as that conveniently we might do, and we could feel no savour of any spices or waters, and we think verily by the favour of her visage and cleanness of her complexion and of her mouth that the said queen is like for to be of a sweet savour and well eyred." A more telling complaint was her lack of cash; Henry remained a widower.

That the bad-breathed should have used spices in the absence of toothpaste is perhaps no wonder; but why was it that the smell of spices was considered not merely attractive but sexy? It is, at present, a question with no satisfactory answer. Scientists have long known of affinities between scent and sex drive, though their findings tend to be more suggestive than definitive. It is true that the part of the brain that processes smells also deals with appetites. People lacking a sense of smell commonly report diminished sex drive, and certain odors can indeed stimulate desire. Freud claimed as much in *Civilization and Its Discontents,* admittedly on a somewhat speculative basis, and that the repression of such responses is a necessary condition of civilized life. None of which, of course, says much about spices in particular. The safest argument is the most modest, that advanced by the anthropologists, who have tended to look more at traditions and beliefs, less at innate than learned responses. If the nose "knows" that spices smell sexy, then conceivably the body will respond accordingly; if faith can move mountains, it can move much else besides.

And that the nose has known of spices' sexiness, it should now be clear, is not to be doubted. According to the American sexologist James Leslie McCary, it still does. In his article "Aphrodisiacs and Anaphrodisiacs" he turns a scientific eye on the old belief that the best way of bedding a potential partner is to serve him or her a fine meal. McCary put the hypothesis to the test by preparing a dessert of pears and strawberries soaked in Cointreau, "drenched in a fragrant sauce of beaten egg yolks, confectioner's sugar, cloves and cinnamon." On being questioned in a controlled environment, more than half the subjects commented that the dish was "very 'sexy.' " McCary's reasoning as to why stemmed from texture, taste, and aroma: "The dessert is smooth, rich and creamy in texture—qualities we subconsciously equate with sexuality. In addition, its redolence (cloves, cinnamon, liqueur) is 'exotic,' another word we tend, however vicariously, to identify with sexual concepts." So nourished, we have a perfectly scientific explanation as to why "it is only natural . . . to be well prepared for the ultimate physical and emotional expression—love-making."

By the standards of spices this is mild stuff, advocates of the airborne method having traditionally made still grander claims. Perfumes have the supreme advantage of being delivered invisibly, their effect all the more subtle for being purely aerial. An eighteenth-century charlatan by the name of Dr. James Graham gave public lectures in which he hawked one of his products, a "celestial, or medico, magnetico, musico, electrical bed," an extraordinary contraption guaranteed to increase desire through a battery of the senses. As Graham promised his audience:

> The sublime, the magnificent, and, I may say, the supercelestial dome of the bed, which contains the odiferous, balmy and ethereal spices, odors and essences, and which is the grand magazine or reservoir of those vivifying and invigorating influences which are exhaled and dispersed by the breathing of the music and by the attenuating, repelling, and accelerating force of the electrical fire—is very curiously inlaid or wholly covered on the underside with brilliant plates of looking-glass, so disposed as to reflect the various attractive charms of the happy recumbent couple, in the most flattering, most agreeable, and most enchanting style.

For a small additional fee a rented orchestra would ensure a successful session of great passion, at the bargain-basement cost of £50 a session.

Graham's clients presumably knew what they were letting themselves in for, but part of the attraction of the airborne method—and to others its danger—was that it could be administered to an unwitting recipient. What better than to assault the unsuspecting object of one's attentions with an invisible battery of seductive scents? The most spectacular claim is made in *The Perfumed Garden* by Sheikh Mohammed al-Nefzaoui, a traditional Arab sex manual written in the fifteenth century at the request of the prime minister of Sultan Abdelaziz al-Hafsi, the Hafsid governor of Tunisia and Algeria. Part practical instruction manual, partly a collection of racy anecdotes, it is one of very few works improved by translation, further enlivened by Sir Richard Burton's rendering into fruity Victorian English.

As the title suggests, perfume is the most subtle and refined instrument of seduction: "The use of perfumes, by man as well as by woman, excites to the act of copulation. The woman, inhaling the perfumes employed by the man, becomes intoxicated; and the use of scents has often proved a strong help to man, and assisted him in getting possession of a woman." The most remarkable instance cited by the good sheikh is the tale of the lecherous goings-on and cunning seduction of the false prophet Moçailama, "the impostor, the son of Kaiss (whom God may curse!), that he pretended to have the gift of prophecy, and imitated the Prophet of God (blessings and salutations to him)." When challenged by a second impostor, a prophetess, to prove his skills, Moçailama was perplexed: How could he possibly hope to convince his rival of his fraudulent claims? As he pondered the problem, a lecherous-minded old man approached him with a solution for his perplexity: he should seduce himself out of trouble.

The method was simple. Before his meeting with the prophetess, he should erect a tent and fill it with the scent of flowers and burning spices. "When you find the vapor strong enough to impregnate water, sit down on your throne, and send for the prophetess to come and see you in the tent, where she will be alone with you. When you are thus together there, and she inhales the perfumes, she will delight in the same, all her bones will be relaxed in a soft repose, and finally she will be swooning. When you see her thus far gone, ask her to grant you her favors; she will not hesitate to accord them. Having once possessed her, you will be freed of the embarrassment caused to you."

Moçailama needed no further bidding. He did as the old lecher advised, and when the prophetess was seated there the irresistible perfume worked its tricks: "She lost all presence of mind, and became embarrassed and confused." Moçailama wooed her with his irresistible charm: "Come, let me have possession of you; this place has been prepared for that purpose. If you like you may lie on your back, or you can place yourself on all fours, or kneel as in prayer, with your brow touching the ground, and your crupper in the air, forming a tripod. Whichever position you prefer, speak, and you shall be satisfied."

Befuddled by the perfume, she was unable to decide: "I want it done in all ways!" she exclaimed. "Let the revelation of God descend upon me, O Prophet of the Almighty!"

When Burton was working on this translation, Queen Victoria sat on the throne of England, and the reception for this sort of thing was not unmixed. Such images were grist for the mill of those who saw in spices one of the hallmarks of the sensual decadence of the East. It was perhaps inevitable that spices came to be considered the aroma of the libidinous Oriental. Yet while scholars have generally regarded such attitudes as a modern phenomenon, part and parcel of imperialist assumptions of cultural superiority, in the case of spices the association is apparently as old as knowledge of the East itself. In the eyes of their critics, spices' exoticism, so large a part of their appeal, reappeared as an insidious moral poison, their foreignness not an asset but a problem. It was, moreover, an idea the Hebrew prophet shared with the pagan Roman. In his poem on the civil war that ended the Roman Republic, Lucan (A.D. 39–65) stresses the decadent smells pervading the banquet Cleopatra laid on for Caesar, painting a picture of oriental decay and oily debauch reclining on couches amid the gorgeous splendors of the Nile. In her gilded palace, Cleopatra served her guests every luxurious dainty of her realms, shamelessly showing her décolletage in fashionably fatigued silk (ancient grunge!): luxury, so Lucan would have it, never before seen by the honest Roman soldiers. Conquered, the effeminate Easterners unmanned the conquering Romans:

> Their hair drenched with cinnamon,
> Still fresh in the foreign air and smelling of its native land,
> And cardamom, newly imported . . .

In the works of Christian polemicists the Roman critique of cinnamon as vain and pointless luxury returned with new vigor. In a Christian universe scent acquired a troubling ambiguity: at once a metaphor of beauty and devotion—"You are the odor of Christ," said the apostle—it was also, proverbially so the sense of seduction, harbinger of a dangerous irrationality. Perfumes were particularly insidious corrupters of the flesh for being subtle and invisible. To Clement of Alexandria (ca. 150–ca. 211), leader of the early Christian community in Alexandria, "attention to sweet smells is a bait which draws us into sensual lusts." His opinion was that the model maiden should studiously avoid all perfumers and all other such places, where women cavort like so many whores slouching in the brothel.

From here it was but a short step to argue that to smell bad was to smell good. The Christian ideal was not odorless but malodorous, an instinct admirably summarized in a life of Saint Arsenius the Anchorite (ca. 354–ca. 455) attributed to Rufinus of Aquileia (ca. 345–410/11). Wracked with guilt and shame for the Babylonian luxuriousness of his former life, the sweet perfumes that delighted his senses, Arsenius turned his back on a life of riches and ease and retreated to a cell in the Egyptian desert where he slept on rotting palm mats dampened with old and stinking water. His fellow monks complained of the stench, to which he replied that he had nothing but scorn for the sweet smell of incense and musk. He would rather put up with foul stenches in return for that sweetest of odors that his soul would enjoy in the hereafter. It was a simple trade-off between the pleasures of this life and those of the next, which, as Arsenius saw matters, was no choice at all. Were it otherwise, when the last trumpet sounded the riches and pleasures on which his body had feasted on Earth would condemn his soul to an unavoidable perdition.

As far as spices were concerned, then, proverbial desirability meant proverbial peril. Cinnamon in particular was singled out by no less an authority than Saint Augustine (354–430), bemoaning his misspent youth when he "walked the streets of Babylon, in whose filth I was rolled, as if in cinnamon and precious ointments." There was more to this note of corruption than a Church father's notoriously acute nose for sin. In repudiating cinnamon Augustine was merely repeating the biblical truth. For all spices' appearance in mystic guise in the Song, they also recalled Ezekiel's ruined city of Tyre, with her cassia, calamus, and "best of all kinds of spices," wrecked by the east wind from the heart of the sea. And after Tyre, there was Babylon. The same apocalyptic literature that placed spices in Paradise also located them among "the fruits," as Revelation addresses the fallen city, "that thy soul lusted over":

> *Alas! Alas! Thou great city,*
> *Thou mighty city Babylon!*
> *In one hour has thy judgment come.*
> *And the merchants of the earth weep and mourn for her, since no one buys*
> *their cargo anymore, cargo of gold, silver, jewels and pearls, fine linen,*
> *purple, silk and scarlet, all kinds of scented wood, all articles of ivory,*
> *all articles of costly wood, bronze, iron and marble, cinnamon, spice,*
> *incense, myrrh, frankincense, wine, oil, fine flour and wheat, cattle and*
> *sheep, horses and chariots, and slaves.*

As the Song was to the poet, so this passage was to the predicant: as spices were the food of love, so were they tinder for the jeremiad. In an age saturated in scripture and not short of apocalyptic instincts of its own, it was hard, if not impossible, to look on them as innocent.

Not all, of course, took such an extreme view. It is true, on the one hand, that a dogged minority made heroic efforts to allegorize the shattered city's cinnamon and spices as symbols of vanished virtues, so reconciling the evangelist's searing vision with other biblical passages where spices appeared in more mystical guise. But others, the majority, were more inclined to see spices as symptomatic of the foul excess of Babylon-Rome, symbolic of the "stinking life of the heretics" or the luxurious excess for which it was made desolate, as the Apocalypse phrased it. This, the prevailing view, was at least as old as the hugely influential early Christian martyr Saint Hippolytus (ca. 170–ca. 236), presbyter and antipope, author of the treatise *Concerning Antichrist*. At best Babylon's luxuries epitomized the false glitter and promise of earthly goods; at worst they were yet more symptoms of its fornication and "excessive luxuries," the "maddening wine of her adulteries," on which the great merchants of the earth waxed rich and for which they were annihilated. "How much she hath glorified herself, and lived deliciously, so much torment and sorrow give her."

When the apostle John wrote these words from the Aegean island of Patmos (as tradition would have it), by Babylon he meant not Babylon of Mesopotamia, then a mere satrapy within the Parthian empire, but the real mistress of the world: Rome. And it is no coincidence that the apocalyptist's catalogue of Babylonian riches reads like a summary of the Roman luxury trade—indeed they offer, in a backhanded way, the clearest indication of how esteemed a luxury cinnamon and spices were. The Apocalypse corresponds closely to the official lists of the Eastern luxury articles subject to duty as they entered the Red Sea by order of the (Christian) emperor Justinian (483–565): cinnamon, ivory, linen, pearls, and gold. The same qualities of sensual luxuriousness that recommended spices also condemned them, crying out for the apocalyptist's lash. God would remember Babylon's iniquities.

As, apparently, did everyone else. As the Eastern trade emerged from the long torpor of the European Dark Ages, to the commentators if not necessarily the consumers the scouring of the Apocalypse soured their proverbial sweetness. If anything, the growth of the trade did not so much detract from as inflate their conspicuous perils. The sulfur kept intruding. Early in the twelfth century, precisely at the moment when cinnamon returned to Europe in volumes not witnessed since Roman times, Hugh of Saint-Victor looked to spices as proof that Rome's decadent luxuriousness was repeating itself. Stretching east beyond the new Babylons he saw arising from the twelfth-century "renaissance," Hugh imagined vast trains of camels, merchants burdened with their wares, bearing all manner of spices, rare and precious garments, huge masses of metals, every precious stone, horses and slaves without number—which was, in fact, not a bad description of the caravans that brought the spices west across Arabia. The world was on the move once more, but to Hugh the most conspicuous of the Eastern luxuries represented no triumph of enterprise but the resurfacing of the human avidity for lucre. Cinnamon was the seasoning of calamity.

The moral was not necessarily limited to the apocalyptist's theme of imperial decline, for spices could equally well do didactic duty for what we would now call issues of personal consumption. Indeed, with their libidinous encumbrance there was scarcely a luxury better suited to the purposes of the doctrine, much beloved of the medieval moralist, of "how anything even remotely enjoyable is bad for you." The idea was a sort of inverse epicureanism: the sense, in the formulation of Pope Leo the Great, that "that which delights the outer does most harm to the inner man." Spices surface in this exemplary capacity in the text known as *The Alphabet of Tales,* a collection of edifying stories that circulated in various versions from the thirteenth century on, under the heading of "how misery and disasters frequently follow bodily delights." A fifteenth-century English version includes a story of a duke's wife so addicted to luxury that she would not wash herself with any water but the dew gathered by her maidens on a summer morning. (One wonders what she did in winter.) It being beneath her dignity to eat meat with her hands, she insisted on cutlery—the detail reveals much about medieval table manners—and "she would make her bed so redolent of spice that it was a marvel to tell of. And as she lived in this manner, by the righteousness of God, she was so smitten with cancer and sickness that she rotted so . . . that no creature might bear the smell of her."

It was, in other words, a suitably stinky comeuppance for her too-fragrant hedonism.* On the other hand, spices were not all bad. So foul was the stench of the festering noblewoman that all her servants left but for a single handmaid, who "might not come near her for the stink, but for the many sweet-savoring spices at her neck; and even so she could not tarry with her any length of time for the horrible stink."

In the scheme of these zero-sum morals, of equal and opposite reaction between now and the hereafter, spices made for something of a moralist's bromide. Precisely on account of their proverbial sweetness, their prominence among the luxuries of the medieval nobility, they formed a telling and, or so it was hoped, salutary contrast with a life of

---

*Readers of Dante will recognize the notion of *contrapasso,* a form of punishment befitting the crime.

Christian austerity—or, which amounted to much the same thing, the bitterness of death and hellfire. For sweetness now surely meant everlasting stench later. After the cinnamon came brimstone. So Peter Damian, that mystical author so reliant on spices in evoking his mystical transports but so disgusted with them in the real world, imagined the damned in Hell: "They shall shriek through their teeth, who here delight in their gluttony; will bewail without end those things in which they delight in here voluptuously; who here inhale the aromas of spices, and long for their tang, shall there be wracked by a sulfurous stench, and a pitchy cloud of smoke shall cover the earth." If the wages of luxury did not find you in this life, they would surely get you in the next.

Even when spices were the flavor of the age, then, their aromas were received with ambivalence. There was agreement that they smelled sensual but sharp disagreement as to whether this was a good or a bad thing. They savored of Paradise, yet they were at the same time incitements to carnality; desire was laced with repugnance. It is particularly startling to find this sense of misgiving among those who expended the greatest energies in their acquisition. In Venice the spice trade, despite being a crucial sector of the economy, long contributed to images of a sensual, luxury-addicted city in the throes of imperial decline. Even at the apex of the Age of Discovery, when Europeans returned to the spice lands for the first time since Roman times, there were those who detected a whiff of corruption in their aromas. Peter Martyr, the chaplain to Ferdinand and Isabella, managed at the same time to celebrate Spanish prowess in the search for spice while bewailing their pernicious, emasculating influence. Writing of Magellan's voyage to the Moluccas, he saw no contradiction in dismissing the spices he sought as "delicacies which render men effeminate." He was, moreover, well aware of the antiquity of the notion. Of the Moluccas themselves he said, "From the date of Rome's luxury they have, so to say, glided into our ken, not without serious consequences to us; for characters soften, men become effeminate, virtue weakens, and people are seduced by these voluptuous odors, perfumes, and spices." Yet the same corrupting spices were the point of the exercise.

It is no longer the fashion for historians to draw such moralizing generalizations, yet in this case some of Peter's assumptions still prevail, albeit less conspicuously or less consciously. The guilt has gone, but not the premise of spices' sensuality. For just as he saw them as voluptuous and erotically charged, so too the modern perfume industry, with its breathless promises of sophistication and seduction, remains a major consumer of spices. Calvin Klein's Obsession contains nutmeg and clove; Opium by Yves Saint Laurent contains pepper, and there are many other such examples. Ginger, mace, and cardamom are all common additives. If we are to take the advertising at face value, spices remain as seductive as they ever were, even if we are less conscious of the fact.

Chiefly, however, modern notions of the sexiness of spice are more literary than literal, but no less real for that. In New York City there is a spice store called Aphrodisia—the name says it all. The association runs so deep as to have intruded into modern pop culture. In the late 1990s, the Spice Girls shot like a gaudy, squawking comet through the outer orbits of pop stardom before, in obedience to the Newtonian physics of celebrity, the acrimonious plummet back to Earth and bust-up. Part of what made them spicy was, needless to say, their feisty sex appeal. Subliminally or otherwise, they honored a grand tradition. Here is the entry for "spicy" in the *Collins English Thesaurus:* "Aromatic, flavoursome, hot, piquant, pungent, savoury, seasoned, tangy, broad, hot, improper, indecorous, indelicate, off-colour, ribald, risqué, scandalous, sensational, suggestive, titillating, unseemly"—all in all, not a bad summary of the discussion at hand and the perfect epitaph, oddly enough, for the Spice Girls.

AFTERWORD; OR,
HOW TO MAKE A SMALL PENIS SPLENDID

This chapter was written on the assumption that any aphrodisiac effect of spices existed more in the mind than in the body: that their effect, if any, was a matter of belief, rather than any strictly physiological response. Considering some of the wild claims made on behalf of spices, this seemed both a reasonable and necessary working method. And there was perhaps none wilder than those made in what is in every sense the spiciest of the works on the topic mentioned above, *The Perfumed Garden.*

Here is a work that for once fully merits the academician's notion of phallocentricity. For the sheikh, penis function and size are constant

preoccupations, in which connection he cites spices in all their multi-
farious potency. They can be rubbed on directly—even better, so the
sheikh would have it, than the melted fat of a camel's hump, leather,
hot pitch, or live leeches. His advice, at times, seems rash: "If you
would make the enjoyment still more voluptuous, masticate a little
cubeb-pepper or cardamom-grains of the large species; put a certain
quantity of it on the head of your member, and then go to work. This
will procure for you, as well as for the woman, a matchless enjoyment."
Spices can even inspire a woman to pack up her belongings and move
in: "If you wish the woman to be inspired with a great desire to cohabit
with you, take a little of cubebs, pyrether,* ginger and cinnamon,
which you will have to masticate just before joining her; then moisten
your member with your saliva and do her business for her. From that
moment she will have such an affection for you that she can scarcely be
without you."

But this is small beer alongside the contents of Chapter 18, "Prescriptions for Increasing the Dimension of Small Members and Making
Them Splendid." In light of the extreme importance of the topic, the
author keeps this discussion for the end of the book, "because from a
good-sized member there springs the affection and love of women."
The converse also applies: "Many men, solely by reason of their
insignificant members, are, as far as coition is concerned, objects of
aversion to women."

Fortunately, a remedy is at hand:

A man . . . with a small member, who wants to make it grand or
fortify it for the coitus, must rub it before copulation with tepid
water, until it gets red and extended by the blood flowing into it,
in consequence of the heat; he must then anoint it with a mixture
of honey and ginger, rubbing it in sedulously. Then let him join
the woman; he will procure for her such pleasure that she objects
to him getting off her again. Another remedy consists in a compound made of a moderate quantity of pepper, lavender, galanga,
and musk, reduced to powder, sifted, and mixed up with honey
and preserved ginger. The member, after having been first washed

*An aromatic North African root, sometimes known as pellitory. It has a light aroma and a
persistent, pungent taste.

in warm water, is then vigorously rubbed with the mixture; it will
then grow large and brawny, and afford to the woman a marvellous feeling of voluptuousness.

While this is quite possibly the grandest of all aphrodisiac claims
made on behalf of spices, it may just be true, if somewhat exaggerated.
Alan Hirsch of Chicago's Smell and Taste Treatment and Research
Foundation has recently published a number of findings pointing to
much the same conclusion, provided one substitutes the sheikh's
"splendid" augmentation for the more medically conventional notion
of an increase in penile blood flow. In one study Hirsch exposed male
volunteers to a variety of aromas while measuring their penile blood
flow by means of a small pressure cuff. In the first, preliminary study
carried out on medical students, cinnamon buns were found to produce
the most dynamic response. However, when the study was repeated on
a broader scale, cinnamon buns and unnamed "oriental spice" paled
into insignificance alongside a whopping 40 percent increase for lavender and pumpkin pie, with doughnuts in second place at 31.5 percent.

On the basis of his findings Hirsch has argued that scent can have a
powerful impact on sexuality; and indeed his results would seem to
confirm, in a minor way, the spice-sex association. They do not, however, settle the learned-versus-innate debate, and either way doughnuts
trump a spice, at least as far as the Chicago male is concerned. (Though
Hirsch did find that his "oriental spice" had the greatest effect on the
subjects who had sexual intercourse most frequently. It may also be significant that all the volunteers for the study were recruited by adver-
tisements on a Chicago classic rock station—arguably a particularly
doughnut-friendly demographic.)

But if the jury is still out on humans, there is a scrap of marginally
more promising evidence concerning rodents, stumbled on inadvertently by a team of Saudi scientists who were looking not for aphrodisiacs but at the toxicity of cinnamon, *Cinnamomum zeylanicum.* Studies of
this nature have long been of interest to the scientific community, anxious to determine whether the antibacterial, antimicrobial properties of
spices have potential industrial or medical applications. The results
would have confirmed a monk's suspicions and gratified the sheikh.

In this case the tests were carried out on laboratory mice. The mice
were separated into three groups and fed a diet including varying quan-

tities of cinnamon. The first group was kept as a control and fed no
spice. The second group was fed a diet high in cinnamon, and the third
was practically stuffed with spice, like geese fattened for foie gras.

The cinnamon-fed mice produced some interesting results. As far as
toxicity was concerned, the tests suggested that the spice has very few
or very mild negative effects. The control group showed no observable
change other than a substantial increase in weight—too many calories,
too little scuttling about. The second group showed no major negative
effect, and they did not put on weight. The third likewise showed no
observable negative effect, aside from a minor reduction in their hemo-
globin count. They also stayed thin relative to the other mice. Of
greater interest was an unlooked-for side effect: the cinnamon-stuffed
mice all experienced abnormal genital growth, and the males experienced a dramatic increase in their sperm count. These more abundant sperm also proved to be far more motile than normal—better
swimmers.

So far no similar tests on humans have been published, or none that I
could find (or that seemed worth believing), but the results look
promising, particularly in an age when men around the world are
reported to be suffering from declining sperm counts. Somewhat belatedly, the experiment offers the first shred of scientific evidence that
maybe the advocates of spice were onto something after all, not just in
terms of a placebo effect but in a deeper, physiological sense. Admittedly, there are those who might feel that abnormal genital growth and
more abundant sperm are not necessarily what one looks for in an
aphrodisiac, and perhaps cinnamon cannot deliver erections on demand
à la Viagra. But in the real business of aphrodisiacs it might do a good
deal more. Cinnamon did not exactly make of these lab mice sexual athletes so much as marathon runners. And they stayed thin, too.

IV

SPIRIT

THE CINNAMON PLANT
Acosta, *Tractado de las drogas* (Burgos, 1578)

CHAPTER 6

○

FOOD OF THE GODS

Drive here the finest herds;
Pile the harvests of the Indians on the altars,
Whatever the Arabs pick from fragrant trees;
Let the rich fumes pour forth. . . .

—SENECA (ca. 4 B.C.–A.D. 65), *Hercules Oetaeus*

Some natures are so sensitive to certain odors! It would indeed
be an attractive question to study, as much in a pathological as
in a physiological sense. Priests are well aware of their importance, having always mixed aromatics in their ceremonies with
the aim of numbing the rational faculties and provoking a state of
ecstasy, which is easily accomplished with women, who are more
delicate than men.

—GUSTAVE FLAUBERT, *Madame Bovary,* 1856

HOLY SMOKE

If Ovid is to be believed, a promise of spice helped lubricate the most
famous seduction of all time. In his *Heroides* the Augustan poet relates
the agonies of indecision undergone by Helen of Sparta as she debates
whether to abandon home, reputation, and family so as to run off with
Paris, her smooth-talking, good-looking houseguest. Ultimately, his
blandishments and put-downs of her boorish, "rustic" husband decided
the issue. The ships were waiting offshore, ready to whisk her away:

The Trojan fleet is ready, fitted out with arms and men;
presently wind and oars will make swift our way.

You will go through Dardanian {Trojan} towns, a great queen,
and the common people will believe that a new goddess is among them.
Wherever you are, the flames will offer up cinnamon, and a sacrificial
victim will strike the bloodied earth.

It worked, and Helen of Sparta became Helen of Troy.

If the story is ageless, the terms of Paris's offer are anything but. Poleaxed carcasses and cinnamon-scented flames might seem a curious way to spark a romance and a war, but in the ancient world, something close to the reverse was the case. Whether to the urban sophisticates of Augustan Rome who read Ovid's poem or, if she ever existed, to the Bronze Age queen known to legend as Helen, the precise force of the offer was unmistakable. It was, in fact, of a piece with Paris's offer that Helen would be treated as a goddess. Along with various other spices and aromatics harvested in tropical Asia and ferried across unknown seas and deserts by ship and caravan, cinnamon was the food of the gods.

Long before there is any evidence that spices were eaten, they were put to applications variously described as religious or—the distinction is largely a matter of perspective—the magical. Ovid's dialogue was, needless to say, a wholly imagined version of an event that may or may not have happened more than a thousand years earlier, yet it is, all the same, a reminder of one of the most important and enduring themes in the history of spices. And as to the practicalities of spiced worship, the words he puts into Paris's mouth are accurate enough.

In Ovid's day, in the last decades before the birth of Christ, scenes not unlike those evoked by Paris occurred on a daily basis in hundreds of temples and shrines around the empire. As Paris promised Helen, spices were typically burned in incense or simply added to the flames in the temple brazier during the performance of religious rituals. Alternatively, they could be infused in perfumes and unguents applied to the cultic statues or the worshipers themselves. Exotic, rare, and inexplicable, they were among the most esteemed props of ancient worship. Not the least of spices' attractions was their practicality. Mixed with incense, they released a sweet, penetrating aroma, adding depth and potency to various Near Eastern and Arabian gums and resins—which is precisely what they still do in commercially produced incenses, many of which use cinnamon, pepper, mace, ginger, cloves, and nutmeg. In the backstreets of Indian towns it is still possible to find workers preparing blends of incense, grinding the spices into a paste that is then rolled into cones or rubbed onto thin wooden sticks. It is a custom that has survived intact since antiquity.

Paganism, in not so many words, smelled. A typical scene of worship is described in *The Acts of Sharbil,* an early Christian work composed during the reign of the emperor Trajan (A.D. 98–117). The setting is a festival in the Syrian town of Edessa:

> The whole city was gathered together by the great altar which was in the middle of the town, opposite the Record Office, all the gods [i.e., their statues] having been brought together, and decorated, and sitting in honor. . . . And all the priests were offering incenses of spices and libations, and an odor of sweetness was diffusing itself around, and sheep and oxen were being slaughtered, and the sound of the harp and the drum was heard in the whole town.

Outside the great festivals, the aromas of spices, incense, and perfumes permeated ancient religion as thoroughly as religion permeated life itself. Every town of any size had dozens of temples and cultic centers whose tutelary deities were honored with fragrant offerings and their festivals marked with processions of devotees bearing censers and smoking jars of perfume. Sailors and travelers carried portable incense burners known as *thymiateria,* often shaped in the form of figurines with a concave top; examples have been recovered from the wreck of the Lion Ship, excavated from the silt of Pisa harbor, where it sank early in the second century B.C. Outside the routine of daily worship, special occasions called for special aromas. When the Syrian-born emperor Elagabalus ascended the throne in A.D. 218, he thanked his tutelary deity with the finest wines, animals, and the richest aromatics, while a chorus of Syrian beauties "performed their lascivious dances to the sound of barbarian music."

The Romans hated the luxurious Eastern ways of Elagabalus and his foreign cult, but they could have had no quibble with his spices, for by now Roman religion was thoroughly odiferous. Within the Roman home garlands and fragrances were offered each morning to the Lares and Penates, the ancestral household gods guarding the domestic gates and hearth. (In Bali the locals make similar offerings to this day.) Cicero writes of incense offered to statues of heroes in the streets, and beyond the city walls the countryside was dotted with shrines adorned with the fragrant offerings of passersby. Virgil describes the hundred altars of

Venus fuming with Sabaean incense and redolent of fresh garlands. When Seneca's Hercules thanks the gods for another victory, he calls for the best sacrificial victims and Indian spices.

The gods of love, we have seen, smelled especially divine, but all gods liked a sweet smell. It was to win their favor that athletes hopeful of success in the games used perfumes either on their bodies or in offerings before competition—the original performance-enhancing drug, with the significant advantage that blame for any failures could easily be deflected. To wit, Philostratus (ca. A.D. 170–ca. 245) writes of athletes who put their losses down to poor perfume selection: "If only I had burnt this and not that perfume, I would have won." During games held by King Antiochus Epiphanes (ca. 215–164 B.C.) of Syria at Daphne, spectators were anointed with one of fifteen perfumes, including cinnamon, spikenard, and saffron, then sent away at the conclusion with crowns of myrrh and frankincense. Lovesick Romans burned spices to win over the gods of love, reasoning that any failures were their own doing: "If the experiment does not come off, he [the lover] is as ready as ever to blame some oversight, reasoning that he forgot to burn this spice, or to sacrifice or melt up that."

So potent was perfume's reputation that in republican times its use in a secular context rankled of sacrilege. When Julius Caesar entered Rome in triumphal procession in 46 B.C., he was flanked by attendants bearing censers of sweet-smelling perfumes. However well the gesture went over with the masses, among the senatorial elite Caesar's trespass on a custom previously reserved for the gods was viewed with outrage, as though he were some oriental monarch posturing as the son of Heaven. Within two years Caesar would get his comeuppance, but the assassins' daggers resulted, in the long run, only in Caesar's deification as the martyred head of a new, imperial dynasty. The time was not far off when all of Rome's emperors would be numbered among the gods and propitiated with perfumes, spice, and incense.

There is no knowing what perfumes Caesar burned, but there is a good chance they contained cinnamon. By this time, this was far and away the most esteemed and important of the Eastern spices, followed closely by its poor relation and look-alike, cassia. In powdered form, the spice was easily dissolved in a base of fat or oil; or the sticks could be added to the flames—holy tinder. In a sense they were sacred, magical. Philostratus tells of a magical second-century brew of spices, gems, and chopped snake that supposedly imparted the power to converse with animals. The emperor Vespasian (A.D. 9–79) dedicated crowns of cinnamon covered with beaten gold in the temple of Peace. Pliny the Elder had seen a huge piece of cinnamon kept on permanent display in a gold dish in a temple on the Palatine, much as Christian churches would in due course exhibit their own prodigious, miracle-working relics.

The Romans shared this reverence for cinnamon with older cultures to the east. The Greek ruler of Syria Seleucus II, in power from 247 to 226, dedicated two pounds each of cinnamon and cassia to the temple of Apollo at Miletus. Even at this time the spice had been known in the Mediterranean for centuries: early in the sixth century B.C., the book of the prophet Ezekiel mentions cassia among the exotic luxuries of Tyre. In Greece around the same time, Sappho wrote of the cassia burned at the wedding of Hector and Andromache as they processed through the doomed city of Troy. It was long the assumption among philologists that Sappho's cassia and the modern spice could not possibly be the same thing, but that the poetess was familiar with the spice no longer seems impossible. A little to the south, on the island of Samos, German archaeologists found cinnamon in a deposit dated to the seventh century B.C. The find was made on the site once occupied by the temple of Hera, where it was doubtless offered to the goddess, in or before Sappho's lifetime.

And herein is cause for wonder. There is no evidence that the Greeks of Sappho's day knew India, and for centuries thereafter it remained more a notion than a place, little more than generic shorthand for the East. But if India was a mystery, its spices were doubly so. They were, in a sense, magical if not divine, arriving by unknown means from the vast blank spaces on the map, spaces populated by dragons, gods, and monsters. From mystery grew mystique. In the fifth century B.C., the Greek historian Herodotus started a long tradition with his account of the cinnamon harvest:

> The way they [the Arabians] get cinnamon is even more extraordinary. They cannot say where it comes from and where in the world it grows (except that some of them use an argument from probability to claim that it grows in the parts where Dionysus was brought up). But they say that the sticks which the Phoenicians have taught us to call "cinnamon" are carried by large birds to their nests, which are built of mud plastered onto crags on sheer mountainsides, where no man can climb. Under these circum-

stances, the Arabians have come up with the following clever procedure. They cut up the bodies of dead yoke animals such as oxen
and donkeys into very large pieces and take them there; then they
dump the joints near the nests and withdraw a safe distance. The
birds fly down and carry the pieces of meat back up to their
nests—but the joints are too heavy for the nests. The nests break
and fall to the ground, where the Arabians come and get what
they came for. That is how cinnamon is collected in that part of
Arabia, and from there it is sent all over the world.

Even the sober Theophrastus (ca. 372–287 B.C.), Aristotle's successor as the head of the Lyceum, was scarcely less colorful:

They say that cinnamon grows in deep glens, that in these there
are deadly snakes that have a deadly bite. Against these they protect their hands and feet before they go down into the glens, and
then, when they have brought up the cinnamon, they divide it
into three portions, one of which they leave behind as the lot of
the Sun. And they say that as soon as they leave the spot they see
this take fire.

While the greater part of such explanations was fantasy, it was true
that fires of cinnamon were lit to the sun and various other gods. These
burnt offerings may have been in some sense a reenactment of a mythic
event, understood by the participants as a ritual act of returning the
spice to its divine "owner" or recalling in some sense its solar origins.
According to Pliny, who thought cinnamon grew in Ethiopia, the
plant could not be cut without the sun god's permission, obtainable
only by the sacrifice of forty-four oxen, goats, and rams. No plant
could be cut in the hours of darkness. First some twigs were removed
with a spear and offered to the god, before the rest was cut, peeled, and
given to the merchants who took it to Ocelis on the Red Sea, the port
of the Gabbanites. From there it was conveyed into the Roman world
by the proverbially wealthy Arabians. Shuttling northward through
the shoals and reefs of the Red Sea or following the ancient Arabian
incense route through Mecca and Medina, by camel and dhow they
brought the spice to markets in Egypt or Arabia and on, eventually,
to Rome.

Or so Pliny presumed; this was his best reconstruction of what remained, in the end, a mystery. There was, however, a sense of Eastern origins. According to Ovid, cinnamon was introduced from the East with the cult of Bacchus, god of wine and ecstasy, bringing the sacred aromas back after his conquest of India: "You [Bacchus] were the first to offer cinnamon and incense from the conquered lands." There may be some truth in this, inasmuch as the spice almost certainly arrived with the introduction of older, Eastern cults long accustomed to spiced offerings. Before then, "the altars were without offerings, grass grew on the cold hearth."

Where history and reliable information were lacking, such myths helped fill a gap. And still today some speculation on the ancient spice trade appears scarcely less fabulous than that of the Greeks and Romans. But if the "how" of the ancient spice trade defies an answer, the "why" seems clearer. On some level or another a belief in the auspicious qualities of a pleasant scent is a universal phenomenon. It was, we have seen, an article of Greco-Roman religious belief that the gods smelled divine. And just as the gods, their food, and their clothing were exquisitely sweet-smelling, so there was a fundamental symmetry in mortals offering fragrance to the fragrant immortals. Offering spices to the gods was, essentially, a matter of offering like to like.

For this reason not only spices but many other Mediterranean aromatics served as sacraments before they were seasonings. Saffron, fennel, and coriander all appear in a sacred setting long before there are records of their secular use. Thyme takes its name from the Greek verb "to sacrifice" or "to make a burnt offering." Writing in the fourth century B.C., Theophrastus believed that spices followed incense and locally available herbs to the altar and censer, and no one has been able to come up with a better explanation since. The Egyptians and other cultures of the ancient Near East made use of Arabian and Levantine aromatics such as frankincense, myrrh, balsam, and terebinth* since at least the early third millennium B.C. The name of the principal Phoenician deity, Baal Hammon, means "lord of the perfume altar"; a Sumerian incense stand dating to about 2500 B.C. is shaped in the form of a priest with incense on his head. Throughout the temples and shrines of the ancient Mediterranean the effect of smell was understood more in

---

*Terebinth is obtained from *Pistacia terebinthus*, a tree widespread in the Near East, and the source of Chian turpentine.

spiritual than in aesthetic terms. A sweet smell was a form of "inarticulate prayer."*

As was true of religion in the rest of the ancient world, the Greek and Roman gods came aromatized. In a sense, the gods *were* fragrance. In literary encounters between mortals and immortals the latter are regularly betrayed by their gorgeous aroma. In *The Iliad* Zeus sits perfumed in a fragrant cloud on Olympus, where his fellow gods feast on ineffably fragrant substances called ambrosia and nectar. The latter is some form of supernal beverage, apparently scented with sacramental aromatics such as myrrh or other incenses from the altar, of whose precise nature Homer seems to have had only the vaguest idea. Homeric scholars have speculated whether the nectar and ambrosia of the Homeric epics represent a memory of various Near Eastern aromatics. The word itself is probably derived from a Semitic root meaning "to fume, waft upward as smoke or vapor." If so, nectar was perfume and perfume was nectar, which is to say that the gods ate perfume. Certainly this is how later Greeks understood it. When the physician to Philip of Macedon compared his healing skills to Zeus's own, his employer reprimanded his act of hubris by serving him incense for dinner: if he were indeed fit to compare himself with the gods, then let him feed on aromatic smoke.

Occasionally there are hints that spices themselves were quite literally seen as divine, not merely evoking but in some sense originating from the realm of the supernatural. Spices were regarded as the earthly or not-so-earthly analogue of the gods' nectar and ambrosia. The fourth-century Athenian comic poet Antiphanes compares a particularly sublime perfume to the "cassia-breathing wind of Heaven."

---

*Scientists have looked for the physiological underpinnings of this custom, thus far with modest but suggestive results. It is believed that the part of the brain that processes smells, the limbic system, also plays a role in regulating reproductive behavior, and emotional and motivational states. Some smell-induced recollection can even take the form of a mild "trip." Lyall Watson, author of *Jacobson's Organ,* has gone so far as to suggest that the burning of incense produces a "basic biological euphoria" akin to sexual excitement. Burning incense releases chemicals similar to human steroids that are thought to play a role in human sexual behavior. If so, something along these lines might contribute to a sense of emotional uplift, a feeling of exhilaration amenable to mild religious transport. Less contentiously, perhaps, there is a consensus that smell disrupts and stimulates the conventional workings of the mind: certain aromas have powers of association that can bend perceptions of time and place. As Rousseau observed, smell is the sense of memory and desire, and such evocative powers are arguably not entirely removed from the experience of religious transport. Smell is as ineffable and elusive as the gods themselves, wafting beyond the reach of the rational intellect.

Intriguingly, by the third century B.C., nectar is referred to as the name of a wine. The *Geoponica,* a medieval compilation of ancient manuscripts, gives a recipe for a spiced honey wine: "6 scruples of myrrh, 12 scruples of cassia, 2 scruples of costus, 4 scruples of nard, 4 scruples of pepper, 6 pints of Attic honey, 24 pints of wine, and store in the sun at the rise of the dog-star for 40 days. Some call this nectar." When Agatharchides of Cnidus sailed around Arabia in the second century B.C., he imagined that the "wondrous scent" of its cinnamon and myrrh was none other than the ambrosia of myth. Nearby, so he believed, were the Happy Isles where the illustrious heroes of Homeric epics enjoyed a blessed afterlife.

Yet there was more to the logic of spiced sacrifice than offering of like to like. If spices smelled heavenly, perhaps even originating from some mythic realm, this is also where they went. What strikes moderns as a curious idea was to ancients so obvious as to need no explanation. The gods of the ancients were sky dwellers, celestial beings of the air and the heavens. Though invisible and remote, they were capable of epiphanies, manifesting themselves in more or less physical form, whether in human guise or as a storm, an animal, or a burning bush. And if the air and sky were where the gods were, that was precisely where their burnt offerings ascended.

The literalness of this belief did not prevent the Greeks and Romans from having fun with the idea. Horace, in an ode to Venus, speaks with typically gentle humor of the goddess inhaling incense. In Aristophanes' *Birds* of 414 B.C., the birds of the title form a blockade between Heaven and Earth, preventing the smoke from mankind's sacrifices from rising and thereby starving the gods into a more accommodating mood. The conceit was a long-running joke. Aristophanes' contemporary comedian Pherecrates suggested in his *Tyrannis* that Zeus had created Heaven so as to prevent the gods from hanging around the sweet-smelling altars. Heaven itself is described with the word for a primitive chimney, a hole in the roof for the smoke to pass through. In Roman times the boastful cook of Plautus's *Pseudolus* claims that his food smells so good that the odors fly up to Heaven, where Jupiter gobbles them up.

Later, when the pagan gods were facing a final, fatal challenge, the comic writer Lucian played with the idea more cheekily still. (His irreverence would, ironically, help ensure his popularity among Christians and thus the survival of his works.) In his *Icaromenippus,* or *Sky*

Man, the smoke of the sacrifices functions as a sort of celestial telephone. High on Olympus, Zeus receives prayers by lifting lids in the floor of his palace—manholes to the mortals—accepting the fragrant prayers and rejecting the malodorous. Leaning over one hole, Zeus rejects an impious prayer—"O ye gods, let my father die soon!"—and moving on to the second obliges the pleasant-smelling smoke of the sacrifice with rain for drought-struck Scythia, lightning in Libya, and snow for Greece. He gives the south wind a day off, dispatches a storm to the Adriatic, and sends a thousand bushels of hail to Cappadocia.

Both the gods and the playfulness were quintessentially Greek, but ultimately these were beliefs that reached back to the far older cultures of the Near East. In ancient Mesopotamia and Egypt alike, the notion of the accessibility of Heaven and the possibility of direct communication were clearer still. Just as the ziggurats reached up to the skies, so too was smoke another route to the gods—and for that matter a more accessible stairway to Heaven. In its simplest terms this same rationale of fragrant sacrifice to curry divine favor was common to all major civilizations of the ancient Mediterranean, finding perhaps its clearest expression in one of the oldest texts, an Assyrian version of the flood myth dating from early in the second millennium B.C. Like the more famous Noah, Uta-napishti sits out the deluge in his ark. For six days and seven nights he listens to the rain, until finally "the ocean grew calm, that had thrashed like a woman in labor, the tempest grew still, the Deluge ended." When the floodwaters finally subside, the grateful survivor returns to dry land to thank the gods with a sweet-smelling offering. Like so many diners around a summer barbecue, the gods are drawn to the aromas:

> *I made a libation on the summit of the mountain*
> *By sevens I set out the vessels*
> *Under them I heaped up calamus, cedar-wood, and* rig-gir,
> *The gods smelt the savor; the gods smelt the sweet savor;*
> *The gods gathered like flies about him that offered the sacrifice.*

On emerging from his ark the Hebrew Noah did the same, so mollifying and appeasing his God: "And when the Lord smelled the pleasing odor, the Lord said in his heart, 'I will never again curse the ground because of man, for the imagination of man's heart is evil from his youth; neither will I ever again destroy every living creature as I have done.'"

In Egypt, where the gods carried different names and dressed themselves in the bodies of animals, the premises of aromatic sacrifice were fundamentally the same. When the Greek historian Herodotus traveled through Egypt early in the fifth century B.C., he noted that the Egyptians added spices to their animal sacrifices so as to make them all the more sweeter to their divine recipients. The oldest extant references to aromatics in worship date from the time of the fifth dynasty of ancient Egypt, midway through the third millennium B.C., by which time unguents were used to anoint pharaohs, priests, and the cultic statues of the gods. In the *Pyramid Texts,* a collection of religious formulae dating from the middle of the third millennium B.C., the sacred incense serves a threefold purpose. On the one hand, the texts make it clear that the incense was believed to attract gods, evoking an invisible, numinous presence. Some texts suggest that the incenses were themselves divine, the chosen vessels of the gods or the form in which they appeared. The counterpart and in some sense the cosmic corollary was that the incense drove off demons, attracting good and expelling evil. In practical terms, the holy unguents were used to anoint the priests and the high priest of them all, the pharaoh god-king. An inscription on the base of the Sphinx depicts the pharaoh Thothraes IV, around 1425 B.C., offering aromatic libations to the gods with which he himself is anointed. The hieroglyph used to designate the sacred aromatics means, literally, "that which makes divine." To be anointed with a fragrant substance was to be godlike.

To the Egyptians, moreover, incense not only was pleasing to the gods but also came from the gods. Dating from much the same time is the famous manuscript of the Shipwrecked Sailor, a briny yarn of a castaway lost in the "land of incense"—Arabia? Somalia?—where he is confronted by a terrifying serpent god who threatens to turn him to ashes. To appease his wrath, the terrified sailor offers the god a range of unidentifiable aromatics: "I will cause *ibi, hekenu, iudeneb,* and *khesait* to be brought to thee, and incense of the temples, *wherewith every god is made content,*" pleads the terrified sailor. But his offer is a case of coals to Newcastle, the god replying with a laugh that it is he who made them. So central were these notions to the Egyptian conception of worship that there was a professional class whose job it was to prepare the sacred oils and unguents. Among the bewildering, animal-headed pantheon of the Egyptians there was even a god of perfumers, Shezmou. Over exactly what perfumes Shezmou was god is, unfortunately, largely guesswork. The effort of extracting modern botanical names from the hieroglyphs and substances such as those offered by the shipwreck is a messy business. Like the dazed and terrified castaway, the Egyptians themselves were scarcely any clearer on the source of their aromatics, a semimythical land they knew as "Punt." Located somewhere on the southern shores of the Red Sea, Punt was supplier to the temples and god-kings of the Nile for well over two thousand years. The earliest recorded expedition took place in the time of the pharaoh Sahure, ruler from 2491 to 2477 B.C., although a slave from Punt appears in the court of Cheops (ca. 2589–2566 B.C.), builder of the great pyramid at Giza. For the sake of its aromatics, Punt was the destination of history's first recorded merchant fleet, a representation of which is still to be seen jinking an angular course around the walls of the temple of Deir al-Bahri, carved there by order of the female pharaoh Hatshepsut around 1495 B.C. The reliefs depict a fleet of five ships, complete with sailors climbing aloft, teams of rowers, and steersmen fore and aft, navigating through a sea populated by giant squid and enormous fish. Judging by the nature of the products they acquired in Punt and the appearance of their interlocutors (including a grossly fat, apparently negroid woman; she may represent an early example of a crude racial caricature), modern scholarship generally concurs in situating Punt somewhere in the vicinity of modern Somalia, a voyage of some two thousand miles southward through the treacherous, reefbound waters of the Red Sea. In the words of the accompanying inscription, these intrepid ancient mariners brought back to the Nile "all goodly fragrant woods of God's-Land, heaps of myrrh resin, with fresh myrrh trees, with ebony, and pure ivory, with green gold of Emu, with cinnamon wood, *kheyst* wood, with *ihmut*-incense, *sonter*-incense, eyecosmetic, with apes, monkeys, dogs, and with skins of the southern panther, with natives and their children." The plants were brought back alive, in pots, so as to grow an indigenous supply in the temple gardens. As we shall see, this was far from the last effort to steal the fragrant plants from the lands of their origin.

It was long thought that Punt was the scene of another, more fundamental beginning, the scene where the spice trade first came into being. For lurking among the list of luxuries brought back for Hatshepsut is a hieroglyph that some scholars have translated as cinnamon. Since the first serious scholarly study of the reliefs more than a hundred years ago by James Breasted, sometime professor of Egyptology and oriental history at the University of Chicago, the relevant hieroglyph has been transliterated so as to yield a word bearing a close resemblance to ancient Chinese and Semitic words for cassia. If they are correct, Hatshepsut's spices locate the gods and god-kings on the Nile at the end of a trading network that spanned the Indian Ocean.

Ancient history, alas, is seldom so simple, and Hatshepsut's "cinnamon" remains at best an intriguing possibility. (A similar debate splutters over medical papyri of the Eighteenth Dynasty, ca. 1543–1292 B.C., which may likewise contain references to the spice.) The debate hinges on muddy issues of transliteration, with the unsatisfying upshot that the precise identity of Hatshepsut's aromas remains scarcely less mystifying than Homer's nectar and ambrosia. Yet in another sense the exact composition of Hatshepsut's cargo is irrelevant, and cinnamon or no cinnamon, her exotica constitute a beginning of sorts. For if the inscriptions at Deir al-Bahri show nothing else, they certainly demonstrate the extraordinary significance the ancients ascribed to aromas and the lengths to which they were prepared to go to get them. It was worth sending a fleet nearly two thousand miles south, and worth recording among the greatest achievements of her reign: look on my luxuries, ye mighty, and despair. (Hatshepsut's boastfulness seems to have worked rather too well, as her successors felt obliged to deface the monuments to her greatness.) The Egyptians were prepared to go to extraordinary lengths for the sake of aromas because the trade served sacred purposes. In the long account of the expedition accompanying the temple reliefs, Amon-Re, lord of the gods, states that he has made Punt, the land of incense, "to divert his heart." If we can discern a motive behind the early trade, it was to retain the favor of a fickle Heaven.

In a world of many gods where pharaohs were themselves divine, it was an imperative with all the gravity of issues of state. Thus, if cinnamon was not among the exotica of Punt, the reliefs offer at the very least a clue as to why it was present later, and why spices were so valued as to warrant a trade over such vast distances.* For a culture accustomed to thinking of trade in terms of profit, and of spices as mere seasonings, it is a reminder of how easily our assumptions glide into a past

---

*Some scholars have long argued that not only this trade but *all* trade first existed in order to serve sacred purposes. When the word for "merchant" first appeared in Mesopotamian texts of the second millennium B.C., it carried sacred associations, designating "the official of a temple privileged to trade abroad."

where they don't belong. The first identifiable impulse for maritime contact between Egypt and the world beyond, by any measure one of the defining moments in global history, appears to have come not from gourmets but from the gods.

Thus when Ovid placed a promise of cinnamon-scented sacrifice in the mouth of Paris, his poetic fancies rested on a certain historical truth. And in the case of Helen's Troy he may have been even closer to the mark than he could have imagined, for it is certain that aromatics were used in the era of the Trojan War and even earlier. Incense burners, some still with traces of spices, have been unearthed from the same period, and small stirrup vases of the Mycenaeans' perfumes have been found as far afield as Egypt and Sicily. Various aromatics have been recovered from a Mycenaean ship wrecked off the southwest coast of Turkey, possibly returning from the Levant. At the Mycenaean palace complex of Pylos, built sometime around 1300 B.C. and destroyed around 1100 B.C.—the era generally identified with the Trojan War— archaeologists found that no less than 15 percent of the clay tablets recording the palace inventories dealt with various herbs and aromatics. When the language of the tablets was deciphered and found to be an early form of Greek, the names of numerous aromatics emerged. Coriander was there, easily recognizable as *ko-ri-a-da-na.* Tablets from the contemporary palace complex at Mycenae, according to legend the home of King Agamemnon, Helen's brother-in-law, contain cumin (*ku-mi-no*) and sesame (*sa-sa-ma*), both words of Semitic origin.

As the language was transmitted through the centuries, so the belief. Through the long intermission of the Greek Dark Ages, when invaders rampaged down the Greek peninsula and the palaces collapsed into ruins, the Greeks retained a faint memory of the perfumes that had once served their gods. In classical times, the tragedian Aeschylus (ca. 525–ca. 456 B.C.) wrote of the sacrificial flames in the palaces, "drugged by the simple soft persuasion of sacred unguents, the deep stored oil of the kings." The Pylos tablets mention four perfumers charged with their manufacture, one of whom, astonishingly, went by the name of Thyestes, a name familiar to students of Greek myth as the unfortunate individual duped by his brother Atreus into eating the flesh of his own son. In Mycenaean times his name was simply a professional title like Smith or Wright, meaning "Perfumer." His role was to provide the palace with the perfumes dedicated to the gods Potnia and Poseidon, a supernatural bulwark against divine disfavor.

Later, as myth would have it, Thyestes' misfortunes would spawn the curse of the house of Atreus, played out in none other than the palace of Mycenae, the scene where according to legend his brother served his gruesome family meal. And it was the ruins of that palace that yielded perhaps the most striking find of all, if the most ephemeral. Here the archaeologist Fredrik Poulsen found a small stirrup vase dating from the second millennium B.C. When he removed the stopper, "there was a sweet fragrance within, a perfume 3,500 years old, which vanished in a moment."

Ovid would have been gratified, though probably not surprised: the Mycenaeans and their gods did, indeed, have a refined sense of smell. And so Ovid is vindicated, at least poetically, if not—or not quite— historically. For such, if she ever existed, was the perfume smelled by Helen of Troy.

GOD'S NOSTRILS

Moreover the Lord spake unto Moses, saying,
Take thou also unto thee principal spices, of pure myrrh five hun-
    dred shekels, and of sweet cinnamon half so much,* even two
    hundred and fifty shekels, and of sweet calamus two hundred
    and fifty shekels,
And of cassia five hundred shekels, after the shekel of the sanctu-
    ary, and of oil olive an hin:†
And thou shalt make it an oil of holy ointment, an ointment com-
    pound after the art of the apothecary: it shall be an holy
    anointing oil.

—Exodus 30.22–23

As far as Pliny was concerned, it was all a colossal waste. In the good old days, the gods had been happy with a simple offering of salt, in the ancient Roman fashion—a modest but adequate sacrifice. Why, then, were his contemporaries intent on sending a small fortune up in aro- matic smoke, all in the name of a misguided piety? Worse still, profli-

---

*About 6.5 pounds.
†About 4 quarts.

gate Romans were now taking products once reserved for the immortals and burning them over the remains of dead mortals. This must be why, concluded Pliny, the land where the spices grew was known as "Happy" Arabia: a happiness attributable "to the extravagance of mankind even at the time of death, when they burn over the deceased the products which they had originally understood to have been created for the gods."

Theologically, Pliny had a point: if the gods were eternal and unchanging, it followed that the modest offerings of yesteryear were perfectly adequate. But Pliny was more bothered by the economics. When he tried to estimate how much of Arabia's perfumed goods went up in smoke each year, he concluded that a truly vast sum poured into Arabia—and out of Rome. Rome's other suppliers of spices—India, China, and what Pliny knew vaguely as "the Arabian Sea"—siphoned off some 100 million sesterces per annum: "So much our luxuries and women cost us." The beneficiaries were not gods but men.

Others took Pliny's complaint further. After all, Pliny was a pagan who, however parsimonious, at least believed in the gods' existence. But for those for whom those same gods were demons, the money spent on spices rankled more of idolatry than profligacy. In theory if not always in practice, there was no room for spice in the holy places of a single and incorporeal Yahweh, God, or Allah. In the religious ferment of late antiquity, as a waning paganism collapsed in the face of the monotheistic challenge of Judaism, Christianity, and Islam, this was an issue worthy of impassioned debate, alongside which Pliny's lament seems a trifle. In the days when Rome's energies ebbed and the new lone gods spread across the empire, it was, for a time, a matter of life and death.

The implications of the rejection of spices by the monotheists are considerably clearer than its origins. The older books of the Bible contain numerous references to spices in a sacramental context. The God of Genesis, we have seen, had nose enough to appreciate a fragrant offering from Noah, just as he appreciated "pleasing odors" from his followers. Genesis tells of Joseph's being sold into slavery to Ishmaelite merchants en route from Gilead to Egypt with "camels bearing spicery and balm and myrrh." In all likelihood the spices the queen of Sheba brought Solomon were destined for a similar use.

There are several biblical allusions to the early long-distance trade in aromatics, in which Solomon was involved, apparently for largely religious reasons. In cooperation with his ally Hiram the Phoenician, Solomon dispatched an expedition to the land of Ophir for the sake of its gold, peacocks, and an unidentified aromatic wood with which to build "the rails of the house of the Lord." As with Punt, Ophir's location remains the subject of scholarly wrangling. One of the more tantalizing possibilities is suggested by the Hebrew word for the peacock included among Ophir's exotica, which looks to derive from the ancient Tamil name of the bird. The peacock is native to India, and since the word does not occur elsewhere in the Bible it seems conceivable that Hiram sailed there. But wherever Ophir was to be found, it is clear that like the polytheist Egyptians the ancient Israelites were prepared to go to extraordinary lengths for the sake of the sacred aromatics, warranting the admiring comment of the scribe: "Never again were so many spices brought in as those the queen of Sheba gave to King Solomon." This was one of the achievements of his reign.*

That had apparently changed, or was beginning to change, by the time of the prophet Jeremiah, late in the seventh century B.C. Yahweh is no longer interested: "What do I care about incense from Sheba or sweet calamus from a distant land? Your burnt offerings are not acceptable; your sacrifices do not please me," thunders the vengeful god of the prophet. To Isaiah, "bringing offerings is futile; incense is an abomination to me." This change of tone was apparently the consequence of a fundamental doctrinal development, marking a shift away from the external act of sacrifice toward an emphasis on personal purity and obedience. God would no longer be appeased by burnt offerings, only by the sacrifice of a contrite heart. In theological terms, the reasoning is clear—at least after the event. God himself was evolving. By the later books of the Hebrew Bible, the more physical God of Genesis, coming and going in the Garden, has withdrawn into a more remote, truly metaphysical being. As a consequence, the whole notion of sacrifice had to be reappraised, since physical offerings made no sense to a god lacking physical form; why offer material goods to an immaterial being?

Yet, as we have seen, the clarity of the theology rests uneasily with the older archaeological and textual evidence. Prophetic choler apparently belies—indeed, may be explained by—a more muddled past.

---

*Exactly which aromatics he obtained from Sheba and Ophir remains a mystery. One of the more intriguing spices mentioned in the Hebrew Bible is *shelet,* which Greek translators rendered as *onyx,* meaning "claw" or "nail"—was this the clove? It is a suggestive coincidence that in practically every major language group, East or West, the name for the spice means "nail."

That the God of the older books appreciated a sweet savor has led some scholars to argue that the deodorization of the Hebrew religion was a relatively late development, written into the holy books by later generations of scribes and editors; that is, by those responsible for the Bible as we now know it. In his study of the use of incense in ancient Israel, Kjeld Nielsen has argued that the widespread early use of aromatics is only dimly remembered in the surviving Bible, thanks to later rewriting by the so-called Reform Movement, a body of scribes and editors responsible for imposing their own contemporary views on any parts of the ancient texts that showed alarming discrepancies from current (or their own) religious practice. The most striking of several references occurs in the older book of Exodus, where Yahweh demands of Moses a "holy anointing oil" made with cinnamon and cassia. The oil is to be applied to the tabernacle of the congregation, for the temple fittings "that they may be most holy . . . for a sweet savor before the Lord." So esteemed was the oil that its use was reserved for the priest. It was not to be used for any secular purpose upon pain of excommunication: "Upon man's flesh shall it not be poured, neither shall ye make any other like it, after the composition of it: it is holy, and it shall be holy unto you. Whosoever compoundeth any like it, or whosoever putteth any of it upon a stranger, shall even be cut off from his people."

For all intents and purposes we have here a reverence for aromatics much the same as shown by the Egyptians and Assyrians: a deity-delighting savor; aromas whose use outside the temple was sacrilege. And indeed it may well have been precisely this shared tradition with the polytheists that accounts for the subsequent exclusion of spices and incense from Hebrew religion. For a priestly class acutely conscious of its uniqueness and jealous of its prerogatives—and one, moreover, that was increasingly coming to conceive of its faith in terms of opposition to polytheist idolatry—spices were a troubling reminder of a past when the lines had been less clear. This thesis fits with other idolatrous lapses of the pre-exilic kings outlined by the different biblical scribal traditions. The Book of Kings relates that in later life Solomon—who was, after all, the pharaoh's son-in-law—dabbled in idolatry: "On a hill east of Jerusalem, Solomon built a high place for Chemosh the detestable god of Moab, and for Molech the detestable god of the Ammonites. He did the same for all his foreign wives, who burned incense and offered sacrifices to their gods." Passages such as this appear to reflect a more fluid religious reality, one that accommodated the extensive use of aromas in worship but rested uneasily with the theology of later generations and was duly excised from the holy books.

The exclusion of aromas would therefore seem to have been a process more evolutionary than revolutionary. During the Second Temple period (536 B.C.–A.D. 70), spices were still burned on the golden altar of the Temple. The spice mixtures were prepared in the Temple itself in the Avtinus Chamber, so named after the family of perfumers who supplied the ingredients. The family claimed to know of a secret ingredient that would make the smoke rise straight up in a column; they refused to divulge the secret lest it be used in the worship of idols.

Elsewhere certain aromatics lingered on. Dating from the second half of the third century A.D., the mosaic floor of the synagogue of Severus at Hammath Tiberias features an incense shovel, apparently still a part of everyday worship. Dating from much the same time is the text known as *The Revelation of Moses,* an early Christian composition based on Jewish sources, in which Adam asks of God, immediately before he is expelled from Paradise, "I beseech you, allow me to take sweet odors out of Paradise, in order that, after I go out, I may offer sacrifice to God, that God may listen to me." In the time of the historian Josephus, writing around A.D. 93, the high priest was still anointed with cinnamon. The most explicit reference occurs in the late-fourth-century account of the sack of Jerusalem by the author known as the Pseudo-Hegesippus, which tells of a priest handing over the sacred vessels and vestments of the Temple to the conquering Romans, among which were "cinnamon, cassia, many spices, incense and many sacred vessels of the sacraments." The context makes it clear that these were reserved for religious use and were numbered among the Temple's most precious furnishings.

Even to this day Judaism may retain a faint reminder of spices' sacral past. Spices are still used in the Havdalah ceremony marking the end of the Sabbath, during the course of which the speaker blesses the wine and spices with the words "Blessed art thou, O Lord, our God, creator of the universe, creator of all the kinds of spices." The precise origins of the custom are impossibly obscure; however, it is at least clear that the practice was current by the early third century A.D., perhaps as early as the first, since it is mentioned in the *Mishnah,* or commentaries. Modern scholars are inclined to see the custom as an outgrowth of an unknown food ritual of the Greco-Roman period; however, it seems equally likely that the spice box is an ancient mutation of a still more ancient religious practice, when spices themselves served as offerings. One of the more tantalizing possibilities is suggested in the apocryphal apocalyptic text known as 3 Baruch, composed by a Jewish author some fifty or so years after the destruction of the Temple in A.D. 70, surviving antiquity only in a modified Greek version. During the course of a vision, an angel escorts Baruch on a tour of the heavens, where he sees the phoenix. The bird "excretes a worm, and the excrement of the worm is cinnamon, which kings and princes use." One scholar has seen in the "kings and princes" of the Apocalypse a reference to the mystical sages of the Jewish community who used cinnamon in their rites.

On the whole, however, it is clear that among the Jews spices were slowly but surely shorn of their magical aura, progressively downgraded to offerings regarded as more symbolic than sacred. It was a pattern followed by the other faiths that followed the Jews in positing a single and immaterial God, but most thoroughly by Islam. Like Judaism, Islam emerged in conflict with a pagan universe, and the aromas that had once played such a part in pagan worship were expunged. So Sura 51 of the Koran: "I have not created genii and men for an other end than that they should serve me. I require not sustenance from them; neither will it that they feed me." Allah's Prophet was well placed to comment on such matters. His native Mecca was an ancient cultic center whose commercial vitality owed much to its commanding position as an entrepôt astride the Arabian caravan routes—along which, among other things, traveled the incenses and spices of the Yemen. As a former camel driver Mohammed surely knew the trade as well as anyone. His first wife, Khadija, was herself the widow of a wealthy spice trader and presumably a supplier to the smoking altars and idols that Mohammed would soon set about destroying. Within the Prophet's lifetime spices effectively disappeared from Arabian religion. No other major religion is so thoroughly devoid of aromatics or physical offerings.*

*Although spices played no direct role in Muslim worship, medieval Islamic scholars produced perhaps the most poetic vision of their origins. According to the great Islamic scholar at-Tabarî (ca. 839–923) and the Arab geographers who followed him, on Adam's expulsion from Paradise he was overcome by remorse and wept with grief. From his bitter tears sprang gems and spices, the medicines and consolation for mankind after the fall.

With Christianity, like Judaism, the picture is considerably more confused. The inherited books of the Hebrew Old Testament, we have seen, contain numerous references to spices; however, the writings of the Church Fathers show a remarkable clarity and unity on the subject: aromas were out. The most serious objection was simply that pagans used them. From the time of the first preaching of the Gospels until the final suppression of pagan religions in the fifth century, early Christians lived cheek by jowl with polytheists and their fuming altars. Like a form of religious air pollution, these were daily and intrusive reminders of the pagan associations of spice. In his *Exhortation to the Martyrs,* the great theologian Origen (ca. 185–ca. 253) claims that the chief outward sign distinguishing a pagan from a Christian is the telltale presence of incense at the domestic altar. No devout Christian would offer incense, for demons were drawn to the sweet-smelling smoke. And if demons could be fed, it followed that they could be starved: the best way of deterring unwanted infernal visitors was to deprive them of the incense on which they fed. For this reason Tertullian (ca. A.D. 155–ca. 220) thought that Christians who bought spices for "solace at funerals" were complicit in idolatry, aiding and abetting the demons that fed off the smoke: "The work of idolatry is perpetrated . . . without the idol, by the burning of odors."

If anything, the odium intensified with the passage of time. To veterans of the persecutions, spices reeked not only of demons but of bitter personal experience. During the persecutions of the emperors Decius in 249–251 and Diocletian in 303–304, believers were identified and offered a chance to recant by sacrificing, offering a libation, or burning incense before an image of the emperor. On doing so, they were granted the appropriate certificate; if not, they were promptly executed (many Christians seem to have survived the persecutions by bribing corrupt officials). Those Christians who elected idolatry over martyrdom were sneeringly called the "Turificati," or incense burners. To Saint Jerome (ca. 347–419/420) the tag was a form of shorthand for the weak or vacillating Christian who was unwilling to die for his faith.

To pagan Romans, Christians' refusal to offer incense to the emperor was, in strictly religious terms, as puzzling as it was perverse, but scarcely threatening. Far more important, refusal to sacrifice to the emperor amounted to an act of political dissidence, an overt rejection of the imperial cult that, in an age when emperors were regularly murdered by their own soldiers, was becoming an increasingly significant prop of imperial legitimacy (and to which, ironically, the Christian emperors were the heirs). But to a devout Christian offering was an act of spiritual suicide, recognition of an evil demon; to a Roman, it was revolt. Hence the periodic insistence by the emperors of the third century on the necessity of sacrifice in front of witnesses, at once a litmus test of allegiance and a convenient way of identifying the rebels. During one such phase, recorded in the document known as *The Martyrdom of Habib the Deacon,* composed late in the third century or early in the fourth, the emperor Diocletian commanded libations and sacrifices, "and that the altars in every place should be restored, and that they might burn sweet spices and frankincense before Zeus." Habib disagreed, preached the scriptures, and promptly went to a martyr's death.

Not all Christians, of course, came to such a dramatic end. Yet the influence of the martyrs was out of all proportion to their relatively small numbers, their salutary deaths adding pungency to what must have seemed to many as more or less abstract theological debates. Like the Hebrew prophets before them, Christians had a sense that the offering of material spices to an immaterial god was misconceived: Why offer perishable spices to an immortal and immaterial being? The second-century philosopher Athenagoras was perhaps the first to state the anti-incense line in terms pagans could understand, arguing that God did not need sweet incense, although his own reasoning has more than a whiff of paganism—since "He is Himself perfect fragrance." So too the Christian apologist Lactantius (ca. 240–ca. 320) argued that "whatever is . . . perishable . . . is inconsistent with the whole subject of immortality."

In liturgical terms, the implications of the position were clear. Isaiah had said it first: "Incense is an abomination unto me," a line reiterated by the God of the fourth-century *Apostolic Constitutions.* Likewise a commentary on the same passage, attributed to Saint Basil (ca. 329–379): "For truly it is an execrable thing to think that God values the pleasures of the sense of smell . . . and not to understand that the hallowing of the body, effected by the sobriety of the soul, is the incense unto the Lord. . . . Corporeal incense that affects the nostrils and moves the sense is by a necessary consequence regarded as an abomination to a Being that is incorporeal." Saint John Chrysostom (ca. 347–407) was still more succinct: "God has no nostrils."

ODORS OF SANCTITY

With sweet-smelling cinnamon,
You are, Our Lady, to be compared;
To myrrh of the Orient,
That distant aroma.

—PEDRO LÓPEZ DE AYALA, *Rimado de palacio,* ca. 1385

Some Christians, however, were not so sure. If the fathers of the Church had little room for doubt about their deity's receptiveness to fragrant offerings, their flock was apparently more muddled. For on the tangled question of aroma and worship, spices and incense were more durable, and apparently more convincing, than doctrine. Long after the temples and altars of the pagan gods were reduced to ruins, the spiced aromas that had once graced the altars of Apollo and Aphrodite lingered on in the holy places of the West.

In the liturgy and literature of the early medieval church, spices reappeared for all intents and purposes in much the same role as they had formerly served the pagans. This return to religious orthodoxy occurred very early. In the first half of the sixth century, the Scythian Christian writer Dionysius Exiguus wrote of the head of John the Baptist, severed by Herod but honored by multitudes of monks and angels, sprinkled with the aromas of "nard, saffron, cinnamon and all spices." We have already seen that by this stage Paradise had acquired a strong smell of spice. Marius, a Christian grammarian born in Africa around 300, located cinnamon in the Garden of Eden. Saints Jerome and John Chrysostom situated India and its spiced exotica next to Paradise. Spices once more were at home in Heaven.

As they were, apparently, in church. The earliest unambiguous reference is the late-fourth-century *Testament* of Ephraim the Syrian, who explicitly stipulates that his fellow Christians should "burn sweet spices in the Holy Place." Some of the earliest references occur in the *Liber pontificalis,* a rattlebag of papal records and pious forgeries composed, in its present form, from roughly the first half of the sixth century on. Many of the oldest records in the *Liber* are based on older documentary records of the papal treasury (*vestiarum*), apparently dating from the fourth century and consisting for the most part of an unadorned record of Church decrees and events, church furniture, reliquaries, treasures, and liturgical equipment. Included in the latter are several huge stockpiles of spice dating from early in the fourth century, in the time of Pope Sylvester, the pontiff traditionally credited with baptizing Constantine. Of the basilica of Constantine (built, as it happens, on the site of the *horrea piperataria,* or spice stores) the *Liber* records an annual gift from the emperor of 150 pounds of unspecified aromatics accompanied by a golden censer. On the site where Saint Peter's Basilica now stands, then occupied by an older church built by Constantine and his mother, Helena, the emperor donated a small tonnage of sacred equipment: gold, bronze, and porphyry, candelabra and gifts from the Eastern Church consisting of 225 pounds of balsam, 800 pounds of oil of nard, 650 pounds of unspecified aromatics, 50 corn measures of pepper, 50 pounds of cloves, 100 pounds of saffron, and 100 pounds of fine linen, "obtained by Constantine Augustus for Saint Peter." In total, the emperor donated a staggering 150 pounds of cloves to various churches.

The *Liber* contains similar records from other great churches around the empire. If the figures are genuine—and they have an air of precision about them—they suggest a complete about-face on the part of the first Christian emperor. If, on the other hand, they are forgeries, they at least show the assumptions a pious forger of the sixth century might have harbored about the treasury of a great church. Either way these spices were evidently Church equipment; they were not there to be eaten, no more than the candelabras or censers with which they are grouped. To all appearances we are very close here to customs excoriated by earlier writers, not far from the cinnamon stored in a golden dish in a pagan temple on the Palatine or the dedication of cinnamon to Apollo at Miletus by King Seleucus. A little over one hundred years after Tertullian had railed against the sweet, demon-attracting bait, and within living memory of a time when martyrs had chosen death ahead of burning incense, God had reacquired his nostrils. Who had converted whom?

Doubtless the new ecclesiastical receptiveness to spice can be attributed to the fact that many of the old beliefs were easily adapted to the new religious circumstances. One pagan myth that lent itself to a Christian repackaging was that of the cinnamon-immolated phoenix, dying so as to be reborn into eternal life. The parallels between the careers of Christ and the phoenix were obvious. Saint Ambrose, the fourth-century bishop of Milan, saw the phoenix and its life-restoring cinnamon as symbols of Christ and his teachings. In a work conventionally attributed to Lactantius, the phoenix

> *Builds a nest, or sepulchre,*
> *For she dies that she may live.*
> *Here she gathers juices and perfumes*
> *That the Assyrian, the opulent Arab gather from the riches of the forest;*
> *That the Pygmies or the Indians harvest,*
> *Or that the land of Sabaea grows in its tender bosom.*
> *Here she piles cinnamon, and the scent of far-diffusing cardamom,*
> *And balsam mixed with cinnamon leaf.*

On account of its pagan imagery, scholars have debated whether the work is Christian or pagan in inspiration, but to some extent the question is misconstrued, for by now phoenix and spices were both. In this sense the formerly pagan phoenix, reborn in Christian plumage, was, after all, immune to death.

However, Christians did not need to look to pagan myths to credit spices with the odors of divinity, for they had their own. Besides numerous references in the Hebrew Bible, some of the brightest images were drawn from early Christian and Jewish apocryphal literature that emerged in the ferment of the second and third centuries. Though most were later excluded from the canonical Bible, these were widely read in the Middle Ages. The apocryphal *Apocalypse of Peter,* dating from the first half of the second century, places the spices in Paradise. Likewise the somewhat older *Book of Enoch,* an apocalyptic work narrating Enoch's visionary transport to Paradise, where the winds from the flapping wings of the cherubim waft spicy aromas:

> And in the midst of the Garden they [the winds] join together and blow from one side to the other and are perfumed with the spices of the Garden even from its remotest parts, until they separate from each other, and, filled with the scent of the pure spices, they bring the odor from the remotest parts of Eden and the spices of the Garden to the righteous and godly who in time to come shall inherit the Garden of Eden and the Tree of Life.

In the hands of medieval commentators references such as these ripened and blossomed into a rich store of metaphor. Spices transcended the terrestrial and heavenly spheres, it being something of a commonplace that in the heavenly Paradise the just would be rewarded for their virtuous lives with eternal bliss and nourished on celestial seasonings. Honorius of Autun, who lived in the middle of the twelfth century, imagined Paradise smelling of cinnamon and balsam while the blessed feasted in the sight of God. This was an enduring image. The English author of a fifteenth-century sermon envisaged the just eating spices on the Day of Judgment, gathered among the stars and in God's radiance. Foods that were immensely problematic on Earth—just how problematic we shall explore in a moment—were fine in Heaven. In the company of saints and seraphim there would be no cabbage and mashed potatoes.

The Middle Ages read the Bible historically, allegorically, morally, and so it was with the Bible's spices. To Rabanus Magnentius Maurus (ca. 780–856), abbot of the Benedictine abbey of Fulda and archbishop of Mainz, Sheba's famous spices (*pigmenta*) were sublimated into symbols of rare force, signifying not mere spices but the various "ornaments of the virtues." Did not the Book of Ecclesiasticus say of holy Wisdom that she smelled of cinnamon? Rabanus lived in a symbol-hungry age, and the expensive, rare, and mysterious spices lent themselves to endless allegorizing. To the Venerable Bede and dozens who copied him, pale, ashen-brown cinnamon was taken as a symbol of inner worth over outward display, of substance over style, redolent of inner virtue. This humble package concealed potent healing gifts within a plain exterior, invisible to the eyes, evanescent, and intangible. The tree (which of course no one had seen) was held to be short and humble, of an ashen color: plain on the outside, but worthy within. Pierre de la Celle, bishop of Chartres (?–ca. 1183), saw spices, and cinnamon in particular, as symbols of incomparable worth, miraculous in their effects, mysterious, sweet, and effective in their healing power.

As has previously been noted, in every sense the spiciest biblical authority—and far and away the most influential—was the Song of Songs. Quite apart from its influence on erotic poetry, there was something in the disembodied, dreamy quality of the Song that reverberated in the mystical imagination. Spices and aromatics are an integral part of the Song's naturalistic, fertile imagery. It was, perhaps, the very elusiveness of the aroma that gave the imagery its force. Spices evoke a rapturous transport:

Awake, O north wind; and come, thou south; blow upon my garden, that the spices thereof may flow out. Let my beloved come
into his garden, and eat his pleasant fruits.

A convenient solution to some awkward possibilities suggested by
such spicy language was to allegorize, reading the spices in question as
a metaphor for mystical ecstasy. By this reading, the poem was a declaration of a love not so much physical as spiritual, its desire shared not
by two lovers but by Christ and the Church, the Church and the soul,
God and the believer, or some variant thereof.

Thus spices, figuratively at least, found their way back into ecclesiastical favor. Shorn of their pagan odium, they signified the holy virtues
and their effects, preserving from corruption and the contagion of sin.
As Pope Gregory the Great interpreted the passage quoted immediately above: "What is signified by these various types of aromas if not
the odor and effect of the holy virtues?" (What indeed?) Clerical writers
from one end of the Middle Ages to the other saw spices signifying
spiritual manna in all manner of forms. To Saint Ambrose, cinnamon
signified the "gifts of the spirit"; Pierre de la Celle saw the Song's cinnamon and cassia as almost platonic in their abstraction, ideals of godliness, the more powerful for their very allusiveness. Cinnamon
symbolized "the odor of good opinion," diffusing its qualities far and
wide. To Philip of Hainault (ca. 1100–1182) the Song's unguents were
confections of precious, healing spices, to be understood here as symbols of the healing gifts of God, working not on the body but on the
spirit. Some efforts to allegorize the more fruity verses into innocence
could be more contorted still. According to Charlemagne's schoolmas-
ter Alcuin, the verse "I would cause thee to drink of spiced wine of the
juice of my pomegranate" refers to nothing other than "the glorious triumph of the holy martyrs."

Fatuous as such efforts may seem, there is no doubting their seriousness; nor, however dimly anyone other than a medieval mystic might
sense it, that spices' sacred past infused their medieval reception. On
biblical authority they were lodged somewhere between this world and
the next, between Paradise and the mundane here and now. If spices did
not literally smell divine (or if divinity did not smell of spices), the two
were at least evocative of each other. If the "he" of "his cheeks are a bed
of spices, as sweet flowers" was a symbolic representation of the divine,

then here was scriptural authority that spices and holiness were in some
way associated. The effect was redoubled by Jerome's Vulgate translation of the Bible—the version most literate Europeans knew—the
Latin of which had the effect of transposing the vocabulary of the present day back into the biblical past. The spicer (*pigmentarius*) of the Song
was the mythic forerunner of the real-world spicer who supplied the
courts and clergy of medieval Europe. In spices scripture and reality
intertwined. The spice routes were the aromatic threads that joined the
present to a sacred past.

In the medieval present, the most immediately apparent implication
of this intertwining, and one that was central to the medieval experience of mysticism, was the odor of sanctity. Medieval holiness came
perfumed and, not infrequently, spiced. By late antiquity Christ, Virgin, and saints had acquired a strong note of cinnamon in particular—
which was perhaps ironic, given the spice's erotic history. To Saint
Idelfonso, bishop of Toledo from 659 to 668, only the aroma of cinnamon came close to conveying the Virgin's odor of sanctity, "more fragrant than cinnamon." This was one of the most enduring conventions
of medieval literature. In an English sermon of the fifteenth century,
spiced wine (*piment*) appears as a metaphor for Christ's blood, shed as
generously as a good host dispenses to his guests: "He humbly shed his
piment, to make his good guests glad."

Underlying these figurative images were literal beliefs. From the earliest times it was a convention that the saintly one smelled of spices
after his death. When the relics of Saint Stephen were found in 415, he
came up smelling not of roses but of spices: incontrovertible proof of
his divinity. Early in the fourth century, Eusebius, bishop of Caesarea
(?–ca. 340), wrote that the martyr Polycarp gave off a smell of fragrant
spices on the pyre: a human incense stick. The hagiographers of the
desert-dwelling hermits seldom fail to mention their pleasant smell.
However bad these unwashed ascetics must have smelled in real life,
legendarily indifferent to physical comforts in their cramped desert
cells, they invariably smelled sweet on papyrus (or posthumously). The
truly divine had no need of spice—they already had it.

With time this spiciness of God's favored ones became a well-worn
feature of the medieval lives of the saints, or *vitae*. Saint Meinrad was a
celebrated Swiss hermit dwelling in a cave on the slopes of Mount
Etzel, killed in a bungled robbery in 861 by thieves drawn by all the
treasures left at his shrine. No sooner had the hermit been suffocated

than "an odor of such sweetness filled the entire space of his cell, as though the odors of all the spices were diffused there." A holy corpse could smell even sweeter than spices. William of Malmesbury (ca. 1090–ca. 1143) wrote of the Venerable Bede that as he expired he filled the nostrils of all present with an odor "not of cinnamon and balsam, but paradisiacal, like the delight of spring breathing everywhere." The Netherlandish Saint Lidwina (1380–1473), after a life of semistarvation, permanently bedridden after a skating accident, smelled of ginger, cloves, and cinnamon. Even a truly worthy person from secular life might be granted a whiff of spice (or better) on the way out. In the early-fourteenth-century *Romance of Guy of Warwick,* the dead Guy gives off a heavenly "sweet breath . . . that no spices might surpass."

There was something more to this convention than a pious or poetic effort to evoke the ineffable. Some scholars have attempted to account for the odor of sanctity in terms of real aromas given off by a corpse, but this is surely either too sophisticated, or too naive, by half. (Nor does this line of reasoning easily reconcile with the progressive deodorization of the saints from roughly the seventeenth century onward.) Spiciness was essentially a function of faith. The *vitae* are not histories in any modern sense of the term; they were written by passionate believers who, convinced they would smell a sweet fragrance, surely did. There was, after all, an important symbolic point to be made, and it was one that medieval readers would have recognized immediately. The *vitae* were written and read by people with an acute feeling for the deeper symbolism of aroma. A pleasant smell was a marker, a revelation of Christian qualities; of inner, invisible virtue over outward display.

And as sanctity and Paradise were understood literally to smell of spices, so it was with the opposite. Devils were often betrayed by their horrible stink. Smell was a writer's means of conveying a moral point. After his death by lamprey, as we have seen earlier, King Henry I died in the bad odor of his ill deeds, emitting a stench so foul it slew the men entrusted with watching over the corpse. The last of Henry's many victims was the man who "had been hired for a great sum of money to cut off the head with an axe and extract the stinking brain . . . so he got no benefit from his fee." (Readers of Dostoyevsky will recall the mixed feelings provoked by the dead Father Zossima. As his cadaver began to smell, his admirers were downcast, whereas his enemies rejoiced that his saintliness had been proven a sham.) So too the medieval Hell smelled supernaturally foul. When Dante toured the underworld he saw flatterers "plunged in excrement" and smelled infernal farts. He met Alessio Interminei of Lucca, "his head so covered in shit, I couldn't tell if he were priest or layman." As Chaucer's Parson said of the damned, "Their nostrils shall be filled with a stinking stink." In Heaven, on the other hand, there was sweet celestial music and a smell of spices. They were a taste of Heaven on Earth.

OLD AGE, NEW AGE

For the medieval Church, spices' aroma of sanctity had several practical implications.

If spices smelled divine, symbolizing if not in a sense summoning a holy presence, there was a certain consistency in supposing they might counteract the malodorous influence of the Devil. The use of a strong, pleasant aroma to dispel a foul-smelling, malign force was yet another direct inheritance from antiquity, albeit one with a Christian twist. In his *Partheneia sacra* of 1633, Henry Hawkins cited an ancient magical tradition in claiming that cinnamon was a prophylactic against devils. To Nicolas Oresme, bishop of Lisieux and an academic at the University of Paris in the third quarter of the fourteenth century, spices worked a potent white magic. Thanks to their scripturally sanctioned powers, they might overwhelm pagan magic, such as the intoxicating fumes of the Delphic Oracle. A meal of spices beforehand was all the vaccination required, although it seems unlikely that many of Oresme's readers would have been at much risk of Delphic contamination.

Oresme's claim is the more striking for the fact that the same author penned trenchant attacks on occult magic. In much the same vein, others claimed that spices might put diabolical forces to flight: the exact reverse of Tertullian's claim that burning spices attracted demons. In his *Romance of Sorcery,* Sax Rohmer — he of the Fu Manchu books — cites a fragrant yarn told by Sinistrari of Ameno. A young nun of the seventeenth century suffered from what a modern psychologist would perhaps classify as a morbid erotic obsession, at the time explained as an incubus. Day and night the demon visited her in the form of a handsome young man tempting her to sin, resisting the concerted power of prayer, relics, and exorcism. Eventually the nuns consulted a learned theologian, who tried an aromatic fumigation:

A new vessel, made of glass-like earth, was accordingly brought in, and filled with sweet cane, cubeb seed, roots of both aristolochies, great and small cardamom, ginger, long pepper, caryophylleae [gillyflowers], cinnamon, cloves, mace, nutmegs, calamite, storax, benzoin, aloes-wood and roots, one ounce of triapandalis [a mix of various types of sandalwood], and three pounds of half brandy and water; the vessel was then set on hot ashes in order to distil the fumigating vapour, and the cell was kept closed.

This worked after a fashion but did not quite complete the job. Still more potent spices were required:

As soon as the fumigation was done, the Incubus came, but never dared enter the cell; only, if the maiden left it, for a walk in the garden or cloister, he appeared to her, though invisible to others, and, throwing his arms around her neck, stole or rather snatched kisses from her, to her intense disgust.

At last, after a new consultation, the Theologian prescribed that she should carry about her person pills made of the most exquisite perfumes, such as musk, amber, chive, Peruvian balsam, etc. Thus provided, she went for a walk in the garden, where the Incubus suddenly appeared to her with a threatening face, and in a rage. He did not approach her, however, but, after biting his finger as if meditating revenge, disappeared, and was never more seen by her.

To many in the Church this sort of mumbo jumbo was precisely that: it was magic and as such had no place in the Church.

Spices were far less problematic in incense and unguents, in which role they had reappeared shortly after the emperor Constantine's conversion. Pope Gregory the Great, pontiff from 590 to 604, argued that the sweet spices rose heavenward with the incense, sweetening the prayers and symbolizing their ascent to Heaven. Elsewhere he writes of spices used in "royal unguents," by which he apparently meant the chrism, the anointing oil used for the consecration of bishops and ordination of priests. Chrism was—is—also used for the sacraments of Baptism, Confirmation, and Holy Orders, as well as the consecration of churches, chalices, patens altars, and altar stones, and for the solemn blessing of bells and baptismal water. One or more of these were, in all likelihood, the destination of Constantine's spices, since the tally of the great Roman churches' aromatics occurs in the same passage relating Pope Sylvester's ordinations on the composition and use of chrism. One possibility is that the spices were used in an effort to create a paradisiacal effect. The Constantinian basilica of Saint Peter's, the church to which the emperor donated the largest amount of spices, was entered via an atrium that was itself called Paradise,* enclosing a garden with fountains: a scaled-down version of the real thing. And if garden, waters, and enclosure of Paradise were imitated, why not its smell? Constantine's spices were, after all, the same aromas that Christian writers conventionally imagined in Paradise.

In the time of Dionysius the Pseudo-Areopagite, a fifth-century Syrian writer, the anointing oil was prepared with whatever aromas were to hand. The early Greek Church used forty different spices and herbs. Rabanus Maurus (ca. 780–856), archbishop and abbot of the great Benedictine abbey of Fulda, apparently based his mix on the Exodus recipe but with the addition of balsam to the cinnamon, the two sharply contrasting aromas symbolizing suffering and sweetness respectively.

In western Europe, however, there never emerged a definitive consensus on the acceptability of spices. To some a sense of their pagan odium never entirely vanished. Though figuratively sublime, in practical terms they were more problematic. Haymo, bishop of the Saxon city of Halberstadt in the middle of the ninth century, felt that spices were "common to idols" and should therefore not be offered to God. Another and probably more serious problem for the early Church was that with the economic and political collapse of the Roman world the spices needed for chrism and incense became harder to come by. Until its final conquest by the Turks in 1453, the surviving eastern half of the empire acted as intermediary to the Far East. Midway through the sixth century, the Persian dynasty of the Sasanids closed the trade routes and entrepôts to Byzantine traders, forcing them to buy from the Persian state at exorbitant prices. In 575, the Persians shored up the last remaining gap in their monopoly with the conquest and annexation of the then-Christian kingdom of the Yemen, where the Romans had acquired the spices and incense used across Christendom. The East was now closed to the West.

---

*The word derives from the Persian, via Greek, meaning "enclosure."

The upshot was that Christians now relied on Zoroastrians for the aromas they—or some of them—employed in their liturgy. Yet the Persians would not have it their own way for long. In 628, the emperor Heraclius sacked the royal Persian residence of Dastagird, carrying off a huge haul of silk, aloes, ginger, pepper, sugar, and "other spices without number." A more lasting defeat came in 642, when the Sasanids were utterly vanquished by the unstoppable armies of Islam and the spice routes passed under Islamic control. For the next thousand years, Christians relied on Jews and Muslims to supply aromas for their worship.

It was long thought that the division of the Roman world into two warring zones of Islam and Christendom brought trade and contacts to an all but complete halt, but the persistent presence of spices in the West puts a serious dent in the thesis. Since they remained an important component of religious practice, they clearly were getting through somehow. In this sense religion, far from being a barrier to trade between faiths, is more likely to have encouraged it.

For it is clear that throughout the early and central Middle Ages, spices and incense alike were regular features of religious practice. They were, however, more a luxury for special occasions than an item of daily use. When Saint Ulrich returned triumphantly from a relic-gathering trip to the monastery of Reichenau in 952 (or possibly 953), bringing with him the remains of Saint Maurice, the residents of Augsburg honored the two saints, dead and alive, with processions, holy water, music, songs, and burnt spices. The Italian chronicler Falcone of Benevento describes the celebrations for the visit of Pope Calixtus II in August 1120, when the air was filled with the scent of incense and cinnamon wafting from gold and silver censers. The Holy Roman Emperor Henry VI was crowned in Rome in April 1191, his entry to the city perfumed with balsam, incense, aloes, nutmeg, cinnamon, and nard. The religion was different, but for all intents and purposes spices served much the same purposes as they had in classical times—the scene is not far removed from Sappho's description of Hector and Andromache's wedding procession, accompanied by the sound of lyres and the smell of cassia.

Many of the references to spices from these centuries begin to make sense only in a sacramental context. There survive a number of letters from Roman church functionaries addressed to Boniface, the Apostle of Germany, martyred by the pagan Frisians in 754, concluding with a gift of spices: in one case, four ounces of cinnamon, two pounds of pepper, and one pound of storax. Another ends with an unspecified quantity of incense, costus, pepper, and cinnamon. This holy ascetic would hardly have shown such attentiveness to his diet: food parcels from Rome do not fit the image of the apostle of the Germans, contemptuous of his personal comforts and safety, roughing it out in the wilds of heathen Germany. In one case a deacon at the Vatican attaches to the spices the request that Boniface should pray for him—with the strong implication that the spices, like the incense with which they are paired, should serve to this end. A letter from the archdeacon Theophylacias, written in 752, describes the spices he is sending as "a little gift of blessing." Language and context strongly suggest that Boniface's cinnamon did not end up in his stomach but in the chrism dabbed on the brows of the Germans he converted, priests and bishops, or the altars, chalices, and walls of the churches he built in the pagan wilderness.

Or, more tendentiously, on kings. Since it was Boniface who presided over the coronation of Pepin the Short, some of the apostle's spices may conceivably have ended up in the chrism with which he anointed the first of the Carolingians at Soissons in 751. Beginning with Pepin's coronation, the Carolingian ritual of royal anointing self-consciously followed Old Testament coronation accounts, in which the holiness of the oil was integral to the symbolism of the ritual, conferring on God's anointed the stature of king and priest, his robes "fragrant with myrrh and aloes and cassia." While the associations were sacred, the need was political. The problem was particularly pressing for the Carolingians, who despite holding effective power as mayors of the palace were constrained to recognize the divine right of the last surviving member of the Merovingian dynasty, an imbecile driven around in an oxcart. The solution was provided by the Church by anointing with the chrism, thereby confirming Pepin's legitimacy as both king and priest, more than a merely secular ruler. Given the conscious following of the Old Testament precedent, it is conceivable that the Carolingians used cinnamon for the chrism and subsequent rituals. Such at least is the implication of the account of the coronation of Berengar, king of Italy from 888 and Holy Roman Emperor from 915, anointed with an "unguent of nectar," as the anonymous poet narrates the event, according to the recipe of the anointing oil given in Exodus; that is, with cinnamon.

At the very least, the literature leaves no doubt as to cinnamon's sacramental associations. Even pepper may have served as commonly as a sacrament as it did as a seasoning.* Before the eleventh century, many of the references to the spice occur alongside those to incense, whether because the two were sold by the same person or because they were used for similar purposes. One of the miracles of the eleventh-century pontiff Saint Leo concerns a shyster who sold pepper and incense to be offered at the pope's tomb. On account of its potent essential oil, the spice is still used in perfumes, oils, and unguents. Among the documents of the abbey of Mont-Saint-Michel is a record dating to 1061, outlining arrangements between Abbot Ranulphus and John, bishop of Avranches, whereby the former undertakes to supply the monastery with the equipment necessary for the celebration of the Feast of the Purification (February 2). This was an important event in the medieval year, celebrated since the time of Pope Sergius I late in the seventh century with processions of candles (hence "Candlemas"). The bishop provides (in the order given) a vestment for the abbot, three pounds of incense, three pounds of pepper, six blocks of wax, and three candles. The context seems odd only if we assume the pepper was there to be eaten; perhaps it was consumed at the feast afterward. It is equally likely that the pepper served some liturgical function, either mixed with the incense used in the censer or, alternatively, as an ingredient in the anointing oil.

There are many such cases where culinary assumptions rest uneasily with the context. As the Venerable Bede lay dying in 735, he told his disciple Cuthbert to run and collect "whatever things of value" he had in his cell, which the hagiographer lists as pepper, linen, and incense: "Run swiftly, and bring the monks of our monastery to me, so I may give them such little gifts as God has given me." The presence of the pepper is startling enough in eighth-century Northumbria; but it would have been more startling still if the hagiographer had sought to portray the holy man Bede gasping out his last words with the diet of his fellow monks foremost among his concerns. For this was an age when such attentiveness to diet was utterly incompatible with the spiritual life of which Bede was—and as the hagiographer intended—a shining exemplar. His parting gift makes sense only if the spice was valued as a sacrament or medicine, or quite possibly both. After bestowing the spices, according to his hagiographer, his final words

---

*In the temple of Kali in Cranganore in southern India, black pepper is offered to the goddess "so that spice vessels sailing abroad have a safe voyage."

were to contrast the pepper, linen, and incense with the gorgeous but worldly gold and silver that the rich were accustomed to distribute from their deathbeds. The force of the comparison relied on pepper having, in some forgotten and unknowable sense, a deeper symbolic force that somehow suited it to a life of holy poverty. And herein, in this mingling of sacred and physical well-being, lay the spice's inner value, whether for Bede or, more to the point, for the edified reader.

That such incidents have lost their force is, of course, because spices' air of sanctity has long since vanished. This seems to have been not so much a conscious, doctrinal departure as a consequence of the growth of the trade. In all likelihood the increasingly common use of spices at the table argued against their sacramental use, depriving them of their symbolic force. Spices simply disappear from view in the later Middle Ages, leaving balsam behind, more or less arbitrarily, as the sole surviving aromatic regularly used in the sacraments. In a twelfth-century sermon attributed to Werner of the Black Forest monastery of Saint Blaise, the use of cinnamon in the anointing oil is referred to in the past tense; evidently this was by now something that needed to be explained to the congregation. In the directions for the preparation of chrism given by the mid-fifteenth-century Pope Eugenius IV, only balsam is mentioned.

Spices survived better in the Eastern churches. In the thirteenth century, the Coptic Church was still using an anointing oil based on the Exodus recipe, with the addition of nutmeg, cloves, and cardamom. According to a contemporary Coptic treatise on liturgy by Ibn Kabar, *The Luminary of Church Services,* the oil used by the apostles was based on the recipes given to Moses by God, with the addition of myrrh and aloes in memory of the spices brought to Christ's tomb by Nicodemus and Joseph of Arimathea. Coptic tradition held that the apostles had mixed the oil in the "upper room," which they then took to the four corners of the earth as they dispersed on their evangelizing mission. In Ibn Kabar's day a new batch was made annually with the remnants of the old. It was believed, accordingly, that the oil used by the Coptic Church still contained some of the spices that had anointed Christ himself.

To this day the Russian Church uses spices in its chrism. Over the course of Holy Week, the Moscow patriarchate prepares a year's supply, during which time a blend of oil, wine, flowers, and spices is stirred, boiled, and reduced, during the last three days to the accompaniment of nonstop gospel readings. There is no strict definition of the ingredients, but a typical mix is still built around the Exodus template of olive oil, cinnamon, and cassia, with the addition of other spices such as cloves, ginger, and cardamom. When the chrism is ready, it is blessed by the patriarch, poured into consecrated vessels, then distributed to dioceses around the country. Authority for the use of the spices stretches back to the time of Dionysius the Pseudo-Areopagite, signifying "the grace-giving aroma of the variegated gifts of the Holy Spirit."

But even this is a far cry from the Heaven-ascending spices of antiquity. In practical terms, with minor exceptions, Christianity has put its spicy past behind it. Religion is deodorized; the very notion of sacred aromas is arcane in the extreme, known to present-day Christians largely as a matter of style: bells and smells versus the whitewashed minimalism of the low church. Some priests still use spices alongside balsam in preparing the chrism, but apparently on an ad hoc basis, the mix being up to the priest in question. The wife of the Reverend Richard Fairchild of Golden, British Columbia, uses allspice, cloves, and cinnamon to prepare chrism for her husband, but hers is, apparently, a rare instance. Even here the spices' role is reduced to the purely symbolic; no longer are they allegorized lovingly.

They linger today only on the new-age margins. A random trawl through the wilder fringes of the Internet suggests that the belief in spiced incenses and aromas is in ruddy health. Claims can vary widely. Some say that spices create a mood for spiritual communication, aiding a state of calm, reflection, or concentration. To one authority pepper brings "the startling awakening of superconsciousness"; others recommend spices to cover the telltale smell of marijuana. (Even this is perhaps not so far removed from ancient use. The spices and incenses used in the temple probably had the added advantage of covering the smells left over by animal sacrifices. In the heat of the Near Eastern summer the altars must have smelled like an abattoir from the "foul remains of months-old sacrifices," as Apuleius put it.) The Web site of the Theosophical Society of America advocates the use of cinnamon in incense "to create a spiritual atmosphere."

Others make more grandiose claims. The TechnoDruid suggests ginger in a "money fast oil," clove and pepper in a "courage oil," pepper "for protection against all kind of attacks," and cinnamon in an "astral travel oil": "Anoint the stomach, wrists, back of the neck and forehead. Lie down and visualize yourself astrally projecting." So potent are these ingredients that they should be used with due caution. Lisa of the Sibylline Order and Ancient Ways writes that during a Goddess Ritual she inadvertently stained her forehead with cinnamon oil, which made her look foolish. Spices require careful handling: "For magical purposes it's best not to blend oils while you're watching TV or having a tense conversation with your mother on the phone; your attention will be diverted, and unwanted negative crap may get into the oil."

●

CHAPTER 7

SOME LIKE IT BLAND

Unnecessary and contaminating seasonings must be avoided.
>
> —GUIGO DE CASTRO, fifth prior of the
> Grande Chartreuse, ca. 1083–ca. 1137

The Spartans flavored their dishes with hunger and toil. These
are the seasonings of our order.
>
> —HÉLINAND OF FROIDMENT, Cistercian monk,
> ca. 1150–ca. 1230

SAINT BERNARD'S FAMILY TIFF

Making a small penis splendid was hardly a recommendation to endear
spices in the eyes of a celibate clergy. And it was this, though he
phrased the matter a little differently, that was troubling Saint Bernard.

One of the most famous clerics of his age, Bernard of Clairvaux
(1090–1153) was a spiky combination of mystic, ascetic, and poet, lac-
ing transports of true lyric genius with a scouring asceticism:
Wordsworth meets Jeremiah. He was, in his day, a towering figure of
the European scene, with the authority to abash a haughty queen or
send a rampaging feudal thug scurrying for penitence; an upbraider of
popes, bloodhound for heretics, preacher of the Second Crusade, propa-
gandist, and recruiter in chief for the Knights Templar. Yet this glittering career was nourished on the meager soil of the Valley of Wormwood,
a wild and narrow defile carved by the river Aube through the hilly borders of Champagne and Burgundy. It was here in 1115 that Bernard
founded the monastery of Clairvaux, shepherding a small group of
monks through a life of extreme privation and isolation, scorched in the

summer, freezing and starving in the winter, renouncing all that was beautiful or precious in the world to find their way to God. Within this barren, cramped tract the sheer force of Bernard's personality would work a miracle as new recruits flocked to rumors of a monastic renaissance. They arrived in such numbers that Clairvaux fast outgrew its original site, necessitating a move downstream to new and more salubrious premises. In a matter of decades, Clairvaux was less a monastery than a minor city of clerics.

Yet in the summer of 1120, the fame of Clairvaux and Bernard still lay in the future. The infant community, still struggling to survive, was smarting from a particularly wounding affront, an affront wherein Bernard detected a lingering, troubling note of spice. Though like practically every other medieval mystic Bernard repeatedly turned to spices to evoke the ineffable, seeing them as symbols of devotion, love, and immortality, on this occasion they brought only bitterness. For as far as Bernard was concerned, they were, if not the primary culprits, certainly accessories to the injury he and his foundling community had suffered. They were the fuel of scandal.

It was not any effect spices might have on his own loins that concerned Bernard, but on those of his young protégé and cousin, Robert. The trouble began during Bernard's twelve-month absence in a hermitage—"like a leper's hovel"—followed by his attendance at the Chapter-General of the Cistercian Order in the autumn of 1119. While Bernard's back was turned, Clairvaux played host to a visitor sent by the "prince of priors," the grand prior of the great Burgundian monastery of Cluny. Whispering encouragement and blandishments in Robert's ear, this "wolf in sheep's clothing"—Bernard's description— succeeded in luring young Robert from the safe if not necessarily warm sanctuary of Clairvaux, abandoning its rigors, rocks, and woods for the comforts of Cluny.

It was, in other words, a poaching, and a particularly underhanded one at that. That Robert was family, that he had once begged to be admitted to Clairvaux and had freely sworn his vows—all this was more than enough to try the patience of this particular saint. But in the disputatious, fractious world of twelfth-century monasticism his defection was a particularly stinging betrayal. Cluny was, by some distance, the greatest monastic establishment of the age, home to some three hundred monks and another ten thousand or so in its dependent houses, with 115 establishments in France alone. Most of the popes of the previous century had been Cluny's alumni. Clairvaux, in contrast, was as yet a monastic minnow, its few dozen monks still in need of a watertight roof. This clerical class divide fed Bernard's sense of betrayal. Physically, Robert did not have far to travel from Clairvaux to Cluny, south from the hilly borders of Champagne through the rolling hills, plains, and valleys of northern Burgundy. Spiritually, however, at least as far as Bernard was concerned, Robert's was a step on the broad, easy road to perdition. If not quite the apostasy he hinted at, it was, in anyone's terms, a defection.

Particularly worrisome for Bernard was the thought of the food that Robert would eat once he got there; indeed, he suspected that the softness of the life at Cluny had had much to do with the young turncoat's decision. There was little that Bernard's white monks of Clairvaux prided themselves on more than the rigor of their dietary observance, and nowhere was monastic degeneracy better exemplified, at least in Bernard's eyes, than at Cluny. He made little secret of the fact that he regarded Cluny as an ecclesiastical fleshpot, where gluttony, loquaciousness, curiosity, and intemperance went by the name of discretion; where preachers commended drunkenness and damned parsimony. It was doubly galling for Bernard—a monk who "went to meat as it were to torment," and then only on doctor's orders—that Robert would be living it up in the vast spaces of Cluny's refectory. He had abandoned tunics for furs, vegetables for delicacies, poverty for riches. In place of the purifying austerities of Clairvaux, he would luxuriate in the Cluniacs' soft cloths, the cozy woolens and long-sleeved tunics of the monks, the opulence of their feasts, the vivid colors of the manuscripts and the gorgeous carvings of their churches, the "misshapen shapeliness" and "shapely misshapenness" of their sculptures, the comforts of their lifestyle—all fed the body, not the spirit; they were the seeds of weakness, not weapons for the battle.

If Bernard is to be believed, not the least of Cluny's temptations were the spices that the monks had no qualms about quaffing: "Pepper, ginger, cumin, sage, and a thousand such types of seasonings, which delight the palate but inflame the libido." It was a foolhardy monk who nourished his body but hazarded the security of his soul on such dangerous foods. Discreet, sober conversation was more than enough entertainment for a clean-living Cistercian; salt and hunger were the only acceptable seasonings for his cabbage, bread, beans, and lentils.

In the years that followed, Bernard's reproaches to his nephew became a minor classic, a Baedeker for the perils and pitfalls of the monastic lifestyle. The Cistercians saw to it that Bernard's reproach to his nephew was widely disseminated—it stands at the head of Bernard's voluminous correspondence—and on the subject of spices in particular his criticisms became a monastic refrain. His hagiographer and follower William of Saint-Thierry spread much the same word to the friars of Mont Dei, imploring them to abstain from "concupiscent and delightful" spices and seasonings on the grounds that they "endanger abstinence": "It is good enough," he argued, "that our food be edible." In due course even the story of the letter's composition became the stuff of legend. The same William tells the tale of the saint returning from his year's absence to find Robert departed for Cluny and its comforts, whereupon he stormed out to the mountainside with a secretary, to whom he began dictating. A sudden downpour appeared in the summer sky, but Bernard insisted that the secretary keep writing; "This is," he reproached his timid companion, "God's work." Chastened, the monk continued, and though both he and Bernard were soaked to the skin the parchment, mirabile dictu, remained bone dry. To mark the miracle a chapel was built on the site, where it stood until the Revolution.

Helped along by such tales, Bernard's opinions on the subject were ensured a wide audience; some of the reverberations, we shall see, are still with us today. But Bernard was far from alone in decrying the corrupting, eroticizing influence of spice. As the trade picked up after the tenth century, the risqué reputation of spices was if anything enhanced, gaining, if not in luster, certainly in currency and notoriety. And as spices moved to the fore in medicine, cuisine, perfumery, and aphrodisiacs, so in the moral economy of high medievalism the sense of their insidious, cheating charms was raised to a level undreamed of before or since. As spices were conspicuous to their admirers, so they were conspicuously disliked. Though the terms of the squabble were generally couched in the language of Christian morality, for centuries after Bernard fired off his reproaches in the "rain without rain," spices served as a touchstone for deeper debates, both clerical and secular, on the vexed questions of food, luxury, economy, poverty, and abstinence. And as is often the way with dissent, these criticisms offer an insight into the last and most ambivalent of the many attractions of spice.

On one level it should come as no surprise that an ascetic Christian monk such as Bernard should have objected to these most worldly of foodstuffs. It is more remarkable that this marked clerical distaste for spice coexisted with celebration. For spices were, as we have seen, metaphors for godliness and the ineffable: odors of virtue, the only thing remotely comparable to the Virgin. Bernard's fellow mystic and forebear Peter Damian possessed a similarly spiced imagination, comparing the shelter of a monastery (Cluny, no less) to a spiced paradise of delights, redolent of sweet-smelling spices, flowers, and the odors of virtue. It tended to be precisely those mystics who praised the heavenly spices who most deplored their use on Earth. There is scarcely a major mystical writer who does not show the same duality: what was fine in Heaven was on Earth distasteful, even dangerous.

There was a good deal more to this ambivalence than a particularly monkish double standard. Indeed, it relied on an opposition central to the mind-set of medieval mysticism, in the form of a radical separation of this world and the next. It was precisely because the Bernards viewed the divide between Heaven and Earth as so profound that the symbolically sublime might be base, even sacrilegious, in reality. It was the context and intent that mattered. For this reason Peter Damian even went so far as to compare spices to the forbidden apple of Eden. To his horror, one Christmas Day he was served spiced wine in the hermitage of Gamugno: "For what was good by nature, is made bad by the sin of disobedience; and what the Creator had soundly forbidden, is made deadly by man through usurpation of his freedom of will." If a mere apple had sufficed to cast man out of Paradise, how much worse was a luxurious, libidinous delicacy?

From the distance of the twenty-first century, the sheer intensity of his or Bernard's complaint cannot fail to strike us as overdone—easily dismissed as yet more medieval harping on the old saw that anything remotely pleasurable must be bad for you. Yet in medical terms, as we have seen, Bernard was merely repeating the orthodoxy. Given their aphrodisiac reputation, it was manifest that there was a problem in reconciling spices with the profession of celibacy. To Bernard's mind, even without spices the flesh was so frail as to need no encouragement to sin. Even for intellectuals like Bernard, demons were real and all around, few of them as insidious and opportunist as goatish Asmodeus, the demon of lust.*

---

*On one occasion Bernard found himself inflamed with desire for a young woman, whereupon he promptly threw himself into an icy pond and stayed there until he had cooled off a little, presumably to the amusement of the woman concerned.

After lust came gluttony. As their pagan critics had never tired of pointing out, spices and seasonings served no evident nutritional purpose, merely making food taste better and thereby whetting the appetite for more. The message was easily translated into Christian terms. To Saint Augustine pepper was a hallmark of the glutton, gorging himself on rare and exotic vegetables and course after course "well sprinkled with pepper"—a telling contrast with Augustine's ideal, a frugal, sparing diet of just enough cabbage and lard to take the edge off hunger.

Given the premises, then, the fact that spices occupied a conspicuous place in Christian dietary jeremiads was all but inevitable. They epitomized everything that food should not be, for which reason it comes as no surprise to find that an ingrained wariness of spices is present in some of the founding documents of the monastic tradition. In the East, Serapion, the fourth-century companion of the Egyptian hermit Saint Antony, knew cloves and pepper as potent aphrodisiacs. At roughly the same time the Rule of Saint Basil forbade sumptuous dishes prepared from expensive seasonings. In the West, his contemporary Saint Jerome laid out the founding principles of the medieval Christian diet in a series of letters to aspirant monks and nuns. In a letter written from Rome around 394, he stipulated that the would-be monk should refrain from pepper and other such delicacies as pistachios and dates, for "while we follow after dainties we distance ourselves from Heaven." Poverty was safer for the soul, and one should eat accordingly: "For we, the poor and the humble, have no riches, nor do we deign to accept offerings. Peasants buy neither balsam, pepper or dates. Those who seek to be rich fall into temptation and the snares of the Devil."

Jerome's objections would play a huge role in shaping Christian attitudes about diet in the years and centuries to come. When in the sixth century Saint Benedict wrote his Rule for the monastic life he insisted that the monks' food should be plain, nutritious, and no more than adequate. The rejection of spices was made still more explicit in a fourth-century letter long attributed to Sulpicius Severus, one of the pioneers of Western monasticism, addressed to the head of a small monastic community in Roman Gaul. The author writes that he has sent the community a new kitchen hand, not excusing but reveling in his lack of culinary sophistication:

After I heard that all your cooks had abandoned your kitchen, I believe because they disdained to perform their duties with common seasonings, I sent a small boy from our own staff, adequately well taught to cook beans and pickle humble beets in vinegar and juice, and to provide an ordinary porridge for the gullets of the hungry monks; he is ignorant of pepper, innocent of laser [another costly seasoning much esteemed in Roman cooking], but comfortable with cumin, and a dab hand at plying the noisy mortar with sweet-smelling herbs.

Besides being a bad cook, he was a psychotic gardener ("If admitted to the garden he will mow down anything in his reach with a sword"). All exotic and expensive seasonings were expelled from the cloister kitchen.

And outside was where they stayed, at least in theory, for well over a thousand years—which was where, more or less, we met Bernard firing off his letter in the rain on the mountainside. Thus on the subject of spices Bernard was merely repeating ancient if somewhat dusty commonplaces. These were, moreover, commonplaces that for his fellow Cistercians had the force of law, the superiors of the order having decreed that "in the cloister we generally use no pepper, nor cumin, nor spices of this type, but only common herbs such as our own land produces."

This situation would not change for the remainder of the Middle Ages, at least on paper. But while such odium may well have put spices beyond the pale, it certainly did not put them out of use, whether in literal or strictly literary terms. Just as Bernard used spices to shame a runaway nephew, so too spices constantly recur in Christian polemic as a convenient badge of dishonor, a token of the unmonastic monk. Even in Bernard's day the character of the gluttonous friar, more concerned with his stomach than his (or anyone else's) soul, was established as a feature of the literary landscape. Typical of the genre is a twelfth-century satire of a slothful, gluttonous, and lustful abbot who naturally loves his spices and sauces. He wakes up puking from the excess of the night before, meditating "more on his sauces than on sacraments, more on salmon than on Solomon," interspersing his "*laudate*"s and "*miserere*"s with stinking farts and belches. He stuffs himself with eggs smothered in pepper, fifty-five at a time. "Of his sauces and condiments what can I tell? He is served the blackest, thickest, hottest, richest, sharpest pepper sauces. . . . These are the sufferings he endures for Christ." In similar vein a monk at the French abbey of Ligugé punned

bitterly of his fellows "who ought to speak religiously of celestial spir-
its [*esprits*], but talk instead of terrestrial spices [*espices*]!"

The sense of inconsistency on which these satires depended took still
more visceral form in the works of Alain de Lille (ca. 1128–1202), a
monk who outdid even his fellow Cistercian Bernard in inventing new
and more lurid consequences of too much spice, the most startling
being the claim that spices and sodomy go together like a horse and
carriage. His poem "Nature's Complaint," probably the most sustained
and splenetic work on sodomy* ever written, takes the form of an ago-
nized dialogue between Alain and a personification of Nature, each
fretting over how it is that "the entire world is imperiled by the flames
of impure love," as Nature puts it. The poem begins with a vision
granted Alain in a dream, in which a grieving Nature confronts Alain
with a harrowing vision of a world turned upside down, where laughter
is turned to tears and joy to weeping, the seals of chastity are shattered,
the grace of nature's bounty is squandered, men are unmanned, and
society is wrecked by the monster of sensualism, "hims made hers,"
predicate turned subject, and the whole modern world generally gone
to pot, shipwrecked in a flood of gluttony and swallowed up in a raven-
ing Charybdis of the gullet.

Of this foul wrong, spices were at once totem, symptom, and cause.
To Alain gluttony was a deadly sin of a thousand forms, one of its most
pernicious and perverse mutations being overelaborate food, particularly the complex spiced sauces so sought after by the aristocracy and, if
Alain is to be believed, the clergy. As Nature complains, "For although
my liberality provides men with so many different types of food, rains
on them such copious dishes, they are nevertheless ungrateful for my
favors, abusing lawful things to illicit excess, loosening the brakes of
gluttony, exceeding the measures of eating and extending their capacity for drinking ad infinitum; seducing their palates with the tang of
sauces, so they might drink more and more frequently, to be thirsty
more often." The worst gluttons she identifies are the prelates, the
worst foods the spices. In Alain's hands, clerics' spice consumption
becomes almost a satanic, perverted rite. Like idolaters worshiping
their sacred pepper, their sexual depravity was mirrored and egged on

---

*For the medieval monk this was a more germane topic than one might imagine. Readers of
Umberto Eco's *The Name of the Rose* will have a sense of some of the sexual tensions bubbling
away in the all-male but celibate community of the cloister.

by the perverse ingenuity of their cuisine, the spiced fish and fowl wallowing in their thick and spicy sauces. Ungrateful and unsatisfied with nature's bounty, they seek out new sauces, slathering on the spice and whipping up their carnal appetites for yet more indulgence:

> This pestilence is not content with common, humble folk, but is widely found among prelates, who, befouling the rite of baptism, baptize salmon, pike, and other equally special fish in a font of their sacred pepper, crucifying them in several martyrdoms of cookery, so that, baptized by such a baptism, they might acquire an agreeably complex flavor. Meanwhile, at the same table, the beast of the earth is overwhelmed by a flood of pepper, the fish swims in pepper, birds are ensnared in its viscosity.

Inverting the eucharistic imagery of a simple, God-given meal of the bread and blood of Christ, the rites of the gourmand's dinner were an antibaptism, a mock martyrdom.

Like many a scene of clerical debauch, Alain's sodomitical spice quaffers are best taken with a pinch of salt; understatement was not a weapon in his or any other medieval polemicist's armory. Indeed, the very forcefulness of the complaint is arguably more suggestive of high standards than of hypocrisy, of cultural rather than material realities. What, then, are we to make of that reality? Were Alain and Bernard at least justified in suggesting that this prohibition of spice was a dead letter among some if not necessarily all monastics?

The answer to this question varies with time and place. Monastic discipline (and wealth) differed from one place to another, and spice consumption with it. Certainly, spices were seldom if ever eaten with such gay abandon as Alain and Bernard were willing to suggest; they were never quite as innocent or acceptable as the critics would have us believe. Even at Cluny their consumption was hedged with conditions. A generation before Bernard's day, Ulrich of Cluny took evident pride in the fact that his monastery never lacked an ample supply of pepper, ginger, cinnamon, "and other healthy roots," which he pointed out were primarily for the infirmary. On food pepper was permitted only once a year, on the last Sunday before Lent, when it could be sprinkled on eggs. A peppered wine was occasionally served after Mass. On the rare occasions when spiced dishes were allowed, they were on no condition to be cooked by the monks but by the servants, safely sequestered in a separate kitchen. Otherwise this was a regime of vegetables, bread, and fish.

The interpretation and the enforcement of such rules varied with the times. In Bernard's day, Cluny's former rigor was relaxed under the abbacy of the worldly nobleman Pons de Melgueil, abbot from 1109 to 1122, although before too long Bernard had what was undoubtedly the supreme satisfaction of seeing even mighty Cluny make an about-face, in large part due to the sheer force of his own example. Two years after Bernard fired off his letter, Pons was deposed by the pope. After an unsuccessful attempt to force his way back, he was succeeded as abbot by Peter the Venerable (abbot from 1122 to 1156). The new abbot, whose rule was extremely unpopular at the start, promptly banned the monks from drinking spiced wine altogether, his one concession to luxury the feast of Maundy Thursday, when a little honey could be added to the wine, minus the spices. (It must have been doubly gratifying for Bernard that besides tightening up on Cluny's diet Peter wasted no time in sending his runaway nephew back to his rightful home. Bernard proved as good as his promise of forgiveness, and Robert ultimately showed himself sufficiently Cistercian—and presumably sufficiently spice-averse—that in due course Bernard promoted him to abbot of a monastery of his own, Maison-Dieu in the diocese of Dijon.) Under Peter's regime "royal spices" were forbidden in terms scarcely less severe than Bernard's: "By what authority is a foreign or oriental spice, sought with such great effort, bought at such great expense, afterwards to be mixed in the wine of poor and abstinent monks?"

But if there were victories over spices, clerics of Bernard's ilk were inclined to see them as isolated battles in a larger war. The Devil was a tireless worker, and the need for vigilance was constant. Even in the shelter of the cloister there were traps and snares, and few places were so fraught with danger as refectory, kitchen, and cellar. If the spirit of the rules was clear, all but the hardiest of souls could find qualifications, if not exceptions, in the letter. Even in the sternest order, the consumption of spice was permitted on special occasions. Some monasteries allowed spices in case of medical necessity, the earliest explicit ruling perhaps that of Saint Ansegisus (ca. A.D. 770–833/4), abbot of Fontanelle. Yet even then there was a risk in throwing spices out the front door that they might creep in at the back. Since a spell in the infirmary meant meat and spice, the sickbed was not necessarily such a bad place to be. Sickness could be feigned, and it seems that it commonly was. The twelfth-century cleric Peter of Blois poured scorn on hypochondriac monks who, affecting to be ill, and weary of the unrelenting diet of fish and vegetables, took electuaries and refused sauce unless it was made with cinnamon, cloves, and nutmeg: "Such clerics are disciples more of Epicurus than of Christ."

In terms of the medical theory of the day, these cassocked Epicureans were justified in fretting over the effects of their cold diet, although their worries tended to contravene their ethos of abstinence. To Bernard's fellow mystic and contemporary Hugh of Saint-Victor, not only spices but even homegrown garlic and cumin were off limits. He lambasted those persnickety monks who insisted on their dinner being just so, picking out various dishes and seasonings on the grounds of their suitability for their constitutions — not too hot, not too cold; here a little cumin, there a little spiced salt and a little remedial pepper, "as fastidious as pregnant women." To Hugh all such bodily attentiveness was synonymous with the deadly sin of gluttony, which he identified with bakers' fancy breads, sauces made with the cook's art, the meat of quadrupeds and birds, sea and river fish, pepper, garlic, cumin, and seasonings in general.

For the hard-liners the use of spices even in a medical emergency was to be overly attentive to the flesh. *The Ancrene Riwle,* a thirteenth-century book of advice for an aspiring anchoress, takes the stern line that "if a man is ill and he has something to hand which will do him good, he may, of course, make use of it, but to be so solicitous about such things, especially if one is a religious, is not pleasing to God." Health of the soul came before health of the body. This grim little injunction was illustrated with the story of three holy men, one of whom

used to resort to hot spices on account of his cold stomach, and he was more delicate in matters of food and drink than the other two, even though they were all ill. They paid no attention to what they ate or drank, as to whether it was wholesome or unwholesome, but always accepted whatever God provided for them, without examining it. They did not attach great importance to ginger, or zedoary, or gillyflower cloves. One day, when the three of them had fallen asleep and the first of whom I spoke was lying between these two, the queen of Heaven came to them accompanied by two maidens, one of whom appeared to be carrying an electuary, the other a small spoon of gold. Our Lady took some of the substance from the electuary with the spoon and put it into the mouth of the first, and the maiden went on to the middle one. "No," said Our Lady, "he is his own physician. Pass on to the third."

That the monasteries were at the forefront of medical studies is a strangely enduring myth, since they were in fact more inclined to frown on anything that smacked of bodily indulgence: "You are a monk, not a physician," as Saint Bernard phrased it. "Though a man has severed himself from pleasures, what is the profit if every day he spends his energies and thoughts investigating differences of constitutions, or in devising new ways to cook food?" It was better to be ill than to eat spices and get better.

If the excuse of sickness opened a chink in the monks' defenses, whether feigned, feared, or real, feast days opened another. Some of the spiciest events in the monastic calendar were funeral banquets, such as those decreed by Burchard the Venerable, count of Vendôme (958–1007), who had churches built posthumously and masses sung for his soul, followed by banquets of rich and precious spices for the monks charged with the obsequies. When Suger of Saint-Denis lay dying of malaria in 1137, he summoned the monks and decreed two pittances* of spiced wine, plus wheat and wine for the poor. Having summarized the historically Spartan diet of the monks, Udalric of Cluny proceeds to tell of the *apocrisarius,* the treasure keeper, charged with supplying the monks "if he can lay his hands on the ingredients, with well-peppered fishes, and piment." Between the austerity of the rules and the periodic indulgence of feasts, it is very hard to extract a sense of the daily realities, but that some spices were eaten at least occasionally is beyond dispute.

Elsewhere across the monastic world, the impression is much the same, that of a muddy line between theory and practice. Even as Bernard thundered about decadence and corruption in the kitchen, his contemporary the abbot Rudolph wrote unblushingly and in great detail of the spicy diet of the monks of Saint Trudo in Brabant. Having commented on the laxity of some monasteries, the lamentable corruption of monastic life, he writes, with no sense of contradiction, of the feast days of Saints Rémy and Trudo, when the menu was a series of

---

*The original sense of a pittance was a bequest to a religious house, whence it came to designate a small dietary allowance to the monks. The sense here is of modest sufficiency.

variations on the theme of fish and pepper. For a first course there was a dish of fish marinated with pepper and vinegar, topped with eggs and more pepper. This was followed by poached salmon with pepper, then more salmon, grilled and generously peppered. To finish there were various other fish and peppered caviar.

But these were special occasions. More startling is the reference in a slightly earlier eleventh-century work by the Blessed William, abbot of the Benedictine foundation of Hirsau in Württemberg, celebrated in his day for the exceptionally strict discipline he had imported from Cluny. Although his was a monastery of perpetual silence (an exception was made for confessions) and one with particularly harsh punishments for any infractions, the monks were apparently allowed spices when they so desired (although, as at Cluny, the spices were cooked not by the friars but by their servants and eaten under supervision in the refectory). The monks used a complex sign language: "For the sign of ginger, use the same sign as set out above for herbs, but with your right hand clenched in a fist, raised up high, moving it round in a circle around your jaw; keep moving it around your jaw; then stick out your tongue, and lick your index finger."

If a conclusion can be drawn, it is that warnings against spices were reiterated so frequently because they needed to be. Over the longer term, the monastic kitchen shows every sign of having succumbed to one of the constants of culinary history: the effort, on slender resources, of turning a fast into a feast.

The result, in short, was the return of spices to the monastic menu. Such was cooks' ingenuity that many dishes of the fast days could scarcely be described as penitential. As mitigation for the hardship of the season, some monasteries used spices *particularly* during Lent. Even in Bernard's day, his contemporary Peter Abelard was scandalized by this monkish hypocrisy. In one of his letters to Héloïse he noted that spices made the food of Lent better, not worse: "What's the point in abstaining from meat if we then proceed to stuff ourselves with other luxuries? . . . We buy various fishes at huge expense. . . . We mingle the flavors of pepper and other spices, bloated with wine, we wash it down with chalices of liqueurs and phials of spiced wine—and the excuse for all this is abstinence from mere meat!"

Others said much the same even of feast days, when, so the critics complained, a brief relaxation of the rules was taken as carte blanche for a binge. When the prior of the Great Church of Canterbury served the

visiting Giraldus Cambrensis a banquet on the day of Holy Trinity
1179, his guest found the meal totally at odds with monastic protesta-
tions, the festal circumstances notwithstanding. The table was duly
meat-free but so burdened with dozens of different fish and spiced delicacies in dozens of "sumptuous and superfluous dishes" as to render
any abstinence purely nominal: "So many types of fish, grilled and
roasted, stuffed and fried, so many dishes prepared with eggs and pepper, all the arts of the kitchen, so many flavors and sauces prepared by
this art, in order to incite gluttony and whet the appetite." All this was
washed down with spiced wines. The vegetables, he adds, were hardly
touched.

The lesson to be drawn is one, ironically, close to the hard-liner's
heart: that in the battle between spirit and flesh, the flesh was never
quite defeated. Doubtless many clerics were as good as their word, but
in the longer run (and perhaps from the start), the hard-liners' was a
losing cause. With time exceptions became the norm. At a monastery
at Worcester in 1300, monks were given an allowance of 18 pence with
which to buy themselves spices "as they know to be suitable to their
own bodily complexions." (Not only a contravention of dietary rules,
this was also an infringement of the prohibition of private property.)
And while the accounts of some monasteries record sparse spice expenditure, by the late Middle Ages others rivaled the lusty appetites of the
nobility. In 1418 the thirty-five monks of Abingdon Abbey spent £53
15 s. on spices, a sum equivalent to the annual income of a middling
country vicar.

To an extent, this laxity was symptomatic of a broader relaxation of
monastic norms—or, as Martin Luther and company would have had
it, of their corruption. With time the intensity of Christian worries
over diet faded. A French monk at the abbey of Ligugé argued that the
rules developed for Eastern ascetics did not apply with the same force to
a Frenchman, because, well, the French are different: "That a Cyrenean
can bear to eat nothing but cooked herbs and barley bread is because
nature and necessity have accustomed him to eating nothing." What
was true of an Eastern eremite did not suit French conditions: "We
Gauls, we cannot live like angels."

The higher up the ladder of ecclesiastical authority one looks, the
spicier things get. Many feasts put on by prelates or monasteries differed little if at all from secular occasions. At the lavish installation
feast of John Morton, bishop of Ely, in 1478, guests were treated to

elaborate mixtures of meat, eggs, fruit, and spices in a sort of aspic jelly. But for the scriptural themes of the elaborate, allusive constructions of sugars and spices to puzzle and delight the guests, this could have been a nobleman's debauch. But even Morton's bender was small beer alongside the installation-day feast for Ralf de Born, proclaimed prior of Saint Augustine's, Canterbury, in 1309. The six thousand guests ate their way through 100 hogs, 30 ox carcasses, 1,000 geese, 500 capons and hens, 473 pullets, 200 piglets, 24 swans, 600 rabbits and 9,600 eggs. Of a total expenditure of £287 8 s., more than £28 was spent on unnamed spices, plus another £1 14 s. on pepper and saffron. Except for the £30 spent on two hundred "muttons," spices constituted the largest single item.

The clerical propensity for spice went all the way to the top. A Vatican ceremonial drawn up by Pope Gregory X shortly after 1274 provides for copious wines and spices for the pope and his retinue after the Christmas Eve Mass. By the following century, the feast of Saint Stephen was celebrated with a magnificent meal followed by a collation, or evening assembly, at which pepper was served. Standards may have slipped, but spices still retained their capacity to cause offense. *The Legend of Celestine and Susanna,* a Middle English poem written sometime before 1425, features a pontiff summoned down to the gates of Hell, where he is accosted by a jubilant personification of Gluttony: "I fed you with rich meats and spicery, spiced wines. . . . Your soul is mine!" Duly accused and convicted, the pope is dragged off to join the legions of the damned.

For at no point was there a downgrading or dismissal of spices' perils. Spices remained dangerous, laced with contamination, even as their consumption became more common. A reform of Cluny undertaken by Pope Martin V in 1428 reveals just how far dietary standards had evolved—or fallen—in the three centuries since Bernard's day. Outside the fast periods of Advent and Lent, the monks were now allowed spice and meat with few qualms, based upon the historically dubious claim that a "heating meal" of meat, eggs, cheese, and spices was "approved according to the ancient custom of the Apostolic Seat." The Cluniacs' excuse for such luxury was that there was not enough water around to supply all the fish necessary for such a large community (although Cluny had apparently coped in the time of Peter the Venerable). Seasonings and meat would nourish the body and obviate tedium—provided, of course, they were not taken in excess. The Easter

Sunday feast must have been a particularly eye-watering meal, as the monks were allowed bacon, cheese, four fried eggs, and half a pound of pepper.

Even then, however, a sense of the need to regulate spices was retained; the framers of the reform saw fit to stipulate when and how they could be eaten. They were still sufficiently volatile material as to warrant inclusion in a papal directive, with a due nod to the laxity of the preceding regime. It was not that spices were suddenly safe; what had changed was the interpretation of the limits, the sense of what was acceptable. As late as 1690, the Benedictine monk and scholar Edmond Martène had no doubt that the dietary stipulations of the Benedictine Rule amounted to a blanket ban on condiments of any sort.

Which leaves us, once more, looking over an uneasy divide between theory and practice. But to point out the existence of this divide is not to say that all who flouted or forgot the rules were backsliders or hypocrites. One of the more humane theologians to touch on the question was Caesarius of Heisterbach (ca. 1170–ca. 1240), author of *The Dialogue of Miracles,* one of the most popular books of the Middle Ages. In his discussion of temptation, Caesarius relates an anecdote by a certain Abbot Gisilbert, who permitted his monks the daily consumption of three grains of spice (peppercorns, presumably). Challenged by a fellow religious, Gisilbert explained that improving the flavor of humble fare with a small amount of spices made the monks eat all their vegetables, lentils, and peas, thereby preventing ill health and malnutrition: "When a monk avoids his peas or lentils out of melancholy or humors, he commits a greater sin than when he eats too much." For if their food was intolerable they would not eat it, and a malnourished monk would weaken and so be unable to fulfill his duties. Moderation in all things was best.

Prohibition, on the other hand, was not only ineffective but counterproductive. According to Caesarius, temptation "arises from the incitements of the flesh and the devil or both, *especially after a prohibition. . . .* It is very deplorable that human nature should always strive after that which is forbidden." So far as Caesarius was concerned, far from making a dent in spices' ancient reputation for magical and erotic potency, clerical hostility burnished it. In an age with its own, decidedly mixed experience of prohibition, it would be hard to disagree. This was surely the undertow of the great torrents of condemnation clerics poured out on spices since the time of the Church fathers. This is not to label as naive all the banners and damners, Saint Bernard and company—who after all knew a thing or two about restraint—but rather to point out a paradox, the eternal quandary of the prohibitionist. To forbid something was to inflate its value and vivify its attractions, and in this sense those who would have had spices expunged from the medieval diet could not help but subvert their own intent. And maybe this was the critics' most lasting legacy: of all the many attractions of spice, real and imagined, perhaps none was so tempting as the allure of forbidden fruit.

FILTHY LUCRE

What a prince does seems like a command.

—QUINTILIAN (ca. A.D. 35–ca. 96), *Declamations*

Needless to say, where one stood on the fraught issues of spices, the libido, health, and appetite depended considerably on one's walk of life. It is no coincidence that clerics' objections to spices tended to single out precisely the same qualities we have already met with in previous chapters. What nobles prized, the clerics decried. Instead of adequate nutrition, spices brought flavor; instead of sufficiency, the desire to eat more; instead of economy, profligacy; instead of celibacy, ruddy sexual vigor. For critics and admirers alike, many of these qualities, good or bad, were covered under the deeply ambivalent notion of luxury. Here too the intensity of their attractions cannot be fully appreciated minus an understanding of their ambiguities.

In recent centuries the idea of luxury has undergone a transformation. Whether in a holiday, a house, or a hotel, luxury is, so the advertisers tell us, a good thing. Even the muesli I buy for my breakfast is, according to the label, a luxury. In the Middle Ages, on the other hand, had there been such a thing as advertising (or muesli), the tag of luxuriousness would have been more fraught, ripe with ambiguity: indeed, for many it was not so much a recommendation as a reproof. Luxury was, after all, one of the seven deadly sins. Caesarius of Heisterbach felt that "luxury, like gluttony, has wrought the greatest evils in the world"—which he listed as the Flood, the destruction of the five cities of the plain with fire and brimstone, the imprisonment of Joseph, the abasement of Israel, the blinding of Samson, the demotion and death of the children of Eli, the adultery and murders of King David, Solomon's idolatry, Susanna's condemnation, and the beheading of John the Baptist. Like the other six deadly or cardinal sins, luxury was both a wrong in itself and the wellhead of greater evils: the notion of a cardinal sin derives from the Latin *cardo,* meaning "pivot" or "hinge," the opening through which greater evils enter. It was not so much an issue of personal consumption as a cosmic wrong.

Or at least "luxury" is one of many inadequate translations of what went by the untranslatable term *luxus,* a wrong of rank, coruscating awfulness, conveying a sense of excess, superfluity, otherness, perversion, illicitness, and—which was but a subset of the same—lust. To Caesarius, luxury and her daughters included "wanton and unbridled prostitution of mind and body, arising from unclean desires," manifested in several degrees of fornication, debauchery, adultery, incest, and unnatural vice. The word itself is cognate with the Roman word *luxuria,* conveying a sense of sprawling extravagance that is only faintly retained in its modern derivatives. The term was originally used of vegetation, implying abnormal and unbounded growth beyond the norm, surpassing its natural limits.

Just how far spices surpassed natural limits emerges obliquely, from the words of those for whom spices were conspicuously luxurious in this latter, intensely negative sense. To those who preferred their consumption inconspicuous, they were the epitome of waste and profligacy: expensive foods, as one critic complained, "wherewith many poor men might be fed sufficiently." What bedazzled a nobleman bent on parading his munificence represented to others a grotesque misuse of resources, a "great outrage of expense." To the anonymous author of *Mum and the Sothsegger,* an early-fourteenth-century polemic, the profligacy of spices stuck in the throat. In contrast with the simple living and hard work of "simple men on ploughs," at court all restraint was abandoned. The king should spend his days, not his nights, sleepless; nor should he spend more than was strictly necessary on dainties, dancing, jesters, "mirrors of sin,"* spices, wax, wine, and waste. Fools, dancing, and mirrors aside, *Mum*'s list is familiar from an episode covered earlier: wax, wine, and spices were precisely the luxuries singled out by Zurara as freely dispensed by the munificent Henry the Navigator.

---

*The mirror was long derided by critics as a spur to vanity.

Above and beyond the sheer costliness of the spices, it was the vanity of their uses that most riled their more puritan critics. Underlying this stance was the conviction that our needs are simple and amply provided for by God. Since God had made the world, he clearly had not meant it any other way: the lilies of the field were more beautiful than the raiment of Solomon. It was no more than consistent—indeed, it was almost a logical corollary—to hold that any disruption of that order was a disruption of God's will, a meddling with what He had intended. Anything that smacked of artifice was an alteration of the divine creation, a perversion of nature. Applied to the table, this purist instinct took the form of a culinary iconoclasm: if the correct purpose of nutrition was nourishment, it followed that the cook's art was unnatural, its sole function to delight the palate, thereby transforming God's creation into a debased, perverted form. Introducing foreign flavors to local foods was both to inflate our own simple needs and to meddle with what had been amply provided for, merely for the sake of a transient pleasure. Thus Chaucer's Pardoner accused cooks of degrading God's creation with their sauces "made of spicery of leaf," all of which he dismissed as "abominable superfluity" and converting "substance into accident," the real essence of a thing into mere external form. They were a sort of antifood, transforming and concealing what God had made. Worse than superfluous, they were impious. The spice eater was not merely a glutton, worshiping the false god of his stomach; he was guilty of the Luciferian sin of rebellion.

That these concerns were something more than abstract theological debates can be sensed from Dante's peopling of the eighth circle of Hell, where a Sienese gourmet by the name of Niccolò wallows deep in leprous horrors, his crime the discovery of "the costly use of cloves."* Revealingly, he shares his corner of Hell with those whom Dante classes as "the counterfeiters." There in the slime with the clove-eating Niccolò are Caccia d'Asciano and Abbagliato, two members of Siena's *brigata spendereccia,* or Spendthrift Brigade, who made themselves notorious by gorging themselves on food and wine, then smashing the plates and glasses. Another resident is Griffolino d'Arezzo, a heretic

---

*This would appear to be one of several unwarranted Dantean slanders. In the previous century, England's King Henry II had already discovered the "costly use of cloves" (in wine), and an Anglo-Norman recipe book of the twelfth century contains a recipe for a clove-flavored dish called "mawmeme."

and falsifier of metals burned to death for claiming he could fly, and the Florentine Capocchio, an alchemist burned at the stake in 1293. All are sentenced to languish for eternity in a dank malarial ditch for the crime of tampering with the natural order.

Dante evidently liked it bland. Of all of the black marks set against spices, this stigma, as the unnatural food of the rich few, was one of the most tenacious. To the clerical reformer John Wycliffe, spices were nothing less than diabolical. In his late-fourteenth-century treatise "Of Antichrist and His Followers," the latter appear eating ornate food "seasoned with hot spices and extra-hot with sauces and syrups." He returned to the theme in his tract *Of the Leaven of Pharisees,* fulminating over the false monks who guzzled hippocras, feigning a life of holy poverty even as they lived off their flock like parasites. The spiced wines they drank and shared with their noble patrons were at once a trapping and a symbol of a life conducted contrary to clerical principles. Greedy, rapacious hypocrites, their lifestyle made them worse than "common thieves and outlaws," who took from the rich but at least shared the proceeds with the poor. In a similar vein, the Franciscans of the late-fourteenth-century poem *Pierce the Plowman's Crede* ought to live poorly and walk barefoot but on closer inspection turn out to have fur lining for their tunics, fancy buckled shoes, and revealing hose. They carry spices everywhere they go. Another poet claims that the begging friars turned a tidy profit from selling spices to "grete ladys & wenches stoute"—pleasant enough for the woman, but the husband had to foot the bill. Still worse was to follow, since the mendicant "will not blink at winning a woman privately and leaving a child within—and maybe two at once!" A contemporary writes of the Jacobins and Augustines "of Judas' kin," who come knocking at the door and taking bribes in the form of spices. If one wanted to ask a priest to intercede on one's behalf or say a wedding or funeral Mass, one had better have some spices ready, since the average member of the clergy "spendeth no speech minus the spice."

Most of the sting of the accusation would disappear as the cost of spices plummeted, yet their air of grubby worldliness outlasted the Middle Ages in at least one corner of the world, albeit in a highly ritu-alized form. Since at least the thirteenth century, it had been customary in France to lubricate judicial proceedings with spices, for which reason François Villon dedicates a verse to a greedy lawyer, to whom he leaves a whole basket of cloves, taken from another, still greedier advocate. As late as the end of the eighteenth century, it was still the custom in the French courts to use spices as thinly veiled bribery, as competing plaintiffs advanced their suits with "gifts" of spices to judge and jury. The expression "to pay the spices" meant to win one's court case—a form of corruption of which the comedians Molière and Racine made merry. It would take a revolution to put a complete stop to aromatic bribery.

From cloister and courthouse, complaints of the worldly excess of the spices were easily extrapolated to the level of national economics. Perhaps more than any other trade, the long-distance luxury trade with the East was open to the charge of needlessly enriching foreigners—and impoverishing one's countrymen. Who those foreigners were was of course a matter of perspective. For most Europeans they were Italians. In an anonymous English polemic of the early fifteenth century, *The Libelle of Englyshe Polycye,* the author slated the Genoese merchants in their great carracks "with cloth of gold, silver, and pepper black," who he felt should be banned from English waters. He reserved special scorn for the "commodities and nicetees" of the Venetians and Florentines, who kept the kingdom supplied with spices and other luxuries, with their galleys laden with "thyngs of complacence." Grouped among such fripperies as apes, marmosets, and other "nifles and trifles," the "dear and deceitful" spices and other such "wasteful goods" amounted to nothing more substantial than a particularly efficient means of redistributing wealth into the hands of the enemy.

The Libelle would have brought a sardonic smile to the Venetians, the Florentines, or the citizens of any of the other Italian trading republics, since they were themselves often at the receiving end of the identical complaint. From the Italian perspective, those cash-guzzling foreigners were for the most part Muslims or the orthodox Christians of Byzantium. Indeed, the complaint could be shunted back down the spice routes as far as the clove and cinnamon groves, just as it had been shunted down in time from one moralist to another, ever since Pliny had bemoaned the costly magnetism of India's pepper. Perhaps the most startling occurrence of the complaint was as the Age of Discovery got under way, in precisely those kingdoms that were expending the greatest efforts on acquiring the spices for themselves in both East and West. Columbus's patron King Ferdinand was apprehensive of an outflow of scarce Spanish currency to Portugal merely for the sake of pepper and cinnamon. "Let's put an end to that," came the royal decree. "Garlic is a perfectly good spice."

It would have been no solace to Ferdinand that identical concerns
were expressed over the border. Even during the heady days of the first
discoveries and conquests, the Portuguese Crown found itself grap-
pling with problems that belied the glamour and the martial glories of
its eastern empire. There to see with his own eyes was the Portuguese
poet Francisco de Sá de Miranda (1481–1558). Not one to be carried
away by the headlong rush to empire, he singled out spices as a sort of
fool's gold. However, it was not so much the drain on the kingdom's
finances as the cost in terms of human capital that concerned him:

> I have no fear of Castile,
> Whence comes no sound angry of war;
> But I'm afraid of Lisbon,
> That at the smell of this cinnamon,
> Unpeoples our kingdom.

These complaints of demographic and economic drain were destined
to outlast the medieval world, passing in due course from one European
power to another as the focus of the spice trade shifted from the
Mediterranean to the Atlantic. In the seventeenth and eighteenth centuries, both the Dutch and the English East India Company regularly
had to field the complaint that their eastern traffic was beggaring the
country. In England the matter was repeatedly raised in Parliament,
where the East India Company had to defend itself from the charge of
putting the country's scarce capital to flight for the sake of spices. The
issue was especially acute for the English, since aside from a strictly
limited amount of pepper smuggled out from under the eyes of the
Dutch in India or squeezed from the wretched, malaria-plagued Suma-
tran port of Benkulen, all of England's spices arrived via middlemen.
For this reason, in 1662 King Charles II issued a proclamation forbidding the purchase of cinnamon, cloves, nutmeg, and mace from parties
other than the producers themselves—a measure aimed at the Dutch
and those "foul traders at home" who dealt with them, treasonously
draining the kingdom of its bullion.

Similar complaints would persist until events finally pushed the
trade into irrelevance. Over time, many causes combined to deprive the
refrain of its potency, until it fizzled out and was forgotten. Though in
absolute terms the spice trade grew larger from medieval into modern
times, in relative terms spices suffered a loss of visibility. New trades
appeared, and other imports overshadowed spices as conspicuous gob-

blers of cash. Moralizers found other commodities to single out as more reprehensible, more ethically dubious: sugar, tea, coffee, and chocolate, all of which have long since been trumped by still more potent stimulants.* So too Enlightenment economics would chip away at and finally demolish the mercantilist logic that had long given complaints against spices such clout; or which, conversely, had for so long made of spices such an effective symbol of worldly means. But by this time both spices and the spice trade had long since ceased to be a pressing national concern beyond a handful of exporter countries, much less a matter for national economic or moral debate. As to why and when this occurred we now turn.

*Though sugar's critics are perhaps staging a comeback.

❶

THE END OF THE SPICE AGE

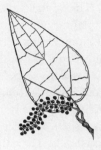

A leaf of the pepper plant. Acosta,
Tractado de las drogas (Burgos, 1578)

> The rarer something is, the more it is sought after. In India penny-royal is dearer than pepper.
>
> —SAINT JEROME (ca. 347–419/420), "To Evangelus"

In February 1755, a battered frigate flying a French ensign and bearing the name of *La Colombe* hove into view off the remote Moluccan island of Meyo. The voyage had left the ship much the worse for wear; it was barely seaworthy, its ancient rigging so decrepit that it was incapable of sailing to windward. On board was a one-armed Frenchman with a cunning plan. His name was strangely appropriate to the task at hand: Pierre Poivre, a Gallic Peter Pepper. Like many others who had traveled to the Moluccas before him, he was there not to trade, but to steal.

The Moluccas had been the sole home of the clove since cloves existed, and so they remained, with some qualifications, when Poivre dropped anchor. Originally confined to five islands to the west of Halmahera, by Poivre's day the spice grew on a few dozen islands of the surrounding archipelago, under the watchful eye of the Dutch East India Company, or VOC. After the final expulsion of the Portuguese in 1605, the VOC had set about making each and every clove on Earth a Dutch possession. Under Dutch rule the islands were exploited with a ruthlessness and efficiency never seen before. Gaps in what had been a porous Portuguese monopoly were plugged, and all clandestine trading was ruthlessly suppressed. The Moluccas were squeezed by a rule as harsh as the better-known plantation regimes of Caribbean sugar and cotton. The inevitable rebellions were mercilessly put down. In 1650, the Dutch governor, despite being bedridden, insisted on personally knocking out the teeth of a Ternatean rebel commander, smashing the roof of his mouth, cutting out his tongue, and slitting his throat.

To prevent all such uprisings and to stamp out smuggling, it was Dutch policy to concentrate the clove on the central Moluccan island of Ambon and a few outlying islands. The sultans of Ternate and Tidore were pensioned off and kept amenable by a combination of cash and the ever present threat of superior force. The clove groves were torched.* From the VOC fortress on Ambon annual expeditions set off to destroy illegal clove trees and to punish renegades. Smugglers were blown out of the water; all unauthorized cultivation was punishable by death. Dutch troops crushed the smuggling center of Macassar, where English, Chinese, and Portuguese bought illicit cloves. By Poivre's day, through cannons and subsidies, the spice was scarcely more widespread than it had been for thousands of years; as closely guarded, as one observer wrote, as ever a jealous lover watched his sweetheart.

Nutmeg, the second spice of the Moluccas, was guarded with a similar ruthlessness. The ethos was summarized by Jan Pieterszoon Coen, an early and particularly brutal governor-general: little profit would come from being "virtuous and good"; it was better "to ride the natives with a sharp spur." And this the Dutch certainly did. By the 1620s, the VOC had worked to death or expelled practically the entire indigenous population of the Bandas. The company imported slaves to work the plantations; Javanese convicts and Japanese mercenaries were called in to mop up any local resistance, which was in any case more imagined

*With some rare exceptions: on the slopes of Ternate's Gamalama volcano there is a clove tree more than four hundred years old.

than real. The headmen of the islands were tortured and duly confessed to all sorts of lurid conspiracies. From the battlements of their forts Dutch artillery looked over the world's entire supply of nutmegs. To be doubly sure, after harvest all nutmegs were treated with lime so that none could be sown elsewhere.

Having themselves stolen the spices from the Bandanese, and having seen off their European rivals with bloody efficiency, Dutch paranoia was understandable. They had much to lose and much to gain. Throughout the seventeenth century the markup on cloves and nutmeg between purchase and final sale was on the order of 2,000 percent, a profit that brought yet more luster to the Dutch Golden Age and paid for many a burgher's elegant house and fittings. To maintain the price at an artificially high level, the Dutch regularly staged spiced bonfires that unconsciously evoked the spiced holocausts of pagan antiquity. In 1735, 1,250,000 pounds of nutmeg were burned in Amsterdam alone. One witness saw a bonfire of nutmeg so great that the oil flowed out and wet the spectators' feet. An onlooker was hanged for taking a handful of nutmegs from the flames.

It was to pilfer company spices on a grander scale that Poivre sailed to the Moluccas. The stakes were as high as they had ever been for earlier spice voyagers: success meant fame and fortune; failure, certain death.

The latter prospect seems not to have troubled Poivre unduly. He was the sort of figure who belonged only in the eighteenth century, his life a Candide-like succession of adventures and narrow scrapes, including several tangles with the Royal Navy, stints in prison, a flirtation with the priesthood, brushes with the ecclesiastical authorities, and flashes of entrepreneurial bravado and polymathy, spiked throughout with intense personal vanity, much of it played out in the swashbuckling surrounds of the Indian Ocean. He arrived off Meyo by a convoluted route. Born in Lyon on August 23, 1719, he was educated by the missionaries of Saint Joseph before continuing his education at the Missions Étrangères in Paris. It was under the auspices of this thoroughly internationalist institution that he developed an interest in natural science and an ambition to see Asia. At the age of twenty, while he was still a novice, the missionaries sent him east, where he spent two eventful years in China and another two in Cochin China (modern Vietnam). Here he had the opportunity to study Asian plants and had his first serious run-in with the authorities. At some stage his superiors began

to have grave doubts about his vocation, sensing that his deepest
instincts were not so much spiritual as commercial. A meeting at Canton with the Irish adventurer and entrepreneur Jack O'Freill set him
thinking of more worldly opportunities in the East. His interest in the
cloth wilted.

His superiors, sensing his disaffection, decided he should return to
France. The superior at Canton concluded he was an opportunist who
had joined the order merely to see the world on a free ticket. And so in
1745 he embarked on the *Dauphin* with his career under a cloud,
headed for home and an uncertain future.

The voyage did not go as planned. As the *Dauphin* passed through
the Bangka Strait, off the east coast of Sumatra, it had the extreme misfortune to run into the *Deptford,* an English man-of-war commanded by
a veteran privateer with the suitably briny name of Captain Barnett. It
was an unequal contest, and after a brief and bloody combat, the
Dauphin was taken. Poivre was hit in the wrist by a musket shot, taken
prisoner, and thrown belowdecks. His ruined right hand quickly
turned gangrenous. Twenty-four hours later he found himself stretched
out on what passed for an operating table, the blood-smattered surgeon
of the *Deptford* standing over him, matter-of-factly informing him that
his lower right arm was now bobbing on the waves, dinner for a hungry
seagull.

More than any other moment, this gory encounter shaped Poivre's
subsequent destiny. Short on rations, the English were anxious to rid
themselves of any extra mouths, so Poivre and the other captives were
dropped at the Dutch town of Batavia (modern Jakarta), to await the
arrival of a more friendly ship. Poivre's enforced four-month sojourn in
the capital of the Dutch empire in the East marked the nadir of his fortunes. It was clear that his missionary career, already troubled, was at an
end—having only one arm, he was unable to consecrate the host. He
did, however, have time on his hands (or hand) to reflect on alternative
careers and give free rein to his fertile imagination. He began making
plans for a brighter future.

The commercial vitality of Batavia soon set Poivre thinking. This
mosquito-infested, unhealthy, but vibrant town was both the epicenter
of Dutch trade with Europe and the hub of the still more lucrative trade
of the archipelago and Asia. Ships came and went from Japan, China,
Siam, Bengal, Malabar, Ceylon, and Sumatra. In an atmosphere of min-

gled squalor and opulence, merchants of all nationalities provided plenty of stimulation for his convalescence. In particular, he was struck by the prosperity of the Dutch spice merchants. He spoke with several Dutch traders who, confident in the company's secure hold on the Moluccas, willingly shared information with the innocuous-looking invalid. Others painted a picture of lax safety measures, of smuggling and evasion that went on under the noses of the authorities, of clandestine spice plants that grew beyond the reach of the Dutch patrols. It struck Poivre that the company had, so to speak, left the house unlocked.

And so an idea took root in Poivre's fertile imagination: he would steal spice plants from under the noses of the Dutch and transplant them to French colonies in the tropics, thereby shattering the VOC's monopoly. (Although he was perhaps unaware of the precedent, in contemplating the transplantation of spice plants he partook of a tradition that stretched back to Hatshepsut's expedition to Punt more than three thousand years earlier.) By acquiring spices he would bring a potentially vast source of income to France, her colonies, and not least himself, in the process delivering a devastating blow to Dutch power in the Indies. He allowed himself to imagine that if all went as planned this would be the single greatest piece of industrial espionage of all time. In Poivre's own words: "I then realized that the possession of spice which is the basis of Dutch power in the Indies was grounded on the ignorance and cowardice of the other trading nations of Europe. One had only to know this and be daring enough to share with them this never-failing source of wealth which they possess in one corner of the globe."

It was to this end that Poivre found himself, several years of plotting and planning later, standing on the deck of his listing ship, peering through a telescope at the clove groves of Meyo. In the end he would succeed—after a fashion—but not this time. The winds were in the wrong quarter and his ship was in such a poor state that he was unable to make a landing. Like Moses in the wilderness, he was forced to content himself with gazing at the promised spice groves, tantalizingly out of reach. In his report on the mission Poivre blamed the ship and, by implication, the tepid support of his patrons, the authorities of the Compagnie des Indes: "Nothing will console me for having been a stone's throw from this island, so fertile in cloves, and yet having been unable to set foot on land, recover these precious fruits, and carry off the much-desired plants which could have made the Compagnie's fortune. . . . Why did I not have anything for an expedition of this nature besides the worst vessel that has ever put to sea?"

There was no option but to look elsewhere. With the monsoon gathering and the condition of his vessel rapidly deteriorating, he charted an erratic course around the Spice Islands, north to the territory of the modern Philippines, and south to Timor, scouring the islands in vain for the precious spice plants. Time after time promising openings came to nothing. At one point he hoisted the Dutch flag to prevent capture by a passing Dutch vessel. Finally he managed to obtain a few second-rate nutmeg plants from the Portuguese possession of Timor, which he succeeded in getting back to the other side of the Indian Ocean, to the French colony of Île de France (Mauritius).

It was, not for the last time, a false dawn. His seeming success rapidly unraveled as the plants failed to thrive. Relations on the island turned sour, and Poivre turned peevish. Poivre saw factional infighting, the tricks and jealousies of enemies both real and imagined. A rival botanist declared the nutmeg plants to be false; given that Poivre had obtained them from Timor, where relatives but not the real thing are documented, he was probably correct. In due course Poivre claimed that a jealous rival had killed the precious seedlings with boiling water or "some mercurial drug." The authorities were uninterested at best, at worst actively hostile to the entrepreneurial, one-armed gadfly who was forever demanding money and ships to pursue his spiced schemes. No one seemed to care. It looked, for a time, as if Poivre's plans had come to nothing.

And so, in 1756, he headed back to Europe, his career again under a cloud. Once more the English attacked and captured the ship he was traveling in, resulting in a stint in an Irish jail. After seven months in Cork, he returned to France. His plans and plants had apparently failed to thrive, but he did at least have time to write his memoir, the grandly titled *Voyages d'un philosophe.*

It was Poivre's efforts with the pen that belatedly revived his project of purloining spices, deliverance coming in the form of an appreciative reader who also happened to be a minister in the government of Louis XV. Troubled by the parlous finances of France's colonial possessions in the Indian Ocean, he was impressed by Poivre's ideas and offered the mercurial entrepreneur the *intendance* of the islands. Perhaps Poivre's scheme was the answer to the endless flow of subsidies to France's costly colonies. Poivre headed back east in 1767. Now at last he could rise above the petty rivalries that beset colonial affairs; he could also employ others to take his risks. He settled on two reliable Indian Ocean hands, Evrard de Trémignon and *le sieur* d'Etcheverry, whom he placed in charge of two swift corvettes, the *Vigilant* and the *Étoile du Matin.* They sailed for the Moluccas in January 1770.

His deputies enjoyed better fortune than Poivre had the first time around. Shortly after making a clandestine landfall on Ceram, just to the north of the Dutch headquarters on Ambon, Etcheverry met a lone Dutchman mending his boat on the beach. Over a drink the Dutchman soon divined the intention behind his visitor's questions but, fortunately for Etcheverry, was so thoroughly disenchanted with island life that he was willing to bare all. He directed the French to the island of Gueby, where the islanders kept illicit clove and nutmeg plants hidden deep in the jungle.

Bidding a grateful farewell but nagged by the suspicion that he might be double-crossed, Etcheverry duly made straight for Gueby. After some initial confusion—at first the islanders mistook the French for a Dutch raiding party—the locals were more than happy to help; anything to harm the Dutch. Though their plants had recently been detected and burned by a Dutch patrol, they directed the French to a nearby island. Here Poivre's men carried off thousands of fresh young nutmeg seedlings suitable for propagation.

There was, however, still no sign of any cloves. Despite the assurances of the village headman, who had promised to bring some seedlings from a neighboring island, the French were getting jittery. After a further eight nerve-wracking days, with the monsoon building on the horizon and the risk of a Dutch patrol ever present, they resolved to sail with only half the task achieved, only to have their departure delayed by adverse winds. It was a fortunate development, for as they waited for the wind to shift, a small flotilla of islanders arrived with hundreds of young clove seedlings.

Their mission accomplished, the French promptly set sail for Île de France. Their last serious obstacle came in the form of a Dutch coastal patrol, which they fooled by pretending to be lost travelers. After an uneventful voyage west across the Indian Ocean, they made a triumphant return on June 25, their holds crammed with no fewer than 20,000 nutmegs and 300 clove seedlings. Their haul was planted in the Jardin du Roi on the Île de France, where, after a few years in which the

majority of the seedlings died, a core group of plants successfully accli-
matized. The first crop of cloves was produced in 1776 and nutmeg two
years after. Each occasion was marked with great ceremony, "as the
Romans were wont to celebrate their triumphs with the trees of the
countries they had conquered," in the words of a Parisian pamphlet. A
ceremonial consignment of the first creole spices was dispatched to the
king. Poivre foresaw more plantations in France's other tropical possessions, the Seychelles, Cayenne, and Haiti. The contemporary Abbé
Raynal compared Poivre's feat to Jason's theft of the golden fleece.

Yet despite all the accolades Poivre's plants were never quite the success they had promised to be; his adventures, ultimately, packed more
panache than punch. Though their descendants can still be seen today,
Poivre's core group of stolen spice plants on Île de France apparently
never produced a profitable crop, plagued by official indifference and
the local monkeys. On the eve of the Revolution, France was still
importing some nine thousand pounds of cloves per annum, the entire
proceeds of which went into Dutch pockets. Perhaps the most bitter
defeat came in 1778. It was now nearly a decade since Poivre had transplanted a few of his beloved spice plants to the new colony of Mahé in
the Seychelles, where they were kept and nurtured in conditions of the
utmost secrecy. But all came to naught when a warship flying the
Union Jack appeared in the harbor, whereupon the gardeners torched
all the spice plants so as to prevent them from falling into enemy
hands. They turned out to have been a little too enthusiastic in carrying
out their orders, for the ship was nothing more threatening than a mis-
directed slaver—and a French one at that. Its crew had hoisted the
Union Jack under the mistaken impression that Mahé was a British
possession.

In the longer run, however, Poivre's overanxious gardeners had good
reason to fear the Royal Navy. During the Napoleonic Wars the Moluccas were twice occupied by British forces, first from 1796 to 1802 and
again from 1810 to 1816. Industrious officers had time to spare in
which to transplant the spices to British possessions around Penang and
Singapore, where, with the encouragement of Sir Thomas Stamford
Raffles, plantations were laid out with full state subsidy and support. In
1843, the nutmeg was introduced to the Caribbean island of Grenada
by Captain John Bell, "because he liked his punch." Poivre's efforts
paid dividends only when he was long in the grave, although France

derived no profit therefrom. Around 1818, descendants of Poivre's stolen cloves were transplanted from Mauritius to Madagascar, Pemba, and Zanzibar, where they did spectacularly well. Nearly two hundred years later, the flow of spices across the Indian Ocean has been reversed, with Indonesia now a net importer of cloves.

Yet if Poivre was ultimately more flamboyant than effective, he remains something of an iconic figure in the waning of the spice trade. For however belated or mixed the fruition of his efforts, they neverthe-less encapsulate some of the deeper trends already under way, trends that account for the rapid fading of spices' ancient attraction. Their proliferation meant that they were on the road to being commonplace.

Poivre, as we have seen, was far from alone in dreaming of spreading spices around the globe. By a royal order of 1678, the Portuguese, robbed of their Asian possessions by the Dutch, had tried to send cloves, cinnamon, nutmeg, and pepper to Brazil, efforts that continued through the eighteenth century. In the sixteenth century, the Spanish had attempted the same in their Central American possessions, though only ginger and cinnamon seem to have done well at this early stage. There was an early attempt, two hundred years before Pierre Poivre, to filch the clove. The other spices had started their steady diffusion much earlier. Pepper is generally believed to have moved east from its native Malabar to Sumatra and through the archipelago as early as the first centuries of the Christian era, accelerating rapidly thereafter. At this time cassia already grew through much of southwest China, Assam, and Southeast Asia.

One of the last spices to set off around the world was the cinnamon of Ceylon. After the fall of the island to the Dutch in the 1630s, the VOC maintained the high price of the spice with a combination of monopoly and blockade, in its essentials the same system as applied to the clove and nutmeg, with a similar pattern of hopeless local revolts and pitiless Dutch reprisals. In June 1760, visitors to Amsterdam witnessed the conflagration of some 16 million French livres' worth of cinnamon. The fire, which burned for two days outside Amsterdam's Admiralty House, gave off a fragrant cloud that passed over all of Holland. The system came to an abrupt end in 1795, thanks once more to the guns of the Royal Navy. Ceylon became a Crown colony, the monopoly system was abandoned, and the plants were transplanted to other tropical pos-sessions.

The hermetic isolation of the spices had been shattered; the ancient combination of rarity and value was now a thing of the past. And as the means of supply was transformed, so too demand was changing. Even as Poivre drifted around the Moluccas, spices were being overtaken by newer and more profitable goods, such as tea, silver, rubber, and textiles. When the British arrived, the VOC was already tottering and bankrupt; spices were no longer the money-spinners they once had been.

This was a process, arguably, that had its beginnings in the earliest days of Europe's eastward rush to the spices. The apex of the Spice Age was the beginning of the end of their attraction. It was, admittedly, an end that took several hundred years to play itself out, but thanks to the very success of the Portuguese and Spanish discoverers, as well as the English and above all the Dutch East India companies that came after, spices were on the way to becoming affordable and familiar. Market manipulation slowed but could not halt the trend. Although the spice lands remained prizes to be fought over (or to be robbed), their ancient glamour and mystery were long gone. Now they were studied, mapped, horse-traded, their products reduced to commodities. Mandeville and Marco Polo made way for tales of surviving and making it big in the perilous, profitable East; of extracting a fortune among the grafters and mosquitoes, the drink and dissolution, of Batavia or Colombo.

By the discoverers' succeeding too well in acquiring the spices, then, the legacy they left was the erosion of their charm. The old myths and legends died hard, but spices were never the same again. In 1556, Francisco de Tamara claimed that cinnamon and laurels covered the water when the Red Sea rose, but by now this sort of thing was sounding increasingly medieval. The tone of the future was set by Garcia da Orta, who as a subject of Portugal's Estado da India had ample opportunity to inspect the reality for himself. With cool Renaissance precision his *Colloquies* dismantle the ancient myths one by one. The most glamorous of the flavors that spices brought to the table—the heady mix of profit, danger, distance, and obscurity—was fading fast.

All of which was a far cry from the Middle Ages, when spices had arrived in Europe from beyond the known world. Spices were now a means of getting rich for anyone willing to take his chances with the perils of the voyage and the deadly monotony of tropical life, with all its loathsome, strange diseases. They had been dragged into the modern world, and with modernity came that deadly quality, attainability.

◗

"The East," ejaculated an old Scotsman once—"the East is just a smell!"   —DAN MCKENZIE, *Aromatics and the Soul,* 1923

As spices lost their attractions across the spectrum of their many former uses, from the temple to the bedroom, their most significant fall from grace occurred in the kitchen. As with any discussion of changing tastes, it is extremely hard to pin down a specific reason. Early modern cuisine was no less spicy than its medieval predecessor, but much had changed. Spices had ceased to be the last word in taste, sophistication, and health. Even as the East India Company and the VOC brought spices to Europe in ever increasing volumes, there emerged a current of thought that looked on the highly spiced cuisine of the Middle Ages with mingled disgust, condescension, and amusement. More became less.

The exact border between medievalism and modernity is a fuzzy one, and this is as true of cuisine as of any other area. Spices still figure prominently in a selection of cookbooks published across western Europe late in the sixteenth century. The English *Proper New Booke of Cookery* (1576) and Diego Granado's *Libro de arte de cocinar* (1599) contain dozens of classically medieval spiced sauces and confections—much as is to be expected of an age that expended such prodigious energies in acquiring spices. Meanwhile, in absolute terms, the spice trade more or less doubled in volume through the course of the hundred years after Columbus, peaking around the end of the eighteenth century.

Yet as early as the middle of the seventeenth century, in some circles the heavy use of spices was seen as something of a culinary joke. In 1665, the French satirist Boileau produced a barbed lampoon entitled *The Ridiculous Meal,* in which the narrator makes fun of the *ancienne cuisine.* The host of Boileau's meal is a pretentious boor who likes to pose as a man of taste and refinement when in fact he is nothing of the sort: "In the whole world, no poisoner ever knew his trade better." Noting that the guest has barely touched the disgusting meal set in front of him, the host inquires if he is unwell and encourages the reluctant diner to partake: "Do you like nutmeg? It has been put into everything." The reference may be to a historical figure, the abbot of Broussin, a nutmeg addict who was mocked for putting the spice in all his sauces. Having long since anesthetized his taste buds with excessive spice, he was always in need of a stronger flavor that his jaded palate could recognize.

Boileau's satire is, then, not so much a sign of the widespread use of spices as it is evidence of their fall from grace. The host's heavy hand with the nutmeg is indicative of his tastelessness. He was a culinary dinosaur, presenting unsophisticated medieval slop as the latest in *nouvelle cuisine,* comically unaware of his failure to keep up with trends. Tastes had moved on.

It is probably no coincidence that this fall from favor occurred just at the time when spices had to compete in an increasingly crowded marketplace. The world was getting smaller, and its bounty was coming to the dinner table. The advent of potatoes, squash, tomatoes, and peppers created new possibilities for cooks, at the same time lessening the workload of spices. American chili was both cheaper and stronger than pepper, and it could be grown practically anywhere. After Columbus first returned with a sample, the plant spread so fast around the world that many Europeans assumed it was of Asian origin. Paprika put down roots from Spain to Hungary. Pepper, for which there had long been no substitute, could now be outgunned.

The chili was only one of several new stimulants competing for attention. A craving for tobacco swept the world in the sixteenth and seventeenth centuries, with coffee and tea following not far behind. Although sugar had been known in the Middle Ages (classed, incidentally, as a spice and used largely for medical purposes), its consumption began to increase dramatically from the sixteenth century on. Late in the century, sugar began to be mass-produced in Brazil and somewhat later in the West Indies, the apparent result a general sweetening of the Western palate, an upward curve that has continued, much to the cost of our teeth and the profit of our dentists, to this day. The carousing cavaliers of the great Dutch artists endured a dental hell. Sugar had something of the glamour and forbidden attraction formerly reserved to spices, and its air of dangerous newness probably did no harm to its attraction.

Meanwhile, the social setting that had so long shaped aristocratic cuisine was gradually but utterly transformed. The seventeenth and

eighteenth centuries witnessed an unprecedented convergence of aristocratic and bourgeois tastes, the effects of which are still very much with
us. By the 1700s, the distinctions between food for great princes and
food for the middling sort of person looked increasingly antiquated; in
a word, medieval. The new spirit was captured by the publication in
England in 1665 of *The Queen's Closet Opened,* offering a glimpse into the
food and manners of the monarchy but aimed at a wider audience—a
taste of royalty, however vicarious, in the bourgeois home. Across the
Channel, in 1691, François Massialot published his *Cuisinier royal et
bourgeois*—a title that little over a century earlier would have sounded
as offputting to one class as absurd to the other. By the end of the century there were 100,000 copies in print. A little later the pioneering *La
Cuisinière bourgeoise* was a runaway success, running to thirty-two editions between 1746 and 1769.

The aesthetic of this distinctively middle-class cuisine was radically
unlike its precedents, marked above all by a shift away from the color,
cost, and elaboration that had been the hallmarks of Roman and
medieval cuisine. It would be misleading, however, to suggest that
food became classless and therefore spiceless; it was rather that spices
were no longer as appealing, medically, socially, even spiritually. With
the Renaissance there was a reordering of the cosmos along less theological, less allegorical lines, with the result that spices lost their symbolism, their ancient significance of health and holiness. (Gold, also
common in aristocratic medieval cooking, went the same way, for much
the same reasons.) Meanwhile, the conspicuous outlets for consumption
were increasingly channeled away from the table, to jewelry, music,
dress, houses, art, and carriages. The modern dinner was a more private
affair than its medieval predecessor. The coded messages of land and
money remained the same, but refinement and affluence were expressed
by different means.

Although some of the hallmarks of aristocratic cuisine—game, in
particular—lingered on, even aristocrats turned to simpler, fresher flavors. Across all orders of society (except the poor, who had never had
much choice), there was a shift to simpler and more local flavors. In
place of the transmutation sought after by the medieval cook, the new
ideal was that food should taste of itself. The new cookery stressed natural, inherent flavors, the ingredients cooked in such a way as to
enhance their particular character. In the cookbooks of the later seven-

teenth century food begins to appear recognizably modern. Often the new taste took the form of an appetite for supposedly rustic food: the idea of the "rustic" table, however contrived, became a good thing.* An upper-class fascination with a supposedly Arcadian peasant life brought country cuisine to the upper-class table—the same instinct that saw Marie Antoinette build faux cottages and cowsheds in the gardens of Versailles. The medieval or Roman delight in witty or exotic subtleties, fish trussed as flesh, came to seem artificial and overwrought.

In this respect, changes at the table reflected trends in the wider world. The age of the emergent nation-state was also the age of national cuisines, none of which had much room for spice. Nowhere was the new trend more fully or more successfully expressed than in Italy, both regionally and nationally, where the delight in fewer, simpler, and fresher tastes remains the quintessence and genius of Italian cooking. Anglo-Saxon cuisine went down a different and bleaker route, but one that led equally far away from spices. In the cookbooks of the seventeenth and eighteenth centuries, elaboration and costliness make way for economy and practicality. In Hannah Glasse's *Art of Cookery* of 1747, for nearly a hundred years the most popular cookbook in the Anglophone world, the use of spices is strictly limited. Pepper survives in much the same role as it has today, no longer the central element as in medieval black pepper sauces. Across the Atlantic, the trend was much the same. There were relics: galantine survived, now transformed from the original spicy sauce into a jelly. The general trend was to relegate spices to desserts such as mince pies and puddings. Which is where, until very recently, they remained.

It was an outcome that would have gratified a Saint Bernard or a Peter Damian, and indeed some of their more puritanical successors may have played a part in marginalizing spices in the modern Western kitchen. For as social and economic change pointed in the direction of bland food, so too did religion. Insofar as diet was concerned, the Reformation and Counter-Reformation succeeded in popularizing what had hitherto been strictly monkish debates on diet; and unlike the Jeremiahs of the previous chapter, they seem to have had a good deal of success in taking that message beyond the cloister. The Puritans felt the ancient Christian wariness of cooking on a visceral level, a fact that goes a long way toward

---

*As of course it still is—the rate at which "rustic Tuscan" cookbooks are published shows no signs of faltering.

accounting for Protestant cuisine's well-deserved reputation for bland-
ness. There was no small irony in the fact that the Protestant powers
were also the leaders in the spice trade. In the seventeenth-century
Netherlands, even as the VOC brought back cargoes of cloves, cinnamon, and nutmeg, Calvinist preachers railed against the corrupting
influence of Eastern spices and their redolence of pagan sensualism. In
Cromwell's England, propagandists took aim at seasonings along with
bear baiting and theaters. Dull food was on the way to becoming both a
religious and a patriotic duty, as one poet lamented:

> *All plums the prophet's sons deny,*
> *And spice-broths are too hot,*
> *Treason's in a December pie,** *
> *And death within the pot.*

The Commonwealth soon faltered, but its legacy in the kitchen
endured long afterward. After the Restoration, the scent of treason still
lingered over spices, and in due course what had apparently begun with
mercantilist economics and religious belief acquired the force of habit.
In the cuisine of the seventeenth and eighteenth centuries, bland was
beautiful. This is the age when the English travelogue acquires the figure of the Englishman abroad, complaining about the unpalatable
spiciness of foreign food. In 1679, the writer John Evelyn thought the
food served at the Portuguese embassy "not at all fit for an English
stomac which is for solid meat." More bluntly, his contemporary Lord
Rochester expressed his preference for "our own plain fare . . . hard as
the arse of Mosely." (Mother Mosely was a famous London brothel
keeper, evidently a hard bargainer.)

Spices hung on in isolated pockets, but they were not what they had
once been. Today the astute culinary archaeologist can still find such
relics as spiced bread in Devon, and further north there is a plethora of
richly spiced puddings—Scotland's national dish, the spicy haggis, is
essentially a medieval pudding. Scandinavia and the Baltic have preserved several remnants of medieval cooking, largely in biscuits,
breads, cakes, and liqueurs. One of the most interesting and unexpected survivals lives on in Mexico's *mole poblano,* a fusion of American
ingredients with the flavors of medieval Spain: turkey, chocolate,
vanilla, and chilies married with almonds, cloves, and cinnamon. If tra-

*A spiced pudding, forebear of the modern Christmas pudding.

dition is to be believed, the combination was dreamt up by a nun of Santa Rosa Convent in Puebla, asked to come up with a meal for a visiting viceroy. It is as though the tastes of Montezuma and the Catholic kings meet on the plate.

Yet such survivals represent the exception, and they tend to be confined to peripheral areas. Perhaps more to the point, there was an acute consciousness of this fact. Western European visitors to more spicy climes did not hesitate to regard spices' longevity as a symptom of provincialism or backwardness. When the Abbé Mably visited Kraków in the late eighteenth century, he snootily dismissed the locals' best effort, "a very plentiful meal which might have been very good if the Russians and the Confederates had destroyed all those aromatic herbs [sic] used in such quantities here, like the cinnamon and nutmeg that poison travelers in Germany." His scorn was more than an isolated instance of the still-flourishing French tradition of lofty contempt for cooking à l'étrangère; rather, it marks a more general shift. The perception had taken hold that spices were all power and no subtlety, best left to the coarse palates of Easterners.

And the further east one got, the hotter and coarser food became. In an age of intensifying nationalism, food came to be seen as a projection of national virtues—or, looking elsewhere, vices. What you ate was a proclamation of national authenticity or, alternatively, decadence. Dryden, we have seen, translated the satires of Juvenal and Persius, in which the importation of Eastern or fancy foods was repeatedly scorned as degrading and debilitating. Spices were increasingly associated with oriental habits; they were exotic and mysterious, effeminizing and voluptuous. An early example was the "cruell Sarazin" of Spenser's Faerie Queene, a character who prefigures the opium-smoking Chinaman or hashish-addled Turk of the nineteenth century, in this case deviously bolstering his strength with illicit stimulants, "dainty spices fetched from furthest India, secretly to kindle their machismo"—not playing it straight like his gentle Christian knight.

Spices became a mark of the exotic and a decadent, incompatible Other. The sensuous Easterner was pictured sauntering through spice bazaars or reclining on his velvet couch, feasting on aromatic banquets as the houris danced around him. In "Hermione," Ralph Waldo Emerson imagined an Arab "drugged with spice from climates warm"; Swinburne's Laus Veneris oozes

Strange spice and flavour, strange savour of the crushed fruit
And perfume the swart kings tread underfoot,
For pleasure when their minds wax amorous,
Charred frankincense and grated sandal-root.

Intriguingly, this sense of the foreignness of spices was most acute in the nineteenth century, precisely when exposure to "swart kings" and their perfumes was greater than ever before. In the early days, Europe's pioneers in the East had had little choice but to assimilate, Portuguese, Dutch, and English alike eating Indian food and developing their own fusion cuisine, of which vindaloo is perhaps the classic example.* Whereas in the days of the Raj there evolved a parallel white man's cuisine, the dreadful white and brown sauces that still linger on in some of India's wealthy households and boarding schools. Meanwhile, in Europe, Antonin Carême (1783–1833), the founder of the French style of *grande cuisine* and arbiter of nineteenth-century taste, regarded the abuse of spices as the antithesis of good cooking. The sense of spices' inherent Eastern dangers was summarized by the dour Scots writer Dan McKenzie, who was repelled by the "strange vices" of those "outlandish Eastern *aromata,* redolent rather of vice and its excitements than of virtue, and its placidity." Fortunately, his native land had undergone a thoroughly Presbyterian fumigation: "I may, therefore, with justice, raise a song of praise to our fathers who have had our country thus swept and garnished, swept of noxious vapours and emanations and garnished with the perfume of pure and fresh air, to the delight and invigoration of our souls." Even as Western penetration of the East reached new levels, East and West went separate ways at the table. In that sense, at least, Kipling got it right.

But historically, of course, Kipling was wrong, for nowhere is the history of East and West more incestuous than at the table. For the sake of spices East and West had an ancient relationship. In light of the appearance of spices in the most remote periods, it is a reasonable possibility that it was *because* of spices that they first met. Yet so thoroughly implanted is the sense of the otherness of spices that native

---

*The name derives from the Portuguese for "wine" (*vinho*) and "garlic" (*d'alho*): wine and garlic sauce. The dish is effectively Portuguese India on a plate, the pork and vinegar of Europe married with the ginger and cardamom of India.

Mediterranean aromatics such as cumin, coriander, saffron, and fennel have come to be associated more with the cuisine of the countries that adopted them than with the lands of their origin—a reminder that the cultural traffic that traveled along the spice routes went both ways. Outside the Essex town of Saffron Walden, few would guess that in medieval times England was long Europe's greatest producer of saffron. Today, when spices are making a comeback, with an upsurge of interest on both sides of the Atlantic, it is often claimed that spices were introduced with the great wave of migration from the former colonies. It is a claim that would have startled the first Europeans who went to Asia, particularly since it was spice that lured many of them there. The Englishmen and Portuguese who ate at the courts of India's Moghuls and rajahs in the sixteenth century found there a cuisine which, in spite of several unfamiliar ingredients, they immediately recognized as showing all the hallmarks of refinement and taste, in its qualities of spiciness and elaboration not at all dissimilar to the cuisine their kings and nobles ate back home.

○

> But what is myrrh? What cinnamon?
> What aloes, cassia, spices, honey, wine?
> O sacred uses! You to think upon
> Than these I more incline.
> To see, taste, smell, observe is to no end,
> If I the use of each don't apprehend.
>
> —THOMAS TRAHERNE (1637–1674), "The Odour"

In the 1660s, the English physician Thomas Sydenham, once hailed as "the Shakespeare of medicine," claimed to have found a wonder drug. His laudanum, he boasted, was an unrivaled "cordial." Made from a pint of sherry or Canary wine, its chief added ingredients were saffron, cinnamon, and cloves, beefed up with a two-ounce slug of opium. For a long time Sydenham's laudanum was immensely popular with his fellow physicians. The spiced opiate was regularly prescribed for restless children, nervous orators, light sleepers, pregnant women, a string of prime ministers and their wives, poets, and artists. It helped them sleep, brought relief from pain, and made them feel terrific.

Like opium, spices had a future after Sydenham's day, but not, for the most part, as medicines. Here too spices went into eclipse no less thoroughly than at the table, for similarly diverse reasons. Only very recently, when spices have come to attract increasing scientific attention, has it once more become possible to justify their use in medical terms, although modern discoveries seldom correlate with the claims historically made on their behalf. No longer is it credible to claim cinnamon as a panacea.

As with cuisine, the decline did not come overnight. In the seventeenth century, it still made sense for Milton to write of Ternate and Tidore, "whence merchants bring their spicy drugs." In 1588, Walter Baley wrote a book dedicated purely to the merits of pepper; in 1677, the Scottish savant Matthew Mackaile wrote another on mace. Pierre Pomet, druggist to Louis XIV, said of cinnamon that "we have few drugs that we use so much of"; he regarded cinnamon oil as "the greatest cordial [remedy] we have." Nutmeg was so widely used that "it would be needless to say any Thing of it." Even in the nineteenth century, sweet smells were still used as a defense against disease, although the practice came to be seen as increasingly folksy. Describing the trial of Charles Darnay in *A Tale of Two Cities,* Dickens pictures the court "all bestrewn with herbs and sprinkled with vinegar, as a precaution against gaol air and gaol fever [typhus]." The Galenic theory of olfactory sensation came under attack during the second half of the seventeenth century, but it was only with Pasteur's discovery of the microbe that the old fallacy of bad air was finally taken out of the equation. With the advance of empirical methods of medicine, subject to verification, humoral theory was dealt a deadly blow. Smells and miasmas, the invisible death-dealing airs that had hung over medical thought since antiquity, were dismissed as fallacious. As bad air and humoral theory were on the way out, with them went spices.

In the medical schools of Europe and America the study of pharmacy became vastly more empirical and accordingly far less reliant on traditional herbal remedies. By the start of the eighteenth century, the divorce between the physicians and apothecaries, descendants of the medieval spicers, was already well advanced, with the reputation of the former in the ascendant. In London the "Chymists" and druggists split from the apothecaries; in Paris in 1777, the *pharmaciens* of Paris split away from the *épiciers.* With their chemical and synthetic medicines the newer disciplines were seen as more scientific, credible, and trustworthy. The apothecary was viewed as an increasingly bogus pur-veyor of folk remedies. In London the College of Physicians denounced the herbalist Nicholas Culpeper as a "physician-astrologer": a quack.

As spices fell from favor with the living, so it was with the dead. Robert Herrick (1591–1674), we have seen, makes numerous refer-ences to spiced embalmings, and a little later Louis Pénicher used spices on the dead dauphin en route to Saint-Denis. It was not until the nineteenth century, with the development of formaldehyde and the improvement of techniques of arterial embalming—first discovered by Dr. Frederick Ruysch (1665–1717)—that the practice was finally ren-dered obsolete.

Spiced aphrodisiacs lived on awhile longer. Pécuchet of Flaubert's *Bouvard and Pécuchet* fretted that spices would "set his body on fire." In at least some parts of the world the faith survived until relatively recently. Writing of early-twentieth-century Morocco, one authority knew of a restorative mix of ginger, cloves, galangal, and honey, for which one of his interlocutors made grand claims: "My grandfather has never failed to take this remedy, since his youth, and now that he is extremely old and full of years, he remains as solid and as lively as a young man. He keeps himself busy with his business, he travels, he has several wives, and they bear children every year." Even in the bedroom, however, spices had to compete in a more crowded field. They regularly crop up in modern books of aphrodisiac cooking, but they have become just one aphrodisiac among many, long since shorn not only of the med-ical logic but also, and perhaps more important, of the costliness and rarity on which faith in aphrodisiacs has always depended.

Something similar occurred with perfumes, although anyone who wears perfume is likely to have splashed on a little spice at one time or another. In the eighteenth century, perfumery tended toward fresher, more floral aromas, and with the advent of organic synthesis in the nineteenth century, perfumery became vastly more complex, accord-ingly reducing the perfumer's reliance on spices. As spices became less expensive, they lost much of the cachet upon which top perfumes have always depended; today they can be substituted or even re-created with artificial substances, new combinations, and, perhaps most important, a barrage of imagery proclaiming this or that scent to be more exclusive, more expensive, more luxurious, worn by celebrities. Cinnamon oil, once the absolute top of the line, is now just one ingredient among thousands.

Last, and perhaps most significant, spices lost their mystical, quasi-magical quality. Already by the late medieval period the religious applications of spice were a faint though vaguely troubling memory for only a handful of learned theologians. With the Reformation, even incense was banished from some (but not all) churches as Protestant polemicists revived old worries about aroma in worship:

> *As if the pomp of rituals, and the savor*
> *Of gums and spices could the Unseen One please.*

The true, reformed religion stripped the altars, scrubbed and white-washed the churches, and threw out the censer. Even the purely figurative force of spices went into abeyance. The modern saint, unlike his medieval predecessor, is generally odorless.

With irrelevance came innocence. The sense of spices' latent temptations, long framed in the medieval moral matrix of gluttony, lust, avarice, and worldliness, was downgraded to strictly individual issues of personal consumption. Falling costs and widespread availability would combine to strip spices of the potency of their symbolism, to the point that the idea of their incompatibility with Christian doctrine or for that matter a life of poverty now seems faintly absurd. In the modern world it tends to be the poor, not the rich, who eat spices.

In short, spices lost their air of dangerous attraction. Yet, as I have tried to point out through the course of this long ramble through their past, spices undeniably do still have a certain something. Faint reminders and echoes are still with us. Most are, admittedly, more literary than literal, the faint cultural echoes that still reverberate around this charged word. The allure of the exotic remains as alive as when Keats wrote in 1819 of

> *Lucent syrups, tinct with cinnamon;*
> *Manna and dates, in argosy transferred*
> *From Fez; and spiced dainties, every one,*
> *From silken Samarcand to cedared Lebanon.*

The nouveau gourmet who savors the cross-cultural mix-and-match of fusion cuisine is not so far removed from the self-consciously exoticizing aesthetic of the medieval nobleman; indeed, some of the more postmodernist combinations of the trendier restaurants of London and New York recall the culinary chiaroscuro of medieval food more directly.

Spices may even lie at the heart of modern capitalism's most closely guarded secret. Mark Pendergrast concluded his history of Coca-Cola with a leaked copy of the formula of the world's most popular and symbolic soft drink, which is, it would seem, spiced with cinnamon and nutmeg. Earlier leaks of the formula, while differing among themselves, suggest the same. If Pendergrast's source can be trusted, it would seem that spices remain as much the flavor of the age as they have ever been, albeit in disguise, hidden away in the basement of Coca-Cola headquarters in Atlanta. Is Pendergrast right? It would, one feels, be wholly appropriate.

SOURCES AND BIBLIOGRAPHY

○

The sources on spices are as diverse and as far-flung as the spices themselves. As I hope this book has shown, spices have a habit of attracting commentary whose inspirations range from scholarly to culinary, from literary to sexual, from bookish piety to the way-out bizarre, for which reasons a bibliography such as this is necessarily highly selective. Among the best general treatments are J. W. Purseglove et al., *Spices* (London: Longman, 1981); Elisabeth Lambert Ortiz, *The Encyclopedia of Herbs, Spices, and Flavorings* (New York: Dorling Kindersley, 1992); *Terre, planète des épices* (catalogue of the exhibition in the Palais de la Bourse, Marseilles: Jardins botaniques de la Ville de Marseilles, 1990); J. O. Swahn, *The Lore of Spices* (London: Senate, 1991); and Andrew Dalby, *Dangerous Tastes: The Story of Spices* (London: British Museum, 2002).

My two indispensable sources of primary material were J. P. Migne's colossal *Patrologia latina* and the even fatter *Acta sanctorum* of the Bollandists. I made liberal use of Charles du Fresne du Cange's *Glossarium mediae et infimae latinatis,* the *Oxford English Dictionary,* the *Dictionary of Middle English,* and the *Oxford Dictionary of Medieval Latin from British Sources.*

Unless indicated otherwise, all translations are my own.

INTRODUCTION: THE IDEA OF SPICE

The account of Terqa and its enigmatic cloves may be found in Giorgio Buccellati and Marilyn Kelly Buccellati, "Terqa: The First Eight Seasons," *Les Annales Archéologiques Arabes Syriennes* 33, no. 2 (1983): 47–67. Although a vast amount has been written on the subject of spices, there is as yet no comprehensive, single-volume history of the spice trade; nor, given the sprawl of the subject, is there likely ever to be one. A useful bibliography can be found in Jeanie M. Welch, *The Spice Trade: A Bibliographic Guide to Sources of Historical and Economic Information* (Westport, Conn.: Greenwood Press, 1994). Some classic essays are collected in *Spices in the Indian Ocean World,* edited by M. N. Pearson (Aldershot, England: Variorum, 1996). R. H. Crofton, *A Pageant of the Spice Islands* (London: John Bale, Sons and Danielson, 1936), and Sonia E. Howe, *In Quest of Spices* (London: Herbert Jenkins, 1946), are two entertaining introductions. The enduring myth of American spices is mentioned in A. Nevins and H. Steele Commager, *America, the Story of a Free People* (Boston: Little, Brown, 1943), p. 27. On the pitfalls of "monocausal" history, see Carlo Cipolla, *Le Poivre, moteur de l'histoire* (Paris: L'Esprit Frappeur, 1997). On some of the linguistic and cultural fallout of the spice trade, see Anne E. Perkins, "Vanishing Expressions of the Maine Coast," *American Speech*

3, no. 2 (Dec. 1927): 136; and, in passing, Edward Said, *Orientalism* (New York: Random House, 1979), p. 4, and Schele de Vere, *Americanisms: The English of the New World* (New York: Scribner and Co., 1872). On the chemical properties of spices: G. S. Fraenkel, "The Raison d'Être of Secondary Plant Substances," *Science* 129 (1959): 1466–1470; *Natural Antimicrobial Systems and Food Preservation,* edited by V. M. Dillon and R. G. Board (Wallingford, Conn.: CAB International, 1994). On the pleasures and perils of nutmeg abuse, see Andrew T. Weil, "Nutmeg as a Narcotic," *Economic Botany* 19 (1965): 194–217.

I
THE SPICE RACE

CHAPTER 1: THE SPICE SEEKERS

The Taste That Launched a Thousand Ships

The sole eye-witness account of Columbus's reception in Barcelona is given by the historian Gonzalo Fernández de Oviedo in his *Historia general,* edited by Juan Pérez de Tudela Bueso (Madrid: Ediciones Atlas, 1959); see also *Le Scoperte di Cristoforo Colombo nei testi di Fernández de Oviedo,* edited by Francesco Giunta (Rome: Istituto Poligrafico e Zecca dello Stato, 1990), p. 96. For an accessible narrative of where exactly Columbus went and what he found, see Samuel E. Morrison, *Admiral of the Ocean Sea* (Boston: Little, Brown, 1942).

Until relatively recently, the economic considerations behind his voyage were remarkably neglected in favor of more personal or "romantic" themes. Felipe Fernández-Armesto, in an extremely cogent and refreshingly sober account, *Columbus* (Oxford: Oxford University Press, 1991), has put the financial motivation into proper perspective. The pre-voyage agreement specifying precisely what Columbus hoped to find can be found in Morrison, *Admiral of the Ocean Sea,* pp. 105–106. On the influence of Toscanelli and his hypothesis of a western route to the spices of the East, see Leonardo Rombai, "Paolo dal Pozzo Toscanelli e la cosmographia nel XV secolo," in *Miscellanea storica della Valdelsa* 98, no. 3 (1992): 173–188; Henry Vignaud, *The Columbian Tradition on the Discovery of America and of the Part Played Therein by the Astronomer Toscanelli* (Oxford, England: Clarendon Press, 1920). The best way to fathom Columbus's optimistic misreading of the evidence is to read his own letters. They are collected in *Select Documents Illustrating the Four Voyages of Columbus,* edited by Cecil Jane (London: Hakluyt Society, 1930); Cecil Jane, *The Voyages of Christopher Columbus* (New York: Da Capo Press, 1971); Clement S. Markham, *The Journal of the First Voyage of Christopher Columbus* (London: Hakluyt Society, 1893); and *Journals and Other Documents on the Life and Voyages of Christopher Columbus,* edited by Samuel E. Morrison (New York: Printed for the Members of the Limited Editions Club, 1963). Other misplaced enthusiasm over American spices may be found in Bartolomé de las Casas, *Obras completas,* vol. 13, *Cartas y memoriales,* edited by Pantino Castañeda et al. (Madrid: Alianza

Editorial, 1995); *Cartas de relación: Letters from Mexico,* edited by Anthony Pagden (New Haven, Conn.: Yale Nota Bene, 2001). On early disillusionment with America's botany see Kirkpatrick Sale, *The Conquest of Paradise: Christopher Columbus and the Columbian Legacy* (New York: Knopf, 1990), p. 143. Citations from Peter Martyr's descriptions of Columbus's samples are from *De Orbe Novo de Pierre Martyr Anghiera,* edited by Paul Gaffarel (Paris: Ernest Leroux, 1907), and *De Orbe Novo: The Eight Decades of Peter Martyr d'Anghiera,* edited by Francis MacNutt (New York: Knickerbocker Press, 1912).

Christians and Spices

The best account of da Gama's voyage available in English is by Sanjay Subrahmanyam, *The Career and Legend of Vasco da Gama* (Cambridge, England: Cambridge University Press, 1997). The only surviving narration of the expedition by one of the participants is the anonymous account known as the *Roteiro,* available in English translation as *A Journal of the First Voyage of Vasco da Gama, 1497–1499,* edited by E. G. Ravenstein (London: Hakluyt Society, 1898). For an overview of the Indian Ocean at the time of the Portuguese arrival see Geneviève Bouchon, "Un microcosme: Calicut au 16ᵉ siècle," in *Marchands et hommes d'affaires dans l'Ocean Indien et la Mer de Chine,* edited by Denys Lombard and Jean Aubin (Paris: École des Hautes Études en Sciences Sociales, 1988), pp. 49–57; *India and the Indian Ocean, 1500–1800,* edited by Ashin Das Gupta and M. N. Pearson (Calcutta: Oxford University Press, 1987). Cabral's voyage is narrated in *The Voyage of Pedro Alvares Cabral to Brazil and India, from Contemporary Documents and Narratives,* edited and translated by W. Brooks Greenlee (London: Hakluyt Society, 1938).

For an overview of Portugal's rise and demise in Malabar, see C. R. Boxer, *The Portuguese Seaborne Empire, 1415–1825* (London: Hutchinson, 1969); M. N. Pearson, *The Portuguese in India* (Cambridge, England: Cambridge University Press, 1987); and Anthony R. Disney, *Twilight of the Pepper Empire* (Cambridge, Mass.: Harvard University Press, 1978). There is a lucid discussion of the empire's ideological underpinnings and its peculiar blend of spiced messianism in Luís Felipe F. R. Thomaz, "Factions, Interests and Messianism: The Politics of Portuguese Expansion in the East, 1500–1521," *The Indian Economic and Social History Review* 28, no. 1 (1991): 97–109; the same author's "L'Idée imperiale manuelino," in *La découverte, le Portugal et l'Europe,* edited by Jean Aubin (Paris: Centre Culturel Portugais, 1990): 35–103, is a handy overview.

The Estado's economic frailties are discussed by Sanjay Subrahmanyam, *The Portuguese Empire in Asia, 1500–1700: A Political and Economic History* (London: Longman, 1993). Debate over the economic impact of the Portuguese démarche in the East, and its effect on Venice in particular, is surprisingly ample and, occasionally, arcane in the extreme. Some of the more readable discussions are Donald F. Lach, *Asia in the Making of Europe,* vol. 1, book 1 (Chicago: Chicago University Press, 1965); Frederic C. Lane, "Venetian Shipping During the Commercial Revolution," *American Historical Review* 38 (1933): 219–233; R. Romano, A. Tenenti,

U. Tucci, "Venise et la route du cap: 1491–1517," in *Mediterraneo e Oceano Indiano: Atti del VI colloquio Internazionale di Storia Marittima* (Florence, Italy: Leo S. Olschki, 1970), pp. 109–140; V. Magalhães Godinho, *L'Économie de l'empire portugais aux XVᵉ et XVIᵉ siècles* (Paris: SEVPEN, 1969); Niels Steensgaard, *The Asian Trade Revolution of the Seventeenth Century: The East Indian Companies and the Decline of the Caravan Trade* (Chicago: Chicago University Press, 1974); C. H. H. Wake, "The Changing Pattern of Europe's Pepper and Spice Imports, ca. 1400–1700," *Journal of European Economic History* 8 (1979): 361–404; "The Volume of European Spice Imports at the Beginning and End of the Fifteenth Century," *Journal of European Economic History* 15, no. 3 (1986): 621–635. For contemporary assessments of Portuguese prospects, Fernão de Queyroz, *The Temporal and Spiritual Conquest of Ceylon,* translated by S. G. Perera, S.J. (Colombo, Sri Lanka: A. C. Richards, 1930); Hakluyt Society, *A Selection of Curious, Rare, and Early Voyages* (London: R. H. Evenas, 1812).

Debate and Stryfe Betwene the Spanyardes and Portugales

The classic account of the geopolitics of Magellan's quest for the Moluccas remains Jean Denucé, *Magellan: La Question des Moluques et la première circumnavigation du globe,* Académie Royale de Belgique, Classe des Lettres et des Sciences morales et politiques. Mémoires, 2nd series, vol. 4 (Brussels: Hayez, Imprimeur des Académies Royales, 1908–1911); see also Lach, *Asia,* pp. 153–154, 226–227). Some of the technical aspects of locating the antimeridian are discussed in *A Viagem de Fernão de Magalhães e a questão das Molucas: Actas do II colóquio Luso-Espanhol de História Ultramarina,* edited by A. Teixeira da Mota (Lisbon: Junta de Investigações Científicas do Ultramar, 1975); Lotika Varadarajan, "The Question of the Anti-Meridian: Economic and Technical Aspects," in *A carreira da India e as rotas dos es treitos* (Angra do Heroísmo: Actas do VII Seminario Internacional de Historia Indo-Portuguesa, 7 a 11 de junho, 1996): 687–697. The text of the Treaty of Tordesillas is reprinted in *European Treaties Bearing on the History of the United States and Its Dependencies to 1648,* edited by Francis G. Davenport (Washington, D.C.: Carnegie Institution of Washington, 1917).

There are several vivid contemporary accounts of the "Debate and Stryfe" between Spain and Portugal over the Spice Islands. (The phrase belongs to the Englishman Richard Eden, sixteenth-century translator of the *History* of Francisco Lopez de Gómara, in *The First Three English Books on America,* edited by Edward Arber (New York: Kraus Reprint, 1971). The foremost are Leonardo de Argensola, *Histoire de la conquête des Îles Moluques par les Espagnols, par les Portugais et par les Hollandais,* 2 vols. (Amsterdam: Jacques Desborde, 1707); João de Barros, *Asia: Segunda decada* (Coimbra, Portugal: Imprensa da Universidade, 1932); Fernão Lopes de Castanheda, *Historia do decobrimento e conquista da India* (Coimbra, Portugal: Imprensa da Universidade, 1924–1929); *The Suma Oriental of Tomé Pires,* edited by Armando Cortesão (London: Hakluyt Society, 1944); Mansel Longworth Dames, *The Book of Duarte Barbosa* (London: Hakluyt Society,

1918–1921); *Travelers in Disguise, Narratives of Eastern Travel by Poggio Bracciolini and Ludovico de Varthema,* edited and translated by John Winter Jones (Cambridge, Mass.: Harvard University Press, 1963); Gabriel Rebello, *Historia das Ilhas de Maluco, escripta no anno 1561,* edited by Artur Basilio de Sá, in *Documentaçao para a historia das missoes do padroado portuguese do Oriente,* vol. 3. (Lisbon: Agencia Geral do Ultramar, 1954–1958), pp. 193–344. Several of these sources as they pertain to the Moluccas are compiled by W. A. Hanna and D. Alwi, *Turbulent Times Past in Ternate and Tidore* (Banda Naira, Indonesia: Yayasan Warisan dan Budaya Banda Naira, 1990). For a scholarly dissection of Portuguese control of spices see Tikiri Abeyasinghe, *Portuguese Rule in Ceylon, 1594–1612* (Colombo, Sri Lanka: Lake House, 1966); C. R. de Silva, "The Portuguese and the Trade in Cloves in Asia During the Sixteenth Century," in *The Eighth Conference: International Association of Historians in Asia: Selected Papers,* edited by Mohd Amin Hassan and Nik Hassan Shuhaimi Nik Abd Rahman (Selangor: Universiti Kebangsaan Malaysia, 1988); C. R. de Silva, "The Portuguese Impact on the Production and Trade in Sri Lankan Cinnamon in Asia in the Sixteenth and Seventeenth Centuries," *Indica* 26 (1989): 25–38.

The most entertaining narrative account of Magellan's voyage remains the first, by Antonio Pigafetta, available in English translation as *Magellan's Voyage: A Narrative Account of the First Circumnavigation,* edited by R. A. Skelton (London: Folio Society, 1975). Francis H. Guillemard, *The Life of Ferdinand Magellan and the First Circumnavigation of the Globe, 1480–1521* (New York: AMS Press, 1971), is dated but still useful. The discharge document is in *Colección de los viages y descubrimentos que hicieron por mar los españoles desde fines del siglo XV,* vol. 4, edited by Martín Fernández de Navarrete (Madrid: Imprenta Real, 1825–37), pp. 247–248.

The Scent of Paradise

One of the best accounts of European rivalry in the East is Holden Furber, *Rival Empires of Trade in the Orient, 1600–1800* (Minneapolis, Minn.: University of Minneapolis Press, 1976). John Keay's *The Honourable Company* (London: HarperCollins, 1991) is a rollicking narrative history of the English East India Company; see also Kenneth Andrews, *Trade, Plunder and Settlement: Maritime Enterprise and the Genesis of the British Empire, 1480–1630* (Cambridge, England: Cambridge University Press, 1984). On Drake's voyage, see Henry R. Wagner, *Sir Francis Drake's Voyage Around the World* (San Francisco: John Howell, 1926). For readers of English, the classic work on the Dutch in the East remains C. R. Boxer, *The Dutch Seaborne Empire, 1600–1800* (New York: Knopf, 1965). Pepys's account of a captured Dutch spice ship is from *Pepys's Diary,* vol. 2, edited by Robert Latham (London: Folio Society, 1996), p. 218. On the issue of Amboyna, old animosities lingered remarkably long, and there has been much credulous reporting and inflation of the consequences. For a sober discussion see D. K. Bassett, "The 'Amboyna Massacre' of 1623," *Journal of Southeast Asian History* 1, no. 2 (1960): 1–19; for a

sense of contemporary outrage there were few more outraged than Abraham
Woofe, *The Tyranny of the Dutch Against the English Wherein Is Exactly Declared
the (Almost Unvaluable) Loss Which the Commonwealth of England Hath Sustained by
Their Usurpation* . . . (London: Printed by John Crowch and Tho. Wilson, 1653).
M. A. P. Meilink-Roelofsz, *Asian Trade and European Influence in the Indonesian
Archipelago between 1500 and about 1630* (The Hague: Martinus Nijhoff, 1962), is
a good discussion of the consolidation of Dutch control; so too Peter Musgrave,
"The Economics of Uncertainty: The Structural Revolution in the Spice Trade,
1480–1640," in *Shipping, Trade and Commerce,* edited by P. L. Cottrell and D. H.
Aldcroft (Leicester, England: Leicester University Press, 1981), pp. 9–21. For an
overview of the VOC's fortunes see Bernard H. M. Vlekke, *Nusantara: A History of
the East Indian Archipelago* (Cambridge, Mass.: Harvard University Press, 1945).

For Western visions of the East in medieval times, see J. Le Goff, "L'Occident
médiéval et l'Océan Indien: Un Horizon onirique," in *Mediterraneo e Oceano Indiano. Atti del VI Colloquio Internazionale di Storia Marittima* (Florence, Italy: Leo S.
Olschki, 1970), pp. 243–264; I. Hallberg, *L'Extrême Orient dans le littérature et
la cartographie de l'Occident des XIIIᵉ, XIVᵉ, et XVᵉ siècles* (Göteborg, Sweden:
W. Zachrissons Boktryckeri, 1906); George H. T. Kimble, *Geography in the Middle Ages* (New York: Russell and Russell, 1968). The Eastern sources give a much
better sense of what was happening in these centuries: see Roderich Ptak, "China
and the Trade in Cloves, circa 960–1435," *Journal of the American Oriental Society*
113 (1993): 1–13; F. Hirth and W. W. Rockhill, *Chau Ju-Kua: His Work on the
Chinese and Arab Trade in the Twelfth and Thirteenth Centuries Entitled "Chu-Fan-
Chi"* (New York: Paragon Book Reprint, 1966). References from medieval literature are from Migne, *Patrologia latina*; see also E. Curtius, *European Literature and
the Latin Middle Ages,* translated by Willard R. Trask (Princeton, N.J.: Princeton
University Press, 1953); *Diccionario medieval español,* vol. 1 (A–C), edited by Martin Alonso (Salamanca, Spain: Universidad Pontificia de Salamanca, 1986); James
M. Dean, *Richard the Redeless and Mum and the Sothsegger* (Kalamazoo, Mich.: Western Michigan University Press, 2000); Jean de Joinville's *Vie de Saint Louis,* edited
by Jacques Monfrin (Paris: Garnier, 1995); Giovanni Boccaccio's *Decameron,* translated by Mark Musa (New York: W. W. Norton, 1982); *Mandeville's Travels,*
edited by M. Seymour (Oxford, England: Clarendon Press, 1967). The physical
presence of Europeans underlying these fables remains shadowy and intriguing in
the extreme. Much of the primary material is gathered by Henry Yule, *The Book of
Ser Marco Polo,* revised by Henri Cordier (London: J. Murray, 1903). Also good on
this are *Lettera di Giovanni da Empoli,* edited by A. Bausani (Rome: Istituto Italiano per il Medio ed Estremo Oriente, 1970); E. Cerulli, "La via delle Indie nella
storia e nel diritto del Medioevo," in *Mediterraneo e Oceano Indiano. Atti del VI Colloquio Internazionale di Storia Marittima* (Florence, Italy: Leo S. Olschki, 1970),
pp. 3–24; R. S. Lopez, "Nuove luci sugli italiani in estremo Oriente prima de
Colombo," in *Studi Colombani,* vol. 3 (Genoa, Italy: International Meeting for
Studies on Columbus, 1951), pp. 337–398. References to early spices in England
are from Pamela Nightingale, *A Medieval Mercantile Community: The Grocer's Com-*

pany and the Politics and Trade of London, 1000–1485 (New Haven, Conn.: Yale University Press, 1995).

As to how some of the wilder fancies emerging from this obscurity informed Columbus's thinking, see Valerie I. J. Flint, *The Imaginative Landscape of Christopher Columbus* (Princeton, N.J.: Princeton University Press, 1992), and Pauline Watts, "Prophecy and Discovery: On the Spiritual Origins of Christopher Columbus' 'Enterprise of the Indies,' " *American Historical Review* 90, no. 1 (1985): 73–102.

II
PALATE

CHAPTER 2: ANCIENT APPETITES

The Aromanauts

The subject of Roman traffic with India is well covered. J. Innes Miller's *The Spice Trade of the Roman Empire, 29 B.C. to A.D. 641* (Oxford, England: Clarendon Press, 1969) was an utterly original work. Though prone to fanciful conclusions it remains an excellent companion for the ancient geographers. On Oberaden see F. De Romanis and A. Tchernia, *Crossings: Early Mediterranean Contacts with India* (New Delhi: Manohar, 1997); on Vindolanda see Alan K. Bowman, *Life and Letters on the Roman Frontier: Vindolanda and Its People* (London: British Museum Press, 1994). On trade with the East more generally, see Federico De Romanis, *Cassia, cinnamomo, ossidiana: Uomini e merci tra Oceano Indiano e Mediterraneo* (Rome: L'Erma di Bretschneider, 1996); Lionel Casson, *Ancient Trade and Society* (Detroit, Mich.: Wayne State University Press, 1984); Lionel Casson, *The Periplus Maris Erythraei* (Princeton, N.J.: Princeton University Press, 1989); Lionel Casson, *Travel in the Ancient World* (Baltimore: Johns Hopkins University Press, 1994); S. Sidebotham, *Roman Economic Policy in the Erythra Thalassa, 30 B.C.–A.D. 217* (Leiden, Netherlands: E. J. Brill, 1986); Romila Thapar, "Early Mediterranean Contacts with India: An Overview," in F. De Romanis and A. Tchernia, *Crossings,* pp. 11–40; E. H. Warmington and M. Cary, *The Ancient Explorers* (London: Methuen, 1929). Older but still worth a look is M. P. Charlesworth, *Trade Routes and Commerce of the Roman Empire* (Cambridge, England: Cambridge University Press, 1926). G. Hourani, *Arab Seafaring in the Indian Ocean in Ancient and Early Medieval Times* (Princeton, N.J.: Princeton University Press, 1995), provides a useful setting on the subject of ancient trade in the Indian Ocean. On the Egyptian leg of the journey, see D. Meredith, "Annius Plocamus: Two Inscriptions from the Berenice Road," *Journal of Roman Studies* 43 (1953): 38–40; also Manfred G. Raschke, "New Studies in Roman Commerce with the East," *Aufstieg und Niedergang der römischen Welt,* part 2, 9 no. 2 (1978): 605–1378. On Greek gastronomy, Andrew Dalby, *Siren Feasts* (London: Routledge, 1996) is a good guide.

Of Spiced Parrot and Stuffed Dormice

For a sober and scholarly discussion of Roman cuisine, see J. André, *Alimentation et cuisine à Rome* (Paris: Belles Lettres, 1981), and Barbara Flower and Elisabeth Rosenbaum, *The Roman Cookery Book of Apicius: A Critical Translation and the Art of Cooking by Apicius* (New York: British Book Centre, 1958). On *piperatoria,* see D. E. Strong, *Greek and Roman Gold and Silver Plate* (Ithaca, N.Y.: Cornell University Press, 1966), pp. 154, 179. The economic data are from T. Frank, *An Economic Survey of Ancient Rome,* vol. 5, *Rome and Italy of the Empire* (Baltimore: Johns Hopkins University Press, 1940), pp. 284–287.

The literary and philosophical setting of Roman cuisine is brilliantly discussed in Emily Gowers, *The Loaded Table* (Oxford, England: Clarendon Press, 1993). For traditional puzzlement and disgust on the subject of Roman appetites, see M. F. K. Fisher, *The Art of Eating* (London: Pan Books, 1983), p. 32; and J. D. Vehling, *Apicius: Cookery and Dining in Imperial Rome* (New York: Dover, 1977), p. 26. Some of the enduring literary echoes of the Roman taste for pepper may be found in *The Poetical Works of Robert Herrick,* edited by F. W. Moorman (Oxford, England: Clarendon Press, 1951), p. 293; and *The Poems of John Dryden,* edited by John Sargeaunt (London: Oxford University Press, 1925), p. 596. The purported perils of the spice trade are discussed by E. H. Warmington, *The Commerce Between the Roman Empire and India* (London: Curzon Press, 1928), p. 80.

Decline, Fall, Survival

The spice trade of the early Middle Ages remains poorly understood and fitfully studied. For a sketchy outline, see Henri Pirenne, *Mahomet et Charlemagne,* 2nd ed. (Paris: Félix Alcan, 1937); Robert S. Lopez, "The Trade of Medieval Europe: The South," in *Cambridge Economic History of Europe,* vol. 2 (Cambridge, England: Cambridge University Press, 1952), pp. 257–354; Richard Hodges, *Dark Age Economics* (London: Duckworth, 1982); Archibald Lewis, *Naval Power and Trade in the Mediterranean, A.D. 500–1100* (Princeton, N.J.: Princeton University Press, 1951).

The bishops' spices are mentioned by Denys Gorce, *Les Voyages, l'hospitalité et le port des lettres dans le monde chrétien des IVᵉ et Vᵉ siècles* (Wépion-sur-Meuse, France: Monastère du Mont-Vierge, 1925), p. 54; the document is reproduced by Karl Joseph von Hefele, *Histoire des conciles d'après les documents originaux,* vol. 1 (Paris: Letouzey et Ané, 1907), p. 407, cited by Casson, *Travel,* p. 301.

For the economic and numismatic data, see M. Rostovtzeff, *Social and Economic History of the Roman Empire* (Oxford, England: Clarendon Press, 1957); Miller, *The Spice Trade,* pp. 218–220. There are general discussions of the rise of the Arab trade in K. N. Chaudhuri, *Trade and Civilisation in the Indian Ocean: An Economic History from the Rise of Islam to 1750* (Cambridge, England: Cambridge University Press, 1985); *Islam and the Trade of Asia,* edited by D. S. Richards (Oxford, England: Bruno Cassirer, 1970); Patricia Risso, *Merchants and Faith: Muslim Commerce and Culture in the Indian Ocean* (Boulder, Colo.: Westview Press, 1995).

Cosmas's account is translated by J. W. McCrindle, *The Christian Topography of Cosmas* (London: Hakluyt Society, 1847).

On the emergence in Europe of a "medieval" view of Asia, see Georges Coedès, *Textes d'auteurs grecs et latins relatifs a l'Extrême-Orient depuis le 4ᵉ siècle* (Paris, 1910); J. Daniélou, "Terre et Paradis chez les pères de l'Eglise," *Eranos Jarbuch* 22 (1953): 433–472; Le Goff, "L'Occident médiéval," pp. 243–264. Anthimus's work on food is edited and translated by Mark Grant, *Anthimus, De Observatione ciborum* (Totnes, England: Prospect Books, 1996).

There are several studies touching on various aspects of the reemerging luxury trade of the eighth, ninth, and tenth centuries. See Steven Runciman, "Byzantine Trade and Industry," in *Cambridge Economic History of Europe*. Vol. 2, *Trade and Industry in the Middle Ages* (Cambridge, England: Cambridge University Press, 1952); Eliyahu Ashtor, "Aperçus sur les Radhanites," *Revue suisse d'Histoire* 27 (1977): 245–275, and "Gli Ebrei nel commercio mediterraneo nell'alto medievo," *Settimane di Studio del Centro Italiano di Studi sull'Alto Medievo XXVI* (Spoleto, 1978): 401–464; C. Barbier de Meynard, *Le Libre des routes* (Paris: Imprimerie Impériale, 1865); S. Y. Labib, "Les Marchands Karimis en Orient et sur l'Océan Indien," in *Sociétés et compagnies de commerce en Orient et dans l'Océan Indien,* edited by Michel Mollat (Paris: SEVPEN, 1970). The early ascendancy of the Venetians is discussed by François L. Ganshof, "Note sur un passage de la vie de Saint Géraud d'Aurillac," in *Mélanges Offerts à M. Nicolas Iorga par ses amis de France et les pays de langue française* (Paris: J. Gamber, 1933), p. 303; see also Carlrichard Brühl and Cinzio Volante, *De "Honorantiae civitatis Papiae"* (Cologne, Germany: Böhlau Verlag, 1983). Abbot Mayeul's unfortunate incident is mentioned by Richard Fletcher, *The Cross and the Crescent* (London: Penguin, 2003), p. 44. On the galvanizing effect of the luxury trade, see Richard Southern, *The Making of the Middle Ages* (London: Hutchinson, 1953), pp. 42–43. On the subject more generally, see Georges Duby, *The Early Growth of the European Economy: Warriors and Peasants from the Seventh to the Twelfth Century,* translated by Howard B. Clarke (London: Weidenfeld and Nicolson, 1974).

CHAPTER 3: MEDIEVAL EUROPE

The Flavors of Cockayne

On the subject of European dreamworlds see the fascinating work by Herman Pleij, *Dreaming of Cockaigne,* translated by D. Webb (New York: Columbia University Press, 2001). The Old English poem of the same name can be found in *The Oxford Book of Medieval English Verse,* edited by Celia and Kenneth Sisam (Oxford, England: Clarendon Press, 1970).

A good introduction to the subject of the spice trade in the central and late Middle Ages is J. Favier, *De l'or et des épices: Naissance de l'homme d'affaires au Moyen Age* (Paris: Fayard, 1987); Nightingale, *A Medieval Mercantile Community;* Eliyahu Ashtor, *The Jews and the Mediterranean Economy, 10th–15th Centuries* (London: Variorum Imprints, 1983), and *The Social and Economic History of the Near East in the Middle Ages* (London: Variorum, 1978); William McNeill, *Venice: The Hinge of Europe* (Chicago: Chicago University Press, 1974).

Some of the more startling references to spices in this period can be found in Étienne Baluze, *Historiae Tutelensis* (Paris: Ex Typographia Regia, 1717), p. 171; *The Laws of the Kings of England from Edmund to Henry I,* edited by A. J. Robertson (Cambridge, England: Cambridge University Press, 1925), pp. 72–73; *Ælfric's Colloquy,* edited by G. N. Garmonsway (London: Methuen, 1939), p. 33; "Chronica of Jaufré de Vigeois," in Philippe Labbe, *Nova bibliotheca manuscriptorum* (Paris: Sebastian and Gabriel Cramoisy, 1657), vol. 2, p. 322; François Marvaud, *Histoire des viscomtes et de la vicomté de Limoges,* vol. 1 (Paris: J.-B. Dumoulin, 1873), p. 177; *Guglielmo IX: Poesie,* edited by Nicolò Pasero (Modena, Italy: S.T.E.M.-Mucchi, 1973), pp. 127, 130; W. FitzStephen, *Norman London* (New York: Italica Press, 1990), p. 54; A. Asher, *The Itinerary of Benjamin of Tudela* (London: A. Asher, 1840), p. 157; Anatole de Montaiglon and Gaston Raynaud, *Recueil général et complet des fabliaux des XIIIe et XIVe siècles* (Geneva, Switzerland: Slatkine Reprints, 1973), pp. 123–124.

Salt, Maggots, and Rot?

Jeanne d'Evreux's spice larder is mentioned by A. Franklin, *La vie privée d'autrefois,* vol. 3 (Paris: Plon, 1889), pp. 44–46. On Humphrey Stafford see Christopher Dyer, *Standards of Living in the Later Middle Ages: Social Change in England, c. 1200–1520* (Cambridge, England: Cambridge University Press, 1989), p. 63.

Recent decades have witnessed a reappraisal of medieval cuisine and a reinterpretation of its spices. Some of the best works on the topic are B. A. Henisch, *Fast and Feast: Food in Medieval Society* (University Park: Pennsylvania State University Press, 1976); Bruno Laurioux, *Manger au Moyen Âge* (Paris: Hachette, 2002); Terence Scully, *The Art of Cookery in the Middle Ages* (Woodbridge, N.J.: Boydell Press, 1997); *Food and Eating in Medieval Europe,* edited by M. Carlin and J. T. Rosenthal (London: Hambledon, 1998); P. W. Hammond, *Food and Feast in Medieval England* (Stroud, England: Sutton Publishing, 1993); *Food: A Culinary History from Antiquity to the Present,* edited by Jean-Louis Flandrin and Massimo Montanari (New York: Columbia University Press, 1999); Charles Cooper, *The English Table in History and Literature* (London: S. Low, Marston, 1929); J. Harvey, "Vegetables in the Middle Ages," *Garden History* 12 (1984); Massimo Montanari, *L'alimentazione contadina nell'alto medioevo* (Naples, Italy: Liguori, 1979); Toby Peterson, "Arab Influence on Western European Cooking," *Journal of Medieval History* 6 (1980): 317–341.

On the subject of spices in particular, see Bruno Laurioux, "De l'usage des épices dans l'alimentation médiévale," *Médiévales* 5 (1983): 15–31.

Some primary sources mentioning spices can be found in T. Austin, *Two Fifteenth Century Cookery Books* (London: Early English Text Society, Original Series 91, 1888); *Babees Book,* edited by F. Furnivall (London: Early English Text Society, Original Series 32, 1868); Terence Scully, *The Viandier of Taillevant* (Ottawa:

University of Ottawa Press, 1988); *Curye on Inglysch: English Culinary Manuscripts of the Fifteenth Century,* edited by Constance B. Hieatt and Sharon Butler (London: Early English Text Society, New Series 8, 1985); *The Goodman of Paris,* translated by Eileen Power (London: Routledge, 1928).

For some representative literary references to spices in food and wine see Eustache Deschamps, *Oeuvres complètes,* edited by Gaston Raynaud (Paris: Firmin Didot, 1891), vol. 3, pp. 75–77, and vol. 7, pp. 186–188, 218–219; *A Volume of Vocabularies,* edited by Thomas Wright (London: Privately printed, 1856), p. 127; E. Barbazan, *Fabliaux et contes des poètes français,* vol. 1 (Paris: B. Walée, 1808), p. 153; G. G. Coulton, *Chaucer and His England* (New York: Russell and Russell, 1957), p. 91; Jean Molinet, *Le faicts et dictz de Jean Molinet,* vol. 2, edited by Noël Dupire (Paris: Société des Anciens Textes Français, 1937), pp. 752–754; G. G. Coulton, *Medieval Panorama* (Cambridge, England: Cambridge University Press, 1938), p. 456; Conrad Gesner, *Trésor de Euonime, philiâtre des remèdes secretz* (Lyon, France: Balthazar Arnoullet, 1555); *Sir Gawain and the Green Knight,* edited by I. Gollanz (London: Early English Text Society, Original Series 210, 1940); F. Rabelais, *Oeuvres complètes,* edited by Mireille Houchon (Paris: Gallimard, 1994); Achille Jubinal, *Nouveau receuil de contes, dits, fabliaux,* vol. 1 (Paris: Édouard Pannier, 1839), p. 300; *King Ponthus and the Fair Sidone,* edited by F. J. Mather, in *Publications of the Modern Language Association of America* 12, no. 2 (1897): 61; Montaiglon and Raynaud, *Recueil général,* vol. 2, 142; Migne, vol. 172, col. 1138; vol. 207, col. 47–48, 1155. On spices' role in preserving wine, see *John Trevisa's Translation of Bartholemeus Anglicus'* De Proprietatibus Rerum, edited by M. L. Seymour et al. (Oxford, England: Clarendon Press, 1975–1988), lib. 7, cap. 187.

The Regicidal Lamprey and the Deadly Beaver

King Henry's lamprey-induced demise is recounted by Henry of Huntingdon, *The History of the English People, 1000–1154,* translated by Diana Greenway (Oxford, England: Oxford University Press, 2002), p. 64; "Gesta Stephani regis Anglorum," in *Chronicles of the Reigns of Stephen, Henry II and Richard, Rolls Series,* vol. 82, edited by R. Howlett (London: Longman, 1884), p. 14.

The medieval blurring of gastronomy and dietetics is well discussed by Terence Scully, "The Opusculum de Saporibus of Magninus Mediolanensis," *Medium Aevum* 54, no. 1 (1985): 178–207. See also his *Art of Cookery.* Lynn Thorndike, "A Medieval Sauce-Book," *Speculum* 9, no. 2 (1934): 183–190, contains several illustrative recipes and recommendations. John C. Super, "El concepto de la nutrición en Juan de Aviñón," *Medicina Española* 82 (1983): 167–173, is a revealing case study. Also useful is M. Weiss Adamson, *Medieval Dietetics* (New York: P. Lang, 1995).

Some primary sources pertaining to the subject are *Le Régime du corps de Maître Aldebrandin de Sienne, texte français du XIIIᵉ siècle,* edited by Louis Landouzy and Roger Pépin (Paris: Honoré Champion, 1911), p. 124; *Three Prose Versions of the Secretum Secretorum* edited by R. Steele (London: Early English Text Society, Extra Series 74, 1898), p. 75; also Furnivall, *Babees,* p. 50. On the perils of beaver, see Edward Topsell, *The History of Four-Footed Beasts and Serpents* (London: G. Sawbridge, 1658), p. 36; Laurence Andrew, *The Noble Lyfe & Natures of Man, of Bestes, Serpentys, Fowles, & Fishes* (Antwerp, Belgium: Jan van Doesborgh, ca. 1521), published in facsimile edition as *An Early English Version of the Hortus Sanitatis* (London: B. Quatrich, 1954), p. 146. Erasmus's observations on the English diet are from J. Jortin, *The Life of Erasmus,* vol. 3 (London: R. Taylor and J. White, 1808), p. 44. On the intersection of humoral medicine, spices, and cuisine, see R. Fleischakker, *Lanfrank's "Science of Cirurgie"* (London: Early English Text Society, Original Series 102, 1894), p. 76; *Secretum Secretorum: Nine English Versions,* edited by M. A. Manzalaoui (London: Early English Text Society, Extra Series 276, 1977), pp. 3–9; Sir John Harrington's translation of the *Regimen sanitatis salerni: The School of Salernum* (Salerno, Italy: Ente Provinciale per il Turismo, 1959), p. 70; *Le Livre des simples médecines,* edited and translated by Carmélia Opsomer et al. (Antwerp, Belgium: De Schutter, 1984); on Lenten variations, see Anonimo Genovese, *Poesie,* edited by Luciano Cocito (Rome: Edizioni dell'Ateneo, 1970), p. 228; *Book of Vices and Virtues,* edited by W. Nelson Francis (London: Early English Text Society, Original Series 217, 1942), p. 53.

The spices of the Avignon papacy are catalogued by H. Aliquot, "Les Épices à la table des papes d'Avignon au XIVe siècle," in *Manger et Boire au Moyen Âge. Actes du Colloque de Nice, 15–17 octobre, 1982* (Nice: Centre d'Études médiévales, 1984). Spicers to English royalty are discussed by G. E. Trease, "Spicers and Apothecaries of the Royal Household in the Reign of Henry III, Edward I, and Edward II," *Nottingham Medieval Studies* 3 (1959): 19–52; see also "Ordinances of the Household of Edward IV," *Proceedings of the Society of Antiquaries of London* (London: J. B. Nichols, 1790). On spice consumption in a representative noble household, see *The Household Book of Alice de Bryene,* 2nd ed., edited by Vincent Redstone (Bungay, Suffolk: Paradigm Press, 1984). Burton's quote is from his *Anatomy of Melancholy,* edited by Holbrook Jackson (New York: New York Review Books, 2001).

Keeping Up with the Percys

The description of Henrique's spice bender is from *Crónica da Tomada de Ceuta,* edited by Reis Brasil (Lisbon: Publicações Europa-America, 1992), pp. 100–101. The subject of dining and rank is discussed by Bruno Laurioux, "Table et hiérarchie sociale à la fin du Moyen Âge," in *Du manuscrit à table: Essais sur la cuisine au Moyen Âge et répertoire des manuscrits médiévaux contenant des recettes culinaires,* edited by Carole Lambert (Montreal, Canada: Presses de l'Université de Montréal, 1992), p. 87. On spice plates see J. Gairdner, *The Paston Letters,* A.D. 1422–1509, vol. 3 (Edinburgh: J. Grant, 1904), p. 167; also *Testamenta Eboracensia, Publications of the Surtees Society,* vol. 30 (London: J. B. Nichols, 1855), p. 17. The affair of the court of solace is recounted by Rolandini Patavini, *De factis in Marchia,* book 1, chap. 13, in Ludovico Muratori, *Rerum italicarum scriptores* (Milan: Ex Typographia Societatis Palatinae, 1723–51), vol. 8, col. 180–181. Some illustrative primary sources are *Libro de los enxiemplos del Conde Lucanor,* edited by H. Knust (Leipzig, Germany: Seele, 1900), p. 140; *Jacob's Well: An Englisht Trea-*

tise on the Cleansing of Man's Conscience, ca. 1440, edited by Arthur Brandeis (London: Early English Text Society, Original Series 115, 1900), p. 144. On Van Maerlant see Pleij, *Dreaming,* p. 97. On correspondence, see E. Martène, *Veterum scriptorum et monumentum historicorum* (Paris: Montalant, 1729), vol. 4, col. 244–245. For Henry V, Alberico Benedicenti, *Malati, Medici e farmacisti: Storia dei rimedi traverso i secoli e delle teorie che ne spiegano l'azione sull'organismo* (Milan, Italy: Ulrico Hoeph, 1947), p. 391. On the great ship see *Documents Illustrative of the History of Scotland,* vol. 1, edited by J. Stevenson (1870), pp. 149, 186–92, cited by Michael Prestwich, *Edward I* (New Haven, Conn.: Yale University Press, 1997), p. 361. For a sense of spices' noble connotations, see William Caxton, *Dialogues in French and English, c. 1483,* edited by Henry Bradley (London: Early English Text Society, Extra Series 79, 1900), p. 304; "The Debate of the Body and the Soul," in *The Chief Middle English Poets,* edited by J. L. Weston (London: G. G. Harrap, 1914), p. 304.

The relationship of the English Crown to its spicers is covered by Nightingale, *Medieval Mercantile Community,* pp. 52, 71, 122. A revealing source on dining at the court of Henry II is *Urbanus Magnus Danielis Becclesiensis,* edited by J. G. Smyly (Dublin: Hodges, Figgis, 1939). For Genoese boasting, see Cocito, *Poesie,* pp. 563–565. On ranking by spice, see Hammond, *Food and Feast,* p. 114; also *Liber cure cocorum,* edited by R. Morris (London: Transactions of the Philological Society, 1862), p. 42. The economic data is from F. Flückiger and D. Hanbury, *Pharmacographia,* 2nd ed. (London: Macmillan, 1879), pp. 503, 578, 635; also Nightingale, *Medieval Mercantile Community,* p. 59. The topic of famine is covered by Piero Camporesi, *Bread of Dreams: Food and Fantasy in Early Modern Europe,* translated by David Gentilcore (Cambridge, England: Polity in Association with Basil Blackwell, 1989). Pepper's fall from grace is charted by Bruno Laurioux, "Et le poivre conquit France . . . ," *Histoire* 67 (1984): 79–80. On the "seasoning of rustics," see *De conservanda bona valetudine, liber scholae salernitanae* (Paris: Lud. Billaine, 1786), p. 300. The Montaigne quote is from *The Essays of Michel de Montaigne,* edited by M. A. Screech (London: Penguin, 1987), p. 300; Froissart's quote is from Simon Schama, *A History of Britain,* vol. 1 (London: BBC, 2000), p. 248. The text of London Lickpenny is reprinted by Eleanor P. Hammond in *Anglia* (1898), p. 414.

III
BODY

CHAPTER 4: THE SPICE OF LIFE

The Pharaoh's Nose

Ramses' autopsy is discussed by Lionel Balout, C. Roubet, and C. Descroches-Noblecourt, *La Momie de Ramses II: Contribution scientifique à l'egyptologie* (Paris: Éditions Recherche sur les Civilisations, 1976–77), pp. 87, 174.

On the subject of Roman and early medieval embalming, some of the more informative works are Laura Chioffi, *Mummificazione e imbalsamazione a Roma ed in altri luoghi del mondo romano* (Rome: Quasar, 1998), and J. M. C. Toynbee, *Death and Burial in the Roman World* (London: Thames and Hudson, 1971). Christian attitudes are discussed by Edmund Martène, *De antiquis ecclesiae ritibus libri tres,* vol. 2 (Antwerp, Belgium: J. B. Novelli, 1763–64), pp. 366–367. Some instances of early Christian embalming are to be found in Flavius Cresconius Corippus, *In laudem Iustinii Augusti minoris,* edited and translated by Averil Cameron (London: The Athlone Press, 1976), lib. 3, pp. 24–25; Jacob Burckhardt, *The Age of Constantine the Great,* translated by Moses Hadas (New York: Dorset Press, 1989), p. 267; *Li Dialoge Gregoire lo Pape* (*Les Dialogues du pape Grégoire traduits en français du XIIe siècle accompagnés du texte latin*), edited by Wendelin Foerster (Paris: H. Champion, 1876), pp. 244–245.

The theological setting and the attraction of cinnamon in particular are discussed by Jean Hubaux and Maxime Leroy, *Le Mythe du phénix dans les littératures grecque et latine* (Liège, Belgium: Faculté de Philosophie et Lettres, 1939), p. 85; R. van den Broek, *The Myth of the Phoenix* (Leiden, Netherlands: E. J. Brill, 1972), p. 167. On the chrism see Theodoure of Tarsus, *Paenitentiale,* II.5.1, in *Councils and Ecclesiastical Documents Relating to Great Britain and Ireland* (200–1295), vol. 2, edited by A. W. Haddan and W. Stubbs (Oxford, England: Clarendon Press, 1871). For the mummy of Maria see César E. Dubler, *La "Materia Médica" de Dioscorides: Transmisión medieval e renacentista,* vol. 4 (Barcelona, Spain: Tipografía Emporium, 1953), pp. 105–106.

The transmission of Roman customs is mentioned by Alain Erlande-Brandenburg, *Le Roi est mort: Étude sur les funérailles, les sépultres et les tombeaux des rois de France jusqu'à la fin du XIIIe siècle* (Geneva, Switzerland: Droz, 1975), p. 27; see also A. Guérillot-Vinet and L. Guyot, *Les Épices* (Paris: Presses Universitaires de France, 1963), p. 65. Baldwin's evisceration is recounted by Albert of Aix, Migne, *Patrologia latina,* vol. 166, col. 711. Techniques in the later Middle Ages are discussed in Patrice Georges, "Mourir c'est pourrir un peu . . . Intentions et techniques contre la corruption des cadavres à la fin du Moyen Age," *Micrologus* 7 (1999): 359–382; C. Beaune, "Mourir noblement à la fin du Moyen Age," in *La Mort au Moyen Âge: Actes du colloque de la société des historiens médiévistes de l'enseignement supérieur public* (Strasbourg, France: Librairie Ista, 1977), 125–126; Louis Pénicher, *Traité des embaumements selon les anciens et les modernes; avec une description de quelques compositions balsamiques et odourantes* (Paris: Barthelemy Girin, 1699). The spiced homecoming of King Henry V is recounted in *The Brut, or Chronicles of England,* reprinted in C. L. Kingsford, *English Historical Literature in the Fifteenth Century* (Oxford, England: Clarendon Press, 1913), p. 430.

Abbot Eberhard's Complaint

For an introduction to the theory of medieval medicine, with due emphasis on its nonempirical aspects, see Lynn Thorndike, *A History of Magic and Experimental Science* (New York: Macmillan, 1923–58). Laura Balletto, *Medici e farmaci, scon-*

giuru ed incantesimi, dieta e gastronomia nel medioevo genovese (Genoa, Italy: Università di Genova, Istituto di Medievistica, 1986), is a fascinating case study with much broader applicability. Similarly, the prominence of the medieval spicer is discussed by L. Irissou, "Les Épiciers-apothicaires et les poivriers de Montpellier dans le cadre communal au Moyen Âge," *Bulletin des Sciences Pharmacologiques* 38, nos. 8–9 (1931): 511–529; Joseph Shatzmiller, "Herbes et drogues dans la médecine provençale du Moyen Age," in *Herbes, drogues et épices en Méditerranée: Histoire, anthropologie, économie du Moyen Âge à nos jours,* edited by G.-J. Aillaud et al. (Paris: Editions du Centre National de la Recherche Scientifique, 1990), pp. 157–167. The broader significance of the European demand for spice is discussed by John M. Riddle, "The Introduction and Use of Eastern Drugs in the Early Middle Ages," *Sudhoffs Archiv für Geschichte der Medizin und der Naturwissenschaften* 49, no. 1 (1965): 185–198. On Saint Gall's medicine cabinet see Henry Sigerist, *Studien und Texte zur frühmittelalterlichen Rezeptliteratur* (Leipzig, Germany: Barth, 1923), pp. 78–99.

There is no shortage of modern editions of medieval medical works. Several of the more influential and representative works I have consulted are Ernest A. W. Budge, *The Syriac Book of Medicines: Syrian Anatomy, Pathology and Therapeutics in the Early Middle Ages* (Amsterdam, Netherlands: Philo Press, 1976); Henry P. Cholmeley, *John of Gaddesden and the Rosa Medicinae* (Oxford, England: Clarendon Press, 1912); Avelino Domínguez García and Luis García Ballester, *Johannis Aegidii Zamorensis Historia Naturalis* (Salamanca, Spain: Junta de Castilla y León, Consejeria de Cultura y Turismo, 1994); Michael R. Best and Frank H. Brightman, *The Book of Secrets of Albertus Magnus* (Oxford, England: Clarendon Press, 1973); Roger Bacon, *Opera hactenus inedita,* edited by R. Steele et al. (Oxford, England: Clarendon Press, 1909–40); Winifred Wulff, *Rosa anglica: Seu rosa medicinae Johannis Anglici* (London: Simpkin, Marshall, 1929); *John Trevisa's Translation of Bartholemeus Anglicus De proprietatibus rerum,* edited by M. L. Seymour et al. (Oxford, England: Clarendon Press, 1975–88). Galen's works were edited by Carolus Gottlob Kühn, *Galen: Opera Omnia* (Leipzig, Germany: Teubner, 1821–28). For Avicenna's *Canon* see D. Cameron Gruner, *A Treatise on the Canon of Medicine of Avicenna* (London: Luzac, 1930), and André Soubiran, *Avicenne, prince des médecins* (Paris: Librairie Lipschutz, 1935).

There is an ample literature on the Salernitan school. B. Lawn, *The Prose Salernitan Questions* (Oxford, England: Clarendon Press, 1963), is a standard work. On influences from the Arab world see F. Gabrielli, "La medicina araba e la scuola di Salerno," *Salerno* 1, no. 3 (1967): 12–24; M. Levey, "Ibn Masawiah and His Treatise on Simple Aromatic Substances," *Journal of the History of Medicine* 16 (1961): 394–403; L. García Ballester and C. Vázquez de Benito, "Los médicos judío-castellanos del siglo XIV y el galenismo arabe: El *kitab al-tibb al-qastali al-maluki* (Libro de medicina castellana regia), ca. 1312," *Asclepio* 42 (1990): 119–147.

For literary references expressing skepticism over the spicer's integrity, see C.-V. Langlois, *La Vie en France au Moyen Âge, de la fin du XIIe siècle au milieu du XIVe siècle,* vol. 2 (Paris: Hachette, 1926), pp. 11. 26754, 11. 29118; also *Thomas Wright's Political Songs of England, from the Reign of John to That of Edward II,* edited by Peter Coss (Cambridge, England: Cambridge University Press, 1996), p. 333; *Oeuvres complètes de Rutebeuf, trouvère du XIIIe siècle,* vol. 2, edited by Achille Jubinal (Paris: P. Daffis, 1874–75), p. 59. Kathryn Reyerson, "Commercial Fraud in the Middle Ages: The Case of the Dissembling Pepperer," *Journal of Medieval History* 8, no. 1 (1982): 63–73, is a revealing study. On veterinary medicine, see Juan Manuel, *Libro de la caza* (Halle, Germany: H. Niemeyer, 1880), pp. 61–62.

Pox, Pestilence, and Pomanders

There is an excellent introduction to the study of smell and medicine by R. Palmer, "In Bad Odour: Smell and Its Significance in Medicine from Antiquity to the Seventeenth Century," in *Medicine and the Five Senses,* edited by R. Porter and W. F. Bynum (Cambridge, England: Cambridge University Press, 1993), pp. 61–68. Though the focus is more recent, Alain Corbin's *The Foul and the Fragrant* (Cambridge, Mass.: Harvard University Press, 1986) was a pioneering work in this regard. There have been several studies attempting to place odors in a cultural setting. They include Constance Classen, David Howes, and Anthony Synnott, *Aroma: The Cultural History of Smell* (London: Routledge, 1994); Ruth Winter, *The Smell Book: Scents, Sex, and Society* (Philadelphia: J. B. Lippincott, 1976); Constance Classen, *Worlds of Sense: Exploring the Senses in History and Across Cultures* (London: Routledge, 1993).

Medieval and early modern works on the plague seldom fail to touch on the subject of aromatic self-defense. Some representative examples are J. Gouerot, *The Regiment of Life, Whereunto Is Added a Treatise of the Pestilence* (London: E. Allde, 1606); Francis Herring, *Certaine Rules, Directions, or Advertisments for This Time of Pestilential Contagion* (London: Thomas Paine, 1636); Ambroise Paré, *A Treatise on the Plague* (London: Printed by R. Y. and R. C., 1630); J. Woodall, *The Surgeon's Mate* (London: John Legate, 1617); William Bullein, *Bullein's Bulwark of Defence Againste All Sicknes* (London: John Kingston, 1562). An indicative prescription may be found in Lynn Thorndike, "Advice from a Physician to His Sons," *Speculum* 6, no. 1 (1931): 113. Frank P. Wilson, *The Plague in Shakespeare's London* (Oxford, England: Clarendon Press, 1927), is a helpful study. For some Eastern parallels, see E. C. Sachau, *Alberuni's India* (London: Kegan Paul, 1910), and Edward H. Schafer, *The Golden Peaches of Samarkand* (Berkeley: University of California Press, 1963). The Genoese death ship is mentioned by Philip Ziegler, *The Black Death* (London: Folio Society, 1997), p. 4.

CHAPTER 5: THE SPICE OF LOVE

"Whan Tendre Youthe Hath Wedded Stoupyng Age"

For a concise biography of Constantine and a discussion of his influence, see Maurice Bassan, "Chaucer's 'Cursed Monk,' Constantinus Africanus," *Medieval Studies* 24 (1962): 127–140. His work on sex has been edited by Enrique Montero

Cartelle, *Constantini liber de coitu* (Santiago de Compostela, Spain: Universidad de Santiago de Compostela, 1983). Pope Joan's appetites are discussed by Cesare D'Onofrio, *La papessa Giovanna: Roma e papato tra storia e leggenda* (Rome: Romana Società Editrice, 1979), and M. Rinaldi and M. Vicini, *Buon Appetito, Your Holiness,* translated by A. Victor (London: Macmillan, 2001). For the opinions of Jean Auvray, see his *Le Banquet des muses ou les divers satires du Sieur Auvray* (Rouen, France: D. Ferrand, 1636). Villon's dedication is from his *Poésies,* edited by Jean Dufournet (Paris: Flammarion, 1993), p. 428.

Hot Stuff

There are several general works on medieval sexuality and aphrodisiacs. Among the best are Danielle Jacquart and Claude Thomasset, *Sexualité et savoir médical au Moyen Âge* (Paris: Presse Universitaire de France, 1985); *Handbook of Medieval Sexuality,* edited by Vern L. Bullough and James A. Brundage (New York: Garland, 1996); J.-L. Flandrin, *Sex in the Western World,* translated by Sue Collins (Philadelphia: Harwood, 1991); *Sex in the Middle Ages,* edited by Joyce E. Salisbury (New York: Garland, 1991); and Joyce E. Salisbury, *Medieval Sexuality: A Research Guide* (New York: Garland, 1990). Some representative examples of spiced aphrodisiacs I have cited are to be found in *Medieval Woman's Guide to Health,* edited by Beryl Rowland (Kent, Ohio: Kent State University Press, 1981), p. 147; Helen Rodnite Lemy, *Women's Secrets: A Translation of Pseudo-Albertus Magnus's* De Secretis Mulierum (New York: State University of New York Press, 1992), p. 145; Cristóbal Acosta, *Tractado de las drogas y medicinas de las Indias orientales* (Burgos, Spain: Martín de Victoria, 1578), pp. 414–415; Roger Bacon, *De retardatione senectutis,* edited by A. G. Little and E. Withington (Oxford, England: Clarendon Press, 1928); *The Seven Books of Paulus of Aegineta,* vol. 3, edited by Francis Adams (London: Sydenham Society, 1844), p. 47; Thomas Dawson, *The Good Huswifes Iewell* (London: E. White, 1610). On the delicate topic of public humiliation, see Jacqueline Murray, "Hiding Behind the Universal Man: Male Sexuality in the Middle Ages," in Bullough and Brundage, *Handbook,* p. 139.

Maimonides' *On Sexual Intercourse: Fi 'l-kima* has been edited and translated by Morris Gorlin (Brooklyn, N.Y.: Rambash, 1961). The study of Arab influence on Western sexual practice is still fragmentary. Some useful studies are Radhi Jazi, "Aphrodisiaques et médicaments de la reproduction chez Ibn al-Jazzar, médecin et pharmacien maghrébin du Xe siècle," *Revue de l'histoire de la pharmacie* 34, no. 273 (June 1987): 155–170; Norman Roth, "A Research Note on Sexuality and Muslim Civilization," in Bullough and Brundage, *Handbook,* pp. 319–328. See also *Il Liber de Ferculis et Condimentis di Giambonino de Cremona,* a late-fourteenth-century translation of the *Minhāj al-bayān* of the Baghdad doctor ibn Jazla (ob. 1100), edited by Anna Martellotti (Brindisi, Italy: Schena Editore, 2000), p. 211. Some modern works with suggestive parallels in the Western tradition are Paul de Régla, *El ktab des lois secrètes de l'amour, d'après le Khôdja Omer Haleby, Abou Othmân* (Paris: Georges Carré, 1893), and Sehban-ul-Hind, *Prophetic Medical Sciences* (Karachi, Pakistan: Darul Ishaat Urdu Bazar, 1989). Al-Tifashi's work was translated by the pseudonymous "English Bohemian" under the title of *Old Man Young Again, Or, Age-re-juvenescence in the Power of Concupiscence* (Paris: C. Carrington, 1898).

On clerical disapproval, some representative samples may be found in *Instructions for Parish Priests by John Myrc*, edited by Edward Peacock (London: Early English Text Society, Original Series 31, 1902); Thomas Wright, *The Anglo-Latin Satirical Poets and Epigrammatists of the Twelfth Century* (London: H. M. Stationery Office, 1872); Richard Lavynham, *A Litil Tretys on the Seven Deadly Sins*, edited by Johannes P. W. M. Van Zuitphen (Rome: Institutum Carmelitanum, 1956).

As I have suggested, spices have remained a fruitful source of sexual inspiration through more recent times. Some revealing sources are Paul Lacroix, *Secrets magiques de l'amour: Octante et trois charms, conjurations, sortilèges et talismans* (Paris: Académie des Bibliophiles, 1868); Pierre Pomet, *A Compleat History of Druggs, Written in French by Monsieur Pomet, Chief Druggist to the Late French King Lewis XIV* (London: John Walthoe and Tho. Ward, 1725), p. 122; M. Toussaint-Samat, *History of Food*, translated by A. Bell (Oxford, England: Blackwell, 1994), p. 497; Nicolas Venette, *Tableau de l'amour conjugal* (Paris: Georges-Anquetil, 1926); John Davenport, *Aphrodisiacs and Anaphrodisiacs* (London: Privately printed, 1869); Marcel Rouet, *Le Paradis sexuel des aphrodisiaques* (Paris: N.O.E., 1971). The incident in Naestved is recounted by Swahn, *Lore*, p. 97. The curious case of Ambon's enthusiastic tree-huggers comes from J. G. Frazer, *The Golden Bough*, vol. 1, part 2 (London: Macmillan, 1931), p. 100, citing Baron van Hoëvell, *Ambon en meer bepaaldelijk de Oliasers* (Dordrecht, Netherlands, 1875), p. 62.

Spice Girls

For a discussion of the ancient attractions of spices see Paul Fauré, *Parfums et aromates de l'antiquité* (Paris: Éditions Fayard, 1987), and Saara Lilja, *The Treatment of Odours in the Poetry of Antiquity*, Commentationes Humanarum Litterarum, no. 49 (Helsinki: Societas Scientiarum Fennica, 1972). The technology is discussed by R. J. Forbes, *Studies in Ancient Technology III*, 2nd ed. (Leiden, Netherlands: E. J. Brill, 1965); Domínguez García and García Ballester, *Johannis Aegidii Zamorensis*, vol. 3, pp. 1540–1544.

King Henry VII's wife hunt is recounted by G. G. Coulton, *Life in the Middle Ages* (Cambridge, England: Cambridge University Press, 1928), part 3, pp. 155–163. For representative concerns over aromatic sensuousness, see Richard Sennett, *Flesh and Stone: The Body and the City in Western Civilization* (New York: W. W. Norton, 1994), p. 223; *An Alphabet of Tales*, edited by M. M. Banks, part I (London: Early English Text Society, Original Series 126, 1904); MacNutt, *De orbe novo*, vol. 2, p. 287. Moçailama's success is recounted in *The Perfumed Garden of the Shaykh Nefzawi*, translated by Richard Burton (St. Albans, England: Panther, 1976). McCary's article on aphrodisiacs and anaphrodisiacs is cited by Philippa Pullar, *Consuming Passions* (London: Penguin, 2001), p. 236. On Dr. Graham, see Amanda Foreman, *Georgiana, Duchess of Devonshire* (London: Harper-Collins, 1998), p. 70. On the subject of smell and sexual attraction, see K. Larsson, "Impaired Mating Performance in Male Rats After Anosmia Induced

Peripherally or Centrally," *Brain, Behaviour and Evolution* 4 (1971): 463–471; for a less scientific approach see Henriette Touillier-Feyrabend, "Odeurs de séduction," *Ethnologie française* 19, no. 2 (1989): 123–129; also Alan Hirsch, *Scentsational Sex: The Secret to Using Aroma for Arousal* (Boston: Element, 1998). For cinnamon-charged sperm see A. H. Shah, A. H. Al-Shareef, A. M. Ageel, and S. Qureshi, "Toxicity Studies in Mice of Common Spices, *Cinnamomum zeylanicum* Bark and *Piper longum* Fruits," *Plant Foods and Human Nutrition* 52, no. 3 (1998): 231–239.

IV
SPIRIT

CHAPTER 6: FOOD OF THE GODS

Holy Smoke

Flaubert was taken with the idea of worship and aromatics. In the *Temptation of Saint Antony* there is a fanciful description of a rite in which the goddess Cybele is honored with pepper and all the perfumes of Arabia: Flaubert, *Tentation*, in *Oeuvres complètes de Gustave Flaubert*, vol. 4 (Paris: L. Conard, 1920), pp. 258, 470. The quote from *Madame Bovary* is found at part 2, chap. 13. The best general treatment of aromas and ancient religion is Marcel Detienne, *The Gardens of Adonis: Spices in Greek Mythology*, translated by Janet Lloyd (Hassocks, U.K.: Harvester Press, 1977). Some relevant sources and discussion may be found in James Breasted, *Ancient Records of Egypt* (Chicago: Chicago University Press, 1906–07); Agatharchides of Cnidus, *On the Erythraean Sea*, translated and edited by S. M. Burnstein (London: Hakluyt Society, 1989), p. 162; *Publii Ovidii Nasonis, fastorum libri sex*, edited by James G. Frazer (London: Macmillan, 1929); E. Gibbon, *The History of the Decline and Fall of the Roman Empire*, vol. 1 (London: Folio Society, 1995), p. 147. On the Near Eastern use of aromatics, see Nigel Groom, *Frankincense and Myrrh: A Study of the Arabian Incense Trade* (London: Longman, 1981); Kjeld Nielsen, *Incense in Ancient Israel* (Leiden, Netherlands: E. J. Brill, 1986); E. Rimmel, *The Book of Perfumes* (London: Chapman and Hall, 1867), pp. 72–73. On Punt, see M. Liverani, *International Relations in the Ancient Near East, 1600–1100 B.C.* (New York: Palgrave, 2001), pp. 240–46; E. Naville, *The Temple of Deir el Bahari* (London: Offices of the Egypt Exploration Fund, 1898). The identification of Punt's aromatics is discussed by Casson, *Ancient Trade*, pp. 244–245.

For a discussion of similar Greek practices, see Cynthia W. Shelmerdine, *The Perfume Industry of Mycenaean Pylos* (Göteborg, Sweden: Paul Åströms Förlag, 1985); Saul Levin, "The Etymology of νέκταρ: Exotic Scents in Early Greece," *Studi Micenei ed Egeo-Anatolici* 46 (1971); Michel Wylock, "Les Aromates dans les tablettes Ge de Mycenes," *Studi Micenei ed Egeo-Anatolici* 15 (1972): 105–146. Lyall Watson speculates on a possible physiological basis for these beliefs in *Jacobson's Organ* (New York: W. W. Norton, 2000).

God's Nostrils

The standard treatment of aromas and incense in the Judaeo-Christian tradition is
E. G. C. F. Atchley, *A History of the Use of Incense in Divine Worship* (London: Long-
mans, Green, 1909). On spice boxes, see Felicitás Heimann-Jelinek, "Die Hav-
dalah," in *Eine Gute Woche!: Jüdische Türme aus Schwäbisch Gmünd* (Schwäbisch
Gmünd, Germany: Einhorn-Verlag, 2001), p. 97; F. Landsberger, "The Origin of
the Ritual Implements for the Sabbath," in *Beauty in Holiness,* edited by J.
Guttman (New York: Ktav, 1970), pp. 167–205; M. Narkiss, "Origins of the
Spice Box," *Journal of Jewish Art* 8 (1981): 28–41; Marilyn Gold Koolik, *The
Tower-Shape Tradition in Havdalah Spiceboxes* (Jerusalem: Israel Museum, 1982).
For speculation on spices' mystical associations, see J.-C. Picard, "Trajet du corps,
trajets célestes: Élements d'une cosmologie mystique juive," in *Moïse géographe,*
edited by A. Desreumaux and F. Schmidt (Paris: Vrin, 1986); for the vision of
Baruch, see Daniel C. Harlow, *The Greek Apocalypse of Baruch (3 Baruch)* (Leiden,
Netherlands: E. J. Brill, 1996), p. 14.

Odors of Sanctity

Two standard works concerning medieval notions of the odor of sanctity are J. P.
Albert, *Odeurs de sainteté: La Mythologie chrétienne des aromates* (Paris: Éditions de
l'École des Hautes Études en Sciences Sociales, 1990), and W. Deonna, *Croyances
antiques et modernes: L'Odeur suave des dieux et des élus* (Geneva, Switzerland: Musée
d'Art et d'Histoire, 1939). The dead King Henry's stench is mentioned by Henry
of Huntingdon, *The History of the English People, 1000–1154,* translated by Diana
Greenway (Oxford, England: Oxford University Press, 2002), and discussed by
Ruth Morse, *Truth and Convention in the Middle Ages: Rhetoric, Representation, and
Reality* (Cambridge, England: Cambridge University Press, 1991). Some suitably
aromatic saints may be found in *The Eight Feasts (Festivals) of the Church: Legends of
the Holy Rood,* edited by R. Morris (London: Early English Text Society, Original
Series 46, 1871), p. 22; see also *Acta Sanctorum: Aprilis, Collecta, Digesta, Illustrata,
a Godefrido Henschenio et Daniele Pepbrochio,* vol. 2 (Antwerp, Belgium: Apud
Michaelem Cnobarum, 1675), p. 283; and *A Select Library of Nicene and Post-Nicene
Fathers,* edited by Philip Schaff and Henry Wace, 2nd series, vol. 13 (Grand
Rapids, Mich.: W. B. Eerdmans, 1964), p. 135.

Old Age, New Age

On Hawkins, see John B. Broadbent, *Some Graver Subject: An Essay on "Paradise
Lost"* (London: Chatto and Windus, 1960), p. 183. On Oresme, see Thorndike, *A
History,* vol. 3, p. 431. The Sax Rohmer quote is from *The Romance of Sorcery* (New
York: Causeway Books, 1973), pp. 299–301. His source is apparently Lodovico
Maria Sinistrari's *Demoniality,* available in English translation by Montague Sum-
mers (London: Fortune Press, 1927). For Yemen and the early medieval spice

trade see Roger Collins, *Early Medieval Europe, 300–1000,* 2nd ed. (Basingstoke, England: Palgrave, 1999), p. 139. On the chrism in the early Greek Church, see Jacques Goar, *Euchologion, sive rituale graecorum* (Paris, 1647), p. 627. Concerning the anointing of kings, see C. A. Bouman, *Sacring and Crowning . . . Anointing of Kings and the Coronation of the Emperor Before the 11th Century* (Groningen, Netherlands: J. B. Wolters, 1957); René Poupardin, "L'Onction impériale," *Le Moyen Age,* 2nd series, vol. 9 (1905): 113–126; *Gesta Berengarii imperatoris,* edited by Ernst L. Dümmler (Halle, Germany: Verlag der Buchhandlung des Waisenhauses, 1871), I.iv. v. pp. 178–180. For instances of the exchange of spices between clerics in the early Middle Ages, see P. Jaffé, *Bibliotheca rerum germanicum,* vol. 3 (Berlin: Weidmannos, 1864–73), pp. 110, 156, 199, 214, 218.

A discussion of the use of spices in the chrism in the Eastern churches can be found in O. Burmester, "A Coptic Tradition Concerning the Holy Myron (Chrism)," in *Publications de l'Institut d'Études Orientales de la Bibliothèque Patriarchale d'Alexandrie* 3 (1954): 52–58; A. van Lanschoot, "Le MS Vatican Copte 44 et le Livre du Chrème (ms Paris arabe 100)," *Le Muséon* 45 (1932): 181–234; Archimandrite Agafador, "Preparation of the Holy Chrism in Moscow," *Journal of the Moscow Patriarchate* 9 (1987): 25–27.

For a representative illustration of the new-age faith in aromatics, see Richard Alan Miller and Iona Miller, *The Magical and Ritual Use of Perfumes* (Rochester, N.Y.: Destiny Books, 1990).

CHAPTER 7: SOME LIKE IT BLAND

Saint Bernard's Family Tiff

Bernard's letter to his nephew may be found in Migne, *Patrologia latina,* vol. 185. On the circumstances of its creation, see Irénée Vallery-Radot, *Bernard de Fontaines, abbé de Clairvaux* (Paris: Critérion, 1962), p. 178; *Life and Works of Saint Bernard, abbot of Clairvaux,* edited by Dom John Mabillon and translated by Samuel J. Eales (London: John Hodges, 1889).

The medieval monastic diet has been well studied, but the objection to spices has been almost entirely overlooked. Some useful studies are A. de Vogüé, "Travail et alimentation dans les règles de Saint Benoît et du Maître," *Revue Bénédictine* 74 (1964): 242–251; C. V. Franklin, I. Havener, and J. A. Francis, *Early Monastic Rules: The Rules of the Fathers and the Regula Orientalis* (Collegeville, Minn.: Liturgical Press, 1982). Joan Evans, *Monastic Life at Cluny, 910–1157* (London: Oxford University Press, 1931), contains much useful information. Migne's *Patrologia latina* is the indispensable source on the subject. For instances of clerical parody of dietary lapses, and hostile comment on spices in particular, see Migne, vol. 100, col. 465; Migne, vol. 20, col. 242; Migne vol. 181, col. 1735; Giraldus Cambrensis, *Opera,* vol. 4, edited by J. S. Brewer (London: Longman, 1873), p. 41; also his *Speculum Ecclesiae,* in *Rolls Series, Chronicles and Memorials of Great Britain and Ireland during the Middle Ages,* vol. 4, no. 21 (London: Longman, 1873), p. 59. On

Ligu:, see Léo Moulin, *Vie quotidienne des religieux au Moyen Âge* (Paris: Hachette, 1978), p. 95. Monkish hypochondria is touched upon by G. G. Coulton, *Five Centuries of Religion,* vol. 3 (Cambridge, England: Cambridge University Press, 1923–36), p. 413, and in his *Medieval Panorama,* pp. 445–448; see also M. B. Salu, *The Ancren Riwle* (London: Burns and Oates, 1955), p. 163. Secular variations on the same theme may be found in Thomas Wright, *Poems of W. Mapes* (London: Camden Society, 1841), p. 13; and Thomas Wright, *The Latin Poems Commonly Attributed to Walter Maps* (Hildesheim, Germany: Georg Olms Verlagsbuchhandlung, 1968), pp. xl–xliv. For the spice-quaffing pontiff see "Celestin und Susanna," edited by C. Horstmann, in *Anglia* 1 (1878): 67–85. On Ralf de Born see Bishop William Fleetwood, *Chronicon Preciosum* (London: C. Harper, 1707), p. 83. On the evolution of dietary norms, see André Vaquier, "Une réforme de Cluny en 1428," *Revue Bénédictine* 35 (1923): 157–198.

Filthy Lucre

The critique of spices as wasteful and luxurious fripperies is one that recurs over several centuries and crops up across practically the entire literary spectrum. Some useful sources are *The Book of Vices and Virtues: A Fourteenth Century Translation of the Somme le Roi of Lorens d'Orléans,* edited by W. Nelson Francis (London: Early English Text Society, Original Series 217, 1942), p. 47; *Jacob's Well: An Englisht* [sic] *Treatise on the Cleansing of Man's Conscience, ca. 1440,* edited by Arthur Brandeis (London: Early English Text Society, Original Series 115, 1900), p. 144; *Mum and the Sothsegger,* edited by Mabel Day and Robert Steele (London: Early English Text Society, Original Series 199, 1936), p. 20; *Archithrenius* 2.6, in Wright, *Anglo-Latin Satirical Poets,* p. 266; *Three Treatises by John Wycklyffe,* edited by James H. Todd (Dublin: Hodges and Smith, 1851), p. 130; *The English Works of Wyclif,* edited by F. D. Matthew (London: Early English Text Society, Original Series 74, 1880), pp. 13–14; *Pierce the Ploughmans Crede,* edited by W. W. Skeat (London: Early English Text Society, Original Series 30, 1867, repr. 1895), p. 12; *Political Poems and Songs Relating to English History, Composed During the Accession of Edw. III to That of Rich. III,* vol. 14, part 1, edited by T. Wright (London: Rolls Series, 1859), pp. 265–266; Anonmio genovese, in Cocito, *Poesie,* p. 474. On lawyerly greed, see Molière's *Les Fourberies de Scapin* and Racine's *Les Plaideurs;* also Villon's "Testament" in *Poésies,* edited by Jean Dufournet (Paris: Flammarion, 1993), p. 214. Some representative samples of the mercantilist aversion to spices may be found in *The Libelle of Englyshe Polycye: A Poem on the Use of Sea-Power,* edited by George Warner (Oxford, England: Clarendon Press, 1926), pp. 18–19; Juan Sempere y Guarinos, *Historia del luxo y de las leyes suntuarias de España,* vol. 2 (Madrid: Imprenta Real, 1788), p. 2; Francisco de Sá de Miranda, in *Obras completas,* vol. 2 (Lisbon: Libraria Sá de Costa, 1937), p. 81. On the subject of the East India Company's purported profligacy, see the pamphlet by Thomas Mun, *A Discourse of Trade, from England unto the East-Indies: Answering to Diverse Objections Which Are Usually Made Against the Same* (London: Nicholas Okes, 1621).

EPILOGUE: THE END OF THE SPICE AGE

Though Poivre is an occasionally untrustworthy judge of his own achievements, the best accounts of his spice odyssey remain his own—not least because they are an accurate indicator of the scope of his ambitions. His writings have been edited and abridged by Henri Cordier, in "Relation abrégée des voyages faits par le sieur [Poivre] pour le service de la Compagnie des Indes," printed in *Revue de l'Histoire des Colonies Françaises* 6, no. 1 (1918). Also useful is *Un Manuscrit inédit de Pierre Poivre: Les Mémoires d'un voyageur,* edited by Louis Malleret (Paris: École Française de l'Extrême-Orient, 1968). A fuller version of events may be found in Poivre's *Oeuvres complètes* (Paris: Fuchs, 1797). Poivre has had no shortage of later admirers, among them Madeleine Ly-Tio-Fane, in *Mauritius and the Spice Trade: The Odyssey of Pierre Poivre* (Port Louis, Mauritius: Esclapon, 1958), and *The Triumph of Jean Nicolas Céré and His Isle Bourbon Collaborators* (Paris: Mouton, 1970). See also Abbé Raynal's *Histoire philosophique et politique des établissements et du commerce des Européens dans les deux Indes* (Geneva, Switzerland: J. L. Pellet, 1780) and Marthe de Fels, *Pierre Poivre ou l'amour des épices* (Paris: Hachette, 1968). On Spanish-colonial spices, see A. J. R. Russell-Wood, *The Portuguese Empire, 1415–1808* (Baltimore: Johns Hopkins University Press, 1998), pp. 152–156, and N. Monardes, *Historia de las cosas que se traen de nuestras Indias occidentales* (Seville, Spain: Alonso Escrivano, 1574), p. 99.

The VOC's demise and the diminishing returns on the spice trade are discussed by V. Kanapathypillai, "Helen or Costly Bride: The VOC and the Cinnamon Trade of Sri Lanka, 1766–1796," *Modern Ceylon Studies* 2 (1987): 133–146; H. Wright, "The Moluccan Spice Monopoly, 1770–1824," *Journal of the Malayan Branch of the Royal Asiatic Society* 31, no. 4 (1958): 1–116; and E. S. de Klerck, *History of the Netherlands East Indies* (Amsterdam, Netherlands: B. M. Israël, 1975); also Boxer, *Dutch Seaborne.* Fernand Braudel has a telling discussion of the VOC's decline in *Civilization and Capitalism, 15th to 18th Century,* translated by Siân Reynolds (Berkeley: University of California Press, 1992), vol. 1, pp. 220–224; vol. 3, pp. 227–235; see also B. E. L. Carl, *Traité de la richesse des princes et de leurs états et des moyens simples et naturels pour y parvenir* (Paris: T. Legras, 1722–23), p. 236; John Nickolls (pseud.), *Remarques sur les désavantages et les avantages de la France et de la Grande Bretagne* (London: T. Osborne, 1754), p. 253.

On the challenge to spices posed by other flavors, see Braudel, *Civilization and Capitalism,* vol. 1, pp. 224–265. The topic is also discussed by Wolfgang Schivelbusch in *Tastes of Paradise,* translated by David Jacobson (New York: Pantheon, 1992). See also Alan Girard, "Le Triomphe de 'la cuisinière bourgeoise': Livres culinaires, cuisine et société en France aux XVIIᵉ et XVIIIᵉ siècles," *Revue d'Histoire Moderne et Contemporaine* 24 (1977); Barbara Wheaton, *Savoring the Past: The French Kitchen and Taste from 1300 to 1789* (Philadelphia: University of Pennsylvania Press, 1983). The Reformation's implications for cuisine are discussed by Pullar, *Consuming Passions,* pp. 126–130. On some enduring medicinal uses of spice see Walter Baley, *A Short Discourse of the Three Kindes of Peppers in Common Use, and Certaine Special Medicines Made of the Same, Tending to the Preservation of Health* (Place of publication unknown: Eliot's Court Press, 1588); A. Mackaile, *Macis Macerata: or, A Short Treatise, Concerning the Use of Mace* (Aberdeen, Scotland: John Forbes, 1677). On aphrodisiacs, see A.-R. de Lens, *Pratiques des harems marocains: Sorcellerie, médecine, beauté* (Paris: Libraire Orientaliste, 1925); Dan McKenzie, *Aromatics and the Soul: A Study of Smells* (London: W. Heinemann, 1923). The reference to Coca-Cola is from Mark Pendergrast, *For God, Country and Coca-Cola: The Unauthorized History of the Great American Soft Drink and the Company That Makes It* (New York: Scribners, 1993), p. 422.

ACKNOWLEDGMENTS

Many people have contributed to this book, wittingly and unwittingly. I owe a special debt to the Ternatean villager who led me to the mile-high summit of Gamalama volcano, through its clove-scented jungle to the crater's sulfurous brim. From the top we surveyed the handful of islands that had long been the sole home of the clove and for the sake of which great historical forces had been set into motion. The experience imparted a sudden insight into the global implications of botanical happenstance, and a sense of wonderment that has only grown with time.

Long before then, I now realize, the seed of the idea was planted in a very different setting, in classes on the richly scented verse of Sappho and Martial taught by Peter Connor, a sorely missed friend and mentor. Whether in a seminar room or an Aleppo coffeehouse, he was an inexhaustible source of encouragement, inspiration, and fun. There have been many others. Willy Dalrymple showed the way and called me a fraud when I dithered and turned to more mercenary pursuits. Jon Wright; Richard Leonard, S.J.; Paul Kildea; Angus Trumble; and Sam Miller were unfailingly generous with suggestions and criticism. Sandy Knowles and Scott Gilmore provided company, electricity, and air-conditioning during a torrid year in Dili. Barbara Reis helped with my inadequate Portuguese, Hansjoerg Strohmeyer with the German, Flore de Préneuf with the Old French.

My immediate intellectual debts are acknowledged in the sources; however, several titles stand out. J. Innes Miller's wildly idiosyncratic *Spice Trade of the Roman Empire* was an early inspiration; so too the writings of Henri Pirenne. Alain Corbin's *Le Miasme et la jonquille* revealed to me that it was possible to imagine history through the realm of the senses: to explore the past through smell and taste.

In the course of the research I have used many different libraries and archives. I owe a special debt to the librarians at the New York Public Library, the British Library, the New York Academy of Medicine, and the New York Botanical Garden.

In terms of the more practical business of turning an idea into a book, my agents Giles Gordon and Russell Galen deserve special mention for their early faith and enthusiasm. It is a huge regret that Giles is no longer here. He was a wonderful agent and a friend. I would like to thank Lynn Anderson, who copyedited the manuscript, and Peter Andersen, who designed it. My editors, Mike Fishwick and Jon Segal, were exemplars of professional excellence; they showed, besides, astonishing restraint in so seldom asking when I would finish. My parents and parents-in-law, though lacking the least self-control in this last respect, provided a roof over my head, love, company, and support.

Last but above all, my greatest debt is to Helena Fraser, who kept me going even when the attraction of spices seemed as elusive as it must have done to those who sought them across the globe, only to find themselves clutching at a will-o'-the-wisp: a sense of frustration and despair I often shared, and inflicted on her. This book is dedicated to her, my spicy wife.

INDEX

●

Aaron, 176
Abbagliato, 283
Abelard, Peter, 277
Abreu, António de, 30, 31
Acts of Sharbil, The, 229
Addon, 155
Ademar III, Viscount of Limoges, 101
Aelfric, abbot of Eynsham, 101
Aelian, 198
Aeschylus, 240
Aethelred II ("The Unready"), King of England, 100
Afghanistan, 87
Afonso V, King of Portugal, 129
Aframomum melegueta, 45
Agamemnon, King, 240
Agatharchides of Cnidus, 235
agnus castus, 197–8
Ailly, Pierre d', *Imago Mundi*, 51
Alamanni, 87
Alaric, King of the Goths, 86
Alberouny of Khiva, 28
Albertus Magnus, *The Book of Secrets*, 170
Albuquerque, Alfonso de, 38
Alcuin, 160, 253
Aldelm, Saint, 94
Aldfrith, King of Northumbia, 94
Aldobrandino of Siena, 121; *Le Régime du corps*, 119
ale, spiced, 113, 116–19
Alexander the Great, 61
Alexander VI, Pope, 25
Alexis, *The Apothecary*, 176
Alhakam II, Caliph, 194
allspice, 11, 263
Almanzor, Sultan of Tidore, 30

aloes, xiii, 7, 8, 257, 259, 260, 262
Alphabet of Tales, The, 219
Alpinia officinarum, 46n
Álvarez Chanca, Diego, 8
Ambrose, Saint, 250–1, 253
ambrosia, 234
Ammonites, 244
Anacreon, 206
Ancrene Riwle, 275–6
Andeli, Henri d', 115
Andrew, acts of, 150
Andrew, Laurence, *The Noble Lyfe and Natures of Man*, 123
Anglo-Dutch wars, 39
Anonymous of Genoa, 134
Ansegisus, Saint, 274
Anselm of Laon, 103
Anthimus, 88, 89, 121
antidotes, 167–8
Antiochus Epiphanes, King of Syria, 230
Antipater of Sidon, 205–6
Antiphanes, 59, 234; *Anteia*, 206
Antony, Saint, 198, 270
Aphrodisia (New York City), 221
aphrodisiacs, 183–201, 221–4, 269, 308
Apicius, 67, 69–73, 121; *De re coquinaria*, 67, 69–71, 89
Apocalypse of Peter, The, 42, 251
Apollinaris Sidonius, 73
Apollonius of Tyana, 198
Apostolic Constitutions, 248
Apuleius, 63–4, 75, 208, 263; *The Golden Ass*, 67; *Herbarium*, 171; *Metamorphoses*, 208

fennel, 206, 233, 306

Ferdinand, King of Spain, xi, 10, 11, 21, 53, 220, 285–6; Columbus's *Letter* to, *illus.* 9

Fernández de Enciso, Martín, *Suma de geografía*, 30

Fernández de Navarette, Martín, 36

Fiore, Albizzo da, 131

Fisher, M. F. K., *Serve It Forth*, 72

Fitzstephen, William, 103

Flaubert, Gustave: *Bouvard and Pécuchet*, 308; *Madame Bovary*, 227

Flemings, 116

food, *see* cuisine

Forme of Cury, The, 139

Fortunatus of Poitiers, 88

fragrances, *see* perfumes

France, 301, 304, 305; aphrodisiacs in, 189, 196, 200; bribery in, 284–5; in Crusades, 102; cuisine of, 92, 100, 101, 106, 112, 125–7, 130–1, 133, 139; burial practices in, 153–7; medicine in, 161, 165, 172, 173; monasteries in, 96, 276, 278 (*see also* Clairvaux; Cluny); Poivre's missions for, 289–96; spice trade in, 90; wine in, 114–15; *see also* Gaul

Francis of Paola, Saint, 169

Franciscans, 49, 50, 167, 187, 284

frankincense, xiii, 230, 233

Franklin, A., *La Vie privée d'autrefois*, 106

Franks, 87–9, 113, 153

Freud, Sigmund, *Civilization and Its Discontents*, 213

Frisians, 259

Froissart, Jean, 140

Fugger banking dynasty, 32, 135

funerary customs, 145–58, 276, 308

Gabbanites, 232

galangal, 46, 47, 93, 112, 114, 127, 164, 167, 185, 186, 195, 308

Galen, 164–6, 175*n*, 185, 187, 194; *Concerning Antidotes*, 168; *The Healing Art*, 169

Gall, Saint, 161

Gama, Paulo da, 15, 23

Gama, Vasco da, xvi, 12–15, 17–24, 36, 37, 41, 59, 62, 85

gariofilatum, 116

Garland, John, 108, 158

garum, 70

Gaul, 96; Roman, 84–5, 270; Merovingian, 88, 89, 153

Gellia, 211

Geoponica, 235

Gerald of Aurillac, Saint, 97

Germany, 304; ancient, 57, 66, 86, 153; medieval, 92, 95, 100, 118, 172, 259–60

Ghazali, al-, 195

Gilgamesh, xv

gillyflowers, 257, 275

ginger, xxiii, 8, 10, 131, 134; as aphrodisiac, 185–7, 189, 191–3, 195, 200, 201, 222; culinary use of, 46, 70, 88, 106, 111, 112, 123, 127, 133, 267, 273, 277, 305*n*; cultivation in New World of, 297; in incense, 228; of Malabar, 16; medicinal use of, 126, 167, 169, 273, 308; mystique of, 47, 49; in perfume, 207, 221; religious use of, 255, 257, 259, 263; wine spiced with, 113, 114

Gisilbert, Abbot, 280

Glasse, Hannah, *Art of Cookery*, 302

Gloucester, Humphrey, Duke of, 112

Golden Hind (ship), 38

Gospels, 247

Goths, 86, 93

Gouerot, J., *The Regiment of Life*, 174

Gower, John, 132

Graham, James, 214

grains of paradise, 45–6, 106, 114, 141

White pepper on the vine. Gerard, *The Herball or General Historie of Plantes* (London, 1636)